THE SA'DAN-TORAJA II

VERHANDELINGEN

VAN HET KONINKLIJK INSTITUUT VOOR TAAL-, LAND- EN VOLKENKUNDE

118

HETTY NOOY-PALM

THE SA'DAN-TORAJA

A STUDY OF THEIR SOCIAL LIFE AND RELIGION

II

RITUALS OF THE EAST AND WEST

1986
FORIS PUBLICATIONS
Dordrecht-Holland / Cinnaminson-U.S.A.

Published by:
Foris Publications Holland
P.O. Box 509
3300 AM Dordrecht, The Netherlands

Sole distributor for the U.S.A. and Canada:
Foris Publications U.S.A.
P.O. Box C-50
Cinnaminson N.J. 08077
U.S.A.

ISBN 90 6765 207 5

Printed in the Netherlands.

CONTENTS

PREFACE

"The Sa'dan-Toraja; A Study of Their Social Life and Religion. Vol. II: Rituals of the East and West" is a sequel to Volume I: "Organization, Symbols and Beliefs" (VKI 87), and together with it forms a complete whole. Volume II deals with a number of rituals as independent ceremonies, at the same time referring to how they are inter-related. The role of ritual in the Toraja's religious and social system is examined, including the parts played by diverse religious functionaries and traditional forms of participation by different classes. Note is made as well of how family bonds are strengthened through the performance of ritual.

For the Toraja the relation between myths and ritual is an important one. Van Baal's comment about cosmological myths in general is particularly relevant to the Toraja: "Most rituals are connected with such a founding myth which can be looked upon as its charter" (Van Baal 1981:162). Myths were discussed in Volume I, as were some chants and litanies, among which those of the merok feast and the chants for the deceased by Van der Veen (see below and the bibliography); yet I wish also to call the reader's attention to various publications by H. van der Veen which have become available since, and where he reproduced various Toraja myths and songs. A list of these works to which I refer time and again in Volume II appears below; they merit close consultation in combination with reading the following pages:

- The Merok Feast of the Sa'dan Toradja (1965). This book, designated in Vols. I and II as "Merok", contains the Passomba Tedong, the chant recited at the consecration of the buffalo sacrificed during the merok-feast.
- The Sa'dan Toraja Chant for the Deceased (1966). Referred to in Vols. I and II as "The Chant".
- Ossoran Tempon dao mai Langi' (1976).
- Singgi' Tondok, The Chant in Praise of the Community of Villages and other songs included in Overleveringen en Zangen der Zuid-Toradja's (1979).
- "Een wichel-litanie der Sa'dan-Toradja's", Feestbundel Koninklijk Bataviaasch Genootschap van Kunsten en Wetenschappen II:396-411 (1929).
- Ma'biangi, the litany recited during divination (unpublished a).
- Pangimbo likaran biang (unpublished a), a prayer spoken during the sacrifice offered in a vessel woven from biang-reed.
- Pangimbo Manuk (unpublished b), The Prayer over the Hen Sacrifice.
- Tae' (Zuid-Toradjasch) - Nederlandsch Woordenboek (1940). Referred to in Vols. I and II as "Woordenboek".
- Ethnografie (Ethnography), written in the Japanese prison camp during the second World War (unpublished c).

In Volume II Toraja rituals are divided according to the Toraja own way
of thinking into Rituals of the East and Rituals of the West. To some
extent these rituals are contrary to each other, yet one can also speak
of a unity of opposites. Their cohesiveness is discussed in the final
chapter of this volume, which also ventures predictions about their
future.

In the Preface to Volume I, I have expressed my appreciation to the
various institutions whose generosity made it possible for me to carry
out fieldwork among the Toraja for so many successive years. A further
debt of thanks is due to organizations who supported my research in
other ways and made it possible for me to publish the results. The
Nederlandse Organisatie voor Zuiver-Wetenschappelijk Onderzoek (ZWO)
financed the translation of this present volume, as it did of Volume I
previously. The Royal Tropical Institute, Amsterdam, granted me the
opportunity to finish writing the text; the support of P.J. van Dooren,
Director of the Social Research Department, deserves special mention.
Once again Donald A. Bloch turned my Dutch into English.

Prof. J. van Baal provided guidance and inspiration in the completion
of Volume II. His help has been constant and invaluable since the in-
ception of this project which now, at long last, reaches completion with
this publication. No one could wish for a more attentive and tireless
editor, rich in constructive criticism and suggestions.

In the final stage Dr. J. Noorduyn was kind enough to go through
the proofs, and in many places the text has benefitted from his suggestions and remarks.

A special word of thanks is due to Heleen Tigchelaar, who typed the
draft of the manuscript and who made it ready for the press.

Last but not least I wish to acknowledge my indebtedness for the assistance which the Toraja themselves offered me. Without their cooperation and confidence in me this study would never have materialized.

PART I
THE RITUALS OF THE EAST

Makale-Rantepao and surroundings.
Left on top: the new division in kecamatan.

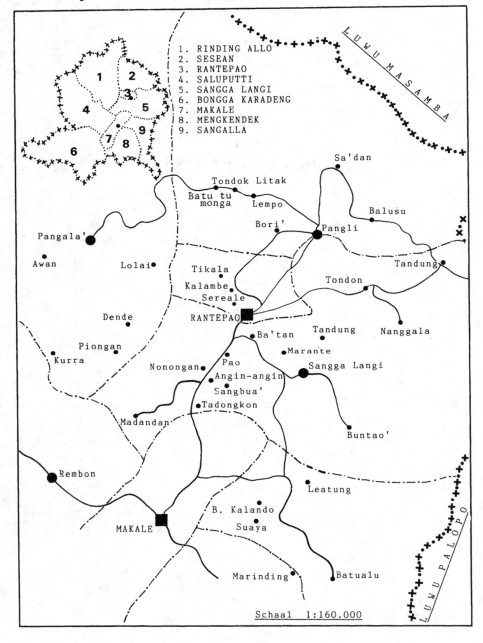

1. RINDING ALLO
2. SESEAN
3. RANTEPAO
4. SALUPUTTI
5. SANGGA LANGI
6. BONGGA KARADENG
7. MAKALE
8. MENGKENDEK
9. SANGALLA

Schaal   1:160.000

Chapter I

DIVISION AND CHARACTERIZATION

Toraja rituals are so varied that it is possible to classify them in very disparate ways. The most obvious division is that which is adhered to by the Toraja themselves. They sort rituals according to their cosmic orientation into Rituals of the East and Rituals of the West. One might also sort rituals, however, into those which a person himself must celebrate or undergo in the course of his lifetime and those which can only be performed by groups or by persons who are rich or whose lives involve certain extraordinary circumstances. Roughly parallel to such a division is classification to scale, for the scope of rituals depends upon the resources of the celebrants. One also might consider a division into transitional and cyclical rituals, but this distinction, as will become apparent, runs into objections. Some rituals which would appear to fit the classification of cyclical are so vast and expensive that they no longer fit into any cycle. Discussion of each of the divisions of rituals proposed above seems a valuable approach to an overall appreciation of what rituals mean to the Toraja, and also a useful prelude to closer inspection of individual rites.

First and foremost is indigenous classification according to cosmic orientation: Rituals of the East (aluk rampe matallo) in direct opposition to Rituals of the West (aluk rampe matampu', cf. Vol.I:112). Rituals of the East promote the welfare of man, the well-being of his animals and plants. Among them are joyous feasts such as bua' kasalle-, bua' padang- and the merok-feast, but also the rice ritual, rituals of exorcism to heal the sick (maro), transitional rites in relation to birth, a first haircut, circumcision, the filing of teeth and body decoration with tattoos. Wedding ceremonies are also "Eastern". It is of interest that the final rites of the death ritual, well-known as a conversion ritual, are classified as belonging to this division as well. Once the entire ritual has been observed, the dead acquire the status of ancestors; thereby they are admitted into the circle of ancestors associated with the East, the deata (which does not negate the fact that people also associate a group of ancestors with the West; these, however, are not called deata, but to dolo, nene' or to matua). Finally, rituals of the East include the death rituals held for a to burake, the priest or priestess who officiates at ceremonies which have to do with heaven, for a to minaa sando, or for a to menani, the priest central to agricultural rituals. These death rituals are thus exceptional.

Rituals of the West have to do with death. Burials and headhunting, usually undertaken in connection with the death of some eminent member of the community, fall into this category. Rituals for laying the dead to rest exhibit a range in scale from modest to elaborate, in keeping with the status and the wealth of the deceased.

The significance of the opposition between East and West is further

underscored by the fact that "Eastern" rites are also referred to as
rambu tuka', smoke that ascends, while "Western" rites may be spoken
of conversely as rambu solo', smoke that descends. This nomenclature
is a clear indication that during rites of the former kind one is addressing heaven, during rites of the latter kind the earth and the
underworld; in both, smoke issuing from the sacrifice is considered to
act as a medium. The emphasis on smoke illustrates at the same time the
vital importance of the sacrificial act to all rituals. Offerings appear to
be the ritual procedure of choice. Animals sacrificed during rituals of
the East are usually light in colour, and the sacrificial offering is
placed down towards the (North)east (for example, of the tongkonan).
By way of contrast sacricifial animals in "Western" rites are preferably
black, at any rate of a dark hue (black hens, for example, instead of
white or yellowish ones), and they are offered up in a (South)westerly
location.

This division is strictly observed. A typical example concerns conversion rituals during which sacrifices for the deceased, previously
enacted with a "Western" orientation, now for the first time shift to the
East. Even during a cycle of rites as complicated as the bua'-feast,
however, one will not neglect to place offers destined for the to dolo
down in the West; this practice differs from the many sacrifices to
higher and lower gods which are offered towards the East.

The opposition East-West also governs the classification for the rice
ritual. Rice belongs totally to the East. It is such an essential food that
men take no risk where rice is concerned. As long as farmers are busy
with the cultivation of rice - for some five to seven months depending
on the district and agricultural conditions - no ritual may be observed
which has to do in any way, however slight, with death. This applies
not merely to actual death rituals. Major feasts classified among rituals
of the East, the bua' kasalle and merok, for example, will be
interrupted until the rice has been harvested. Here, however, not only
ritual but also practical considerations appear to be at work: it is
simply essential that people resume their agricultual activities until the
rice crop has been assured. One can renew his food reserves and at
the same time enjoy respite from the hectic pressures that accompany
the direction of a feast. One can also detect practical thinking in the
saying that a dead man pays for his own burial.

When someone dies, the yield from his sawahs may only be used for
his own death feast. Not until after this feast is the land divided among
his heirs. The main thing, however, is that rice in the fields must
remain far removed from the influence of the dead and of the West.

It is also possible to classify rituals according to their scale. Scale
will be connected to the class and comparative prosperity of those who
are the object of the ritual, or of those who perform it. The strong
stratification of Toraja society is never more unmistakable than it is
within rituals. Every person receives the ritual accompaniment befitting
his class and the resources on which he and his group rely to differentiate them from others. The noble rank of the highest representative of
a group is a source of pride to all members; the recognition of this
nobility through elaborately celebrated rituals is an affair close to the
hearts of everyone in the group, for such events determine their collective status.

Death rituals make such considerations particularly clear. For slaves
or for small children possible observances are limited to the following:

1. dikaletekan tallu manuk ("a chicken's egg is laid out for him who has died");
2. disilli' ("looking after the corpse according to the lowest death ritual");
3. didedekan pangkung bai ("the pig sty is struck with a stick for the deceased"). This makes clear that a single pig is butchered for the dead man;
4. dibai tungga' ("he - or she - is treated in keeping with the ritual of a solitary pig"). One slaughters only a single pig as in the preceding ritual, but this form of burial entails somewhat more elaborate rites;
5. bai a'pa' ("four pigs"). Four pigs are slaughtered.
6. dipasangbongi ("that which happens during one night"). During this ritual a black buffalo and a black pig are slaughtered;
7. dipatallung bongi ("that which happens during three nights"). Three black buffaloes and several black pigs are slaughtered. This ritual would seem rather a costly one. It would therefore not be able to take place unless the dead slave's family made every effort to carry it out. In reality the same range of burial ceremonies (from number 1 onwards) exists for a free man; yet his surviving family members can decide to hold a still higher, more expensive ritual;
8. dipalimang bongi ("that which happens during five nights"). Five black buffaloes and eighteen black pigs are slaughtered. (The word bongi, night, can be associated, as in the dipatallung bongi above and the dipapitung bongi which follows, with the black sacrificial animals);
9. dipapitung bongi ("that which happens during seven nights") is more expensive yet: seven black buffaloes and twenty-four black pigs are slaughtered. The dipalimang bongi and the dipapitung bongi are held in puang-regions only for the family members of the dead prince. For the prince himself the dirapa'i (number 10 in the list of burial possibilities presented here) is usually observed, the funeral rites which entail an interruption, a rest period. At least twenty-five black buffaloes and thirty-six black pigs must be slaughtered during such a death ritual. The toll of dead animals usually exceeds these specified minima.

Elsewhere, beyond the Tallulembangna, the five-night or seven-night or even the dirapa'i-ritual may be observed to honour a rich to makaka (free man) who has died. In Buntao' district the dipalimang bongi is the highest form of death ritual. In Kesu', on the other hand, the dipalimang bongi and dipapitung bongi are seldom celebrated, for people find these rituals, which may not be interrupted, too long. Here the rich prefer the ritual with an intermission, three variants of which are practised. The differences are essentially a function of how much is to be spent on the ritual. The lowest variant is the dirapa'i dilayu-layu (dilayu-layu: that which brings about wilting or fading). The slaughter of nine black buffaloes and thirty-six black pigs suffices for this ritual.Both the rapasan sundun (so named after the rapasan, the temporary coffin in which the dead person's earthly remains lie for some time) and the sapu randanan ("the ritual that sweeps everything away") are more expensive. At the former at least twenty-five black buffaloes and thirty-six black pigs are slaughtered, more if the celebrants so desire. For the sapu randanan "hundreds" of buffaloes and pigs are put to death. In practice both higher forms of the dirapa'i are only held for to parengnge' (a rank of nobility) and their wives. The to parengnge' of Kesu' consider themselves roughly equivalent to the puang of the Tallulembangna.

It is notable that in main distinctions among gradations of death rituals, people don't speak of smaller or larger, but of lower or higher. The extent of the observance is regarded as a factor related to hierarchical ranking within the prevailing system of social stratification. Consistent with this observation is the fact that the scale of feasts in one sphere determines to a large extent the scale of feasts in the opposed sphere as well. Thus one says that the dirapa'i, the death ritual of the highest order, may only be performed for someone who during his lifetime held the bua' kasalle-feast. As it happens this restriction is not so strictly observed, certainly not in Kesu'; indeed it would be difficult to demand compliance there, for the last major bua'-feast in Kesu' took place more than sixty years ago. The principle, however, is clear. High rites are for the mighty, low ones for the humble. This obtains not merely for such exceptional feasts as the bua' kasalle and the merok but also for those that recur regularly such as marriage feasts and the celebration of the maro-ritual to cure the sick. At all levels one sees the potlatch element of status demonstration, a display of one's eminence by incurring expenses by celebrating feasts. There is invariably an element of competition on hand, the challenge of "keeping up with the Joneses".

It would be a misrepresentation of ritual among the Toraja, however, to over-emphasize the show-off aspects of celebrations. The major feasts of the rich also have their social side. They make it possible for the followers (retainers) of those who organize a large feast to celebrate events in their own family circle concurrently; in this way, without extravagant expenses, feasts within feasts can take place to everybody's satisfaction. For example, whenever the merok-feast is celebrated, one spares no trouble trying to reach as many relatives as possible, even those living in regions or cities far from the Tana Toraja, so that every member of the rapu can participate. The festivities have at heart the notion of promoting the well-being of the entire family group. This group actually helps to arrange and finance the feast; the noble family leader is honoured by being designated host and thus assuming responsibility for an appreciable share of the expenses connected with the celebration. His voice carries special weight in making arrangements for the feast, although he is assisted in organizing things by certain persons with the necessary knowledge and experience. These need not be individuals form his own kin group; they might well be priests (expert to minaa, for example) or other to parengnge' or anak patalo. Even slaves (kaunan) who are familiar with proceedings may be consulted about a pending ritual. Yet, the service of a kaunan in such matters is invariably passed over in silence. All honours go to the host - shared on some occasions with several leaders of groups that have cooperated in organizing the feast. Recognition of their contributions, however, in no way belittles the host's position.

Corresponding to different death rituals there are associated conversion rituals. These, however, are not as varied as the former. For the higher forms of the dirapa'i, the required conversion ritual is the mangrara pare, "the sprinkling of the rice with blood"; for the lower dirapa'i, i.e. the layu-layu-ritual, and for the dipapitung and dipalimang bongi, the manganta' ("to accompany") is prescribed. The appropriate conversion ritual after the dipatallung bongi bears the name ma'palangngan para, the significance of which will be explained later in a discussion of the ritual. At the same time conversion rituals will be examined which follow upon completion of lower death rituals: the ma'tadoran bai which is held after the sangbongi; the ma'tadoran manuk that succeeds the dibai a'pa'; and the manglika' biang that serves as the concluding rite to the lowest forms of the death ritual.

There is a suggestion of something cyclical about the way conversion rituals are associated with forms of the death ritual. People gladly imbue this cyclical notion with content by asserting that whoever has performed a dirapa'i for his father or mother is in turn entitled to celebrate a bua' kasalle. Stronger yet, in Kesu' people maintain that after a conversion ritual first a maro- and then a merok-feast should follow. It is apparent that the Toraja like to look upon the rituals as constituting a cycle in which celebration of one ritual is a prerequisite for celebrating another. The reality, however, is often different. The cycle concept may be an ideal, but practice deviates from it. Otherwise social mobility would be precluded. In addition some feasts have grown so extensive and expensive that their renewal, their celebration a second time, has become an impossibility. This is especially true of the bua' kasalle in Kesu'. The cyclical pattern of the rituals is therefore more a matter of appearances than a reality.

Finally certain general characteristics of these rituals deserve mention. The first of such characteristics has already been alluded to during the preceding discussion: the baroque emphasis on all kinds of rules. People act as if there are extremely stringent rules, obligatory conditions which must be fulfilled, such as first having organized a bua' kasalle-feast in order to be eligible to be fêted with a dirapa'i-ritual (Kesu'). A further example is the imperative that a bua' kasalle may only be celebrated once all death rituals within the community (= bua', or circle) have been brought to absolute completion. Reality reveals, however, that special arrangements can be made for participants who do not live up to these demands (see Chapter II.3, rite 13 and note 21).

The baroque tendency is also manifest in a clear inclination to engage in boasting. For every action, every episode, sacrifices are required which participants like to portray as extensive and precious. In descriptions of rituals performed in the past sacrifices of several tens of animals (in itself nothing to scoff at) readily multiply into several hundreds. The exaggerations, indeed, are not without effect; they create a situation in which successive enlargement of the ceremony is inescapable until it becomes so expensive that performance of the ritual becomes cost-prohibitive.

Hyperbole, it should be remarked, is not an element which only catches the attention of a critical outsider. It belongs to the occasion. Eulogizing (singgi') of the brave and the distinguished is an important component of the bua' kasalle- and the maro-ritual. It occurs at the height of the ritual when the scene has been carefully set. The pendant to such praise one discovers in the death ritual where the laudation of the dead takes place during the badong (a chant performed by professionals and/or guests as they dance) and retteng (recitation of topical or satirical poetry).[1]

This correspondence raises at the same time another remarkable point: the parallelism that exists between various rituals. This is especially evident between the bua' kasalle- and merok-feast, two occasions which to a significant extent involve striving towards the same goal: confirmation of the social position of the hosts on one hand, and on the other affirmation of the relation between the community and the gods of the upperworld. In both the Passomba Tedong, laudation of the buffalo, is a crucial component. This laudation is in essence a recapitulation of the history of the tribe. There are, moreover, other parallels to be pointed out, a sufficient number in fact to prompt speculation about whether the bua' kasalle might not simply be a more elaborate version of merok.

Such, however, is certainly not the case for parallels which can be observed between the bua' kasalle and the major death rituals, even though once again these are not confined to the laudation. As part of the great bua'-feast people prepare a vast scaffold which serves as the focus of the final phase of the celebration. Such an elevated platform is also used during the major death rituals. All such matters are part and parcel of a specific style which involves paying special attention to the history of the group and its importance.

The principal point of agreement among all rituals is, to be sure, the sacrifice. The sacrifice can consist of buffaloes, pigs or hens, even now and then a dog. Only few sacrifices are in their entirety offered to the gods. That will happen in the event of more sizable sacrifices (i.e. with a buffalo or a pig) only when the offering is to purify a sin. Incest is the most serious transgression for which such ritual atonement may be sought. The sacrificial animal is then hacked into pieces all of which are burned (see Merok:3-4 and 164-6). This incineration of the sacrificial animal, however, only occurs otherwise on a limited number of occasions, during the ma'pallin, for example, when a black hen together with a bamboo cylinder containing rice which has been cooked in it are burned outside the village. The blood of that hen is allowed to seep into the earth after hollowing out an indentation by striking the ground three times with the heel. This, too, serves as a sacrifice to expiate sin.[2]

What is true about all sacrifices is that only a small share, usually an extremely small share, is set aside for the gods or ancestors themselves. This share, in the form of a pesung (an offering on a banana leaf), is laid out for them in a ritually prescribed place where dogs, birds or pigs end up devouring. Most of the sacrificial animal is divided among celebrants. A modest portion of what they receive is already prepared to eat; the remainder is distributed in the form of raw meat which they will cook themselves at home.

During the sacrifice a presentation should be made to those for whom the offering is intended, the gods or the ancestors. This often occurs in the guise of what one could call prayer (mangimbo: to utter a prayer). At times gods cited during the prayer are spoken of as a trinity. In other instances the gods are hardly specified. Examples of both forms follow:

"Mayest thou, thou trinity, in golden magnificence,
remain on the richly laden cendana tree, while
chewing the betel quid,
Puang Matua, Pong Tulakpadang, God of the Earth!
Then, shining like tiny small gold beads, shalt thou,
the three belonging together, like the stones of the hearth,
sit on the tree whose branches are full of precious things,
in a meeting with thy co-gods, in a gathering with

the ones who, with thee, are revered as lords,
whilst making thy mouths red."

(Merok:181)

"Thou who art our ancestors,
thou who art our forefathers.
The ancestors, the first descending from heaven,
our forefathers from the time beyond memory, who
came down from the stars.
Ancestors, following each other, like the steps of
a stair, forefathers, succeeding each one after
the other, like the rungs of a ladder."

(Merok:167)

Note how in the final lines of the fragment from the first prayer not
only is the trinity addressed, but also the "co-gods", a group of
divinities with no further designation. In other instances the prayer
spins out into a long litany.

In concluding this chapter some justification seems in order for the
manner in which the material will be presented. Presentation conforms
with Toraja categories. This might seem a self-evident choice. Yet it
means that conversion rituals will be discussed at the end of Part I,
preceding the death rituals (Part II) to which they are a logical continuation. This sequence raises objections of sufficient gravity for me to
have considered some other arrangement. The principal reason for
ultimately complying with Toraja usage is that a more logical sequence
runs into diffuculties at other points along the way, for it does not do
justice to the most salient characteristic of Toraja ritual: the baroque
development of functions and rituals, a development which makes a
mockery of the simplicity which is the soul of logic. On these grounds I
have decided to abandon any attempt at simple logic by beginning my
description of rituals with the most elaborate developed feast of all, the
great bua'-celebration that more than any other conveys an idea of what
a religious ritual in Tana Toraja entails. As a close second, the merok-
feast follows. Next come rites which, in whole or large part, have to do
with rice. Then transitional rites, healing rites (exorcism rituals), and,
finally, the conversion rituals to which passing reference has already
been made.

Chapter II

THE GREAT BUA'-FEAST

> "The skilled burake regulated in good order, from
> the beginning to the end, the rites of the women,
> the to tumbang, on the centre part over which the
> wind blows,
> the priestess with supernatural power, ordered in a
> proper manner, in the middle of the front space,
> the required adat-performances of the ones who
> were placed there as dancers."
>
> (Merok:149)

1. Introduction

In addition to the great bua'-feast, the bua' kasalle (also called la'pa'
kasalle or la'pa' banua), a smaller bua'-feast is also known, the bua'
padang. Although the major celebration may have grown out of the
smaller one as the result of flourishing prosperity, I will not speak of
both in the same chapter. The essential character of each of these
rituals is too distinct to handle them together. Furthermore the bua'
kasalle has developed into a "cérémonie totale" in which all aspects of
Toraja society and its increased wealth find expression, while the small
bua'-feast, the bua' padang, has remained in essence a ritual whose
principal object is not to glorify the social community in its entirety but
rather to celebrate its staple food crop, rice. Therefore we examine the
bua' padang at the close of the chapter concerning the rice ritual
(Chapter IV.5.).
   As far as the name of the feast, bua' kasalle, is concerned, A.C.
Kruyt (1935) has associated the word bua' with the Indonesian bua, or
fruit. He thought that he was dealing with a fertility feast, an explanation that seems plausible at the first glance. The Sa'danese bua',
however, has not the significance of "bringing forth fruit" as Kruyt
thought but is related to the Indonesian buat, to make. According to
Van der Veen, bua' (ma'bua') is an obsolete term that once meant "to
work" in the strict sense of holding an adat-feast: an association thus
of work and celebration that also occurs in other Indonesian languages.
Kasalle means: great. La'pa' is to loosen, to free oneself from something, and therefore has the significance of a major sacrificial feast that
is celebrated as the conclusion of preceding rites, during which, as
prosperity has permitted, a series of obligatory sacrifices has been
offered (Woordenboek: v. la'pa'). Banua means "house" and refers to
the tongkonan that is the centre of the feast activities. The term la'pa'
banua is, indeed, not in frequent use.
   Performance of the bua'-feast is not an individual affair, even should

one person assume leadership, but rather the concern of a sangbua', a
bua'-community: a territory of limited extent. In Kesu' this is usually a
village (e.g. Sangbua'), or half of a village, but it can be a larger
area (cf. Vol.I:VI.1.2.). Within the bua'-community leadership of the
feast is the prerogative of a tongkonan that enjoys an eminent position.
The head of the tongkonan, an initiator of the celebration is designated
ampu bua', the host of the feast. He need not perform his responsibil-
ities single-handed, for other important tongkonan in the bua'-commun-
ity will cooperate by lending services and providing goods. Certain
titleholders in the village (in the bua'-community) have set tasks in the
ritual and villagers (the inhabitants of the bua'-territory) contribute
their share by helping with certain jobs that have to be done. This can
be essential, for even if the ampu bua' is a wealthy man, he must bear
the brunt of the costs. The members of the ramage of the host's tongkonan will lend assistance according to their means, but they will also
not hesitate to come from afar to take part in the festivities. The tongkonan with its surrounding compound is the centre of the feast, at
least during the first part of it. During the second part the feast is
transferred to the rante kala'paran, the great plain for village feasts
which are rituals of the East.

The bua' kasalle can be traced back to the myth of creation. In the
Passomba Tedong ("laudation of the buffalo") it is recorded that the
first feast on earth was in fact celebrated in heaven (Merok:147, 151).
A burake was fetched who determined the order of the feast. The to
tumbang, the female functionary who has such a prominent role in the
ritual, is already mentioned in the same verses. After celebration of
this feast, the rice on the sawahs of the upperworld thrived, an indication that the ritual, among its other effects, benefits the rice crop.

For a more specific idea of what people expect of the feast, however,
one must attend a celebration on earth. The myth states that the initial
feast in this world was held in Rura where the first incestuous marriage
on earth was consumated (Vol.I:159-61). The celebration of the bua'-
feast was to cleanse the earth and restore its bond with the upperworld. Commemoration of this incest is a feature of the ritual which is
not passed over in obscurity during contemporary enactment of the prescribed ceremonies.

A death song from Nonongan reports that after Rura bua'-feasts were
held, successively, in Enrekang, Se'ke' (Sinadi), Bangkudu (Kesu'),
Siguntu' and near Singki', a mountain in the area where the dead man
lived who is the subject of the death song. In this and in other songs
the bua'-feast appears to be connected with the migration of the group
which moved from place to place before arriving at its present home.
This migration is seen as a "transfer" of the tongkonan, with a burake
at the head of the migratory procession:

> "And then his clanhouse did he move,
> His shielding force he took elsewhere
> His ancestor who was divine
> His forefather revered as lord.
> His burake preceded him,
> His people followed behind
> The bead-hung drum[1] she struck for him,
> The python skin she hit for him,
> Resounded the snake instrument ..."
>   (The Chant:28)

One can thus also consider the bua'-feast as a feast which accompanies the renewal of the tongkonan, a motif one detects in the ritual in only one action, when a small part of the roof is renovated. Closer study of the myths which are about celebrating the bua'-feast rewards the effort handsomely. In this context it is significant that myths about the bua'-feast in Kesu' (The Chant:25-8) differ from those in Riu where the sequence of mythical bua'-observances is not the same (see below, sections 3 and 4).

Something of the essence of the bua'-feast has been suggested in the preceding text: the restoration of the relation between mankind and heaven achieved through a large-scale purification ritual[2] that takes the form of the presentation of young women to the upperworld. The relation between heaven and earth as a kind of marriage is not only re-presented in the ritual in the person of the burake, the woman who belongs to the upperworld, who even in her death ritual remains a creature of heaven, but above all in the girls or young women (virgins) who may not come in contact with the earth throughout the entire se-quence of rites. The young women stay inside or are carried about in state and finally deposited high in a waringin (banyan) tree or on an elevated platform (the gorang) (Kesu'). These women, the tumbang, are subject to the authority of an important, possibly somewhat older woman who is called tumbang. Just as in Macassar and in Buginese territories marriageable young women stay closeted in their houses until they are married (Chabot 1950:142), the tumbang remain shut up inside. They may not touch the earth and are carried in sedan chairs like some sort of heavenly bride. All these females belong to the ramage which throws the feast; they are not only physically present in the rites, but they are also symbolically identified with the tongkonan in which they abide.

Within the house, next to the central support post, a complicated conglomeration of paraphernalia is introduced known as the anak dara (sister, virgin) or tumba' (= tumbang). Especially this last nomencla-ture shows the identity of the anak dara with the tumbang. And spell-ing things out even more than is necessary, as the feast draws to its end, the anak dara is brought to the waringin which (in Kesu') serves as the temporary residence of the tumbang. As if this wasn't enough, the tumbang are also identified with the white wood of the sandal tree which at a certain moment is used as a sacrificial pole but at the same time symbolizes the tongkonan (marapuan) and its fertility.

The celebration of this ritual is no simple matter. Years in advance (at least in Kesu' where this component is important) a banyan tree is planted so that in the due course of time it will be possible to place the tumbang in its branches. Once the moment has arrived that the rites can begin, first of all, after various introductory ritual behaviour, the anak dara is fabricated and brought in place. A branch of sandalwood is also fetched, which must be of the white variety (white, like yellow, is a colour which is associated with the upperworld and nobility). A rite is carried out which demonstrates the identity of the tumbang with the sandal tree. Trance dances also take place inside the tongkonan. In total these events and the rites which accompany them take about six months to complete. At this point it is time to work in the sawahs. The tumbang are brought into the tongkonan or into a small house that is set up for them on the compound (the tangdo') where the ampang bilik (a symbol that is part of important tongkonan, see Vol.I:241ff.) is also put in place. There they will remain, subject to many prohibitions, until the second part of the feast commences. Several simple sacrifices mark the close of the first part.

After a year or longer, preparatory sacrifices are offered to usher in the second phase of the feast during which the principal celebration takes place. The feast site is shifted to the rante kala'paran outside the village where (when the waringin plays a part) a floor is constructed in the banyan tree upon which the tumbang will spend some time. This floor and its accoutrements is known as a gorang. Most of the time, however, a gorang is a towering construction made of thick bamboo. Eulogizing takes place on the gorang; it is also the point around which the tumbang are carried in specially crafted, beautifully ornamented palanquins. The gorang consists of six struts, about 8 m high, of buangin (Casuarina equisetifolia). In the lowest part of the gorang a floor is laid of bamboo that has been hammered flat. High up on the scaffold cross-bars are fastened which, together with the floor, help to hold the gorang together and keep it stable. The to minaa stand on these cross-bars (thin beams) during the laudation. They climb onto the cross-bars via a ladder with seven rungs which is leaned against the west side of the gorang. Beneath the gorang, on the ground, there is a rectangular frame to which wheels are attached. Is this the object which J. Kruyt has designated ruma-ruma ("small house") (J. Kruyt 1921:62)? Also on the ground in the middle of the gorang a vat of stone or wood is placed that has the shape of a rice mortar. Inside the vat the lumbaa langi', the "pole of heaven"[3], is stood upright, a huge bamboo which rises right through both platform floors. From its end, high in the air, a basket is hung with a white chicken in it. Several springs of sowing rice also hang from this basket. The bamboo fulfils a role in the lumbaa langi'-rite of the bua'-feast (see below, section 5 and note 54).

The parading of the tumbang is an especially festive occasion which entails extensive preparations: the decoration of the sedan chairs, the summoning forth of the tumbang, their visit to the kala'paran and their being settled on the terrain where the feast is to be held (in separate small shelters that have been furnished for them), as well as their being carried around the gorang at a rapid pace, are all actions which are accompanied by many sacrifices. Even a kind of mock battle is part of the programme at the feast site.

The Passomba Tedong belongs to the most important rites which precede the principal sacrifice. The accompanying narrative goes on for many hours. It is no less than a recitation of the myth of the tribe, beginning at the creation of the world and ending with the arrival of the group at their present place of abode. The sacrifice that follows is one of the most significant events in the whole celebration.

Once this sacrifice has been made and the eulogizing of the brave and the outstanding has been finished, the end is near. The tumbang acquire new clothes and are set down again on the ground, bringing to completion their long taboo period. A few simple activities round off the feast.

The celebration, which requires an impressive number of sacrifices, attracts countless guests, in the first place relatives of the host by marriage but also fellow residents of the bua'-community who do not belong to the ramage holding the feast but who help carry out the hard work involved. The unfolding of rites requires the cooperation of many functionaries. We have already mentioned the ampu bua', the burake,

the tumbang and her escort - the latter being women and girls of high
standing in the host's ramage. The burake is a professional priestess
for a larger geographical area whose functions can also be carried out
by a burake tambolang, a transvestite (tambolang, a black and white
stork, see Vol.I:IX.5.). The to ma'gandang deserve special mention,
the drummers who accompany the to burake and usually belong to her
family. The assistance of many other functionaries is indispensable as
well, such as the to minaa and the to parengnge'. This varies from
place to place.

It is impossible to provide a description of this long and extremely
elaborate "cérémonie totale" which does justice to innumerable local variations. The account of the bua'-feasts which follows confines itself
therefore to three celebrations. The first is an excerpt from J. Kruyt's
report covering one (or more) such feasts, a report that pertains especially to Pangala' (J. Kruyt 1921). Allo Rante (Ne' Sangga) has
described the last bua'-feast in Kesu' held in 1923. His account which
prompts a fair number of questions is presented and commented upon in
section 3 below. In section 4 a great bua'-feast in Riu is portrayed.
The text here is based largely on information from Pong Samma' and from
local to minaa, but I have relied on my own observations as well (section 5). In Riu, unlike Kesu', the bua'-feast is still performed rather
frequently, even in several locations at the same time (but not syn-
chronously). One of the reasons for this is that in Riu people have
managed to keep the first phase of the celebration comparatively modest
so that it is easier to finance than elsewhere. Moreover, the spread of
Christianity has also made itself felt here; in Kesu' the process of
conversion is almost complete. In this context Van der Veen's comment
that already in the early 1920s the bua'-feast in Kesu' had all but died
out is of interest (1924:400). Bua' Sarungallo attributes his name to the
bua' (kasalle)-feast that was being held in Kesu', which is consistent
with what Van der Veen has reported. In Nonongan the bua' (la'pa')
kasalle has in fact been celebrated after this year. In addition to the
high cost, which we have already discussed (Kesu'), another reason
advanced for why the ritual has not been observed involves the
quarrels and internal wars which the Toraja frequently fought against
each other in the Sa'dan region during the first quarter of this century. The ritual, as a rule, takes a long time and, it goes without saying, requires calm. The unsettled state of affairs that prevailed is one
explanation for why in certain villages, Angin-angin for one, people
showed an ever-increasing inclination to replace the bua' kasalle with
the small bua'-feast, the bua' padang. Other factors were also of influence on this development, such as a rapid succession of great death
rituals that had to be observed and the imposition of such duties as
statutory labour by the colonial government.

As far as the sacrifices which are part of the bua'-feast are concerned, what was said in Chapter I also applies here: they are for the
most part offered to the gods and the deata in a rather straightforward
way.

2. The sequence of events in Pangala' district [4]

In Pangala' when one is planning to hold a bua'-feast a to minaa is
consulted about the celebration. As the initial rite, the to minaa per-

forms the massuru', a purification rite (massuru' = to comb, here in the sense of to clean). As part of the rite a pig is sacrificed. Next comes the ma'pesung. The sacrificial food consists of a pot of boiled rice and parts of the sacrificed pig. One almost always uses the same parts of the sacrificial animal (see Vol.I:251). Two sets of four pesung are prepared. The first four pesung are placed by the to minaa in the Northeastern corner of the house (in the front room). Sirih and areca-nut are also set out with each pesung. The pesung are offered to: 1. the deata of the earth (the ampu padang, see Vol.I:126); 2. Puang Matua; 3. the ancestor who descended from heaven (Manurun diLangi'); and 4. his son Pondan Padang who farmed the first sawah in Pangala'. Kruyt's description of the ritual act is not consistent with figure 2 in his text, designed to clarify the situation. Conditionally I would hazard the following account of proceedings: there are two sets of banana leaves which are spread on the floor of the tongkonan in front of each other; two pesung belong to each set. While the to minaa holds a bam-boo cylinder with water in the right hand and lays the left hand on the leaf in the foremost position, he addresses 1. and 2.; afterwards, with the left hand on the second set of banana leaves, he calls on the ancestors 3. and 4. The priest performs this act either early in the morning or at about noon. J. Kruyt adds that the to minaa must con-sume the right hip joint, none of which is part of the offering, on the spot; this strikes me as quite an assignment. "Hereupon one (the to minaa?) descends from the house to the ground and repeats what is described above: a pig is slaughtered, and parts are reserved for the dipiong-offering; the to minaa with his face to the Northeast, seated on a mat on the ground, offers the four pesung on two (sets of) banana leaves to the four tribal fathers" (J. Kruyt 1921:50; by the four tribal fathers Kruyt means the gods and ancestors specified above). Presum-ably the mat is situated to the Northeast of the tongkonan. Now, too, the to minaa has his face turned to the East during the prayer (see arrow):

East

	1		2
↑	o Ampu Padang		o Puang Matua
	3		4
	o Pondan Padang		o Manurun diLangi'

During the ma'nene' which now follows, a pig is slaughtered anew. Again the to minaa prepares four pesung on a mat: two pesung next to each other are for the ampu padang and Puang Matua; the other two pesung side by side are respectively for Polopadang, an ancestor in Kesu', and for the most important ancestor of people from Tikala[5]:

o Puang Matua		o Ampu Padang
↓ o Polopadang		o ancestor from Tikala

West

During this prayer the to minaa faces West (see arrow). The nene' (to dolo, to matua) are the ancestors of the (South)West. Yet it is notable that the sacrifices are also intended for Puang Matua who lives in the heavens.

The following rite is the mangrambu langi'. A pig is fastened to a stick together with a stalk of Dracaena. Two men lead the pig to the Northwest of the village. The to minaa goes along with them and upon arrival at a certain place receives his payment. The pig is now slaughtered on the spot by the to minaa. He uses two pointed wooden stakes to spear some pieces of the sacrificed animal and drives the stakes into the ground next to each other aligned in a Northeast-Southwest direction. With his face to the Northwest the to minaa calls out to Puang Matua; for this invocation he inserts two old V.O.C. coins[6] in the opening of his left ear to prevent his going deaf. Aside from the offering to Puang Matua the rest of the pig is burned in its entirety; no one may eat of it (see above; and Merok:3-4 and 164-6). Subsequently, the host and several families go to request the to burake to perform her offices at the feast; "ussumba' to burake" (ask the burake to officiate at the celebration). Upon arrival at the priestess's house, everyone screams aloud and the to burake kills a pig. The host hands her some money; the amount is not mentioned. After the priestess has agreed with what is asked of her, she fashions an anak dara. This anak dara consists of a bundle of tabang-leaves (Dracaena terminalis, bloodwort[7]), pusuk (the young leaves of the Arenga saccharifera), a piece of the aerial root of the banyan tree, the leaves of the nanna', the kamban-kamban, and the lambiri (a kind of palm, called by Kruyt the pseudo sugar palm).[8] Then the burake takes a piece of bamboo and quarters it, decorating the fragments on the top by partially leaving it intact - applying a standard technique for adorning bamboo with motifs. In fig. 4 of his article, J. Kruyt provides an illustration of bamboo that has been treated in the required fashion and provides the names of the engraved motifs (with the exception of bua kapa', the cotton, Kruyt's designations are difficult to identify with known motifs). The four lengths of bamboo, the stalks and the leaves are then all attached to a lance and this anak dara is fastened to the North side of the centre post of the house, a petuo. (For the possible significance of this anak dara, see Vol.I:VIII.1. According to J. Tammu, the former assistant of Van der Veen, the fetish is already erected during the maro-ritual: it is placed in the tongkonan which will be the centre of the bua'-ritual.) After the anak dara has been prepared, the to tumbang is selected. In Pangala' she must be the wife of one of the most eminent members of the host's family. No indication is given of her exact relation to the ampu bua'; all that is said is that the host in consultation with his family members chooses the to tumbang. The to tumbang in Pangala' has seven female companions.[9] The whole group may be referred to as to tumbang or to mangria barang. Little is reported about the marital status of these to mangria barang, "those who support the winnowing fan". They are identical with the to tumbang about which J. Kruyt writes in his article. He tells us that in Ba'tan (Kesu') the to tumbang may be single or married, as long as they have not had any children. Van der Veen's information on Kesu' is different:

"When I was small, I was a tumbang,
     when I was a child, I was a to ma'langi'."
(From Singgi' Kaunan sola Pia (The laudation of the slaves and children) published in Van der Veen 1979:276-95. To ma'langi': a person who is in a state of exaltation.)

The number of women is not limited here. The relevant regulations in other regions are perhaps different: Kruyt reports that elsewhere eight to tumbang are possible. We should interpret what he says to mean most probably that of the seven or eight to tumbang there is always one who serves as the actual functionary and the rest as her escort or replacements (the lady or girl called kampa banaa is in fact the stand-in of the tumbang). The to mangria barang are subject to food and other taboos.

The to tumbang in Pangala' may not eat of the flesh of an animal that has been slaughtered in honour of the dead, or has died a natural death; nor may they consume food that grows in dry land (J. Kruyt 1921:54).[10] This latter prohibition pertains to maize and certain root crops that are the designated food for people in mourning. The great bua'-feast is, after all, a deata-feast. Kruyt's contention that these food taboos are the only restrictions on the behaviour of the to tumbang is not confirmed by the facts, as will soon become clear. After the to burake, her face to the East, has made an offering from beside the anak dara - the offering consists of parts of a slain pig - together with other celebrants she dances the massirri'-sirri' at night. (This dance is unknown to me.) The next day the mekayu busa takes place (mekayu: fetch wood; busa: white). The white wood that is to be collected is that of a variety of the sandal tree. Other sandalwood varieties are dark; they are incorporated into other rituals. Here, however, white sandalwood is required. Before the sandal tree is felled, the to burake kills a small pig. From the parts, intended for the gods, she then prepares four pesung. Afterwards the tree is cut down and the trunk laid on the compound of the celebrating tongkonan with its top pointing to the East. It is left to lie there for three days and three nights.

Meanwhile another scene has already unfolded on the compound. While the to burake is busy slaughtering the small pig by the sandal tree and preparing the sacrifice, a number of men from the group of celebrants has brought in two trees: a kole (I am unable to classify this tree further; it yields good timber) and a buangin (Casuarine). While the men perform war chants (sumapuko), these two trees are carried into the yard and set down whereupon the to burake once again sacrifices a pig. The buangin is used for firewood during the feast (see below), whereas it is not evident what function the kole-tree serves. After the dipalundan sendana, the laying out of the sandal tree, a new task awaits the to burake, one that once again is called dipalundan, but this time it is the "laying out" of the to tumbang. She must lie down at full length on a mat in the house. Then she is covered entirely with cotton that has been plucked but further left untreated. The to burake proceeds to comb out the raw cotton, an action described as mamuso. J. Kruyt (1921:55) provides no explication for this rite, yet the cleansing of the cotton is apparently a purification rite, while the to tumbang, for some reason or other, is associated with the sendana, for she, too, must stretch out flat on the earth.[11]

On the evening of this day, all of the host's (the ampu bua') family come together in the tongkonan. A fire is started in the hearth from the wood of the tabi (?), the nanna' (a common firewood), and the buangin which was hauled into the yard. When the wood has cooled off, several to ma'gandang (drummers) arrive. It is J. Kruyt's assertion that these drummers are constantly in attendance on the to burake (she

and they are from the same family, see Vol.I:27, 144). The embers of
the fire are then shoveled out of the hearth with a pesese (a kind of
wooden spade or scoop, a cultivation tool) and poured onto the floor of
the sali (the central room of the house where the hearth is located).
The ampu bua' and his family trample the coals into ashes as they
dance and sing (gelong).[12] Both the dancing on the remains of the fire
and the singing of the gelong suggest a trance state.

The next action is construction of the tangdo' kalua', a floor which
joins up with the front of the tongkonan to make a kind of front
gallery. The planks of the floor are lashed together with a bambalu-
liana. At the Northeast corner of the tangdo' kalua' a small sacrificial
vessel is placed consisting of part of the stalk of a bamboo-ao' (Dendrocalamus strictus) from the top end of which a small basket (karerang) has been suspended. A pig is now slaughtered on the tangdo'
kalua' and the parts intended for sacrifice are distributed on a number
of pesung (presumably eight although Kruyt does not specify). Remarkably the karerang remains unused. Next the sendana trunk is stuck
into the ground to the Northeast of the tangdo' kalua'. Afterwards the
to burake performs a war dance: "Hereupon the to burake performs the
mangaluk on the tangdo' kalua, i.e. she enacts a dance with a sword in
hand which takes her three steps forward and then three steps back
(nondo), over and over" (J. Kruyt 1921:56). Mangaluk is actually the
invocation of the deata which the to burake performs (see section 4
below), and ondo is the name of a dance which is part of the maro- and
bugi'-rituals. During this dance, performers go into a trance; this
might also hold true for the dance which the to burake executes.

Kruyt tells us that people then disperse to look for a banana tree on
which a comb of fruit is hanging. A sacral cloth, a sarita, is tied
around the comb of bananas. This long cloth is held tightly by all the
family members of the ampu bua' while the trunk of the banana tree is
dragged to the tongkonan and set in the ground to the North of the
house. Afterwards people carry the bananas wrapped in the sarita
inside and attach them to the anak dara so that the two touch each
other. On the same day everyone from the vicinity contributes a pig.[13]
These are slaughtered. The hindquarters of each pig are for those who
gave the animal. The kollong (a ring of flesh around the neck) is cut
from each pig. About half of the pig is still left. The to burake and
the to ma'gandang split half of what remains between them and the rest
is for the celebrant at large.

A simple bench, about as long as the tangdo' kalua' is wide, is then
constructed: the laang-laang. The laang-laang stands in front of the
tangdo' kalua'. At this point the to minaa slaughters a pig "to implore a
blessing for all that exists". He removes the parts of the animal meant
for the deata which are cooked in a length of bamboo. Adding rice,
boiled in an ordinary pot, he now prepares four pesung on two sets of
banana leaves. In front of the middle of the tongkonan a length of bamboo-ao' is placed with its top pointing Northeast (cf. Vol.I:272). To the
West of this bamboo a mat is laid down on top of which the four pesung
are set out. With his face to the East, the to minaa enacts the sacrifice; the pattern is the same that has already been described. A scrap
of the pig's meat hangs from the bamboo-ao' meant for the to minaa.

At night women sit on the laang-laang, with the tumbang at the
Western end. The men stand facing them in a row. Choral songs are
sung (ma'dandan). At the same time, two to minaa also "ngaluk

padang"[14]: one stands to the East, the other to the West, and while they recite the ancient family tree in order to demonstrate the origin of the customs they observe, they change places with each other repeatedly. In this way they continue throughout the night (J. Kruyt 1921:58).

Next on the programme is the ma'tammuan (welcome, greeting). The ampu bua' and the tumbang boil a quantity of yellow-coloured rice in a bamboo cylinder, stopping the open ends with bloodwort leaves. Chicken is also prepared. On the following market day members of the ramage take these bamboos to the market where they make short work of eating the contents. The to minaa goes, too, and besides the sandal tree that always stands on a market, makes an offering of four pesung composed of rice and chicken. The to ma'gandang who have escorted him now proclaim aloud that the bua'-feast has, for the time being, ended because cultivation of the sawah is to begin.

During the taboo situation which lasts until the second part of the feast begins, approximately a half year later, the to tumbang are shut inside the house. On the few occasions when they emerge they must keep their heads covered with a sacral cloth (a maa'-cloth). The only thing they are permitted to do is to cook their own food. They eat rice, meat, and some fruits. Maize is forbidden, for maize is the food of those in mourning (see above). They come in contact with the earth as little as possible. At times this period can indeed last more than a year: under such circumstances, however, after the rice cycle, the to tumbang are brought to the sacrificial terrain, the site which each village (each bua'-community, according to Kruyt) maintains for the celebration of feasts: the kala'paran. Here they are carried eight times around the erected sacrifical platform, presumably the gorang. Afterwards they are borne back home.

After an interval of more than a year has passed, the bua'-feast is resumed once new rice has been sown (J. Kruyt 1921:58).[15] The umba'-rui tangdo' is then the first rite. The to burake sacrifices a pig in the house and puts some meat as an offering on the pesung intended for Puang Matua and the deata who have previously been named (the ampu padang, Manurun di Langi', etc.).

The ensuing rite is the ma'tete' (to make a bridge). To the North of the tangdo' kalua' (to the North of the middle of this floor) three sticks from the buangin-tree are placed on the ground pointing Northwards; two more sticks are put down touching the tips of the first three, and then one last stick just a little bit further on. To the last stick a long rope is tied which leads towards the kala'paran, the feast terrain. Here a small, square platform is erected (tangdo'-tangdo') from banyan branches. The long rope from the six sticks on the ground is attached now to the Southwest corner of the tangdo'-tangdo' (see fig. 6 in J. Kruyt's article). To the Northeast of the tangdo'-tangdo' a sandalwood pole is stuck into the earth (it is not clear whether this is the same pole reported in use during the first part of the feast). In connection with this action, the ma'tambuli (digging of a hole) is first performed. The drummer, face to the Northeast, calls upon the deata. Then the hole is dug. Part of an iron roasting pan and three yellow beads (manik riri) are put into the hole. The purpose behind addressing the deata is to put them in a favourable mood, to ask them not to ruin the soil, but rather - just the opposite - to see to it that the earth yields

a good harvest. Next a pig is half-slaughtered to the East of the
tangdo' kalua', dragged past the buangin sticks and along the length of
rope to the tangdo'-tangdo' where it is put out of its misery.

A second pig is then killed, after which the to tumbang and her companions (the to mangria barang; see section 4 below) follow the same
route as the first pig, past the buangin sticks, along the rope to the
tangdo'-tangdo'. There the women sit in a circle with their legs
stretched towards the centre. A long sarita-cloth is draped around
their shoulders. A large winnowing fan is then laid across the legs of
the to tumbang and the other to mangria barang (see Jannel and
Lontcho n.d.:ill. p.57). The fan contains a number of bamboo cylinders
decoratively carved and filled with palm wine. Two cylinders are
strapped together into one bundle. Each woman picks up such a bundle
in her right hand. Eight kaledo (packets made of folded banana leaves
containing boiled rice) are placed in the fan, and eight belundak (Fig.
11). (The number, arrangement and decoration of the bamboo containers
can vary from region to region.) In addition strips of pork, a pesung
with grains of the Coix Lacryma Jobi and boiled, yellow-tinted rice are
put into the winnowing fan.[16]

It is not certain for whom or for which deata the food on the fan is
intended. Next the to burake prays aloud. She stands to the West of
the to tumbang and the to mangria barang, her face to the East. The
priestess asks Puang Matua to confer prosperity and health. Then she
knots her hair like a man; a second to burake who has joined the proceedings does likewise.[17] Each priestess places a plume of parakeet
feathers on her head, seizes a shield and a sword in her hands and
performs a war dance, encircling the tangdo'-tangdo' several times.
Afterwards they move on to the mangaluk, i.e. while they walk about
calmly they ask Puang Matua for his blessing and for prosperity. Now
the to burake, to tumbang and all her companions go back to the house
where no one any longer, not even the to tumbang, need abide by special rules.

The laang-laang is repaired. To the West of this bench the to minaa
sacrifices some hens; certain pieces are set aside for the nene' (ancestors). The to tumbang and her retinue of women take places on the
Western side of the laang-laang; other women (from the host's family?)
fill up the remaining room. They draw up in a row and begin to intone
a song (ma'dandan, see Vol.I:VIII, note 8). A row of men assembles
facing them and responds with another kind of song, the manimbong
(for this song, see Holt 1939:74-6, illustrations 75-8).

People then proceed to construct a vast tower (gorang) on the feast
terrain (rante kala'paran). Here I will only describe the rite which
accompanies the making of the ruma-ruma (the small table under the
gorang). After this table has been fashioned, the to burake has a pig
slaughtered and from the flesh makes two pesung which are set out on
the ruma-ruma for the deata.

The to minaa then proceeds to the ma'pakande nene', the rite known
in Kesu' as ma'pakande to matua (Merok:2). A pig is again used as a
sacrifice and the usual parts are offered to the ancestors previously
cited. The to minaa officiates at a spot West of the tangdo' kalua'.

The ma'tali tanduk ("decoration of the buffalo horns") follows. A
person carries out this rite who is considered to be especially qualified.
The horns are necessary for the songlo' that takes place the next day.
They will decorate the sedan chairs in which the to sanda karua are

carried. A chicken and a pig are slaughtered for the ma'tali tanduk. The chicken meat is cooked in a piong (bamboo joint), the pig in a pot. Some parts are offered to the deata but who presides at the rite is not reported.

The following day a festive procession takes place. The participants proceed in attractive garb to the rante kala'paran. In front walks the to mano'bo[18], a man in full battle array. The to burake follows him. Behind these two functionaries comes the to tumbang who may not touch the ground. Therefore the to burake sprinkles tabang-leaves (Cordyline terminalis) on the ground for the to tumbang to walk on. In the wake of the to tumbang advances the to ma'tanduk, the man who wears the decorated buffalo horns on his head. Tied to his arm is the end of a long cloth, the pangriu. The ampu bua' and his family members hold on tightly to the pangriu. Last of all follow remaining celebrants, those who may not use a pangriu. The procession travels three times around the gorang. The to burake leads the to tumbang beneath the tower and lays three grains of husked rice on her head. The to burake kills a pig (or has one slaughtered) and offers four pesung to the deata. She places these offerings on the ruma-ruma. The to tumbang and her to mangria barang advance now to the tangdo'-tangdo' where the rite with the winnowing fan is repeated (see above). Kruyt's text makes no mention at this point of any duelling between to burake.

During the evening of the same day, the ma'pulung is held (ma'pulung: come together to consider something, in this instance, presumably, the further course of the feast). The ma'dandan and the manimbong follow once more.

On the following day, a mock courtship is acted out between the to burake and the to ma'gandang. The to burake is inside the house; the to ma'gandang stands on the tangdo' kalua'. The to burake speaks first: "What dog is that barking below? What areca-nut has fallen on the ground? Who is there?" He answers: "I haven't let a nut drop, but I see a woman". She: "If you should perhaps desire me, then I'd tell you I'm not interested". He: "Even if you don't want to, I'll force you". She: "How you're eyeing me! This door is too small, so I don't want you." He: "Then I'll force you". She: "I'll spit on you. If you don't go away, I'll get a piece of firewood." He: "Ah, you really aren't very good-looking. I've seen through the floor how you're covered with lice." She: "If you want to marry me, you may come in, but if you're just interested in a single visit, I don't want you." (J. Kruyt 1921:64).

In advance the sedan chairs (bullean) have been made ready for the to tumbang and her escorts. For each sedan chair, a pig is slaughtered; a pesung is placed on the bullean. At roughly the same time the to minaa commences with the ma'parekke para, a sacrifice made near the para, the triangular protruding section of the front façade of the house. This occurs in the houses of those who take part in the bua'. For whomever may have previously celebrated a bua', however, this rite is not necessary.[19] Everywhere the rite is observed the household head has a pig slaughtered. Some of the flesh is removed; a pesung is placed on a plank in the vicinity of the para; a second pesung is set down on the floor. Each house then prepares the potumabu, a packet from the mabu-leaf (?) in which boiled rice and some pork are wrapped. These potumabu are sent to the to minaa. The to tumbang now proceeds to the next rite, called sumba' to manurak (J. Kruyt gives no translation; the exact meaning of the words is unknown to me, probably: to

call the one who celebrates the buffalo = the to minaa). She has a dog
killed on the compound and boils the body in a pot. The meat when it
has been cooked is conveyed to the to minaa. He immediately has a pig
slaughtered; pesung once again are presented to the deata (to Puang
Matua, the ampu padang, Manurun diLangi' and his son). The bearers
of the dog meat are given pig to eat. A different to minaa makes an
offering to the nene' (ma'pakande nene') to the West of the tangdo'
kalua'.

At cock's crow the next day the to minaa and two to ma'gandang go
to the kala'paran. The ma'tambuli is carried out by one of the to
ma'gandang to the East of the gorang; here s sandal-tree branch will
be planted. The other to ma'gandang digs a hole South of the gorang in
which a rice mortar containing a bamboo-ao' will be inserted (see
below). A buffalo is then led to the North of the gorang where the to
minaa celebrates the beast in song.

One of the to ma'gandang selects a long pole of bamboo-ao' and
severs it. In the stump which remains, three yellow beads and a fragment from an iron roasting pan are placed Then the to ma'gandang
binds a sarita to the top of the ao' that he has severed and while
others carry the bamboo, he pretends to be tugging it forward. Once
they reach the kala'paran he lays the bamboo flat on the ground in
order to ordain it as lumbaa. Meanwhile the buffalo that has been
praised in song has been slaughtered and the to burake has killed a
pig. She now places six pesung composed of meat from the pig on or
next to the ao' together with one kaledo of yellow-coloured rice and a
pesung of grains of the Coix Lacryma Jobi. The bamboo-ao' is now
stood erect with its foot end in the rice mortar that has been stationed
under the gorang. For the role of this bamboo, from this point on
designated lumbaa, the reader should consult section 4 below. Furthermore, for the sequence of actions in the ceremony during which the
buffalo (or several buffaloes) is sacrificed, the final rites of the ritual
in various regions hardly differ from one another.

Here there only remains to report what is done with the anak dara at
the close of the feast (J. Kruyt 1921:70-1). The to burake removes this
artefact from the house. She prepares four pesung. For this sacrifice,
a pig is slaughtered. She extracts the four lengths of bamboo decorated
with carving from the anak dara and inserts a pesung into each one.
Four of the most prominent members of the ampu bua' each take one of
the bamboos and implant it in the most beautiful and spacious of his sawahs. What remains of the anak dara is brought to the banyan tree and
laid at its base.

On the first following market day the ma'tammuan ("to go in order to
greet") recurs. A pig is killed and prepared; concurrently a vast
amount of rice is boiled. At dawn all take the food that has been made
ready with them to the market. Upon their arrival, the to minaa offers
up two pesung under the banyan tree (thus not next to the sendana).
The whole time his face is turned to the East. Afterwards the group
finishes off the food they have with them. Upon their return home, a
pig is slaughtered for the ma'panampani tangdo', the chopping up - of
a sacrificial animal - for the tangdo'. The to burake and the to ma'-
gandang prepare two banana leaves with food for the rite which, while
they face East, is then offered on the tangdo' kalua' to the deata. Subsequently those who have taken active part in the feast are paid with
money and husked rice.

The closing rite of the bua'-feast consists of the to burake's dousing the to tumbang's head in a trough filled with water. The head wash of the to tumbang coincides with purification ritual enacted by all bua'-feast celebrants, who take a bath.

The entire bua'-feast has a great deal to do with the relations between mankind (the inhabitants of this world) and the upperworld. It implores heaven's favour for man, animals and crops. A.C. Kruyt points out that the perching of the to tumbang high up in the banyan tree is comparable to the "journey to heaven" of the Bare'e-Toraja women (A.C. Kruyt 1935). Indeed, their sojourn in the tree does seem an attempt to establish contact with the upperworld, the realm of the gods and divine ancestors. The term tumbang is an indication in the same direction; it means, literally, to leap up. At times it also has the significance of falling into a trance. People who become entranced during the maro-ritual are similarly called to tumbang (see Chapter VI.2.); yet we shouldn't confuse these figures with the to tumbang of the great bua'-feast. These latter women and girls stay free of any trance and for them the word tumbang can only mean that they make their way in an upwards direction: during a certain phase of the feast they climb into the banyan tree and stay there for some time (Kesu') or on the "big day" of the feast they spend a good while in a hut perched on high posts (in Riu; see below).

3. The la'pa' kasalle as celebrated in Kesu'

The material processed in this section derives from a long interview with Ne' Sangga in 1966. It is largely his account of the last la'pa' kasalle-celebration in Kesu' of which he was an eye-witness in 1923. Ne' Sangga's tale is not altogether satisfactory, to be sure. More than fourty years separate the event from his retelling and one detects the consequences of this time lapse rapidly enough in the rather schematic character of Ne' Sangga's presentation. When I reread his recollections, a feeling now and then steals over me that reality has undergone contamination with memories of other ritual celebrations, such as the bua' padang-feast. It is now no longer possible to challenge Ne' Sangga on this score. Comparison with J. Kruyt's report of a la'pa' kasalle, as will become apparent, yields some clarification but not to such an extent that one can construct from Ne' Sangga's narration a living, and in all aspects satisfactory picture of the exciting events which actually took place. It remains primarily a summary of sacrifices and ceremonies in succession which, at least for the first half of the series of rituals, it has seemed advisable to number consecutively in order not to lose track of the progression. The result may not make absorbing reading but it is still impressive when one thinks how much effort and dedication the celebration must have cost.

The la'pa' or bua' kasalle begins with rite 1, the mangrimpung or mangrapu, the assembly of people who belong to the ramage. A pig is sacrificed; the offering is directed in part to the soul(s) of the dead. During the mangrapu, the to minaa officiates.
   The ma'pallin, rite 2, follows; a sacrifice about which more detail is reported in Chapters III.7. and 8. and IV.3. The to minaa sacrifices a

small black hen on the compound so that evil influences will be banished. Here follows rite 3, the likaran biang (see Vol.I:270ff., Merok:158
and Van der Veen, unpublished a) and rite 4, the mangrambu langi',
an expiatory offering for previous transgressions (see Chapter I). For
this rite a pig is incinerated whole; it is thus not divided and consumed
ceremonially. The to minaa makes the offering.

The following sacrifice, rite 5, is the ma'tete ao', a sacrifice to the
gods that derives its name from the vessel which contains the offering
that is suspended from a bamboo-aur fixed in the earth: "across a small
bridge of bamboo-aur". The sacrifice is performed by the to minaa on
the compound of the tongkonan of the host.

Rite 6 is next, the mangkaro bubun[20], "the cleansing of the well"
(for the accompanying sacrifice, see also Chapter III, rite 6 and
Merok:4). During this purification a sella' is sacrificed by the to minaa.
During rite 7, the massali alang ("the laying of the floor in the ricebarn"), the to minaa offers up a chicken (a rame, yellow with brown
spots) and a dog. Then follows rite 8, the membase kandean (kandian),
"the cleansing of the eating bowls"; the to minaa sacrifices a cock
(whose colour is not mentioned). Rite 9, the ma'bubung ("laying the
ridge covering on the roof") is also part of the merok-feast and the
mangrara banua (cf. Merok:4). The to minaa recites the sacrificial
prayer (for the text, see Merok:168-80). This offering consists of a
pesung which is set out on a plank near the para. A pig is the animal
which provides food for this offering.

Rite 10, the ma'pakande to matua, the offering of a sacrificial meal to
the ancestors of the (South)West, is intended as an introduction to a
new series of actions. It is Van der Veen's opinion that "giving food"
to this category of ancestors also involves beating of drums, i.e. those
drums which are used in the rituals of the East (see Merok:5). Yet,
Ne' Sangga makes no mention of the use of these musical instruments;
nor does J. Kruyt. The offering entailed in the ma'pakande to matua
consists of parts of a black hen placed on torn banana leaves to the
Southwest of the tongkonan. The rite occurs during the merok-feast as
well (see Chapter III.7. and 8. and Merok:2, 5) and in the manganta'
(see Chapter VII).

At this point, rite 11, the manglelleng anak dara takes place, the
cutting down of the banana tree and the bamboo necessary to make the
anak dara (see Vol.I:241,244,286). In Kesu' the anak dara consists of:
- four pieces of bamboo;
- the young leaves of the sugar palm;
- the young leaves of the pseudo sugar palm;
- the leaves of the tabang;
- the leaves of a creeping plant, the kamban-kamban.
Upon completion of the ma'parekke para (rite 13, see below), the bamboos and leaves are trussed together. (Later the trunk of a banana
tree and/or a sword will still be added.) For this the smallest sacrifice
of all is made; it is known as piong sanglampa and pesung sangdaun,
the names spoken together in a single breath. Once the leaves needed
for the anak dara have been collected on the compound, rite 12 follows:
the ma'tete ao'. The ma'tete ao' has already been reported as number 5,
but in point of fact rites recur at times during the ritual. Afterwards
the elements required for the anak dara are assembled in the house and
rite 13 ensues, the ma'parekke para just mentioned a few sentences
earlier: a sacrifice is offered on the plank near the para. (J. Kruyt

(1921:64, and note 19 above) reports a different sequence and several
variant rites.) The rite is carried out by those in no position to have
performed the manganta' for a dead family member (for the manganta', a
conversion ritual, see Chapter VII.2.7.). A pig is slaughtered, or
several pigs. These are supplied by family members of the host.[21] The
to minaa is still officiating. The bamboos of the anak dara are filled
with water and bundled together with the banana tree, the young palm
leaves, etc. (didodoi pusuk; literally: "dressed in a skirt of leaves
selected from the young aren palm"). The bundle is adorned with red
cloths. The anak dara is fastened to the top of the most important post
inside the tongkonan, the petuo, which stands on the a'riri posi'
(Vol.I:232, 240). At about seven o'clock in the evening family members
are summoned, those from the same ramage for the next ceremony, rite
14, the ma'mulu. Bamboos are tied in bunches and made into torches
(bia') which are placed to encircle the tongkonan and provide illu-
mination. Once the ma'mulu is over, on the same evening, family members convene to reach an agreement about when they will begin with
the construction of the tangdo'. Hereafter the ritual enters into its
second phase.

Once accord has been reached about the tangdo', the ma'pakande to
matua, rite 15, follows again (for this sacrifice, see Merok:2 and
above). A black chick is put to death by the to minaa who places the
meat then prepared from the victim on the earth to the Southwest of
the tongkonan. The usual banana leaves are spread out first under the
food. On the same day, rite 16 is staged, ma'patama gandang, literally,
"bringing the drums inside", i.e. introducing the drums into the ritual.
These are musical instruments which only may be used in rituals of the
East. The drums are put in the tongkonan. A hen and a pig are slaughtered and some of the meat laid out on the drums as a sacrificial meal
for the deata. Only afterwards are the drums played for the first time.
The drumming takes place, with intervals of silence, during the coming
two days as well. The to minaa continues to preside over the ceremonies.

On the day after the ma'patama gandang, the ma'pasang tedong, rite
17, is staged, the display of the buffaloes. Exactly what the rite entails
is not specified, yet during the merok-feast the buffaloes owned by the
villagers are led outside the village and collected there. The forehead
of the animals is then smeared with the blood of a pig which is sacrificed on this occasion (Woordenboek: v. pasang). This pig is killed on
the East side of the compound.

Later the same day, in the afternoon, rite 18 takes place, the ma'kollong gandang, for which a pig must be slaughtered. The kollong, the
ring of flesh cut from the neck of the sacrificed pig, is placed on the
drums as an offering.

On the morrow, rite 19, the langngan buntu, is observed, "the climbing of the hill" (in order to make a sacrifice on the top). The rite is
also known as melondong datu, "to offer a rooster to the gods", with
the purpose of imploring the blessing of the upperworld (here datu,
actually signifying a prince, is used to convey the same notion as
deata). The to minaa conducts the sacrifice. In Ba'tan he ascends the
hill Malenong, in Tonga he climbs to the summit of the cliff Kesu'.
There the to minaa slays a red rooster with white feet, a sella'. The
same day, rite 20, manglelleng sendana, "the felling of a sandal tree"
occurs. In actuality the rite involves around a branch that is hacked

off and then at the appropriate time planted in the soil of the compound. Rite 21 is the mangke'te' bambalu: the bambalu is the liana
which is used to tie the buffalo to the branch of sandalwood driven as
a post into the compound soil; mangke'te' means "to cut off". What
follows, rite 22, is the manglika' biang, the preparation from reeds of a
container to hold an offering. For the contents of this prayer, see
Merok:158-67, and Van der Veen, unpublished a. In this instance the
offering consists of a manuk rame, a dark yellow hen with brown spots.
Some of the chicken when it has been cooked is placed into the sacrificial reed container together with rice boiled in a piong (bamboo joint).
The to minaa performs the offering.

In the middle of the night after the manglika' biang, rite 23, the
ma'tambuli, "the digging of a hole", takes place. This rite is led by the
sokkong bayu or by the to minaa who stands in for him. The clothing
worn by the person who officiates consists of a long white jacket and a
sacral maa' folded into a headcloth; a manik ata, a necklace in which
old yellow, sacral beads and gold beads alternate, is displayed around
the neck. Meanwhile a buffalo has been led to the spot and to the West
of the buffalo a pig in a litter has been set on the ground. Three of
the host's female relatives sit on the ground of the feast plain, each
with a winnowing fan on her lap; continuously they toss rice into each
other's fans (see Merok:6-7, 184-91).[22] Then the ceremonial planting of
the sendana-branch is carried out, a rite led by a matua ulu[23] and not
by the to minaa. This, the 24th rite, also involves fastening the buffalo
to the sandalwood.

The following rite 25 in the la'pa' kasalle as observed in Kesu', is the
Passomba Tedong, the consecration of the buffalo, the ceremony which
is also of such importance during the merok-feast. The words which are
recited are the same as in the merok-feast but not the tune in which
they are recited. For the arrangement of the buffalo, the pig, the
sandalwood-branch and various functionaries in Kesu', the reader is
referred to Fig. 1. The buffalo is an ordinary black one, just as in the
merok. During this rite the bearers of the same titles take part as
those who will be discussed in the description of the merok-feast.

Fig. 1. Consecration of the buffalo, great bua'-feast, Kesu'.

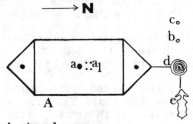

A tongkonan
a a'riri' posi', with the anak dara (a 1) to its North
b the to massomba tedong, "he who consecrates the buffalo"
c the to mangrande londong, "he who holds the cock in the palm of his
   hand"
d the sendana-tree
e the buffalo

In Ba'tan (Kesu') the participants are the already mentioned sokkong bayu (datu muane) who delivers the prayer and offers the sacrifice, the datu baine who officiates at the Passomba Tedong and puts the buffalo to death in the early morning, the to manobok, a to parengnge' in the bua'-community of Ba'tan, and the to ma'sanduk, "he who serves the sacrificial meal". Other functionaries include the to ma'sadi, "he who cuts the meat of the sacrificial animal into pieces", the to ma'nasu, "the one who does the cooking", the to manobok bai (alternatively spelled to mantobok), "the one who kills the pig with a stab", the to mangrande londong, "the one who holds the rooster (for sacrifice) in his hand", and the sipalakuan, the helpers, those who assist the above-mentioned adat-functionaries perform their tasks. As the time approaches when the consecration of the buffalo will take place, the drums are placed on the floor under the ricebarn. During this rite, 25a, pa'po-pengkalao gandang, "the bringing down below (i.e. the removal from the house) of the drums", an offering (ma'pesung) is made. A prayer precedes the consecration of the buffalo, one which is spoken by the sokkong bayu (or by the to minaa who may replace him). The prayer is the mebala kollong, literally "embracing the neck". Its intention is to protect the community from disaster and death and against revenge at the hands of the living or dead who might be roaming about with such a thought. For the contents of the prayer, see Merok:11, 16-8. The secondary motive of the adat-head who utters the prayer (here the sokkong bayu) is to assure himself of the support of the entire community so that no one will disrupt the consecration of the buffalo or interfere in any way with the celebration of the feast. In the prayer the sokkong bayu asks the members of the bua'-community:
"Have you already reached agreement,
that you may hold the end of my ladder?"
The clan members, numerous as bamboo culms growing
together on the same stool, reply:
"We have already come to a decision in our discussions
with the ones who are placed as guardians,
with the ones who are set up as protectors of the land.
We have also reached agreement
with the mighty clan-house
and the supreme seat,
and so we hold the end of your ladder."
(Merok:17)

As the 26th rite, the consecration of the buffalo is enacted. This rite is the same in both great feasts, yet what now follows is not applicable for the merok. On the same day that the sandalwood branch is stuck into the ground, to the East of this post the hut which has already been mentioned is erected (the hut is not depicted in Fig. 1). Next to it the ma'pesung is held: on a few pieces of banana leaf some meat from the animals sacrificed during the preceding rite are laid as an offering. Thus no additional pig is sacrificed. The hut is referred to with the name tangdo' kalua', but it is, to be sure, different from the previously cited tangdo' kalua'.

Three girls, about eight years old, are brought to this hut, where the drums referred to above are also stored. The hut is, moreover, adorned with an ampang bilik[24] which is decorated with the young leaves of the sugar palm. The front of this ampang bilik is turned to

face east. According to information, in Kesu' the girls who stay in the
hut may not exceed the age of thirteen; presumably they may not have
had first menstruation either. Besides to tumbang, they are also called
anak dara, virgin, which would seem to suggest that they have not yet
engaged in intercourse. For their role as "heavenly ones" it is perhaps
prerequisite that they are pure to qualify for their ceremonial functions
(cf. the daha from the village of Tnganan Pagringsingan and other Bali
Aga-villages on Bali; see, among others, Korn 1933:99). The number
three is the minimum required; if need be there can be six, or even
twelve to tumbang. After the tumbang have entered the hut, Ne'
Sangga's narration mentions the appearance of the to burake for the
first time, reporting that she joins the to tumbang. Then a pig is
slaughtered. What subsequently happens with the pig is not mentioned,
yet from the succeeding events it appears that it is used for an offering: rite 27 is an invocation (ma'pangalukan) delivered by the to
burake.

The ramage now come together to consult about when a gorang will be
built (in this instance a platform in the banyan tree). After one to four
days the megorang, rite 28, is observed, the building of the gorang.
From this point on the to burake presides over all offerings. A pig is
sacrificed. [25] The to burake and the to tumbang proceed to the gorang
(rite 29), while the ampang bilik remains behind in the tangdo' kalua'.
Men may not enter this gorang.

The to burake and to tumbang must stay in the gorang for three
days and three nights. Thereafter they come back to the ground again,
a ceremonial descent which symbolizes the coming down of celestial
beings to the earth (personal interpretation). The descent is known as
massonglo' do mai barana', "the descent from the banyan"; it is rite 30,
and a major happening. The to tumbang, the girls, are wrapped in
maa'-cloths carried out of the gorang. A special stairway, or ladder has
been constructed that is wide enough so that three people can stand
side by side on it. The stairway is decorated with golden kris. After
the descent, the to burake and to tumbang sing a litany, the ma'enge
(Woordenboek: v. enge). When the to tumbang are back on earth,
female family members join them. To celebrate this, rite 31, the to
burake – at times there may be more than one – kills and divides a
buffalo, officiating at all the actions. One or more pigs are also
slaughtered. For the ma'pesung, a surasan tallang [26] is put up by the
to burake. The offering is set down on a bloodwort leaf (usually sacrificial food for the gods is placed on a banana leaf; such a ritual presentation of something to eat, served on a leaf, regardless what leaf, is
always called a pesung). After the ma'pesung, the to burake once again
calls on the spirits (ma'pangalukan). [27] Then, rite 32, the to tumbang
and to burake go back to the tangdo' kalua'. When celebrants reach the
compound, the metangdo'-tangdo', rite 33, takes place. (In the Woordenboek, tando'-tando' is listed, a weakened form of tangdo', (the construction of) a small galery in front of the house. Woordenboek: cf.
tangdo' and tando'.) It would seem this rite encompasses the building of
the tando'-tando' reported by Van der Veen.

Ne' Sangga had nothing to say about the interval of approximately
one rice cycle that is so important in the ritual and which should
commence after the rite sketched above. Referring to J. Kruyt's account (1921:73), we can reconstruct what transpires during this period
of rest. The to tumbang remain enclosed in the house throughout a rice

cycle or sometimes even longer. They may only leave to bathe which takes place beside a special well, the well (spring) of the tumbang, bubun tumbang. When they go outside, the tumbang always have their heads wrapped in a maa'-cloth.[28]

After this taboo period, the celebration resumes. The ma'pangissi is staged, "the filling". Under the guidance of the to burake, a buffalo and a pig are slaughtered next to the house where the tumbang had taken up residence. Five pesung are prepared from the meat of these animals. These are set out on the floor of the tangdo' kalua' (the house of the tumbang). The to burake takes eight bamboo cylinders filled with sirih, pinang, lime, a dash of palm wine and a few drops of water. She holds these eight cylinders, strapped together into a single bundle, in both hands and makes a circle over the pesung eight times. She places two pesung on the galla', a small platform of woven bamboo joined to the tangdo' kalua' by a plait of leaves from the sugar palm. She also puts two pesung in the basket that hangs from the bamboo-ao' erected next to the tangdo' kalua'. She deposits the remaining pesung at the foot of the bamboo. She carries out all these actions wordlessly. The significance of this rite is not altogether clear.

At this point we will resume the narration of Allo Rante (Ne' Sangga), but without further enumeration of the sequence of rites. Up to now ritual events unfolded near the tongkonan. The barana'-tree also stands close to the compound. Here the scene shifts to the rante kala'paran. On this feast terrain a platform built on high poles has already been prepared; it, like the platform in the banyan tree, is called gorang, and its construction (megorang) has been accompanied by the sacrifice of a buffalo and a number of pigs. Before the buffalo is killed, the Passomba Tedong again takes place. The parengnge' officiate collectively during this ceremony. There is also a sacrifice made, a pig, for the guest house on the kala'paran.

A date is set for the massonglo', the festive procession of celebrants to the kala'paran. Family members come together three days before. Again a pig is killed, and eaten with relish. The entire ramage as well as friends and spectators assemble.[29] A sedan chair is made ready to transport the to tumbang and the ampang bilik to the rante kala'paran.[30] The to tumbang still may not come in touch with the earth. The sedan chairs are large and decorated with red textiles, including maa'-cloths. The to tumbang leans against the ampang bilik[31], which is likewise decked out with maa'-cloths and with young sugar palm leaves. To tumbang and to burake are dressed in ceremonial attire. En route to the kala'paran the to tumbang carry the sa'pi' decorated with gold and parakeet feathers on the head and with yet another small ornament on top in the form of a triangle (see Fig. 2a and b). The priestess wears red clothing (women's apparel) and a red and white headcloth, the tali burake. At the kala'paran the girls take shelter in a ritual hut.

The gorang, the platform on high piles, serves as a stage for the massinggi', the eulogizing of the members of the ramage. The to minaa enters into proceedings: in fancy dress, he climbs the gorang and in colourful speech he praises the fortunate, those judged worthy of the honour. The platform is decorated with young sugar palm leaves for the occasion and with leaves from the belo bubun (a variety of the Croton with speckled yellow and green leaves); red cloths and kris are also added as ornamentation. Each person being praised during the singing

Fig. 2a. Headgear worn by women and girls during the maro-feast, the merok- and great bua'-rituals.

a tida-tida, spangles of goldleaf
b sa'pi', a cap made of strips of young bamboo with the outer layer peeled away, possibly decorated with figures cut from goldleaf.
c patotti or pana'-pana', an ornament of human hair. The to ma'randing-dancers who perform at major death rituals also wear such an ornament on their war helmets. The hair comes from the prey of headhunting forrays.
d sondong para, a triangular ornament that resembles the triangular part of the façade which is located beneath the ridge of the roof in leading tongkonan. This part of the front wall is called (sondong) para. Literally, disondong para means: "to be made like a part of the façade". The sondong para, situated towards the top of north side of the house, can be considered one of the most sacral parts of dwelling, a symbol of the upperworld. The same holds true for the triangular ornament, made of paper, which is part of the headgear.

Fig. 2b. Sa'pi'; this hat is a variant of that pictured in Fig. 2a. The sa'pi' shown here is worn primarily during the ma'dandan at the bua' kasalle, and during the merok-feast by dancing women and girls from the group.

a patotti or pana'-pana'
b bulu ba'an, a decoration made from parakeet feathers (bulu: feathers; ba'an: parakeet)
c tida-tida, spangles

is pointed out by the to minaa with a staff. He holds fast to one end of
a long cloth while the priest holds onto the other. The to minaa rings a
copper bell (bangkula') in between verses. The first whose praises are
celebrated are the anak patalo, the brave among their number, together
with other eminent office holders. After the men, their wives receive an
accolade.[32] The to minaa does his best, for his later reward will be
proportional to the amount of praise which he has bestowed (for certain
personages there was no to minaa willing to perform the massinggi'; all
feared the eulogy would fall short of the praise that was due). Children
are complimented, too, either singly or as a group, but the boys always
separate from the girls. During the laudation girls wear a gayang
(kris), a rara' as a necklace, and on their heads the sa'pi'. Boys wear
a kris, a cap and a long jacket (bayu lamba'). It is also possible for
slaves to be praised in song, but only if their masters have given instructions for this to be done.
    The Passomba Tedong is then held for the second time, with the to
parengnge' presiding. The buffalo stands to the Northeast of the
gorang. Early in the morning of the following day, the buffalo is
slaughtered (the "big day" of the feast apparently lasts two days).
Once there are a lot of people on the rante kala'paran, the women begin
to dance and sing (ma'dandan); the ma'enge also takes place. People
are dressed up once again, displaying their inheritances. Once people
have withdrawn into the guest houses, the meat of the buffalo and also
of a pig that has been slaughtered is placed down on banana leaves as
an offering (ma'pesung). The sokkong bayu recites the accompanying
prayer.
    After eating, people stream into the open again and intensify the fes-
tive mood by dancing: women dance the ma'dandan, older men the
manimbong, and younger men the manganda' (for a description of the
manimbong, see Holt 1939:74-6 and figs. 75-8; see also the choreo-
graphic sketch on p. 117 of her book. For the manganda', see Holt
1939:66-9 and figs. 65-8 and the sketch on p. 117. Holt does not describe the ma'dandan as a dance.) Performing the manganda', the
dancers hold a copper bell in the right hand.[33] The dance is especially
spectacular thanks to the heavy headgear of the dancers which consists
of real buffalo horns. The dances were said to be held at night (in the
evening?). At the same time the war cry was raised, mangaru' (Woordenboek: v. aroe'). During the same night the ullimbui langi' also takes
place, a rite in which a large bamboo-ao' is stood on end in the
gorang. For the positioning of this bamboo, see section 1 above; for
the rite ullimbui langi', "the sharing collectively in heaven", see below.
On the next night the ma'singgi' described above is observed once
more. While the to minaa is occupied with the laudation, the to burake
invokes the gods and the spirits again (ma'pangalukan). During the
following afternoon the ampang bilik is moved to the tongkonan. This
plank is stored in the house as a sign that the tongkonan has celebrated a bua'-feast (see Chapter II, note 24). Another sign also provides evidence that such a feast has been held: across the whole width
of the floor on the façade of the house a wooden board, notched and
painted yellow, is fastened (bunga allo, "flower of the day").
    Now the close of the taboo period for the to tumbang and her compa-
nions has arrived. The to burake has laid a wooden trough with some
water in it on the tangdo' kalua'. She puts "animals" into the water,
probably fish raised in a flooded sawah. Meanwhile the to tumbang and

companions have walked to the host's house. They replace the maa'-
cloth which they have been wearing as a headcloth with a yellow fillet.
One by one each girl's head is then thrust down into the water (the
yellow bands are first removed). The girls receive a new name, which
usually begins with Tumba' (= tumbang); the name furthermore is associated with springs, whirlpools, rivers or the sea, with all things
related to water; for example, Tumba' Tasik (tasik = sea).

After this rite the tumbang and her escort proceed to the nearby
market carrying packets of pokon (pokon: packets braided from the
leaves of the bamboo-betung in which glutinous rice has been boiled,
see Fig. 11). They distribute the pokon among people at the market.[34]
This act frees them from the prohibitions attached to their status
during the bua'-feast. Many celebrants linger behind a while on the
feast terrain until a feeling spreads that the ritual has reached an end.
The placement of the anak dara in the banyan tree also belongs to the
final phase of celebration (see rite 66 below).

Not only does the great bua'-feast preserve and promote the well-
being of man, his animals and his plants, it is also a concluding ritual
that comes at the end of all rituals (also those of the West). The air
has, as it were, been purified by the celebration of the great bua'-
feast. This is also indicated by the designation la'pa' which is related
to the Indonesian word lepas: free, released from.

4. The great bua'-feast in Riu on the slopes of Sesean

According to the to minaa, the story of the creation of the world, the
origin of the gods and the establishment of ritual (see Vol.I:VI.1.1.,
VI.2.a. and VI.2.3.) should precede the short description of the rites
– translated into Bahasa Indonesia by Yusup Samma' – which follows
below. During this prelude the institution of the important bua'-feast is
mentioned as well.

Although the to minaa did not raise the matter of the proper season
for celebration, it was my impression that in Riu, in the lembang
Suloara, the feast culminated in the months of October or November[35];
in this area of Torajaland it was celebrated in rotation by leading
families, although on occasion they held feasts at the same time. Indeed
in 1970 three bua'-feasts were organized there concurrently, if not syn-
chronously. In Riu the expense of a great bua'-feast does not rival
what it costs in Kesu' which explains why in Riu after 1921 this ritual
has continued to flourish, even down to the present day.

In this region, too, the tongkonan, the centre of a (sub)ramage, is
at the heart of the feast, just as it is during the merok. The host of
the bua'-feast is an elder of the ramage, the most important one. All
his family participate, coming from far and near, just as they do for a
merok-celebration.

According to tradition, the children of Banggai diRante held the original bua'-feast in Rante Bulaan upon completion of the maro-ritual.
The second bua'-feast was celebrated in Rura, the third in Kesu', the
fourth in Riu. Then the ritual returned to Rante Bulaan, i.e. it was
celebrated there for the second time. (Other sources indicate the first
feast took place in Rante Bulaan, the second in Lino, the third in
Rura, the fourth in Kesu' and the fifth in Riu.)[36] From this account it
emerges that Rante Bulaan is not the same as Tana Toraja, but is

regarded as a mythical country, possibly close to the sea, a land where the ancestors reside. The first bua'-ritual in heaven preceded these bua'-feasts on earth.

It was possible for me to attend a number of the rites observed during the great bua'-feast celebrated on the slopes of Sesean in October 1970. Among other ceremonies, I was present on "the great feast day". An account of my observations on that occasion appears in section 5. Here, too, use will be made of information acquired at that time (e.g. concerning the anak dara).

1. The to minaa identifies the first rite of this feast as the mangrambu langi', "to cover the heavens with smoke", an expiatory sacrifice in which the offering, a pig, is burned. The rite lasts one day. The host's family slaughters pigs, chickens and dogs. (Although the subject was not pursued further, it does not seem likely to me that all these animals are incinerated; the burnt offering, I assume, is restricted to the pig mentioned above.) This is thus a sacrifice which man offers the gods to attone for sins of the past; these transgressions consist for the most part of neglecting marriage restrictions, and taboos of a sexual nature between relatives (Woordenboek:274).

2. The following rite of the bua'-feast is the mameleng (the word defies exposition). A pig is sacrificed.

3. Next comes the sitami palilli' (possible translation: to stop struggling with each other. Sitami: presumably sitammi', literally: to chew each other, in the sense of fight with one another. No translation is available for palilli'.) All members in the bua'-circle share in this rite. They may no longer nurture feelings of hatred towards each other - if such feelings ever existed, A pig is killed and offered as a sacrifice (memala'). Pieces of this pig are placed as a sacral meal on a banana leaf (pesung). The sacrifice is consecrated to the deata.

4. On the fourth day a pig is again killed and sacrificed; the offering again is placed on a banana leaf. The rite is called tongkonni sukuran padang (? literally: "to sit on the cubic measure of the earth"). The to minaa conducts the sacrifice, as he also does the preceding ones.

5. The following rite is the ma'suru' do banua, "the purifying of the house". The to minaa chooses a propitious day, a day on which the bua'-feast might be celebrated (which indicates that with the preceding rites the bua'-feast itself is not yet considered to have begun). After a pig is sacrificed, the to minaa implores the blessing of the gods for the feast (which will be celebrated).

6. Hereafter comes the ma'tomatua. A sacrificial meal is offered to both categories of ancestors, the to matua (nene') who live in the West, and the deata in the East (this differs from Kesu', where the term ma'tomatua denotes a rite for the ancestors of the Southwest). This meal, a hen, is the same for both. For the deata it is set out on the East side of the tongkonan (in the afternoon or shortly before noon); for the nene', on the West side of the house, late in the day (makaroen). The offerings are all made on banana leaves. The to minaa pronounces the prayer. The rite lasts a day.

7. On the following day, the ma'tomatua is repeated. Two hens are slaughtered once more, one for the deata, the other for the nene'. The same procedures are followed as specified above. On this, the seventh feast day, a hen is also slaughtered for Pong Tulakpadang, Lord of the Underworld. The offering (pesung) is carried out by the to minaa.

8. A hen is sacrificed (pesung) to To Kaubanan (the epithet of Puang Matua). The colour of the fowl was not specified. This sacrifice keeps the memory of Puang Matua alive.

9. A hen is sacrificed for the sukaran aluk do (dao) melangi', for the 7,777 aluk, the 7,777 fixed adat-prescriptions which were brought down from heaven. The sacrificial chicken may be any colour except white.

10. Subsequently the tutungan bia', "the lighting of the torch", takes place. For this rite a hen is sacrificed. The torches (bia') serve as a guide - "so that we humans can find the way" - an expression which possibly refers to the search for a form of subsistence approved of by the gods. In answer to my question whether these torches were real or symbolic, my interpreter asserted they were symbolic.

Van der Veen has a different interpretation. For him "the lighting of the torches", is, in poetic terms, a metaphor to describe an expiatory sacrifice designed to elicit blessings and well-being. According to the creation myth in Riu this took place for the first time in heaven; on earth such a ritual of atonement was celebrated initially after incest was committed in Rura. It was enacted by Suloara', Bua Uran and Pong Kannabua', three important ancestors from Tikala and Riu. The events are described in the Ossoran nene' lan lino, "De Overleveringen van de Voorvaderen op Aarde" (The Traditions of the Ancestors on Earth), transcribed and translated by Van der Veen (unpublished d):

Dilando lalanni Suloara' sola Bua
Uran anna Pong Kannabua'.

A long journey was made by
Suloara' and Bua Uran and
Pong Kannabua'.

Ratumi ma'rebongan didi, napasi-
turu' pandanan bai lako rampe
matampu' tu rebongan didi.

Upon arrival they established
the various rites; they subsequently called for the sacrifice
of a pig in the direction of the
West.

Balo'mi tutungan bia', tumbu kumuku'mi kaaran ballo marorrong.

The expiatory offering brought
good things, the bundle of the
bright-shining torches meant
prosperity.

Sulemi Sokko kalale' nakadang
tutungan bia'.

Then Sokko kalale' (a buffalo in
the myths) thrived through the
agency of the expiatory offering
that brought good things.

Sule Indo' Pare'-pare' nakadang
tutungan bia'.

Then Indo' Pare'-pare'[37]
thrived through the agency of
the expiatory offering that
brought good things.

11. A hen is sacrificed for the turunan (in Tikala and Riu this is the name for a well). The rite is vital because water is drawn from this source and without water no life is possible.

12. The teppe' uma is the name of this rite, "the making of a small sawah". The ricefield is imaginary. The significance of the rite is not altogether clear, yet it probably is associated with demonstrating the general importance of rice cultivation. A hen is killed and serves as an offering.

13. Massuka' barra' do banua, "the measuring of the rice in the house with a cubic measuring standard". This, too, is a rite whose name

refers to an action that should be interpreted symbolically. A hen is sacrificed; its colour is not mentioned.

14. Urrampun to minaa, "the convening of the to minaa". The underlying thought here is that all to minaa are called together by the ramage; in actuality only one representative of this category of priests is present.

15. Unnoto gelong, "to hit the gelong precisely". A hen is killed as a sacrifice. It was not stated who made the offering, yet presumably it will have been the to minaa. The villagers being to sing the gelong. This rendition of the gelong belongs to the maro-ritual. A certain form of this ritual, discussed in Chapter VI, the maro ma'bate (the maro-ritual in which a flag or banner is carried along) is apparently celebrated in Riu as a prelude to the great bua'-feast and precedes the fabrication of the anak dara. It should be reported that such a combination does not occur in Kesu'. Here I will stick to a brief summary of the rites, maro-rites in fact, which take place prior to the making of the anak dara. The intention of these rites appears to be the warding off of evil influences.

16. Ma'gelong bate. Many chickens are slaughtered, hundreds of them. One chicken is consecrated as an offering (pesung). A bate is rigged up, a bamboo pole with a "flag" (red cloth) attached.

17. Manglelleng tallang. A hen is slaughtered as a sacrifice for the hewing of the bamboo used for the bate which is called the bate bua' and serves to implore a blessing over the feast.

18. A hen and a pig are killed as "food" for (as a sacrifice to) the bate (ma'pesung bate). In the interim the bate is made ready.

The progression of the bate-feast is for the rest roughly parallel to the description of the ma'bate manurun and the maro as a conversion ritual at a burial feast (see Chapter VI.2.7. and 2.8.). The objective of the feast, it seems to me, above and beyond imploring a blessing from the deata, is the purification of the territorium (bua'-circle).

At the end of the bate bua'-celebration a meeting of the family members who organize the bua'-feast takes place together with villagers who wish to participate. A meeting thus of the entire sangbua'. Everything for the bua'-feast should be brought into readiness. Indeed one cannot delay the initial rites too long, for a death could spoil the planning utterly: in that event the feast may not be celebrated.

An important event is the selection of the women who will be central figures during the ritual, the to mangria barang. The families who have taken the initiative to hold the feast have the most to say about this choice. Indeed the disappointment can be bitter among women who think themselves suitable but who aren't even considered to be eligible. Only those women qualify for consideration who are both from prestigious families and rich (to sugi'). This is true especially about the choice of the to tumbang, for after her death she must be buried according to a lofty order of death ritual, the dirapa'i.

As first rite, the to mangria barang celebrate the ma'mulu at six in the evening at the tongkonan of the tumbang. Because this rite is repeated several times it is not assigned any special number here. The to mangria barang sit in a circle with their legs stretched out, the toes pointing to the centre. A great winnowing fan (barang) is laid across their legs. First ordinary rice and then glutinous rice is placed on the fan. A sarita is draped across their shoulders (see also above, and J. Kruyt 1921:60). The women are in festive garb. Each holds a bundle in her hand consisting of belundak (packets of cooked glutinous rice) wrapped in the leaf of the induk-palm (sugar palm). These packets are inserted between suke dibonga, "spotted" suke, bamboo joints which are decorated at the top end with incised motifs (the unfree may not use such suke). Palm wine is contained in the bamboos. Since the opening of the suke is stoppered with a fatty piece of pig's meat, to take a sip of tuak the women must remove these palompo first. Throughout the night and the next morning the to mangria barang must remain sitting in this configuration while holding the bamboos and rice packets in their hands. The to burake circles around them, playing the clapper drum. Gelong-songs are sung as well. This is all done to keep the women from falling asleep.

19. A chicken and a pig[38] are killed on the pasa'. In response to the question which pasar was meant, the answer I received was the rante kala'paran, the plain where the great bua'-feast is celebrated. The chicken and pig are a sacrifice for the anak dara. This anak dara[39] (see also sections 2 and 3 above) consists of:
- four pieces of bamboo;
- daun pusuk (young sugar palm leaves);
- kayu buangin (Casuarina equisetifolia);
- kayu ampiri (probably the lampiri, the pseudo sugar palm);
- kayu nanna'-nanna' (a wood which makes good firewood or charcoal);
- kayu kole (a tree that yields excellent timber);
- kayu kamban (a creeper whose fruits resemble bananas);
- daun tabang (the leaves of the Cordyline terminalis, the bloodwort plant);
- ue baine (a variety of rattan not further specified, the notation of sex may be compared to the bamboo-tallang, which is supposed to be female (Van der Veen 1979:135-53); ue means rattan, baine means woman);
- a la'bo' (a cleaver);
- a doke (a spear);
- a peruru (a ribbon to bind a woman's hair knot);
- dishes;
- spoons;
- a dolong-dolong (a wooden vessel, long in shape, in which vegetables and Spanish pepper are placed);
- a pesangle (serving spoon for rice);
- a kara kayu (a wooden plate with a handle, used to measure out portions of cooked rice);
- a kurin (earthenware crock);
- a mortar for making sambal;
- a lampa (a bamboo for carrying water);
- a baku' (a basket).
In other words all sorts of objects found around the house are added to the anak dara. In a tongkonan in the village of Toyasa in Riu I saw an offering plate with rice, sirih and areca-nuts as part of the anak dara which stood in the middle of the house between the two central house posts (differing from J. Kruyt's observation, the anak dara was not tied to the most important petuo, see above). The anak dara was constructed from eight bamboos, four inside, four outside. The number eight, which is of great significance among the Toraja, apparently is an allusion to the "plenary eight", i.e. the to tumbang and her escorts, ideally eight women who have a task to perform in the ritual. From this

point on the to tumbang keeps watch next to the anak dara. The other women also have chores to carry out, although these are of somewhat less importance (see below).

The four exterior bamboos of this anak dara were encircled by a ribbon adorned with daun pusuk; this ribbon bound not only the bamboos, but a sword, two spears and a section of banana tree with a comb of bananas as well. A sirih-pouch was also one of the attributes. At this stage the anak dara is spoken of as tumba' (tumbang). Is this tumba' identified not only with the leading female in the ritual, but also with the community's staple crop, rice?

I was told that the four exterior bamboos are stored in the ricebarn after the feast (see, however, below), and the rest of the anak dara placed in a barana' (banyan tree). In point of fact the artefact is then called anak dara for the first time, but to avoid confusion with the tumbang, the term anak dara will be maintained throughout the text. Identification of the tumba' with the tumbang is obvious. They are the same word and, when the great bua'-feast ends, the tumbang acquires the (new) name of Tumba' so-and-so (see above).

Before I might inspect the tumba', I had to drink some water from a scoop which was offered to me by the to tumbang who maintained a vigil in the tongkonan beside the anak dara. The various objects which make up the anak dara - with the exception of sword and spear - are things women use, most of them miniature models of household articles. In connection with the preparation of these items, my informant told me that the anak dara is a woman; a virgin, he added. When asked what the function was then of sword and spear, he replied that these had been inherited (it is possible that these are objects which by nature are to protect the anak dara). One component of the anak dara deserves further commentary: the banaa, a small basket set out to the West of the anak dara, wrapped in a sacral maa'-cloth (Van der Veen maintains this term denotes a wooden vat in which husked rice, an egg and three yellow beads are placed; Woordenboek: v. banaa). In Riu the banaa is filled with yellow rice (boiled rice mixed with turmeric). Banaa is also the name of the tumbang's deputy. Only one female informant drew my attention to another object called bua'. The alternate name for this object is talimbung (to rally around something, in the sense of creating a close-knit bond). This object was a small basket braided from the young leaves of the sugar palm. Half-way up the side, threads are pulled through the basket with a basting stitch: the uppermost ring of thread is white; the one below is red, the one below that yellow; and the fourth thread in descending order, black. The to burake makes the bua'. A pig is sacrificed on its behalf. Parts of the pig are removed for a pesung offered up by the to burake during rite 21 (see manglika' bua'). I do not know to which gods or spirits this offering is presented. Afterwards the bua' is preserved in the sumbung (the room at the rear of the tongkonan, the southern end; see Vol.I:233, 237) near the longa (the protruding part of the roof). The modest little basket is the symbol of the bua'-feast in its totality.

As a sacrifice for the anak dara (and for the banaa?), yet another pig is slaughtered. The kinship group pays the to minaa for his services in money (sumba' to minaa). Up to and including the rite mentioned above, for all the rites in succession, the to minaa has led the ceremony and received a share of the offering. Hereafter the to burake usually officiates. In Riu, to be more specific, it is the burake tattiku'.

20. This is the massuru' bua', the purification of the bua'-ritual. A pig is slaughtered. The to burake receives 1,200 rupiah.[40] This priestess, who officiates from this point on, makes the offering.

21. On the 21st day, the manglika' bua' is held (lika': to twist, to weave together).[41] Hens are slaughtered, one of which is a sacrifice for the deata, one for the nene' (ancestors) and one for the anak dara. The feathers of this last chicken are attached to the anak dara. A pig for the bua' is also killed on this day.

22. A hen is slaughtered, a sacrifice for the mangrenden bua', "the pulling (or the pulling onwards) of the bua'-feast". The rite serves to transfer the bua'-ritual symbolically to the house (the tongkonan of the family group which took the initiative for the celebration).

23. A hen is killed for the anak dara. The bird is killed in the tongkonan where the anak dara stands and there an offering is made (pesung).

24. Pakande sallangara onganan banua, "all the household furnishings receive something to eat". For the household goods, a hen is sacrificed (pesung). These furnishings are important, for people rely on them and every tongkonan has its special articles which, at least in part, are household effects. The anak dara is fitted out with all sorts of objects of daily use in miniature.

25. Menggaronto' asu lia ditunna lako banua bua', "as a foundation there is a brown dog who is slaughtered on the way to the bua'-feast". It is not certain for which category of gods or spirits the brown dog is slaughtered that serves as a sacrifice for the great bua'-ritual.

26. A pig and a hen are killed for the to mangria barang ma'pasalian, "the coming out of the to mangria barang", "those who wield the winnowing fans".[42] The to mangria barang (the to tumbang and her escort) go outside where, on the floor of the ricebarn, they sit (in a circle) with their legs pointing to each other; a large rice winnowing fan is laid across their legs. The ma'mulu (see above) repeats.

Above we have commented about the companions of the to tumbang. These women (elsewhere perhaps girls; but in Riu those who participated in the ritual were adults) are referred to as the to sanda karua, "the plenary eight". Their number includes the following persons:

1. the to tumbang;
2. the kampa banaa, "the guardian of the banaa"; she is the tumbang's replacement;
3. the datu bua', "the bua's noble consort";
4. the ponno bua', "she who is entirely replete with the bua'";
5. the rante bua', "the surface of the bua'-feast, the ceremonial plain";
6. the sirri bua', a title that is difficult to translate (sirri: that which is handled with awe because it houses a spirit; see Woordenboek:616);
7 and 8. companions with no special designations.

For these eight women (or girls) it is a memorable day. After a term of protracted seclusion during which they have kept watch over sacral artefacts (anak dara, banaa, etc.), they may show themselves once again to the public. They are attractively clad: the tumbang wears a maa'-cloth on her head, her escorts wear head ornaments made from yellow tarrungfruits. Around her neck the tumbang displays a rara', the others have manik ata-necklaces. Around their wrists the women wear a strip of cloth to which lengths of coloured beads and gilded scraps of silver have been sewn. Their clothing consists of a yellow sarong and matching jacket.

27. The manglelleng sendana pa'tangdo', "the felling of the sandal tree (branch) needed for the tangdo'" (the floor joined to the front of the tongkonan on the occasion of the bua'-feast). My informants had nothing to say about any more elaborate rite in connection with the sendana (see, however, J. Kruyt 1921:53, mekayu busa).

28. The sendana is stuck in the ground. A pig and a dog are slaughtered as offerings (no mention was made of the dog's colour). The sacrificial meal is presented to the gods (pesung).

29. Tiosok laa, "the setting up of the laa" (= laang-laang, the platform or bench of bamboo). The bench is where the women sit who sing the ma'dandan (a sacral song at the great bua'-feast; Woordenboek: v. dandan). A pig is slaughtered (for sacrifice?). The song of the women alternates with song from men who stand opposite them. The song is known as manimbong (see above). In Toyasa Riu I was to attend the ma'dandan but for some reason the choral singing did not take place; perhaps it was the rain that deranged things. In Riu the laang-laang consisted of two bamboo benches, one of which was placed above the other; the whole construction looked like a short, wide ladder. For a ground plan of the tongkonan and the laang-laang, see Fig. 3 (the drawing is not very clear on this point). A sacral maa'-cloth hung over the entire width of the benches. The laang-laang itself is not sacral; after the feast is over, the bamboo is burned for fuel.

Fig. 3. The great bua'-feast, Riu.

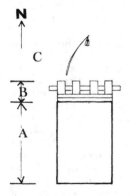

A tongkonan
B laang-laang
C peturo langi'

30. Umpakande nene', "the giving of food to the ancestors of the Southwest". A pig and a hen are slaughtered next to the tongkonan "to fill the banaa". A pig is also killed for the manglese roa, "the treading on glowing coals" (roa or roaya: glowing coals or embers). These embers are mixed with tabang- (Cordyline terminalis) and with Casuarina equisetifolia-leaves. Walking over them is a display of respect for the gods; the men of the ramage must do so. A trance dance is the core of this rite.

31. On this day the unnala punti takes place, "the bringing of the banana plant" (punti: banana). A plant with a comb of bananas is placed beside the anak dara; the to tumbang eat the fruit which is ripe. Three hens are provided for this rite, one as a sacrifice, the other two for the to burake to take home. The hens may be any colour except white.

32. On the day when this rite is observed, many pigs are slaughtered for the massabu tangdo' kalua' or the tiballa tangdo' kalua', "the consecration of the great tangdo'". The ramage slaughters "hundreds" of pigs. One should accept this total with a grain of salt. What takes place does, however, have a potlach element, each family trying to supply the largest pig possible (some if which have a value comparable to that of a buffalo).

During the following rites in Toyasa Riu I was present.

33. On the first day of my stay in this settlement the 33rd event of the feast was staged, the ma'pulung (pulung: assemble to consult about something; Woordenboek: v. poeloeng). A pig, a chicken and a dog were slaughtered. The to minaa examined the gall bladders of these animals (thus not the to burake). The hen was placed on a banana leaf as an offering (pesung); piece of the banana leaf is torn off on the right side (while tearing, one holds the point of the leaf away from the body). The pesung is intended as an offering for the laang-laang (dipodoi to' laang - in Kesu' this also takes place during the merok-feast; in Buntao' I did not witness it while attending the merok, cf. Chapter IV). Stems of biang, sirri-sirri leaves, nanna'-nanna' leaves and passake leaves are laid on the ground. After the rite the leaves are collected and tied fast to the uprights of the laang-laang.

For the ma'pulung two little sacrificial altars were erected: the peturo langi' and the langngan. The peturo langi' (turo: indicate; langi': heaven) is a short bamboo rod prepared from bamboo-aur (see Fig. 3). The tip of this bamboo may even be cut off, in contrast to that of the bamboo for the tadoran. The tip of the peturo langi' must bend towards the North. The pole is stood near the langngan, a "spit", that is used to cook food (rice and meat from slaughtered animals). This spit is situated North of the tongkonan. Pieces of meat should be hung from the peturo langi' as an offering, scraps, for example, from the dog which must be sacrificed after the peturo langi' is in place, at about twelve noon. For one reason or another, however, this offering did not take place during the rite I saw in Toyasa Riu. What did take place the previous night was the killing of a pig which the to minaa presented as an offering (pesung). Beside the langngan, yellow rice, kalosi (arecanuts) and bolu (sirih) are set down. Here, too, a small pig is slaughtered, the second, and roasted on the skewer. Parts of this pig were hung from the peturo langi'. A hen was killed, too.

After this had all happened, the to minaa intoned a prayer. Blood from the slaughtered pig was collected in a suke (a bamboo joint of small dimensions); a small stick, the pa'todiran, was inserted in the suke. This stick would be used like a brush to make a line on the heads of ramage members with the pig's blood. The suke was hung from the peturo langi' along with another suke that was filled with tuak (palm wine) for the deata. When the sacrificial meal (pesung) was prepared, what was left-over from the pig was divided among those present[43], except for the head. The pig's head is chopped off and reserved for the to minaa who eats away the flesh. The skull, however, is not shattered. First it is suspended from the peturo langi' and later, intact, preserved in the house of the to minaa or the host of the feast. The hen, however, is left whole; first it is hung from the peturo langi' and later also kept intact inside the house.

The offering (pesung) is cooked next to the langngan in a bamboo that has been cut off in a special manner, dipamate (as is customary for a death ritual, see Fig. 49). No explanation for this dipamate was forthcoming. Throughout the night the to minaa sang their litanies which they do with their faces turned to the East. The peturo langi' remains standing this and the following days, whereas the laang-laang is dismantled and used for firewood.

34. A pig is slaughtered for the dikande belundak (kande: to eat; belundak: packets of glutinous rice wrapped in the young leaves of the aren palm and then boiled, see Fig. 11). In this instance one should interpret the word belundak figuratively to mean that the pig is not used for the sacrificial meal (pesung).

35. A pig and a hen are slaughtered for the ma'tekken piong (tekken: to employ as a stick - Woordenboek: v. tekken; piong: a bamboo joint in which polished rice, here glutinous, and meat are cooked - in this instance meat from a pig and chicken; ma'tekken piong: "the piong stand there like sticks"). The sanda karua (or members of their family?) prepare the piong. When the piong are ready, each of "the plenary eight" takes one and uses it like a walking staff. All the sanda karua (= to mangria barang) stand in a line, the tumbang up front, piong in her right hand. Her left hand is trussed together with the piong and the right hand of the sanda karua behind her, using a kain sarita to bind them. The cloth is then wrapped around the left hand of the second in line together with the piong in the right hand of the woman next in line, etc. Women sing and dance (ma'dandan).

Everyone who has a function in the great bua'-feast must slaughter a pig and a chicken. Some portion of the slain animals is first used by the to burake for an offering. What remains is mixed with rice and cooked within bamboo joints to be consumed by the family.

36. Sule metamba langngan langi' lako To Kaubanan, "return from the summoning up of 'The One Who Has Grey Hair'". This possibly refers to a prayer spoken by the to minaa; in accompaniment a pig is slaughtered for To Kaubanan (He Who Has Grey Hair = Puang Matua).

37. A hen is slaughtered for the ditunu unnalai rumpang do mai banua (tunu: to slaughter, alai: the removal of[44], rumpang: waste, banua: house). The rite purifies the house (that is the centre of the bua'-feast). In the morning the to burake prepares the chicken as an offering (pesung).

38. Untunu manuk kande punti to banua (manuk: hen, kande: to eat, punti: banana, to banua: members of the house). A chicken is killed so that the tumbang (and residents of the house) may eat ripe bananas. The chicken is prepared as an offering (pesung) which is presented to the deata by the to burake accompanied by a prayer, imbo pangaluk (imbo: a prayer spoken over a sacrifice that is about to be offered up, see Woordenboek:162; pangaluk, cf. ma'pangalukan, all kinds of invocations executed by the to burake during the la'pa', the great bua'-feast; Woordenboek:12).

39. All the rites mentioned above have taken place within a half year. From this point on, a ritual pause begins which lasts a rice cycle. It is

the ampu bua' who prescribes this interval. The period of rest is called ma'torroi (= to stop with something, here with the celebration of the great bua'-ritual; Woordenboek: v. torro). The interval, however, is broken after about half a year by a rite during which a pig is slaughtered, the sipaka to Puang Matua (= To Kaubanan). This was translated by my informant - rather freely it would seem - as, "We give thanks that Puang Matua has preserved and protected us". During the above-mentioned year the tumbang and the kampa banaa stay in their tongkonan (the prohibition against leaving the house applies presumably to the "plenary eight"). After the rice harvest, the celebrants resume the bua'-feast (diba'rui bua', the renewal of the bua'-ritual). From now on rites take place on the kala'paran, the festival plain outside the village.

The to burake is summoned to get the bua'-feast under way once more. On one day a number of rites are enacted during which pigs and hens are slaughtered.

a. A pig is killed for the umba'rui suru' (umba'rui: to renew, suru': an expiatory sacrifice).

b. Misa bai ditunu undodoi tumba': a pig is slaughtered in order to give the tumba' (the to tumbang) a dodo (= sarong). This sarong consists of the yellow-green leaves of the induk, the sugar palm. The leaves hang like a fringe over the tumbang's cotton sarong (which is usually yellow).

c. Misa bai ditunu ma'tete: a pig is slaughtered for the "bridge" (tete). This is a symbolic bridge represented by placing two little bamboos across a small ditch in front of the tongkonan. The rite embodies the idea that the deata will cross this bridge (to attend the feast?). The sacrifice for the bridge is composed of three animals: a pig, a chicken and a dog (J. Kruyt (1921:59) reports a "bridge" of buangin-branches).

d. A pig is also slaughtered for the ussabu tangdo', "the consecration of the tangdo'", the floor constructed against the North side of the tongkonan. The to burake takes a second pig home alive (the expression pasalian, to leave out, is used; this would seem to indicate that this pig is no part of the ritual offerings but serves instead as a form of payment).

40. For the mantanan lolo, "the burying of the umbilical cord", a pig and chicken are slaughtered. The significance is that the great bua'-feast has, as it were, been reborn, so that the "umbilical cord" of the ritual needs to be interred.

41. A chicken, a pig and a dog are slaughtered for the male tama kala'paran menggaronto', "going to the kala'paran to serve as a basis", i.e. for the ensuing rites. The to burake makes an offering of food (ma'pesung). A pig is also dispatched for the lempo to tumbang (lempo: a floor or small platform; in this instance it refers to the hut - lantang - in which the tumbang remain during the bua'-feast).

42. Ma'kapa' ampu bua': a pig is slaughtered for this rite which informants compare to the kapa' for marriage (cf. Vol.I:34ff.). It is not clear what function the kapa' has in this context.

43. A pig is slaughtered for the massabu ruma-ruma, the consecration of the ruma-ruma. This is the name for the ampang bilik in Kesu' (see Vol.I:241ff.); in Riu it is the term for the frame with wheels that is placed beneath the gorang. Added to the above is the expression ditanan lan kala'paran, "the planting - of the feast - on the kala'-

paran", which signifies that the ritual will be celebrated on this special plain. The to burake presides over the offering (pesung) on the kala'-paran at the spot where the gorang will be erected.

44. Untangsui tanduk tedong, "the bone is removed from the buffalo's horns". (This might also mean: "to bring the buffalo horns outside".) For this rite a chicken is slaughtered on the compound of the tong-konan. The to burake carries out the offering (pesung). Thereafter the horns must be attached to the bullean, the sedan chair in which the tumbang are carried around the rante kala'paran, the terrain where the bua'-ritual is completed. A chicken is also killed for the ussarongi, the decoration of the bullean. It is the to burake who makes the sacrifice. In front the sedan chair is graced with a wooden board that has been elaborately carved. For the rest the ornamentation consists of: pusuk, the young leaves of the sugar palm; red, banner-like cloths fastened to bamboo poles; a katik, a bird's head on a long neck. (This wooden carving also adorns the front part of a tongkonan.) A sprig of paddy dangles from the katik. The buffalo horns are fixed to the end of the carved plank.

45. A pig and a chicken are slaughtered for the umpakande nene', "the feeding of the ancestors of the (South)West", a sacrifice which takes place on the rante kala'paran under the to burake's leadership.

46. Manuk ma'parapa' do banua, a hen is slaughtered for the house-hold effects which are set in place. The hen is killed in the tongkonan of the tumbang. It is the to burake who puts the hen to death and utters the prayer (mangimbo).[45]

47. On this day the lolako pasa' (lulako pasa') is staged, literally: "going to the pasar (market)".[46]

48. Ussabu tedong, consecration of the buffalo (that will be sacri-ficed). A pig is slaughtered. The to burake makes the offering (pe-sung). On this day many pigs are killed; as many, it is said, as 40 small and 100 large.

49. People return home, to the tongkonan, for the ma'pulung (pu-lung: come together, gather). The manganda' is enacted on the compound. A pig is slaughtered and feasted upon without an accom-panying sacrificial ceremony (dikande belundak). The ma'pulung occurs in the evening. Afterwards, on a single day, a number of rites are ob-served.

50. The first of these is the ussali para (ussali para: to equip the para with a floor; the para is the sloping part of the façade of the tongkonan). A buangin is felled. Apparently a sacrifice is made on the floor that is constructed; cf. ma'parekke para (see above and note 19). It is also possible, however, that this "floor" is part of the temporary residence of the tumbang; her stay in the most sacral part of the tong-konan symbolizes her relation to the Upperworld (Nooy-Palm 1979:90). During a bua'-feast rite which I attended in October 1976 in the village of Deri, which lies in Tikala, a tumbang wrapped in maa'-cloths was carried out of the house through the door which faces East. She held herself stiff, and resembled a wooden doll. (There was hardly a glimpse of the woman herself.) The men who carried her out of the tongkonan held her straight up; the similarity was marked with the removal of a corpse from the tongkonan, also because the men went shuffling and singing alone. Yet the dead are borne away in a prone position. After the tumbang had been brought out of her house, she was set down on the tangdo'. After freeing herself from the sacral cloths, she climbed

up a ladder to a small floor under the peak of the roof where she
remained until the rite, during which she was carried around the rante
kala'paran (see below, rite 59).

51. The ussabu ianan (ianan: possessions). The possessions of the
ramage are (symbolically) consecrated. As sacrifice, a pig is killed.
Although it wasn't specified that the to burake officiated at the offering
(pesung), that seems likely.

52. Ullisu sarong (ma'lisu sarong: to roll back and forth, like a
sunhat that is leaned against something; see Woordenboek:317). What
the rite signifies remains murky. While it is enacted, a pig is sacrificed
(pesung).

53. Ussabu lolo tau is a sacrifice – a pig – for the consecration of
the umbilical cord, the symbolic navel-string of humanity (here specifically the ramage).

54. A sacrifice is also offered for the tanan laa kala'paran, for the
bringing of the laa to the feast plain. The laa is a platform on which
the to minaa will stand. It is installed on the gorang. It should be
noted that no word was said about building the gorang. Apparently
while other things were going on it was erected. The next day two
rites occur:

55. Ussabu bullean, a sacrifice for the "preparation (= consecration)
of the sedan chairs" of the tumbang. A pig is killed; certain parts are
prepared as an offering. The to burake presides over the presentation
of the sacrificial food (pesung). The ramage consumes the rest of the
pig. The bullean is now assembled. An earlier rite (44) had to do with
fabrication and decoration of sedan chair parts.

56. Umpakande nene', "the feeding of the ancestors", is the most
important rite of the day. As sacrifice, a pig is killed. The to burake
presents the offering on the West side of the tongkonan where the
tumbang resides.

57. The next day is set aside for the umbungka' banaa, "the opening
of the banaa", the wooden vat that has been under the protection of
the tumbang. A chicken is slaughtered. Another chicken is killed for
the umparapa kada, literally: "to silence the words", "to bring to
peace". That is the title of the one who opens the banaa. Should any
hostile feelings linger in the hearts of celebrants, this offering is to
eradicate them and bring harmony. It is in essence a repetition of the
third rite which took place during the first half of the bua'-feast, the
sitami palilli'.

58. Subsequently, the lolako pasa' comes again. Two chickens are
slaughtered and prepared as offering (pesung) in the tongkonan of the
tumbang. One is for the deata, the gods of the Northeast, and one for
the nene', the ancestors of the Southwest.

59. This is the day of the kasongloran ma'mulle, the descent to the
feast terrain where the tumbang and her ritual companions who occupy
such an important place in the celebration are carried about (carry
about: ma'mulle). First a pig and a buffalo, both entirely black, are
slaughtered. The head of the family offers the meat as a sacrifice
(pesung) in the tongkonan. Only afterwards may the sedan chairs, with
the seated tumbang, and the crowd which follows them, depart from the
house. Many men are needed to support a sedan chair; the bearers are
people from the village, not relatives. The to burake organizes this
great feast day, except for the massinggi', the eulogy of the brave that
also is carried out on this day and is arranged by the to minaa.

This day of the feast is also known as kasongloran tama kala'paran, "the descent in procession to the place of the feast". The to mano'bo is an important functionary. He inaugurates, as it were, the events of the day: he is the first to set foot on the feast plain. In so doing he performs the same role that the to usso'boi rante (to massanduk dalle) does in the death ritual (see Woordenboek:618 and Chapter XI.1.2.). He is, to be sure, referred to by the same name as the to massanduk dalle, i.e. to usso'boi rante (kala'paran) and his function is also identical; he, too, is the first to walk on the plain where the ritual is to continue in order to free the place from all evil influences. In his function the to mano'bo wears brass horns on his head and is fully armed.[47] On this day the manganda' should also (again?) be enacted.

Further commentary was provided concerning the sacrificed buffalo. This animal is killed by being pierced by a lance. The part designated as the sepak diruang (a foreleg) goes to him who utters the prayer (the to mangimbo), here the to burake. The other sepak diruang is allotted to the to massurak (he who speaks during the consecration of the buffalo that is sacrificed). This figure is not the to minaa, but presumably one of the heads of a ramage other than that of the feast's host. The to mangimbo and to massurak in this great bua'-feast can be compared to the to mangimbo (sokkong bayu) and the to ussumbo tedong in the merok-feast (see Merok:9). Of the lette undina, the hind legs, one goes to the to ma'gandang, and part of the other goes to the to mano'bo. What is left of the second hind leg is divided in three. A third is then given to:

a. to umpakande to matua, "she who feeds the ancestors" (it is one of the "plenary eight" who performs this sacrificial act under the watchful eye of the to burake);

b. manglika' bua', literally: "the twisted into one = entwined bua'", "she who embraces the bua'", another of the to burake's helpers;

c. the to massuru' bua', "she who cleanses the bua'", a third of the to burake's assistants (see Woordenboek: v. soeroe').

All these chunks of meat are cooked and eaten. The palongko' (hip joint) of the buffalo is split in two: one part goes to the to massadi; the other to the owner of the buffalo. The owner happened to be the tumbang (an adult woman). The bladder is hung from a pole close to the tangdo' which is placed near the langngan (here apparently the peturo langi' is meant). The brisket, a portion from the midriff (aak), is given to the one who has stabbed the animal. This is the to minaa. The buku piso, the shoulder blade, is presented to the to manampan, the one who distributes the meat (usually an eminent to makaka, free farmer, from the community, the head of a saroan, mutual aid organization). Part of the stomach (tambuk) is made into an offering (ditampak pesung, the left-overs, the last of the sacrificial food)[48] which the to minaa consecrates.

The neck of the buffalo is divided into twelve pieces (kollong) which are shared among the ampu bua'. At the great bua'-feast celebrated in Batu Kamban in 1970 there were four ampu bua'.[49] The head of the sacrificial animal is cooked whole (karerang). When it has been picked clean, the skull is later preserved in the house of the to tumbang.

A piece of the liver is prepared as an offering for the gods, placed on a banana leaf.

The rest of the meat from the sacrifice is shared out[50]; during the process, the names are called aloud of those entitled to a portion (the

divider of the meat does the calling?). Yet as soon as someone's name
has been called, another tries to make away with his share. Perhaps
this is all in sport, but just as with sisemba' (calf-kicking, see Woor-
denboek:596), the earnestness and aggression involved make a deep impression. Whoever manages to get a piece of meat home, doesn't need to
divide it further. (For the rules of sisemba', see Andi Lolo 1969.)

60. A pig is slaughtered and eaten (diissong pandan, "the pig is
stretched out lengthwise like a rice mortar"). The animal is thus not
offered as a sacrifice. The laying out of the animal happens in a house,
presumably in that of the tumbang.

61. It is notable that no mention is made during the previous summary of rites of the preparation of the lumbaa langi'; in fact this is an
important ritual artefact. Yet, despite the silence, it happens here,
too, and the erecting of this "celestial pole" is accompanied by offerings; the sequence of actions does not differ in any way worth mentioning from J. Kruyt's description (1921:66-7).

62. On the day of the descent to the feast terrain (no. 59), the massinggi' also takes place, the praising of the men of the marapuan,
during which the to barani, the brave, and the ramage's youngsters
(pia) are extolled in song separately. A man is considered one of the to
barani if he has killed someone; or it may be someone who has travelled
far and returned, or a (successful?) gambler. During the ma'singgi',
the to barani wear a tali padang-padang, a kind of laurel-wreath on
their heads made out of a short, prickly grass. Whoever is being
praised at the moment holds his sword upright in his hand, or one of
his followers does. For more information about the massinggi' in Riu,
see the description below of the "big day" in Batu Kamban.

63. As soon as people come back from the kala'paran, a pig is
slaughtered to commemorate the fact that the anak dara is going to be
brought out of the house (sule lanmai kala'paran unnalai anak dara do
mai banua). The ritual food is placed on a bloodwort leaf as well as on
a banana leaf.

64. Then the ma'tekken piong is enacted once more (cf. rite no. 35).
Numerous pairs of these piong stand arranged next to the ricebarn. A
pig and a chicken are slaughtered, yet not for a sacrifice. Those present make a meal of them.

65. The following rite is the removal of the anak dara. In the village
of Toyasa I was among the spectators when the anak dara was conveyed
to the barana' from the tongkonan in which it had been on display.
Across the compound from the tongkonan stood the ricebarns that
belonged to it. The bamboo poles for the ma'tekken piong stood two by
two leaning against one of the ricebarns. The ritual on this day consisted of a number of rites. At about 9.30 a.m. the to ma'gandang
arrived (also called to burake; in this instance he happened to be the
husband of the to burake).[51] He had a bamboo yoke in which leaves
had been inserted. He acted as if he was completing a long journey and
collapsed to rest a little and to drink something. The pantomime was to
suggest he had come back from foreign places. The symbolism escaped
me.[52] A prayer said by the to burake tattiku' marked the end of the
first ceremony.

66. Towards the end of the afternoon, the anak dara (actually not
the whole anak dara, merely its wrapping) is brought from the tongkonan and carried away. The anak dara is carried in front, followed by
the to burake tattiku' who plays the clapper drum, the to ma'gandang,

the tumbang and her escort, the ampu bua' and several members of his and the tumbang's family walk behind. All the tumbang clutched a kain sarita in their left hand; they carried this cloth at about shoulder height. The anak dara (the bundle of leaves) was laid in a barana', an act which evoked thoughts of the young girls in Kesu' who were also called anak dara (= tumbang) and who stayed in the banyan tree during a certain stage of the la'pa' kasalle-feast. After the leaves had been put into the barana' four bamboos from the anak dara were brought to the sawah (probably the first rice field established by the host's ancestors). The remaining four bamboos, the four in the middle, were put down next to a ricebarn. The "clothing" of the anak dara, its wrapping, is placed in the banyan tree. According to Pong Samma', each of the to mangria barang inserts a length of bamboo into the soil of a sawah which is her property. She places the bloodwort leaves inside the bamboo. The rice which grows at this spot may not be cut. The sawah may not be sold or mortgaged to any outsider, only to a member of the same ramage.

67. Metamba langngan langi' lako Puang Matua (= To Kaubanan), "the calling aloud to heaven to Puang Matua". For this rite three scraps of sacrificial food are removed from a piong and placed on three pieces of banana leaf; these rectangular pieces of leaf lie in a row (these pesung always consist of delicacies). Once the gods have appropriated the essence of these offerings, the people who are present consume them. Next the to burake slaughters a pig and recites a prayer which gives thanks for the protection and help which Puang Matua has provided during the feast.

68. Unnalai rumpang: it is the intention of this rite to purify the house and the compound. A chicken is killed and prepared as an offering (pesung).

69. Metena. This word means to commission a piece of work and in so doing to slaughter an animal for those who will carry the work out. Beside a sawah the to burake kills a pig, a chicken and a dog. Nothing is said about what happens afterwards with these sacrificed animals, nor to whom the sacrifice was directed. The rite ushers in the close of the great bua'-feast. People are now free, the tumbang are no longer subject to prohibitions. They need not observe food taboos either any longer.

5. The "big day" and the days after in the bua'-feast in Batu Kamban, Riu (October 24-27, 1970)

For a map of the plain where the feast was celebrated, see Fig. 4. There were two such plains in Riu; on the second one, shortly before my arrival, a bua'-feast had just ended. The most prominent constructions on the plain were a colossal gorang and the ritual huts on high posts inside which the tumbang and the to mangria barang stayed.

In the morning two calves were slaughtered on the rante kala'paran (as distinguished from the buffalo specified in the description of the great day of the bua'-feast). Their meat was distributed[53] and after people had first prepared an offering from it at home, they came back again to the feast terrain. Until the crowd returned, the five bullean (sedan chairs) might not enter the plain.

At approximately eleven in the morning the first sedan chair with the

Fig. 4. Feast terrain, great bua'-ritual, Riu (October 24-27, 1970).

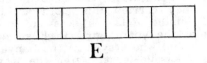

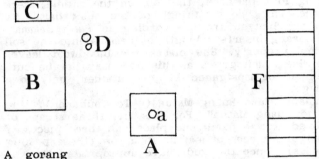

A   gorang
a   lumbaa langi'
B   house of the kepala lembang, the lembang-head
C   ricebarn
D   sendana-tree with menhir
E   accommodations for the tumbang and the to sanda karua
F   guest lodges

tumbang seated in place, the vehicle attractively decorated, began its
journey to the rante kala'paran. While the many bearers shouted, they
bore the sedan chair three times around the towering gorang where
later the to minaa would ascend in order to sing the praises of the men
of the rapu. During the circuits of the sedan chair - a rapid, jolting
ride for its occupant! -, the to burake led the way with her clapper
drum, the to minaa accompanying her. A mass followed behind; the
sequence of the procession didn't have much significance. After each
circuit there was a brief pause. After all of the bullean had been
carried around (they followed hard upon each other), there was a long
interval during which people ate. Then once again the carrying of the
sedan chairs around the gorang recommenced. The bright sun dazzled
on the coloured trappings of the bullean and the celebrants gay apparel; rejoicing reached its highest pitch. Palm wine kept the crowd in
high spirits. At about two in the afternoon, the conveyance of the
tumbang and her escort ended. The ladies went to shelter in the huts
on high posts, which were reserved for them. Then the massinggi' was
to begin. The tumbang had a maa'-cloth folded flat and tied on top of
her head. She wore a yellow skirt, with a fringe of pusuk over her
dress. Her blouse was also yellow. Around her neck hung a splendid
rara' (the jewelry of upperclass women). The tumbang's ritual companions also wore yellow blouses and sarongs; on their heads perched
wreathes of tarrung-fruits (Solanum melongena). They, too, had a
fringe of pusuk over their garments. While not in conveyance, the tum-

bang and the rest of "the plenary eight" remained in the elevated huts which overlooked the feast plain.

The eulogizing (massinggi') got under way at two o'clock. Several to minaa stood during the massinggi' on the gorang and recited words of praise in a peculiar rhythm, punctuated by the ringing of the copper bell which they swung back and forth. A string trailed below from each to minaa's hand; the bottom end was held by the person who, for the moment, was the object of the to minaa's laudation. Both the to minaa and the man being extolled turned their faces to the East. As far as I could make out the recipients of praise could have little idea what actually was being said. Several to minaa delivered eulogies at the same time. Yet, somehow they seemed to know, for if a man felt he was not being given due praise, he pulled on the string. People who had undergone such songs of praise several times before, held a rattan cord in their hand. Usually the string consists of a thin strip of cloth in some solid colour. The eulogizing went on for about an hour. At three in the afternoon, people's favourite sport, sisemba', began.

The beautiful weather abruptly ended. Dark clouds gathered; a strong wind suddenly arose. Everyone dashed for shelter. The sky turned black and rain poured down. I wanted to go outside to look for my interpreter and his companions but people held me back. Towards evening the wind died down. It soon appeared we'd been through a whirlwind. A bad sign: only the plain where the feast was celebrated had been hard hit. The wind had twisted clumps of heavy bamboo-betung into knots as if they were mere wisps of straw. Some of the ritual buildings were damaged, too. The great sendana-tree had fallen on the shed which my interpreter and his companions had deserted just in time in search of a better place to wait out the storm. Even the menhir no longer stood upright. Only the gorang and the lumbaa langi', the bamboo pole from which there hung a small basket with a white chicken meant to confer good fortune, were intact. The poor chicken must have been spun around by the wind like a creature possessed!

The rain kept on for some time but happily by midnight it had cleared enough to let the ma'sulo or ma'bia' proceed. This was the encircling of the gorang with mammouth torches made of several bamboos split in half lengthwise and bound together. Rather than petrol, coconut oil was used for the torches. Some fifty torches were carried about, each torch-bearer making three circuits around the gorang. A pig was slaughtered as a sacrifice for each torch. Every house that participated in the feast contributed a torch. For the significance of the rite, see rite 10 above.

Early the next morning, about five o'clock, the rite was enacted during which various celebrants try to gain possession of the white chicken and the six sprigs of paddy which are fastened to the top of the pole which towers above the gorang. By means of a rattan rope (luntian) the pole has to be pulled to the East without snapping it. Whoever succeeds in doing this is assured of long life. He is to breed more fowl from the white hen and to share the paddy for sowing among the participants of the bua'-feast. The offspring of the white chicken may only be sacrificed during deata-rituals.[54] This rite has the same name as the pole itself, lumbaa langi', celestial pole. The pendant of this lumbaa of heaven is apparently the lumbaa padang (padang: earth), a designation for the tombi, the banners or cloths which are on display at the house of a dead man.

The next morning (October 27, 1970) the to minaa sat in a circle and discussed the cause of the whirlwind. Perhaps someone had violated a prohibition before entering the feast terrain, for example by eating meat that came from a death ritual.[55] The priests couldn't decide for certain, however. For safety's sake a pig and a chicken were sacrificed in atonement. Afterwards, at about ten, the to burake, escorted by her assistent (also addressed as burake), made an offering that was set out in a dulang (a bowl on a pedestal) and in two dishes (in each of these vessels there was an egg). Then the burake proceeded to perform the pangalukan, the invocation of the deata; she faced to the East and held a spear in her hand. She did not play the clapper drum, however. The to minaa were also present and joined in chorus, ringing their copper bells while looking off to the South. The rite was called tabuan tallu manuk (tallu manuk: chicken's eggs; there is no explanation available for the word tabuan, "wasp", in this context). It took place under the gorang. The deata were asked for their blessing.

The same morning the eulogizing of the to barani, the brave, was staged. Although they were supposed to wear a tali padang-padang on their heads, not all those who were praised had on such a wreath made from prickly grass. One warrior, for example, was wearing a black flannel cap. At times, a to barani may have a follower with him who holds up his sword. Just as with the laudation of other men, the to burake first leads a procession three times around the gorang. This also held true for the youths and boys whose praise would be sung later (massinggi' sola to pia, praising all the children). They, too, were in their fanciest clothes with turbans and necklaces. One or two even wore a kris. On the lowest step of the platform set up next to the gorang the small children collected, on the third step children already somewhat older, while the adults mounted onto the platform itself. The to barani were accorded a place of their own. They took seats in the bullean.

Toward four o'clock in the afternoon two buffaloes were said to be slaughtered. Yet, I wasn't there to see it. Nor could I escape the impression that the whirlwind had put a damper on the festivity of the feast. The mood of rejoicing had vanished.

Gorang, Sesean-region.
The gorang is 8 to 10 metres high. It consists of six uprights, two
from buangin- and four from uru-wood (uru: Michelia Celebica). The
ladder is made of three uprights of bamboo-betung across which seven
(at times nine) rungs have been fastened. In the centre of the gorang
a pole is erected, the lumbaa langi', a single, long bamboo-ao' (aur). A
basket is attached to it in which a white chicken sits. Five small
bundles of paddy also hang from the lumbaa langi'. A stone rice mortar
rests on the ground under the centre of the gorang; in its cavity the
base of the lumbaa langi' is propped. See also pp. 13, 20, 29, 44, 45
and 48.
Bua'-feast at Batu Kamban, lembang Suloara.
(Photo: Hetty Nooy-Palm, 1970.)

The bottom part of the gorang including the floor, the ruma-ruma. Wheels are attached to the underside of the gorang which conveys the impression that the tower must symbolize a vehicle. In the foreground the burake tattiku' officiates at an offering. See also pp. 13 and 42.
Bua'-feast at Batu Kamban, lembang Suloara.   (Photo: Hetty Nooy-Palm, 1970.)

Peturo langi' with the piong and both suke; at its top hang scraps of meat from the slaughtered pig. The langngan (on the ground) runs North-South. See also pp. 18, 24, 40, 41 and 45.
Toyasa Riu, lembang Suloara.
(Photo: Hetty Nooy-Palm, 1970.)

The to burake beneath the gorang during the pangalukan. In her right
hand she holds the garatung, in her left, a dish. Bua'-feast at Batu
Kamban, lembang Suloara.
(Photo: Hetty Nooy-Palm, 1970.)

The lumbaa before insertion in the gorang. Twenty pesung are lined up
next to the bamboo, a large number so that none of the deata will be
forgotten. The burake tattiku' (left centre in the photo) prays to the
deata. See also pp. 22 and 40.
Bua'-feast at Batu Kamban, lembang Suloara.
(Photo: Hetty Nooy-Palm, 1970.)

The first bullean enters the ritual plain. The bullean is decorated with
a pair of buffalo horns with tabang-leaves at the tips, a katik (bird's
head carved from wood) from which a sprig of paddy and two bamboo
poles are suspended. To each of these poles a clump of tabang-leaves
and a red cloth are fastened.
The tumbang in the sedan chair has a folded maa'-cloth on the top of
her head; her escorts wear a wreath of tarrung-fruits.
The to mano'bo walks in front, the first to set foot on the ritual terrain; he wears brass horns and holds his sword (la'bo' penai) upright
in his right hand, a shield (balulang) in his left hand. See also pp.
44–45 and 47–48.
Bua'-feast at Batu Kamban, lembang Suloara.
(Photo: Hetty Nooy-Palm, 1970.)

The tumbang and her companions are carried about in the bullean (ma'mulle). The tumbang can be identified by the maa'-cloth which she carries folded flat on her head. In the background are the shacks in which the tumbang remain when they are not riding in the sedan chairs. See also pp. 44-45 and 47-48.
Bua'-feast at Batu Kamban, lembang Suloara.
(Photo: Hetty Nooy-Palm, 1970.)

Laudation of the men at the great bua'-feast in Batu Kamban. The men are seated in the bullean, the sedan chair in which the tumbang are conveyed around the gorang. The bullean is decorated with two bundles of tabang-leaves (Cordyline terminalis). A bundle of rice is suspending from the katik. Around their necks the men wear manik ata. One of the men is holding a rope, the other a long strip of cloth; at the other end, the to minaa on the gorang is holding these, too. Both men also hold spears. See also pp. 46 and 49. (Photo: Hetty Nooy-Palm, 1970.)

Those whose praise is sung hold onto the end of a cord; the other end is held by the to minaa atop the gorang. Some of the men on the ground are also holding a spear. Some men sit in a sedan chair during the laudation. In the background are visible the feast shelters where the leading women of the ramage stay. The lofty dwelling to the left in the photo is reserved for the tumbang. The important men of the celebrating group, those who do not participate in the massinggi', receive shelter in guest houses, in nearby tongkonan, or they sit on the floor constructed beneath the ricebarn. These buildings are not depicted in the photograph. Several men are seated on the ground (centre right). (Photo: Hetty Nooy-Palm, 1970.)

The to minaa singing the praises of the men of the marapuan. They ring the bangkula' (copper bell) with their right hands. Below, whoever is being extolled holds onto the end of a strip of cloth or a length of rope. In the centre of the eight metres high gorang, the lumbaa langi', the celestial pole, juts up into the air; from its tip hangs a basket containing a white chicken and a sprig of paddy. See also pp. 46 and 49.
Bua'-feast at Batu Kamban. (Photo: Hetty Nooy-Palm, 1970.)

Before the eulogizing of the children (massinggi' sola to pia) begins, they pass three times around the gorang with members of their families, just the way adults do before their laudations. Accompanying family members hold the strip of cloth that the children have bound around their upper arm. The children carry a bamboo staff. In Riu only boys are awarded the songs of praise. See also p. 50.
(Photo: Hetty Nooy-Palm, 1970.)

Chapter III

THE MEROK-FEAST

"So that they may continually increase in wealth, in
quantity like the leaves,
in order that the branching of the precious things
may continue to swell still more,
so that they may reach the pinnacle of wealth,
in their possessions, achieving the absolute peak."
(Merok:185)

1. Reasons for holding the feast (Kesu' and Buntao')

The word merok derives from rok or rauk, to stab to death. The
"stabbing to death" refers to the manner in which the buffalo which is
sacrificed at this ritual was formerly slaughtered. At present the beast
is usually not pierced with a spear; it is felled instead by a mighty
blow with a cleaver (la'bo').

In the first place the merok is a feast for the whole ramage (marapuan). Even more than with the bua'-feast, the tongkonan is the centre
of the ritual. The places where rites are staged are in the house itself
and on the compound, where the ricebarn also stands. This barn fulfils
a role as well in the ceremonies. Other places people visit for certain
rites include the site of sugar palm cultivation and the local market.

The merok is not merely a family feast, it can in addition be a ritual
at which one of the most eminent members of the ramage is the head of
the ritual. Van der Veen cites a number of reasons for holding a
merok-feast (Merok:1):
1. Someone has become prosperous and has had no adversity;
2. Someone has been prosperous for some years after atoning for a sin
he had committed with a sacrifice;
3. A former slave, thriving, now holds the feast[1];
4. The merok can be celebrated in thanksgiving after the tallung bongi,
the limang bongi or the dirapa'i (see Chapter I). In Kesu' the merok is
then considered to be a conversion ritual.

The first three motives especially support the categorization of the
merok as a "feast of merit"; such celebrations are also known among the
inhabitants of Nias, the Tontemboan among the Minahasa in North
Sulawesi, the Nga'da on Flores and the Naga, particularly the Angami-
Naga, in India.

My Toraja informants supported the division made by Van der Veen
into four categories, yet they emphasized that the merok was more than
a feast of thanksgiving after a death ritual; in such instances it had
the grandeur of a conversion ritual which enabled the deceased to

attain the status of deata. The person at whose instigation a merok-feast is held is the head of the tongkonan (tongkonan in the sense of a ramage), or one of its most eminent members. The deceased will, to be sure, have been an important member of this ramage.

A fifth reason for celebrating the merok-feast is to express gratitude for a successful rice harvest.

2. Persons with a role in the merok-feast

Those who take part in the feast are ramage members and their affinal kin. In the litanies one speaks of "the members of the tongkonan numerous as culms of bamboo" (Merok:16-7).[2] If possible all members of the rapu attend. They come from as far as neighbouring Luwu' and from Ujung Pandang, the capital of South Sulawesi. The principal sacrifice, the buffalo, is executed in Kesu' by the sokkong bayu. He recites the prayer and for the duration of the ritual is called to mangimbo, "he who utters the prayer". The consecration of the buffalo is the task of the datu baine (Vol.I:98ff.). He acquires the title - once again only for as long as the ritual lasts - of to massomba tedong, "the one who consecrates the buffalo". Both these adat-chiefs can allow a to minaa to replace them if they don't feel conversant enough with the prayers. The tongkonan of either the sokkong bayu or the datu baine can, of course, also be the centre of a merok-feast itself.

During the consecration of the buffalo, the to indo' padang stand to the left of the to massomba tedong. In the Passomba Tedong, the laudation of the buffalo, the ancestors of the to indo' padang are spoken of, Datu Mengkamma and Karaeng[3] Ma'lokoloko, created by Puang Matua. Before this pair of earliest to indo' padang took part in rice cultivation, the rice harvest fell far below expectation. After the intervention of these "rice functionaries", the mythic rice field yielded an abundant crop (see Merok:120-1, verses 615-20 of the Passomba Tedong). Keeping in mind the function of the to indo' padang in the ritual, one can also consider the merok as a thanksgiving after a bountiful rice year or a series of bountiful rice years; in this sense it is the counterpart of the celebration of the bua' padang in which the gods are implored to bless the coming rice harvest. When he appears in the merok, the to indo' padang is also called to mangrande londong, "he who holds the cock in his open hand". He does indeed hold a yellow or brown rooster with white feet while the to ussumbo tedong delivers the consecratory litany. In this context we should note the role of the constellation The Rooster of Tulangdidi', Manukna Tulangdidi'.[4] The position of this configuration of stars indicates when successive phases in the cultivation of rice should be initiated (Vol.I:168).

There are a number of other functionaries:
- the to ma'tambuli, "he who digs the hole with a sharp object"[5] (in which the sandalwood branch is inserted);
- the to mantobok, "he who stabs to death" (the buffalo or pig);
- the to mangrenden tedong, "he who pulls forward the buffalo to be sacrificed";
- the to massanduk, "he who serves the rice" (the rice intended for the sacrifical meal). The to massanduk invites the gods to partake of this meal; after the gods are considered to have eaten their share, the food is consumed by the assembled guests;

- the to ma'nasu, "he who cooks";
- the to massadi, "he who cuts the meat into pieces";
- the to pabalian, "the helper", also called the to masserek (daun) pesung, "he who tears the banana leaves for the offering (pesung)";
- the to sipalakuan. [6]

In the merok-feast women play a far less prominent part than in the bua' kasalle, yet their rather modest contribution should not be overlooked. During a certain phase of the feast, women winnow the rice (Merok:7). This happens during the ma'tambuli (see section 7, rite 13 below). "Three female members of the family of the giver of the feast who are chosen by ballot sit at the place where the feast is to be held. Each has a winnowing basket of husked rice in her lap and they continually throw the rice from one basket to the other." What this winnowing of the rice signifies is unclear. Perhaps it symbolizes the purification of the atmosphere.

Earlier in the ritual another rite is enacted in which women participate: ma'pasa', going to the market (not mentioned below in the summary of rites; see, however, Merok:5). The rite takes place before the ma'patama gandang (see section 7, rite 9). "For this the women adorn themselves with a headband, sa'pi', decorated with gold leaf, parakeet's feathers and human hair, and put on their festival clothing. They take with them palm wine and viscous rice wrapped in a leaf of the bamboo called pattung (Dendrocalamus flagellifer), and offer them to such of the clan members (what is meant here is ramage members) as they find in the market place. After that, arrangements are made regarding the ritual of striking the drums, ma'patama gandang." (Merok:5)

On the evening of the "big day" (allonamo kaperaukan) of the feast, girls and young women from the group again perform: "In the evening the young girls and the young women, dressed in their festival clothes and adorned with ornaments, place themselves in a row and start singing a humming song, ma'dandan" (Merok:9).

3. Clothing and regalia worn by functionaries during the merok-feast

Women's apparel during the merok has been described in the preceding paragraphs. During the Passomba Tedong, the sokkong bayu in Buntao' has a woman's jacket wrapped around his arm. This embodies the significance of women for the group. I am not sure whether this is also customary in Kesu'. The important functionaries in the ritual, the sokkong bayu and datu muane, wear short trousers (seppa tallu buku) and a long white jacket with rather wide sleeves (bayu lamba'). Around their necks, they wear a manik ata, a necklace consisting of alternating gold beads and sacral masak (dark yellow) beads. They wind a maa'-cloth around their heads. The to ussomba tedong in Buntao' also has a barre allo (sun motif) of gold leaf as part of his regalia; in Kesu' and elsewhere this is not customary. The remaining functionaries wear more ordinary clothing.

4. Rice in the merok-feast

The to indo' padang have already been reported as functionaries in the merok. In the creation myth (Passomba Tedong) recited at the ritual, not only is the establishment of the first rice field in the upperworld reported, but also the origin of rice itself (Merok:440) and of the various goddesses who are associated with rice (Merok:347-8). Because the merok is a ritual of the East, (cooked) rice is part of the sacrifices and sacral meals. The ricebarn is also the centre of action in several rites. (For rites pertaining to rice and ricebarns, see section 7, rites 4 and 13.)

5. Sacrificial animals in the merok-feast

Various animals are slaughtered during the ritual, and during the consecration of the buffalo a special pig and a special rooster are also led forward. These animals, just as in the great bua'-feast, are considered to belong together. The animals have a special colour. Of the buffalo it is said: "The one then that was the descendant of the yellow-haired one, the one that was the progeny of the one whose skin was well proportioned" (Merok:133, verse 670).

The colour of the rooster held fast by the mangrande londong during the most important part of the ritual has already been stipulated (yellow or brown with white feet).

No specification is made of the preferred markings of the pig.

6. Buildings, animals and plants in the merok-feast

The tongkonan, to be sure, is of fundamental importance. It has its prototype in the iron house of heaven.

"In order to perform the ritual for the iron house from
start to finish,
step by step, in the right order,
with the object of effecting the required adat-performances
for the poles with strong fibres, in regular order,
following on each other, like the rungs of a ladder."
(Merok:123)

One of the main posts of the tongkonan, the petuo farthest to the North (Vol.I:233) is joined to a sendana (sandal tree; in point of fact, here only a branch of sandalwood). The two are strung together by a bambalu-liana, rattan and a sacral sarita-cloth.[7] The branch is set up to the Northeast or the North of the house. The deata (ancestors become divinities) are invited to take places in the "tree". The sendana decked out with all kinds of valuables has its prototype in the sandal tree of the upperworld which is mentioned in the Passomba Tedong (Merok:227-8). The liana and rattan are strong plants; together with the sacral sarita-cloth they symbolize a tight bond. Together they represent the relation between the ramage, man on earth, and the gods above (who have taken places in the sendana). The façade of the house is hung with inherited treasures of the ramage, such as kandaure and religious maa'-cloths. The buffalo to be sacrificed is tied to the sendana (for the symbolism of this buffalo, see Vol.I:VII.1.). At this spot the buffalo is consecrated and then killed. The ritual ends with the re-planting of the sendana-branch to the Northeast of the ricebarn.

7. The rites of the merok-feast in Kesu'

This section depends upon information from B. Sarungallo which he
provided in 1966. Before the actual feast a series of actions take place:
a. the ma'tomatua (see Chapter X.5.);
b. the mangrara pare (see Chapter VII.2.8. and Merok:1);
c. the massampinni[8], for this ritual see p. 204; sampin = sacral textiles
used in a ritual. The term refers to the collection and preparation of
the sacral textiles for ritual use.

The merok itself then follows. It can be broken down into the following
compounds:
1. Ma'pallin: a sacrifice is made to ward off evil spirits; the to minaa
officiates. A black chicken is placed down along the Southwest side of
the tongkonan. For the prayer which is spoken, see Merok:156-7.
2. The manglika' biang: a dark yellow (or brown) hen with speckles
(rame) and rice cooked in bamboo are offered to the deata. For the
likaran biang, the vessel to hold the sacrifice woven from reeds, see
Vol.I:270, Merok:158, and Van der Veen, unpublished a. This small
basket is set down to the Northeast of the tongkonan. The to minaa
makes the offering. In the prayer he evokes the image of Puang Matua
who summoned the gods together the way a rooster calls his chickens.
Puang Matua is asked to come down from heaven:

> "And shall the door of heaven be opened,
> and shall the window of the all-enfolding be thrown open.
> Shall thy stairs of beadwork be lowered,
> shall thy golden steps be let down.
> Let the rainbow then be thy path,
> thou shallst make thy way along the arch of the sky.
> So that thou arrivest at this blessed region, like the
> coming of a prau", etc.
>   (Merok:161, verses 22-5, see also pp. 158-9)

3. The mangrimpung: the ramage convenes to make sacrifices to the ancestors. A pig is made into an offering (for the prayer, see Merok:
166-7).[9]
4. The massali alang: "to lay a floor under the ricebarn" (metaphorically). The drums which are played on the big day of the feast are
placed on the floor under the ricebarn. These drums are important in
the merok-feast. They may never be used during a death ritual; then
others must be employed. The drums serve to invoke the gods (Merok:
5-6). During the massali alang, a hen (rame) and a pig are sacrificed.
5. The ma'tadoran: see Merok:4. For the offering holder, the tadoran,
that is set up to the Northeast of the tongkonan, see Vol.I:272.
6. The mangkaro bubun, "the purifying of the well", is twofold:
a. untammui lalan tedong, "on the way to meet the buffalo"; this rite is
held to see to it that nothing untoward happens while the buffalo that
is to be sacrificed is led to its destination; a chicken is slaughtered;
b. mangrara kombong, "the covering of the sugar palms of the tongkonan with blood"; the sacrifice, designed to make the palms produce
abundant palm wine, consists of a dog (Van der Veen asserts it is a
hen).

7. Ma'bubung: during this rite a covering of bamboo slats is laid over the ridge of the tongkonan; a pig is slaughtered. The to minaa first addresses Puang Matua and then all the gods of the upper- and under-world as he prepares the sirih pinang-offering (for the prayer which the to minaa speaks, see Merok:II.G, II.H and II.I). This rite is also held to celebrate the building and consecration of a tongkonan (Vol.I:244). The act of roofing symbolizes, as it were, the appeal to the highest figure of the upperworld, Puang Matua, who sits enthroned in the zenith.[10]

8. Umpakande to matua: cf. Merok:2.

9. Ma'patama gandang, "to beat the drums".[11] In the meantime the drums have been transferred from the ricebarn to the tongkonan where they are played by the to minaa. Below, outside the house, another to minaa calls out to ask why the drums are being beaten. The answer: "Because the merok-feast is being celebrated". Hereupon a chicken is sacrificed (and a pig, too, according to Van der Veen). The offering is set out on the drums. Throughout the coming two days, the gandang are played continually.[12]

10. Ma'kollong gandang: a pig is sacrificed, and a kollong, a ring of meat from its neck, is placed on each drum.

11. Ma'pasang tedong: the buffaloes which will be sacrificed are herded together; this is accompanied by killing a pig and sprinkling the heads of the buffaloes (above their eyes) with its blood.

12. Ma'popengkalao gandang: the drums are carried from the tongkonan with non-stop thumping. Inside the tongkonan a young chicken is sacrificed; afterwards the gandang are brought back in.

13. Between 18:00 and 20:00 two rites take place:

a. the ma'tambuli, "the digging of a hole". Either the sokkong bayu or the to minaa digs this hole with a small spade (pesese); he is dressed in a bayu lamba' (cf. section 3 above). Three women from the host's family winnow rice ceremonially, tossing it from one fan into another. Whoever digs the hole utters a prayer which begins, "It may be that one of thy hairs will be frightened, O soil rich with blessings, where I shall stick the iron into it ..." (Merok:185-9). The soil is then compared to a sacral maa'-cloth with special motifs (seleng). Next the kurre sumanga' (a thanksgiving; cf. Glossary Vol.I) is recited over money, over the sugar palm, over chickens, over the sawahs and the ricebarn (yet not over buffaloes and pigs!).

b. Passomba Tedong, "the consecration of the buffalo". The datu baine or the to minaa delivers the litany which lasts from roughly eight in the evening to six o'clock the next morning (for this litany, see Merok: 18-156). In front of the tulak somba of the tongkonan, a sendana (sandal tree) is planted (see section 6 above). After the tallu basongna (section 6 and note 7 above), the buffalo is secured to the sandal-wood.[13] To the North of the sendana a pig is put down. Behind the to minaa, who may replace the to massomba, the to mangrande londong stands. During the ma'tambuli, the to minaa uses a stick of iron rod as staff; during the consecration of the buffalo a spear (originally used to stab the buffalo to death; cf. section 1). It is significant in which direction the buffalo falls once he has been "stabbed" to death (Vol.I: 203). The consecration of the buffalo (Passomba Tedong, literally: tribute to the buffalo) is the high point of the merok-feast. During this long litany many tales unfold: how the cosmos came into being; how the gods emerged; how mankind and its important animals and plants were created; how the rituals in heaven were established and what sacrifices belong to them. The role of slaves is also emphasized and citation is made of the colour and kind of animals that should be sacrificed (Merok:11 and 18-156; see also Vol.I:VI.1.1.).

14. Now begins the big day of the feast (allona). On this day not only the buffalo but also a rooster and a pig are slaughtered (these three sacrificial animals are spoken of in the litany as a trinity). The altar is marked off with a red cloth. A small sacrificial table is made for the meat of the slaughtered animals. Van der Veen's description is vivid (Merok:8-9):

"A large red cotton cloth is hung round the place where the offering is to be made, the to' pangantaran = the place where the woven cloth is hung. Slats of bamboo are laid on stakes and old woven cloths and beadwork are hung on them. Beside this structure a small offering table is erected on four bamboo struts on which motifs are incised. A small platform is constructed in the middle of these struts. The top of each of these struts is hollow, forming a container; palm wine is poured into three of them and water into the fourth. An old woven cloth is hung round the small offering table. Ribs of the leaf of the sugar palm are attached to the tops of these four struts. The outsides of the leaf ribs are scraped and kapok, smeared with the blood of the offering animals, is wrapped round them at various places. These ribs, wrapped in the blood-smeared kapok, are called pandung balo. A pasakke plant, a plant which has red flowers and small fruit, and which is used at various offerings to bring coolness, i.e. blessings, is tied to the four struts of the small offering table. The word sakke = cool and masakke = blessed. In front of the offerer is a plate on which there is a small piece of iron from a roasting dish, pamuntu, and three yellow beads. The offerer is called the to ma'pesung.
...
The offering meal (pesung) consists of parts of the lungs, kidneys, liver, brisket and the fat of the buffalo and the pig, as well as the ring of flesh from the pig's neck, and yellow viscous rice. No part of the cock is used in this offering. In the evening young girls and women dance and sing the ma'dandan."

A few hours previously, following its consecration, the buffalo was slaughtered. The pig, too, was killed. Members of the tongkonan were daubed with the latter's blood. The daubing is called patik. The instrument used is made from the ribs of a palm leaf wrapped with fluffy bits of cotton which is dipped into a bowl full of pig's blood. After patik, the drums sound ceaselessly. Van der Veen continues:
"After sirih pinang has been offered to the gods, the offerer calls upon the gods to wash their hands. For this purpose he holds in his right hand a small container with water in it. Next he takes in his right hand a small container with palm wine in it and invites the gods to partake of the offering meal.
After the offering prayer (Merok:182-3) has been spoken, the members of the clanhouse (= tongkonan) can take up the offering gifts and dispose of them. They bring blessings. People can go and sit in small groups and eat together."

15. The next day a sandalwood tree is planted to the Northeast of the ricebarn so that the group will give birth to many children, fructify like a bamboo with many culms (ma'rapu tallang). Indeed growth and

prosperity of the ramage is the end towards which the merok-celebration is dedicated. If the sendana takes root and flourishes, the family
group will thrive.

8. The rites of the merok-feast in Buntao'

When the merok was celebrated in 1969 in Buntao', I attended the concluding rites (nos. 18 and 19). Sampe Litak Danduru and Izak Sorreng
Palajukan told me about what had already taken place. Their information
has been integrated into the following account. It is clear that on this
occasion the ritual was enacted in keeping with the model of a pesuru'
or rassa papa-ritual.[14] It is but rarely celebrated in Buntao' and consists of a series of rites which depart in certain respects from the
ritual as it is observed in Kesu'.

1. The first rite is the ma'piong sanglampa. The piong is prepared in
the tongkonan which is the central point of the feast. A chicken is
quartered and set out on banana leaves. The four pesung are placed
on side roads.[15] The to minaa presides at the offering which is intended for an evil spirit named Pong Kapero'-pero' (pero': pushed off
course; Pong is a contracted form of puang; the term denotes someone
who is the father of one or more children).
2. The second rite is the ma'pallin. Rice is cooked in a piong in the
Southern part of the house. Then a hen having the colouring known as
rame is killed.[16] The offering is made by the to minaa and serves to
atone for all guilt (an expiatory offering for all transgressions which
have been committed). For the text of the litany which the to minaa
delivers during the ma'pallin, cf. Merok 156-8 (this litany originates
from Kesu').
3. The ma'pakande Tau Bunga' follows. Rice cooked in a piong and the
meat from a hen (karurung, a hen whose light brown feathers have
black speckles) are set down in the Southwest of the tongkonan. The to
minaa presides. The offering is intended for the first inhabitant(s) of
the land. Tau Bunga' may perhaps be translated as "the people who
preceded".
4. The next rite is the ma'pakande Puang. The offering again consists
of rice prepared in a bamboo cylinder and a hen (kollong arae, a
chicken or rooster with prominent comb, and, this time, with black
feet). The to minaa performs the offering in the Northwest of the tongkonan; it is for the dead who belonged to this house.
5. Makolik biang: rice is cooked piong-fashion; the to minaa slaughters
a chicken (rame, with white feet) and presents the offering to the
deata in the Northeast of the house.[17]
6. Ma'pepa'du: rice is cooked in the tongkonan; then a hen is killed
(rame, with white feet). The head of the household presents the offering to the spirits who grant prosperity: sikambi' lindo banua, "the
guardians of the face of the house", the "face" (front) is a holy part
of the dwelling. (Pepa'du means divining the future by inspecting the
bile of sacrificial animals, see Woordenboek: v. pa'doe.)
7. Mangalli uai: the to minaa conducts the offering next to the well; it
is intended for the spirits that protect the source so that the drinking
water remains pure. The sacrificial meal comprises rice prepared in a
piong and a chicken (rame, with white feet).

8. Mangalli kombong: in this rite, celebrated by the to minaa at the base of a sugar palm, rice in a piong makes up the offering, together with a dog (balia', a dog with a reddish coat) and a chicken (uran; the feet may be any colour). The rite is to promote the growth of the sugar palm groves, the palm which yields tuak.

9. Mangrambu langi': an expiatory offering for possible transgressions; a pig is slaughtered on a low hill beside a river. No rice is prepared. The pig is cut into pieces and these are thrown into the river, except for one piece which is roasted over a fire (rarang) and serves as an offering. The to minaa enacts the rite.

10. Mangalli lolok riu: rice is prepared piong-fashion and then a chicken is killed (karurung tedong[18], with black feet). The to minaa sets the offering down on the grass; it is for the spirits who guard the grass, the food of the buffaloes.

11. Mangalli kanan: rice is prepared in the same way as for the preceding rite; a chicken is slaughtered (karurung tedong). The to minaa presents the offering at the side of a spring so that the buffaloes will continue to have clear drinking water.

12. Makambu: again rice in bamboo is cooked (dipiong); a black pig is slaughtered and part of the carcase used for the offering. The to minaa conducts the rite near the buffalo stalls in the hope that the buffaloes will thrive and have many descendants.

13. Ma'bubung: rice is prepared, but not in bamboo holders. A black pig with a white dash on its forehead (todi) is killed. Part of the pig, with rice, serves as offering. The head of the tongkonan is the offerer. Ma'bubung means "to lay the covering of the ridge on the roof" (cf. Merok:4).

14. Untanmui lalan tedong: next to the buffalo stable, rice is prepared in a piong and then a chicken is killed (karurung tedong with black feet).

15. Mangallo tedong: the rice required for the pesung tedong (?) is dried.

16. Mangallo bai (bai = pig). The significance of rites 15-17 is not altogether clear. It would appear they involve offerings (with the drying of rice as one component) directed to the deata who are the protective spirits, respectively, of the buffalo stall, the pig sty and the chicken coop. The rites are to ask the deata to bless these animals.

17. Mangallo manuk (manuk = chicken). See rite 16 above.

18. Ma'ta'da: sacrificial meals are prepared in various colours (mangrangga)[19] with boiled rice as a central ingredient. A black pig is also killed for the offering which takes place on the same day as rite 17. The death priest's helper (to ma'koko) officiates (see below). The offerings for the ancestors of old, the dead who long ago exchanged the ephemeral for the eternal (elsewhere: to matua, "The Old Ones"). The sacrifice is held early during the evening or late in the afternoon near the (North)Western corner of the tongkonan.

19. Matanna allona. Allona indicates that a major event in the feast is at hand. Because I was present at this rite, an extensive account follows presently (section 9). Here what needs to be said is that the person who fells the sandal tree has a special title: to manglelleng sendana (lelleng: to fell or cut down). Three sacrificial animals, a cock, a pig and a buffalo, are slaughtered.

20. Massara'ka: the palongko' (hip joint) and the heads of a buffalo, pig and chicken sacrificed on the occasion of rite 19 are reserved for

this rite which occurs on the morning after the matanna allona. These parts of the slaughtered animals are cooked; rice is prepared as well. After the sendana-branch has been planted on the Northeastern part of the compound, the family members who are present share the food. The planting of the sandal tree thus falls under this rite.

Rites 1 through 14 inclusively last for one to two days; rites 14 through 17 continue for four consecutive days without interruption. Rites 18 through 20 must similarly be conducted without a pause on successive days.

The texts of prayers and utterances which accompany the offerings were not recorded.

9. Ma'ta'da and matanna (allona) in the village of Kadinge' (1969)

After a walk of two kilometres, we reached the site of the feast, the flat top of a hill. Here stood the tongkonan, three ricebarns and a house of more modern design made from woven bamboo slats. At first sight it was not obvious that Bamba Lemo was a tongkonan. It had so many built-on parts; there was no carved ornamentation and no longa. Nevertheless that Bamba Lemo was of respectable antiquity appeared from the fact that the tongkonan had an a'riri posi' and a pata'[20] decorated with carving.

The tongkonan is located in the region where the adat-chief bears the title Issong Kalua' (The Great Rice Mortar); he was the most prominent figure in the merok-feast which was under way. I was introduced to The Great Rice Mortar, a friendly man between 60 and 70 years old. His willingness to provide me with information was an important stroke of good fortune, for he was one of the leading adat-dignitaries in Torajaland (cf. Vol.I:70).

Upon our arrival women were pounding rice, their rhythm so rapid that it sounded like drum beats.[21] We heard the sound already from afar. Other women were seated in front of the tongkonan winnowing rice. It was said, however, that this had nothing to do with the ritual.

The first evening, the night of October 20, 1969, the ma'ta'da was scheduled to take place, a rite comparable to the umpakande to matua in Kesu', "the feeding of the ancestors" (ma'ta'da means literally: to make a sacrifice, to implore). In other regions of Tana Toraja, Kesu' for one, the rite entails making an offering at the site of the cliff tomb of someone who has been dead for at least a year. Then the sacrifice takes place after the rice harvest.

For the ma'ta'da, a black pig was slaughtered. The to ma'koko, the priest who, just as the to mebalun, is a specialist in rites of the West, is the functionary designated to make the offering (the to ma'koko is actually the helper of the to mebalun; this helper in Kesu' has the title to pabalian. Ma'koko signifies: "to dig a hole to use the earth to blacken clothing"; this "soiling" of clothes is a rite of the death feast). In the early evening the pig was killed and cut into pieces. The intestines were placed in a wooden trough with a handle (passeran). Someone brought the trough to the Great Rice Mortar who pored over the intestines, the bile and the gall bladder. From their arrangement he can determine whether prospects appear favourable or not. Other prominent title-holders and to minaa also inspected the bloody contents of the

trough. The signs were judged auspicious. The pig was butchered. In
the meantime a langngan (spit) had been erected. A fire was lit beneath
it and bamboo joints were leaned against the horizontal pole. It would
take a long time, however, before the contents of these piong would be
edible, for intermittent rain broke out repeatedly. It was already far
into the night when the to ma'koko was able to proceed with the
offering; food was placed on a dozen pesung to the West of the tongkonan.

The consecration of the buffalo would take place the next morning,
the morning of the day after the ma'ta'da (at an early hour, but
whether at 4 or 6 there was some confusion). The buffalo, an ordinary
dark grey specimen had already been selected. It was a young animal.
His horns may not exceed one hand and three fingers in length. Usually the horns are a good bit shorter, and the animal still younger.
There was difficulty, however, securing the buffalo. This was the
reason the feast was delayed and the consecration would be taking place
the following morning. Apparently at dawn not much was yet in readiness. The Great Rice Mortar went about, rather nervously, calling for
three pio (loin-cloths) and three bayu (bayu lamba': long jackets).
Finally women brought these forward. The pio were white, decorated at
the ends with coloured motifs woven into the cloth. The clothing was
for the three important functionaries in the feast, all to parengnge':
a. the to mangrenden tedong (= to mangimbo)[22], "he who pulls the
buffalo onwards";
b. the to massomba tedong, "he who consecrates the buffalo";
c. the one who cuts off the sandalwood branch that is of such importance in the rite, the to manglelleng sendana.
In addition there were two further officials, also to parengnge', but
they wore no special ritual clothing (one of the pair was the to mangrande londong, "the one who holds the cock in his hand").

The Issong Kalua' himself actually should perform the function of the
to massomba tedong. If he is not sure of the text, however, he can ask
a to minaa or one of the three other to parengnge' from Buntao' to
stand in for him. The latter took place during the celebration initiated
by tongkonan Bamba Lemo.[23] Functions b. and c. above were carried
out by other to parengnge' from Buntao' (for these to parengnge', see
Vol.I:43ff.). In Buntao' the number of functionaries in the merok is
smaller than in Kesu', but otherwise the feast unfolds along similar
lines.

The sendana was carried in, a straight branch hacked from a sandal
tree; the branch was some two metres long and thick as a man's wrist.
Side branches were trimmed. A hole was dug for the sendana. The
ma'tambuli (digging of the hole) did not, however, seem to be a rite in
itself. A special functionary was responsible for cutting the branch
from the tree: the to manglelleng sendana (literally: the one who fells
the sendana, but in fact the tree is left standing, only a branch is cut
off). He was one of the four to parengnge' and wore a headcloth and a
long jacket. The sendana was to be encased in pieces of bamboo so that
it wouldn't be damaged during the fatal stabbing of the buffalo. Any
injury to the branch might mean it would fail to take root and grow;
this would have significant consequences (see above). The
sendana-branch was encased in bamboo slats which were encircled with
lengths of bambalu-liana. A rattan, a bambalu-liana and a sarita joined
the sendana to the a'riri posi' of the tongkonan (and thus not with the

Northern house post, as in Kesu'). The buffalo is fetched and tied to the sendana with a bambalu-liana. It was the job of a special functionary, the to mangrenden tedong (mangrenden: pull forward, tedong: buffalo), to keep the animal under control while he is tethered. He was one of the three to parengnge' in full regalia. The sandalwood branch was not decorated; nor was the tongkonan. Meanwhile the Issong Kalua's stand-in for the rite had been clothed. He wore a bayu lamba. On his head he had a maa'-cloth, the ends of which trailed down his back. The barre allo (sun disk with rays) was tied in place so that the metal disk rested against his right temple. The sunburst, about 15 cm in diameter, was gilded. Nassa shells are fastened to this ornament in such a way that they form a circle. In Tana Toraja, so far from the sea, shells are scarce, a commodity of great value. The rest of the decoration of the barre allo consisted of an incised tumpal-motif, also in concentric circles (tumpal is a motif that appears on Javanese batiks; it is made up of a row of small triangles). Two large double spirals had been scratched into the centre of the sunburst. As far as I know, this decoration is exclusive to Buntao'.

The moment had arrived for the ceremony to begin. The to massomba tedong (the man with the barre allo) stood before the sendana. He held a spear in his right hand. To the bottom of the spear a green areca nut had been fastened so that the weapon itself never touched the ground. A pouch with daun bolu (sirih leaves) and a small vessel made from a calabash (lau) were also attached to the doke (spear). The spear was not waved about, as in Kesu' (Merok:7). The man with the barre allo launched into his litany. Now and then he hesitated, and looked out in front of him with the embarrassment of a school boy who falters in reciting his lessons. He admitted will all honesty that he had forgotten the text. Indeed, reciting the Passomba Tedong is no everyday affair and he was - people told me later - nervous because so many guests stood (and sat) listening even though all the relatives expected had not yet arrived. The buffalo also listened. I had heard that during the consecration the buffalo stood stock still, but I hadn't given the story much credence. Yet, the animal in fact hardly moved a muscle throughout the Passomba Tedong; with his soft, dark eyes he stared at the man who sang the litany, and every once in a while his ears twitched, that was all.[24] It was as if he was absorbing the story of the darkness which prevailed before heaven and earth were separated; the story of the creation of man and of the first buffalo, here Lilin by name. I mulled over the dreadful fate awaiting the buffalo and found myself hoping that the recitation would go on and on. Further along, between two ricebarns, the pig and the rooster which would also be sacrificed were in readiness. Here it was apparently not the custom as in Kesu' for a man to hold the rooster in his arms during the Passomba Tedong. The consecration of the buffalo began at roughly seven in the morning; two hours later it already ended. The text was drastically abridged. Originally the consecration was to take place at night, but the buffalo had eluded capture. The to massomba tedong's spear was to be the buffalo's death instrument. As so often, this animal, too, perceived that the man who approached him now had a dark goal in mind. He tried to escape his fate by circling around the sendana. The first blow struck home, but it wasn't fatal. The animal, mad with pain, went on turning about the sandalwood branch. He was blindfolded; a mark was made on his breast to assist the executioner's aim. The second stab

Fig. 5. Ground-plan showing disposition of objects, animals and functionaries during the merok-feast in Buntao'.

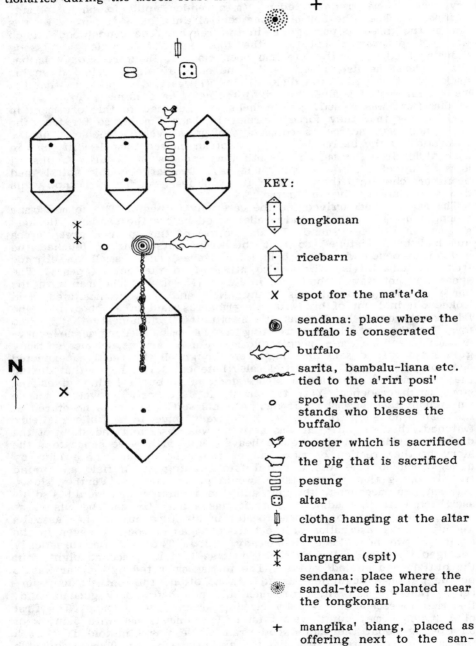

KEY:

tongkonan

ricebarn

X   spot for the ma'ta'da

sendana: place where the
buffalo is consecrated

buffalo

sarita, bambalu-liana etc.
tied to the a'riri posi'

o   spot where the person
stands who blesses the
buffalo

rooster which is sacrificed

the pig that is sacrificed

pesung

altar

cloths hanging at the altar

drums

langngan (spit)

sendana: place where the
sandal-tree is planted near
the tongkonan

+   manglika' biang, placed as
offering next to the sandana

was deadly, but by then I had fled into the house that was to the left of the tongkonan. The buffalo was stabbed in his left side and must fall on his right side. Should he collapse onto his left side, that would presage disaster. In keeping with adat-usage, the animal was hacked into pieces. Only the head was left intact.

The deata were to be feasted on certain buffalo parts (see Vol.I:206). The pig and rooster also belong to the offering presented to the gods. The buffalo, however, is the most important sacrificial animal. The pig was slaughtered in the fashion customary in Buntao' - and only there: a knife was stuck into its ear. The pig was black, as prescribed. (The custom called sipalakuan - see Chapter III, note 6 - was not executed.)

In the meanwhile two drums were brought outside. These gandang are important objects in this feast. They are played almost non-stop to drive off evil. In truth it might be more apt to say they were played to purify the atmosphere. The drumming is less an exorcism than a cleansing; in this way the harm that might threaten the family - and the ritual in general - is banished. A sacral maa'-cloth was draped over the drums; on top of it, on a scrap of banana leaf, lay a small offering (pesung). The rhythm of the drumming modulated constantly; there were, it seems, different ways of playing. It was exhausting work and the to ma'gandang (the drummers) took turns at set intervals. They varied in age from very young to very old. These drums may only be struck during the merok- or bua'-feast. And only a tongkonan that has a pata' may have these drums played during the merok-celebration.

Also by this time the to massomba tedong had inspected the bile and the gall bladder of the slaughtered buffalo: the signs appeared to be extraordinarily auspicious. The afternoon approached and the to parengnge', the wife of the kepala lembang[25], and I ducked under the ricebarn to shelter from the hot sun. The to parengnge' sat on the front edge of the floor there; it was their reserved place during feasts. For the others, even sugar palm branches inserted in the ground failed to provide adequate cover. Groups of every size kept on arriving, family members come as guests to their own family celebration. With every group came pigs, one or more, trussed to bamboo poles in customary fashion. The animals were laid down next to each other in the burning sun. During the day some twenty-five were brought, a dozen or so slaughtered. It took no more than an instant to singe off the hair and scorch the skin, but the meat of the pigs was left almost raw; further cooking would make it difficult to divide the meat. No one indeed should eat of the flesh until the offering was consecrated to the gods. And the food for the offering was anything but fully cooked. The meat consisted of specific parts of the buffalo. The rice had already been put into bamboo joints which had been leaned against the langngan; the outside was black, but it took, as usual, forever until the contents were done. The offering was to be placed on a small sacrificial altar made of four struts of bamboo-tallang stuck in the ground and decorated with carving on top; two platforms of woven bamboo were supported by the uprights (cf. Vol.I:272). Two kandaure and two maa'-cloths hung from an upright pole to the left of the altar. The remaining space was filled with newer fabrics.[26] The sarita, the bambaluliana and the rattan still joined the sendana to the a'riri posi' of the tongkonan. (For the lay-out of buildings, regalia and personages, see Fig. 5.)

The influx of guests went on unabated; they brought pigs, rice and tuak (in long bamboo joints and in vats). By now the contents of the piong were ready to be eaten. And now, on a great many strips of banana leaf, food for the gods was prepared. No more than a few pesung were needed for the offering table, but the number of portions was much larger, a good dozen. Only the four pesung in the middle were for the gods' repast. Women were busy serving rice. There were many busy, but one was in charge, the to massanduk deata (the one who serves the rice for the gods; ma'sanduk: to dish out). This woman can be the host's sister. All the other women were family members, indeed those family members who were part of the female line of the tongkonan.[27] All the women belonged to the to parengnge'-class (women are important in the kinship system; the Toraja themselves call attention to this fact). The stand-in for the to parengnge' who had blessed the buffalo had a woman's jacket knotted around his right wrist. This, too, indicated the significance of women and the female line in the family group; were Bamba Lemo a tongkonan of a lesser order, then the to massomba tedong would have wound cotton threads around his left wrist.

Serving the rice was no light chore, for various kinds of rice had to be arranged in colourful patterns: ordinary rice (white), red rice (in the middle), black rice, rice dyed yellow with tumeric, glutinous rice, and, in the centre on top, a kaledo (see Fig. 11). These were all the varieties of rice which Puang Matua had given to man, with one exception. He had also given yellow rice but then, when the rice was used for an offering in the rambu solo'-sphere, he had taken it back to heaven. Since then white rice has been dyed yellow for the offering meal. The parts of the sacrificed animals were added to the rice. The offering was brought to the altar: one portion for Puang Matua placed on the upper surface; three portions for the three other important gods placed on the lower surface. The same functionary who had consecrated the buffalo, presided over the offering.

Before the gods were fed, they were first offered sirih: people, too, chew sirih before they eat. The areca-nut which had been fixed to the haft of the spear which the to massomba tedong held during the litany and used to stab the buffalo to death, was included in the sirih pinang-offering.[28]

Now might mankind eat and drink as well! Voices droned above the sounds of feasting. How many guests were present? It was impossible to count them - several hundreds.

I was asked to take a photograph of the host and his (close) family members in front of the tongkonan. It was difficult to fit them all in the picture. Wasn't the litany sung during the consecration of the buffalo explicit about a family group as numerous as the culms of a flourishing bamboo?

The next morning the sendana-stake was to be replanted somewhere Northeast of the tongkonan or its compound.

The to minaa who stood in for the Issong Kalua' during
the closing rites of the merok-feast in Buntao', October
20-22, 1969. He wears a maa'-cloth on his head, with the
barre allo attached to it at his right temple. He also is
wearing a bayu lamba', a long jacket open in front.
Around his right wrist, he has a woman's jacket
knotted. In his right hand he holds a spear which rests
on an areca-nut fastened to the bottom of the shaft. See
also pp. 73-74. (Photo: Hetty Nooy-Palm, 1969.)

The to mangrenden tedong and the buffalo at the merok-feast
in Buntao'. See also pp. 72-73 and Fig. 5.
(Photo: Hetty Nooy-Palm, 1969.)

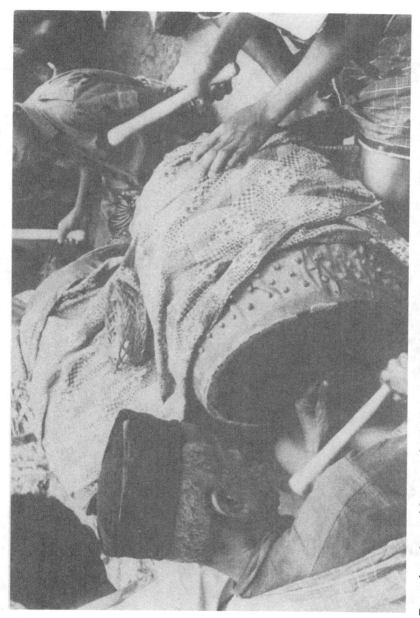

To ma'gandang (drummers) at the merok-feast in Buntao'. The drums are covered with a maa'-cloth. In the centre the pesung are visible. See also p. 75 and Fig. 5. (Photo: Hetty Nooy-Palm, 1969.)

A rooster and pig: animals sacrificed at the merok-feast in Buntao'. See also p. 73 and Fig. 5. (Photo: Hetty Nooy-Palm, 1969.)

Pesung: sacrificial meal for the gods, placed on banana leaves; merok-feast in Buntao'. See also p. 76 and Fig. 5. (Photo: Hetty Nooy-Palm, 1969.)

The panganta' at the merok-feast in Buntao'. Among the hanging cloths is a kandaure (an ornament fashioned from beads). See also pp. 68 and 75 and Fig. 5. (Photo: Hetty Nooy-Palm, 1969.)

Sipalakuan, a custom that is part of the manganta' and the merok-feast:
the offerer and his assistant hold onto the tail of the pig that has been
sacrificed and ask for a blessing for themselves. See also pp. 64 and
75.
(Photo: Archives of the National Research Centre of Archaeology,
Jakarta, 1938.)

Chapter IV

THE RICE RITUAL

"The kaloko' whistles,
The kaloko' brings rice.
The little tattiku'-bird deposits his rice outside the ricebarn,
The dove fills the ricebarn."
(Biung-song, sung during the
ma'belundak, a part of the rice
ritual; Woordenboek:71)

1. Priests and functionaries

The ricefield in heaven is described in the Passomba Tedong. This sawah is situated at the upper end of the firmament (Merok:119). Despite great expenditure of effort, the yield from the upperworld sawah initially was disappointing. Puang Matua then took a journey to the West, to the place of the sinking sun, where pure gold is found. He took this gold back with him and upon his return home he put it in the divine bellows. The bellows began to ply. Two beautiful children were born from the bellows: Datu Mengkamma' and Karaeng Ma'loko-loko. Grown to maturity, they were custodians of the hundred food taboos which had to be observed for the celestial sawah, and of the thousand ritual instructions which have to be obeyed for this ricefield. Then the sawah began to produce a more flourishing crop (Merok:117). Without ritual, rice will not even grow in the best sawah. Datu Mengkamma' and Karaeng Ma'loko-loko[1] were the first to indo' padang, rice priests. To indo' means mother. The rice priests, however, are men; the word "mother" refers to their watchful relation to the rice.

In one village there are usually several to indo' each responsible for a certain component of the rice ritual. In a village divided in two, for example in Upper Ba'tan and Lower Ba'tan, each part has a full complement of rice priests. It is possible for other functionaries, male or female, to officiate at some point as well. In order of rank and significance the to indo' padang can be classified as follows:
1. The bunga' lalan[2], "the one who begins the path, who opens the way". He is the one who takes precedence in whatever has to do with the cultivation of rice and related rituals. Bunga' lalan is also the name of The Seven Sisters, The Pleiades, the constellation which farmers are on the lookout for when they want to begin rice cultivation; when this constellation first becomes visible in the heavens again, the time is right to commence sowing (Woordenboek:82). In Ba'tan doan, the office of the leading priest in the rice ritual and in all matters related to rice cultivation is filled by a member of tongkonan Bamba; in Ba'tan

diongan, by a member of tongkonan Kullin (Kullin Tangnga).

2. The second important to indo' is the to massanduk (sanduk: to serve boiled (rice) from the pot onto separate plates).[3]

3. The third functionary is the to mantobok, "he who stabs (the sacrificial animal) to death". He is also the one who performs the rite of consecration when a small ditch (panta'da) is dug so that water can flow out of the sawah. Before rice is planted, the field must be dry. The rite (massabu panta'da, Vol.I:102) is not mentioned by itself in Allo Rante's (Ne' Sangga) summary (see section 3 below). Presumably the to mantobok sacrifices a chicken during the rite. (Indeed, the chicken is not stabbed to death, but its throat is cut.)

4. The fourth functionary is the to pabalian (the "helper", the "assistant").

5. Foremost among the remaining, less prominent figures with a role in the ritual, is the londong datu. The title may be connected to the sacrifice of a cock once the rice has begun to ripen (londong: rooster; datu: lord). The designation also possibly refers to the melondong: "the female guardian of the shed (lantang) in which the bunu' (strips removed from bamboo which are used to tie bunches of rice) are kept". Little is reported about the task of this "guardian". In this context Nobele mentions two functionaries, husband and wife, who belong to the class of hereditary slaves. The couple guards the bunches of padi which are piled up to dry in front of the lantang bunu'. These bunches are separated into two categories: the pare papanuku, twelve in number, used for rites; and the pare pangrakan, used to pay the rice cutters. The pare papanuku are laid out in the centre of the drying place for rice and sprinkled with water from half a gourd (kandean lau) by the "guardian" (Nobele calls her to ma'pemali, "she who pays heed to the taboos"). The pare pangrakan are set down on the East side of the drying place. As with the pare papanuku, this is done shortly before the rice is stored. When the padi is stored, the male of the couple takes (a bunch of?) pare papanuku from the drying place, his wife picks up (a bunch of?) pare papanuku. She also takes with her the gourd filled with water and an incense burner. The man puts the pare papanuku somewhere in the East side of the ricebarn that originally was the property of the founder of the village and on top of it he places the pare pangrakan. His wife sprinkles the bunches with water and hangs the gourd above the entrance of the ricebarn. Then she ignites tagari and buangin-leaves in the incense burner which she sets down on the ground in front of the barn (Nobele 1926:82ff.). What is being enacted apparently has to do with the later fabrication of a "rice mother"; see section 3, rites 15 and 18, under indo' mangrakan.

6. The to ma'pallin (see Chapter III.8., rite 2 and Merok:2).

7. The mangnganan barodo (mangnganan: to inspire amazement; barodo defies translation). The nature of this rite is unknown to me.

All in all, as so often, there are eight functionaries. For further information about these to indo' padang, see also Vol.I:102ff. and 279ff. For the function of the rice priest (in particular for the bunga' lalan) a person is proposed by the members of his tongkonan. The nomination must be ratified by the anak pare-pare nangka' at the meeting where the anak patalo play a prominent role (cf. Vol.I:44 and 49ff.). The to indo' do not belong to the highest class, but rather to the to makaka direngnge', "the lowest level" of the to makaka. This is connected to

the fact that they may not eat any meat that comes from
a death ritual. Indeed, they should avoid death feasts as much as possible. They cannot be rich because they may not participate in any significant extent in the system of reciprocal exchange of buffaloes and
buffalo meat inherent in funeral rites.

2. Rice cultivation

2.1. Varieties of rice

The Sa'dan-Toraja consider rice to be their leading food. We have
already noted that rice is of heavenly origin and its cultivation is regulated by numerous rules. The Passomba Tedong makes mention of many
additional details, such as the name Takkebuku (= having no bone, no
pit), the ancestor of the cooked rice (Merok:91, verse 440), and the
phrase pare tallu bulinna, "three-eared rice", which appears repeatedly
in transcriptions of invocations (Merok:186-7, verse 24ff.). The phrase
is not a reference to a particular variety of rice but rather gives
expression to the perfection of rice properly cultivated. "Three-eared
rice" has also a ritual implication, referring to the kinallona pesungan
banne, see below, section 3.
   The most complete account of the cultivation of rice among the Toraja
and of related prescriptions, of the distribution of the harvest among
interested parties, of rice sicknesses and of irrigation practices has
been written by Nobele (1926:70-85). His data concerns the territory of
Ma'kale. A reader in search of more complete information than what is
contained in the following text, should consult Nobele's work.
   Some fifteen varieties of rice are distinguished (Woordenboek: v.
pare). As is true among other Indonesian peoples, rice here has
various names depending upon whether one is talking about rice still in
the field, unpolished rice, or cooked rice. Rice that hasn't been cut or
threshed is called pare; rice already husked, barra'; rice ready to eat,
bo'bo'. Although rice is the most important crop, it is not the basic
food of the poor. They may possibly have to make do with maize, which
costs less. They also eat yams (Indonesian ubi, Dioscorea alata L.,
Toraja andoa' or dua'). Among more prosperous families maize is only
consumed during a certain phase of the death ritual (see Chapter IX).

2.2. Sawahs

The Sa'dan-Toraja are excellent rice cultivators. In the past rice was
primarily raised on irrigated fields[4] designated by different terms
depending on their situation and the quantity of water that had to be
supplied. A wet ricefield was called uma or galung. Uma ma'kambuno
lumu', "a field in which the water rises as high as a fan-palm", is the
designation for a sawah which always holds a rich water supply (Woordenboek: v. uma). Dry ricefields are also known. Each field has its
proper name. The fields often lie next to each other in a series of terraces at different heights. The Toraja are skilled at laying sawahs; the
ricefields encroach high up the mountain sides, especially on the slopes
of Sesean, reminiscent of the ricefields of the Javanese, the Balinese
and the inhabitants of the Philippines. Their construction requires a
vast amount of hard labour. In the territory of Pangala', if one looks

down from on high the view reveals land sprinkled with vast stone formations; nonetheless the people have constructed sawahs, often using the rocks as part of the sawah dike. The dikes, seen from the terrace below, are at times more than the height of a man. This is true as well in other parts of Tana Toraja. In the territories of Bori' and Riu, for example, on the mountain slopes terraces can be seen which are separated by perfectly smooth walls up to 10 metres high. These walls of hewn stone prevent the earth from tumbling down. This impressive accomplishment is ascribed to the ancestors. The present inhabitants of the area admit: "we can't do it nowadays". Here, too, the sawahs are often hemmed in by massive rocks. Aa' uma is the name for small sawahs which nestle against a mountain side (aa': slope).

2.3. Tools

Until recently agriculture in Tana Toraja did not involve machines. Now, since the late 1970s, small tractors on a modest scale are being used in the surroundings of Rantepao because manual labour, in Torajaland, too, has become so expensive. Even exploitation of the buffalo as a draught animal was formerly but occasional (since 1966 this has been changing). In 1949 it was reported that such draught animals came from the Buginese, "for our buffaloes don't work". With the exception of precious specimens, however, the buffaloes do work. Usually cows are harnessed to the plough or harrow. The buffaloes do not obey commands to turn, however, as they do on Java, Bali and in Buginese areas. In old songs like the Passomba Tedong, buffaloes are frequently depicted at work in the ricefields (Merok:134-5). On an ancient pio uki', a loin cloth used in rituals, owned by S.L. Pasapan of Tallulolo, buffaloes pulling a plough are portrayed (see Vol.I:194, fig. VII.3.). The plough is steered by two men: one behind the plough itself, the second leading the team of buffaloes.

There are thus reasons to believe that the use of the plough - which, to be sure, depends to a great extent on the composition of the soil -

Fig. 6. Plough (tengko).

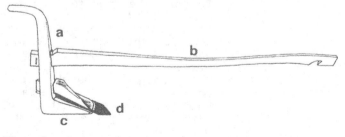

The ploughshare is made of karurung-wood (karurung: the hard wood at the core of the sugar palm). The Golden Plough of the upperworld is mentioned in the Passomba Tedong.
a plough handle (plough tail)
b plough beam
c shove beam or plough head
d ploughshare

is older than the Toraja themselves realize. Plough and harrow are virtually identical to those which are used in Buginese territories (cf.
Matthes [undated]:ill. VI, figs. 1 and 3). An argument in support of
the proposition that the plough was introduced from the Buginese is
that fifty years ago this tool was only found in Tana Toraja in the
territory of Rano which borders on Buginese lands. The plough is of
the so-called Indian type that is popular throughout Indonesia and also
in Burma (Further India). (In addition, in Java the Chinese plough is
used, also found in the Philippines, but not in Sulawesi (Celebes);
information from J. Cattie, former curator Museum of the Royal Tropical
Institute, Amsterdam.) The word for plough is tengko; for yoke, ayoka
(see, too, Fig. 6).

The harrow (see Fig. 7) is to break up the clods of earth on plough-
ed land; kurrik, in fact, has the meaning also of scratching or
scraping. The harrow as well as the plough is pulled by a span of
buffaloes, or by one or two men.

In 1949 I saw a to parengnge' in Tikala struggling on his way home
under the load of a heavy harrow thrown across his shoulder. When I
asked his wife how this harrow was pulled, she answered with a note of

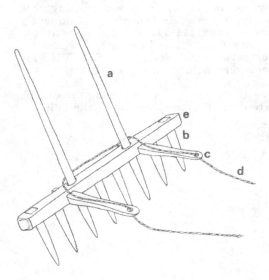

Fig. 7. Harrow (salaga).
a   toeanna, "handle"
b   isi salaga, "the teeth of the
    harrow"
c. inan rari', "the place
    (holder) for the rope"
d   rari', rope or string made of
    buffalo hide
e   batangna salaga, "the beam
    of the harrow"
The harrow is made entirely
from wood, the hard wood at
the core of the sugar palm. The
harrow is pulled by one or two
buffaloes, or one or more men.
To turn the harrow, it must
first be lifted.
At the start of harrowing, the
teeth of the tool face backwards. Once the soil has been
loosened up to some extent,
then, using the handles, the
farmer pushes the salaga
forward so that the teeth stand
more or less perpendicular to
the ground.
The buffalo is led by one man, the harrow is steered by a second. The
steersman holds a whip; he also has a cleaver (la'bo') with him so that
in the event that the buffalo is frightened and runs off, he can cut the
rari' through.

The halter, samban, is twisted out of young sugar palm leaves.
Kurrik is the name of a small harrow that is used in the puang-areas
Ma'kale and Sangalla' on small sawahs.

pride, but somewhat shyly, too, "by my husband". (Her answer made it clear that not only the unfree do strenuous farm work, but nobility as well.)

Harrow and plough, harrowing and ploughing, often are featured in sayings and metaphors. They appear in litanies, too, e.g.: "that which has been settled like a harrow", and "that which is as fixed as a plough". Both these comparisons mean "that which is prescribed" (Woordenboek: v. salaga).

A tool that presumably antedates both the plough and the harrow is the peleko' (Sangalla') or petibak (Kesu'), a shovel that resembles a rowing oar which consists of a shaft about 7 m long and a blade about 20 cm long and 15 cm wide (see Fig. 8). In its original form this tool consisted of a single piece of wood. Later the blade was partly replaced by a piece of iron mounted in the wood; by 1946 such shovels with a wooden blade had all but disappeared. Just as its wooden prototype, the iron blade has various shapes, ranging from diamond-shaped to rectangular. I was told that such differences have to do with the quality of the soil being farmed.

Fig. 8. Petibak or peleko'.

The handle and the wooden blade of this digging implement are fashioned out of a single piece of wood. The darkened area in the figure represents the iron part of the blade. The tool is for sale at the market. Its length is approximately 125 cm.

The peleko' or petibak is for finishing the sawah dikes, i.e. scrapping off the grass, and for tilling the sawah. One holds the handle or the top of the shaft in the right hand, with the left hand somewhat lower down. The tool is stuck into the mud obliquely. The mud (and the weeds which grow in it) is then dragged towards the cultivator in such a way that the weeds become buried under a layer of soil. (Several people perform this work at once in Mamasa, as "neighbour help"; those involved, I assume, are the saroan.) Because the work is done by many, at the same time a thick roll of topsoil is created (Hekstra 1970:12; what happens further to the roll is not mentioned). In Tana Toraja I did not witness this group effort with the peleko'. In many areas, to be sure, this old tool has been replaced by the bingkung (hoe), at least it has been in Kesu', Ma'kale and Tikala. The hoe was introduced shortly after the end of World War II.

Peleko' and hoes are used above all on smaller, more highly situated sawah plots or on extremely swampy fields.

At times when filling the sawahs iron staves are used, a kind of digging stick or crowbar (pekali bassi; pekali: to dig, bassi: iron). These are pointed at the bottom and somewhat flat on top.[5]

Another implement is the lembang or raki', a kind of wooden sled which is pushed forward with the help of two poles which serve as handles (lembang: proa; raki': raft). The sled is used to transport soil to level the ground.

We should also mention scarecrows (payo-payo). They may not exactly be tools but they are artefacts employed during rice cultivation. They differ in appearance, representing human figures or horses and are made of the dry leaf-sheaths of bamboo shoots. La'pa-la'pa are rattles of bamboo that are fastened to a string. If someone pulls on the string, the noise chases off the birds. A garentong, consisting of pieces of bamboo and scraps of tin, works in the same way; joined to a rope, if the rope is set in motion, then the garentong clatters and the sound scares away the birds.

The final object employed in the rice cycle is the rice knife (rangkapan; see Fig. 9). For additional artefacts used in the cultivation of rice, see text below.

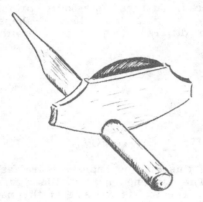

Fig. 9. Rice knife (rangkapan). The handle is bamboo, the guard in which the blade is inserted is wood, the blade itself iron.

2.4. Agricultural tasks

In different parts of Torajaland, agricultural activities begin at different times of the year. In Kesu' farmers begin in November to work the sawahs; planting starts in February; the harvest takes place in August. For the rice cycle in Tikala, Kesu' and Bittuang, see Fig. 10.

Before transplanting of rice takes place, a nursery (panta'nakan), a miniature sawah, is made. Waste and weeds are carefully removed. Seedbeds are protected from animals by arches of bamboo. After the

Fig. 10. The rice cycles in Tikala, Kesu' and Bittuang.

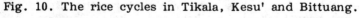

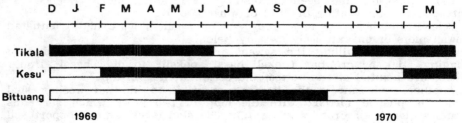

nursery is ready for sowing, seeds - rice grains - are selected. This takes place on the compound. For the selection, ears of rice are spread on a wooden plank and women, in a somewhat bent position, holding onto one of the support posts of the ricebarn, walk on them. This treading process of releasing grains for sowing is called manglullu'. The chance is great that if buffaloes threshed the rice or if threshing flails were used the grains would be damaged and no longer suitable for sowing. The women who perform the manglullu' may not wear black clothing, certainly no black dress. Around their necks they wear the manik ata (a necklace made of gold or gilded beads alternating with blood coral, see Nooy-Palm 1969:fig.4 and plates VI and VII, and Nooy-Palm 1975b:40-2 and photo 12). Ata refers to rice still in the husk among polished grains of rice; possibly the term associates the form of the gold or gilded beads with that of the grains of rice (personal interpretation). Rice is brought into connection with the colours of the upperworld, white and yellow. Black clothing must not be worn during these rites because black falls in the sphere of rambu solo', the sphere of the rituals of the (South)West, those of the to matua.

Many women can take part in the treading ceremony; in the instance of the sawah of a rich man, 50 would not be a surprising number. The rice which is not used for sowing is given in payment to the treshers. Some three days after the manglullu', the selected grains of rice are soaked in water for 24 hours by men. Then they are spread on the surface of the seedbeds (this, too, is the work of men, usually persons with experience). After three days the nurseries are drained of water so that the rice can now germinate.

Next the water is removed from the sawah. On large sawahs the ma'da'dak is then enacted, the trapping of fish with a basket. This takes place when the water is very low. The fish are removed from the basket by hand. A high degree of skill has been developed; one hears the fish floundering in the muddy water. After being caught, a fish is laid in a separate basket. The bamboo spikes that stick out like teeth from the bottom of the fish traps also loosen the soil.

For some time thus the ricefields have served as "fish ponds". Indeed, in many sawahs farmers have dredged out real fish ponds, so-called gusian, a few metres deep and surrounded by a small dam. The water level is kept constant here; during the ma'da'dak some of the fish caught can safely be kept in the gusian. For 3 days after the ma'da'dak the sawah is left dry. The ground is tilled with plough, hoe or peleko'. There are sawahs which are more or less always under water as a consequence of the composition of the soil and the level of the water-table. In such ricefields a large part of the work, including weeding, must be done with bare hands; at times workers even use their feet. In all cases, after the land has been prepared, water is let back onto the sawah.

When the young rice plants in the seedbed are about a month old, the ma'da'dak is sometimes repeated.

Meanwhile, at least if the rains have begun on time, the preparation of the sawah ground has been completed. After ploughing, the land is levelled - with hands and feet, and, at times, with earth transported by sled. Harrowing then follows.

For fertilizer, ash or pig manure, mixed with chaff, is spread. Buffalo manure is not used, for it would make the rice "ill". To be sure sawahs fertilized with buffalo waste sometimes yield rice with empty husks. (Precisely when fertilizers are laid down is not clear to me, presumably before the soil is turned.)

According to Hekstra, in Mamasa farmers prefer to improve the soil of the sawahs by spreading on fresh dry earth removed from the sawah dikes and transported by sled; experience has taught them that this practice improves the sawah's yield (Hekstra 1970:12). After about three months, women uproot the young rice plants from the nursery. A bunch of rice that one can hold between thumb and index finger is tugged free and shaken against some object so that all the soil falls free from the roots. These bunches are tied together and topped and later, one by one, each seedling is planted separately in the sawah. In Kesu' and Tikala women who stand in rows do the transplanting. Because of their simultaneous, rhythmic motion, the scene resembles a dance, a kind of ballet (for a description, see Wilcox 1949:188 and illustration facing p. 176). In Sangalla' men transplant the seedlings.

After a month men weed out the grass growing between the rice plants. Labourers on the sawah are paid with food, tuak, sirih and Rp.100/day (Rp.100 = approx. Dfl.1 at 1969 prices). More is sometimes paid. In 1969 a worker in Kesu' received 2 litres of rice a day, plus food and palm wine.

During work on the sawah, which begins about 8 a.m. and lasts until 5 p.m., women bring the midday meal to the fields. Sometimes labourers bring cooked rice with them to the sawah in a kapipe, a bag of tuyu-reeds that is made in Lolai, in Pangala' or in Dende' (at present people also use plastic bags).

When the rice in the fields is almost ripe, it is protected from birds through manipulation of the garentong and similar devices described above. There is little, however, one undertakes against field mice. They are considered ampu padang, princes of the earth, who are entitled to profit from crops growing in the fields. Modern methods to combat field mice have therefore scarcely been adopted.

Women do the harvesting, using the rice knife. Reaping goes on the whole day through; meals are eaten on the sawah. As a rule there is only a single annual harvest. In the territory of Madandan, however, the rice is cut twice a year.[6]

The yield from the ricefield is calculated in the number of small bunches which are cut. One bunch - sangkutu' - consists of as many ears of grain as a person can surround with thumb and index finger. In La'bo'[7] those who do the harvesting may keep one bunch for every ten they reap; limangkutu' or sangpongo' is the name for a packet of five bunches joined into one.

In some regions certain tasks, such as preparing the soil and harvesting, are performed collectively by the inhabitants of a neighbourhood (saroan). The work is carried out in the form of reciprocal aid (these saroan also care for maintenance of the sawah dikes; see Vol.I:95).

Although irrigation of the ricefields undoubtedly involves mutual consultation, it was impossible for me to learn anything definite about how such arrangements are reached. Informants told me that theft of water did occur, especially as the dry season came closer. There is no institution comparable to the subak on Bali.[8]

During periods when the sawah is not planted with rice, few so-called "secondary crops" are cultivated. Instead, fish may be put out in the ricefields.

After the rice harvest, sisemba' takes place, the sport of "calf-kicking". Two youths grab hands; they are partners in the contest. They hold onto each other so that when they kick they won't lose balance. One kicks - takes the offense, the other wards kicks off - takes the defense. Two villages compete with each other in teams of 10. The sport continues for three days. The fighting is determined by tradition. After the boys have finished "calf-kicking", six days later the adults begin. Whoever is struck a hard blow may harbour no grudge. Rather heavy injury is no exception. This is true, too, for the silangkan-langkan in Bittuang, a duel with sticks of rattan to which nails have been attached. The blows are parried with shields (cf. similar duels with whips in Tnganan Pagringsingan on Bali, on Lombok, in Manggarai, on Flores and on Timor). For a description of the sisemba' (in La'bo'), see Andi Lolo (1969) and Wilcox (1949:227-8).[9] The sport has also a religious significance and thus can be considered part of the rice ritual.

Although there is no longer a taboo on cultivation of "secondary crops" between two rice cycles, people still prefer, as in the past, merely to use the sawahs as fish ponds. Even before 1969 certain sawahs, however, were planted with rice which matures between the two usual rice seasons. Since 1969 experiments have been under way with modern rice varieties that permit more harvests per year.

3. The rice ritual in Kesu'

The ma'tongkonan precedes all rites. The to parengnge' and the village elders (of Ba'tan, for example) are called together to set a time for initiating the first rite. One then begins with:

1. Ma'pallin, an expiatory sacrifice (see Merok:156-8, and Chapter III, section 4, rite 1). Outside the village a black hen is slaughtered. Someone kicks the earth three times with his heel and the chicken's blood is allowed to flow into the depression. Then the hen is burned, together with rice cooked in a bamboo cylinder. The to ma'pallin performs the offering. The contents of the accompanying prayer give evidence that the sacrifice falls in the sphere of the West:

"So that we together may undertake the performing of the
pallin-offering, at the Western side, in order that
we, each one with the other, may concern ourselves with
the holding of the expiatory offering."
(Merok:156-7, verse 2)

2. Hereupon the mangkaro kalo' follows ("the cleaning of the ditch"; kalo': ditch, trench). A chicken is sacrificed. The ditch is figurative; one digs the "ditch" or cleans it so that a lot of water will flow into the sawah, or so that it will rain heavily. The to pabalian slaughters a chicken; the offering he prepares consists of a kaledo and/or a belundak hung from a tadoran. Kaledo and belundak are packets in which sacrificial food is wrapped (see Fig. 11). The rite is also known as mangkaro palembang.

3. Massu'bak signifies the digging up of a little earth and sacrificing a chicken as a sign that cultivation is about to commence. The bunga' lalan observes the Pleiades. During the massu'bak panta'nakan-rite at the start of making the seedbed for the rice, a chicken is sacrificed.

Fig. 11. Packets of rice, which may be used for rituals.

Pokon, glutinous rice cooked in the leaf of bamboo-betung which has been folded double.

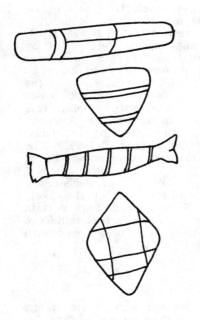

Kaledo, rice cooked in banana leaf.

Belundak, glutinous rice wrapped in packets made by braiding strips of young sugar palm leaves.

Katupa', steamed rice wrapped in packets made by braiding strips of young sugar palm leaves.

The chicken (a rooster, sella', or a chicken, rame) is offered up by the to indo'. (This functionary is selected from the four major to indo'.) Parts of the slaughtered chicken are put into three bamboo cylinders in which rice is cooked (tallu piong). The offering takes place during the tenth month (October).

4. The threshing of the sowing rice, manglullu' pare. Before the rite, at home, a chicken is killed and people wear quantities of gold jewelry so that the rice will become just as yellow. Formerly, this sowing rice used to be blessed by the to burake (in Kesu' by the to burake tambolang).

"When the burake tambolang has entered a ricefield where the harvest is in progress, she is presented with twelve bunches of rice. She gives back two of them after she has tied them together or bent the stalks of the bunches upwards. These two bunches are then reserved for sowing rice. Similar events follow when the burake tambolang passes by a ricebarn where the harvest is being stored, or the drying place of the rice where the bunches of rice are being spread out in the sun. On these occasions the burake tambolang speaks the following words: 'May the rice be abundant, the ricebarn filled, people receive children, the buffaloes calves, the pigs bear young and chickens multiply'." (Van der Veen 1923/24:399)

The rice is then sown. First ten grains are sown, no more. A chicken or a pig is slaughtered. During the spreading of the seeds, cooked rice is put in among the sowing rice. This cooked rice is called bo'bo' ka'do and is intended as "provisions" for the sowing rice. For this purpose in Ma'kale pokon is used, rice cooked in packets made from the folded leaves of the bamboo-betung (see Fig. 11). The rice to be sown is put in a special winnowing fan, bingka' ka'do. This fan is only used during the threshing and the sowing (Woordenboek: v. ka'do). Before the sowing commences, an offering (ma'piong) is brought to the nursery; it consists of a piong with cooked rice. The piong is opened and the rice, together with salt, is placed down on a banana leaf. The sowing of the seed rice itself has already been described above.

5. Ma'padoloi, "transplant (some rice plants) before proceeding to plant the entire sawah". The rice seedlings are transplanted; first the field of the bunga' lalan is planted (ma'padoloi literally means: "to allow to go first"). At this rite a chicken is sacrificed.

6. Mewaka' pare, "the root of the rice standing in the field". The rice is growing; one implores a blessing so that the plants will take root. The londong datu (rice priest) makes the offering. According to J.P. Suna from Tondon, a territory between Nanggala and Rantepao, if the rice was not growing well a search began in the village for who might have committed a transgression; indeed, people would be quick to suspect someone was guilty of incest. The guilty party had to supply a buffalo, pig or chicken, depending on the gravity of his sin. The same holds true in Kesu'. The to minaa investigates who the guilty one is.[10] He also presides over the offering.

Before the next rite begins, a meeting again takes place (ma'tong-konan) on the compound of the sokkong bayu. Just as during the previous ma'tongkonan, exactly where people sit who participate is unimportant. If there are few participants, they may sit on the grass between the tongkonan and the ricebarns. The to indo' may take their places on the floor of one of the ricebarns, the anak pare-pare nangka' on the floor of another.

7. The membase mairi' follows (membase: "to wash the hands"; mairi': all, everything). People gather for "hand-washing", i.e. they purify themselves figuratively. The upperworld is asked for its help. From this point on the to indo' may not eat meat from a death ritual. Three chickens are sacrificed for the membase. First the umpakande (ma'pa-kande) to matua takes place (see Chapter VII.6.). The sacrifice consists of a black chicken and it is placed down to the West of the tong-konan (in this instance next to the house of each family taking part); the rite is carried out between 5 and 6 in the afternoon (see Fig. 12a). The next morning a chicken is sacrificed, a sella'. The offering is presented in the form of a tadoran. Five pesung with rice are also set down; all unfolds on the compound to the Northeast of the tongkonan, for this is an offering to the deata (see Fig. 12b). Inside, on the front gallery, six more pesung are placed on the Northeastern side of the tongkonan (see Fig. 13).

8. Mantanan pemali, literally: the taboo (on the) plants; cf. Van der Veen: marra' pemali.[11] Once the rice has turned yellow, three days of silence are observed (for the rice): this rite is in a sense comparable to the nyepi on Bali. No goods may arrive, no wood may be chopped, no noise is permitted, etc. For this component of the rice ritual, a chicken is slaughtered. The offering, in the form of a tadoran with a belundak and a kaledo, is made by the bunga' lalan. A ma'tongkonan precedes this rite (see rite 6 above).

9. The mangarra'i pemali actually falls within the rite named in 8 above. On the second day the prohibitions are the strictest.

10. Umbukai pemali. The period of silence is ended. The to indo' calls

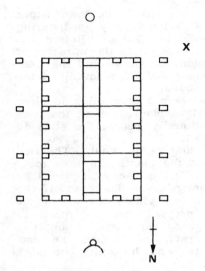

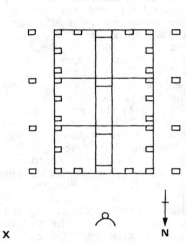

Fig. 12a. Ground-plan of a tongkonan with the place (X) indicated
where sacrifices for the to matua
are set down. For explanation of
the ground-plan, see Vol.I:237-8
and fig. VIII.1.

Fig. 12b. Ground-plan of a
tongkonan with the place (X)
indicated where sacrifices for
the deata are set down.

out that the rite is concluded. The rite apparently is intended to leave
the rice undisturbed, not to startle the rice during ripening (personal
interpretation). The offering consists of a chicken and is made in the
form of a pesung. The pa'sandukan officiates but all the to indo' are
present.
11. Langngan buntu (or melondong datu, "to offer a rooster to the
gods").[12] The to indo' and the to parengnge' climb a hill; this hill,
buntu, is a special site for sacrifices in the rice ceremony. Each functionary slaughters a red rooster. In Kesu' the celebrants climb Kesu'

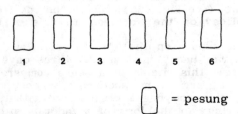

= pesung

Fig. 13. Offering during rite 7. Pesung one and two are placed on top
of each other, which also occurs with pesung three and four. Then, at
pesung five, an offering is enacted during which the ancestors, all of
them, are invoked (no text of this litany was recorded). No information
was provided about pesung six.

Mountain, with the to parengnge' in the following order: 1. sokkong bayu, 2. datu baine, 3. to ma'sanduk. (This obtains in Ba'tan; in Tonga the sokkong bayu is last.) Behind the to parengnge' come the combined to indo'.

12. Menammu pare is the ensuing rite. Menammu literally means: to receive the rice, to bring it in. In other words, the rice is harvested and a thanksgiving offering is made. The sacrifice involved is to be carried out by all families who harvest a rice crop, thus even the common man, in contrast to what happens, for example, during the melondong datu. This thanksgiving offering to the rice is enacted by each saroan separately; all the residents of the saroan must make a contribution, in paddy or money, to secure the pigs needed for the sacrifice. Each house must bring a pan of cooked rice to the site of the celebration (penammuan) and take a portion of it for the offering. For the menammu pare at least two pigs must be slaughtered. According to information acquired in 1969, the rite consists of two parts: the manglelleng bunu' (mangleleng: to fell, to cut down); and the ullelleng piau (piau: ?). The bunga' lalan officiates at the first part, the offering consists of a tadoran set up at a special place on Malenong cliff. For the second rite, two bamboos, each about a finger long and with leaves intact, are laid in a special place next to the sawah (on the sawah dike). A red chicken is sacrificed. The offering consists of a kaledo and also a pesung placed down between the two bamboos on the sawah dike. Hereupon follows the ma'pakande to matua (giving food to the ancestors of the Southwest), which might be considered a third rite. The bunga' lalan officiates.

13. The next rite is the mangimbo, executed by two to indo'. More pigs may be slaughtered now, as many as ten. The to parengnge' put the pigs to death and divide them among the to indo'. According to information collected in 1969 four pigs is a minimum. First the head of the animals is chopped off. The bunga' lalan receives half of one of the slain pigs (the part designated as teba, including the entire buku leso, see Fig. 14). The three remaining pigs are also divided up, each of the other three important to indo' also receiving a teba but one with only half of the buku leso. Then rice is piled on a dulang, first ordinary,

Fig. 14. Illustrations of division of meat, rite 13. Left: buku leso; right: teba.

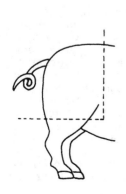
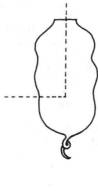

then glutinous rice. The kollong is placed on top. The bunga' lalan is given a whole kollong, the other rice priests only part of one. Next to the dulang, a pesung is set down as well containing pieces of buku leso; each to indo' is allotted a dulang (N.B. the teba is given raw).
14. Ullelleng ta'pan langkan ("clearing the place where the hen-harriers alight"). Paddy is brought to the to indo'. The intention of this rite remains unclear to me.
15. Mangrakan ("to harvest the first bunches of paddy"). A chicken is sacrificed at each sawah before any rice is cut. All the to indo' officiate (exactly what they do, however, was not reported). Each household prepares an offering of three piong with chicken. Scraps of cloth are burned. A fragrant grass, tagari (Dianella ensifolia), is also set on fire as an offering to the gods. Then people begin to reap the first bunches of paddy, an act which is accompanied by an offering of rice cooked in bamboo. The first bunches of paddy are stored in the lantang bunu', a shack or small hut which is customarily set up several days before the harvest begins on the site of the drying place of the rice (pangram-pa'). This pangrampa' is in the immediate vicinity of the house. The name of the hut, lantang, derives from the strips of bamboo used to bind the bunches of paddy. The building also has a ritual function.

What has been described above primarily concerns ritual aspects of the rice harvest. How much rice is reserved for ritual ends depends upon whether or not in that harvest year a conversion ritual is going to be celebrated. If not, then three bunches are sufficient. These for the time being are stored in the lantang bunu', later to be united into a single indo' mangrakan (rice mother) which will be the first rice put into the ricebarn. if there is a conversion ritual in the offering, then together with the makings of the rice mother, a few additional bunches of rice are put into the lantang bunu'. These will be used during the mangrara pare (part of the conversion ritual), and for the ma'billa'i. These extra bunches of rice are then pounded and cooked under the watchful eye of the to ma'pesung pokon, a woman. (She resembles the to ma'pemali in the puang-regions, see above.) While she performs her task this woman may bathe but not wash her hair. It is said she receives three bunches of rice from every sawah. The question is how one is to interpret "every sawah" here. Each ricefield owned by the host of the ritual, or all fields belonging to members of the local community? Whichever is true, her function during the ma'billa'i is limited to preparing three pesung which she places one by one on the three hearthstones inside the lantang bunu'.

When there is no conversion ritual to celebrate, everything follows a much simpler course. In the evening, according to my Kesu' informant, at about seven, a chicken is sacrificed for the entire sawah complex of the family, but this does not appear to be a general custom. According to Van der Veen (Woordenboek:492) ma'billa'i is to make an offering of rice which has just been harvested before continuing with the reaping (see also Chapter VII.2.8.). Until this rite has been observed, one may not eat the newly harvested rice. Once the rice which will be part of the offering has been pounded, then three grains without husk are wrapped in a dongka-leaf (a Colocasia species) together with a sharp chip of bamboo (billa') and buried beneath the stone rice mortar; this is where the rite gets its name from: ma'billa'i.

Yet, it is all rather confusing: first we were told that the offering was made before labourers carried on with the harvest, and later we

were informed that the rite only takes place after the entire crop has
been brought in and people want to eat the newly harvested rice for
the first time.

The only possible conclusion is that local practices vary. In any
event it would seem that three bunches of rice are set aside for the
rice mother that will be kept in the ricebarn and that usually this event
is accompanied by a sacrificial act. Only afterwards does the harvest
begin in earnest and carry on to its conclusion in a single spurt of
action.

16. After the harvested rice has been brought to the pangrampa', the
ma'pongo' takes place, or, as my information from 1969 indicates, the
ma'pakalapu (from lapu, the plumpness of the rice in its husk). Yet the
ma'pongo' and ma'pakalapu are not identical. Ma'pongo' is the simple
practical act of binding five bunches of rice into one, on and on. Only
once this has been accomplished can the ritual take place which aims to
promote the fullness of the grain and for which a rooster or a pig is
slaughtered and the flesh cooked in piong, later to be part of a pesung
offered up by the sokkong bayu.

17. Yet another rite follows, the ma'bo'bo'-bo'bo'i (from bo'bo', the
upper layer of the cooked rice). Some rice is removed from each bunch
and laid on a piece of banana leaf. This is carried once again to the
three hearthstones in the lantang bunu'; if there are twenty bunches,
then twenty banana leaf fragments are brought to the hearth.

Even when no conversion ritual is held, variations in the usual procedure are possible. This may affect events at the drying place described above or the storing of the harvest in the ricebarn, an event
described below.

18. The storage of the harvest in the ricebarn should go paired with
the transportation to the ricebarn of the indo' mangrakan, the rice
mother. All research sources and all my informants, however, were
silent on this score. Only Nobele makes some slight reference in this
direction (Nobele 1926:82-5).

18a. Ma'popemba'ka', "reproduction". A small pig is slaughtered. One
hopes that the rice will multiply, that one as it were will turn into two.
Apparently this is a communal rite, for a bunch of paddy in front of
every house is spattered with the blood of the sacrificial pig. Only
after this has been done, the rice bunches are laid in the ricebarn
(ma'pakise). It seems we should detect here a variation of the
ma'pakalapu (rite 16). That it is, indeed, for in addition we discover it
reported that before the ma'pongo' (which has another siginificance in
this context, seeming to allude to the picking up of the pongo', the
bunches of rice, to bring them to the ricebarn), at three in the
morning, a chicken is killed and placed on top of the rice.

18b. A similar offering is also described for another variant, the
ma'piong pangrampa'. A chicken is sacrificed in front of every pangrampa', the place where rice is dried. A red chicken is indicated, the
meat of which is prepared in a piong; afterwards the food is placed on
a banana leaf. The offering is presented at three in the morning. The
bundles of rice (sangkutu') are carried from the pangrampa' into the
ricebarn. The door to the ricebarn is fastened with a lock. It is opened
again for the first time half a month later. (In the past, the door to
the ricebarn was closed with a wooden bar; this is still done in Buntao'
and elsewhere.)

18c. Once the rice has been stored, a kind of final rite is held, the

ma'piong karoen (karoen: afternoon). At 5 p.m. piong are made ready
(from coconut alone). These piong, however, may not yet be eaten. A
large rooster is slaughtered, a sacrifice for the closing ritual, a
thanksgiving to the deata. After that, people may eat. During the
evening of this day, three men with a torch circle the ricebarn three
times, a purification rite. Also on the same day packets are prepared
for the ma'belundak, the making of packets of glutinous rice, see Fig.
11. Together with the leaves of the a'da' (a kind of grass with pointy
blades), the passakke and the darinding, these packets are hung up
the next day at the following places:
- the East side of the house[13];
- the ricebarn;
- the pigsty with a sendana to the Northeast;
- the buffalo stalls;
- the path to the well;
- the well;
- next to the piong karoen which are set up on the compound to the
Northeast of the house;
- the pangrampa';
- the path leading to the entrance to the compound;
- the lantang pare.
Children eat the belundak-packets. Hunting for them is an occasion for
fun. Afterwards the sisemba' (calf-kicking) is staged.
19. Ma'piong bubun (bubun: well). People go to the well to ask Puang
Matua to keep the water clear so it can be used during sacrifices. An
offering is made which consists of a chicken and piong (the piong may
not be brought home). Then follows:
20. Mangrompo tondok ("to fence in, to enclose the village"). In the to
indo's name, the to minaa presides over the sacrifice. This rite is
enacted because tradition tells how in former times there was someone
who was a master of black magic so that by itself the rice went out
again from the ricebarn and left it empty. To prevent this from
happening, an offering is made.
21. At last the time comes for the ma'bungka' alang, the opening of the
ricebarn (alang). This may only be celebrated if no one has died in the
family whose grave has not yet been sealed. The to indo' opens the
ricebarn. A chicken is cooked in an earthenware port especially for
Puang Matua. A piece of this chicken is placed on a banana leaf (ma'pesung) on the board in front of the door to the ricebarn. First two
pongo' are pulled outside; the pesung is set down on them. Then the
ricebarn is shut again. The two pongo' are pounded and eaten together
with snails (suso) and vegetables. No other combination of foods is permitted. Only afterwards may people eat rice with meat, even with meat
from the rambu solo' sphere. The time of the lo'bang padang follows,
i.e. the time when there is nothing left (literally: "the field is empty").
There is no rice in the sawahs.

In closing this description it should be explained that for offerings
performed at the sawah there is a special place: pesungan banne (pesungan ka'do; see section 5 below and Crystal 1974:121). At times this
is on top of a stone. Three heads of rice are left standing there which
are called kinallona pesungan banne: "provisions for the place of sacrifice in the sawah" (Woordenboek:462).[14] Not everyone in Kesu' places a
stone next to these rice plants. Such a stone indicates that the former

owner of the sawah was someone for whom a dirapa'i (the highest order
of death ritual) was once celebrated. One finds such sawah stones in
other places, too.

In Bittuang, A.C. Kruyt saw a stone in a rice field which had been
painted red on top. The stone represented a phallus. He reports that
such erect stones are only found on the sawahs of the to parengnge'
(A.C. Kruyt 1923/24; and Vol.I:268ff.).

Methods of cultivating rice and observing the rice ritual differ from
place to place in Tana Toraja. For the rice ritual among the Sa'dan-
Toraja, a reader should further consult A.C. Kruyt (1923/24:323-57)
who devotes attention to the ritual riding of swings (while the rice is in
the field) and to playing with tops (after the harvest). Nobele has been
cited already as a valuable source about the rice ritual in puang-states
(1926:70-85). What my informants did not tell me, but A.C. Kruyt mentions (1923/24:126), is that during the ripening and harvest of the
rice, sexual intercourse should be frequent to stimulate the fertility of
the crop. One also narrates myths to promote the growth of the rice
(cf. Vol.I:162). For other taboos concerning rice, see A.C. Kruyt
1923/24:345-50). For rice cultivation in Pantilang (situated in Luwu'),
the Memorie van Overgave by the civil servant Pronk is informative.

4. The rice, the datu and the deata

Before Dutch colonial rule was firmly established in Sulawesi, at the
time when the Toraja were considered to be independent of Luwu'
(which they themselves deny), the custom existed known as medatu
(melondong datu). Toraja from the territories of Sa'dan, Balusu,
Tondon, Nanggala and Pantilang brought a rooster to the Datu of Luwu'
and received sowing rice which they mixed with their own rice seeds.[15]
On such occasions the to burake may have blessed the sowing rice. One
believed that sowing rice reinforced in this fashion would be more
fertile. In this connection it is useful to recall the relation between rice
and the East, the direction where one seeks the gods and the deata,
but also the direction where Luwu' is situated in relation to Torajaland.
Elsewhere I have pointed out that the Toraja, "the people of the West,
are seen in opposition to the people of the East, the residents of
Luwu'" (Vol.I:6). For them the Prince of Luwu' is the Datu Matallo, the
Prince of the East, which explains the relation between this royal figure
and the vitality of rice. Those who may still not be convinced should
consult the passage in Chapter XI.4. (Mantaa bati) describing how the
to minaa during his recitation of prayer turns to the ancestors of the
Datu Palopo, namely the Datu of Luwu'.

5. The bua' padang

At the beginning of Chapter II, I pointed out that in addition to the
great bua' kasalle there was a more modest feast known by the name of
bua' padang, a ritual to promote the growth of rice. One may also
consider the bua' padang as a kind of celebration of the agricultural
new year, held to ask for a blessing for the rice crop (Woordenboek:
74-5, v. boea' padang). The fact that in Ma'kale the feast is also called
menani pare, "to celebrate the rice in song", points in the same direc-

tion. Further confirmation comes as well from the fact that in Kesu'
celebration of the ritual has a cyclical character. One began with the
bua' padang in La'bo', and in the following years observed it in succession in Tandung, Marante, Mengkepe, Tonga (possibly together with
Bonoran), Pao and Angin-Angin (for the location of these places, see
Vol.I:4). Tadongkon and Sangbua' may also have participated (oral information from Van der Veen). The cycle as such, however, is more
important than who exactly took part. In the past it seems to have been
considered important to ask the gods to bless to rice first in one area
and then in another.

Consciousness of this cycle element apparently faded already at the
beginning of the present century. According to my principal informant
(Ne' Sangga, alias Allo Rante), the ritual fell under the suru' padang.
What he meant was that it was primarily an expiatory offering that
followed a transgression (padang: land, suru': to comb , to clean). For
Ne' Sangga, when I spoke with him (November 1966) the bua' padang
was already "a thing of the past". Although it was still celebrated in
Tikala, the last time such a feast was held in Kesu', he told me, was in
1923. His claim appears most likely to be valid. In Nonongan, according
to Johanna Linorante, this ritual was enacted for the last time in 1924.
As a consequence the information which I collected about this feast was,
as far as accuracy and completeness are concerned, seriously affected
by time. Consequently, I will restrict my account to a few major aspects
of the ritual.

The feast that in addition to bua' padang is also called ma'bua'[16] and
la'pa' padang goes under the name of menani pare in Ma'kale. It begins
with the lemun padang (lemun: to form a lump or clod, but no one
could explain the relevance of the term here). This involves slaughtering a pig. The to indo' enacts the mangimbo. Beforehand the drums are
brought to the site of the sacrifice; a pesung is laid on the drums and
after the instruments have been played, they are carried back into the
tongkonan of the to indo' and hung in place. After three months these
drums are beaten again, ma'tundan gandang ("to wake the drums").
With this rite, the feast recommences. A pig is once more slaughtered.
The to parengnge' (and thus not the to indo') officiates at the rite.
The sokkong bayu, or a to minaa as his replacement, utters the prayer
at the offering (mangimbo). Afterwards another pig is killed. A bit
later (see below) the manganta' takes place; in such a case the
manganta' is not a conversion ritual at the close of a death feast, but
rather a ritual of thanksgiving.

Together the ma'tundan and the manganta' comprise the ma'bungka'
langi', "the opening of heaven". Afterwards people confer about when
to put up guest houses and the gorang. These constructions are
erected on the rante kala'paran, the feast plain. Two pigs are
slaughtered, one for the gorang and one for the melantang (the building of the guest houses). Once both the guest houses and gorang have
been completed, then each tongkonan must hold the manganta' (cf.
Chapter VII.2.7.). Since there are several tongkonan in a bua'-com-
munity, virtually every to parengnge' and to indo' is kept busy; each
of these functionaries must enact the mangimbo. The manganta' is
observed last for the tongkonan of the sokkong bayu; this happens
before the celebrants proceed to the rante kala'paran (manganta' ao').

The next day a festive procession advances to the rante (songlo').
The sokkong bayu in full feast apparel walks in front. A maa'-cloth is

folded on his head so that the folds are aligned in such a way that they are compared to the scales of a fish (disissik). The pollo' dodo (a piece of red cloth decorated with coins and beads; actually the hem of a woman's sarong worn during certain feasts) and parakeet feathers are attached to the headcloth as well. One corner of the kaseda, a long red cloth, is tied to the sokkong bayu's right wrist. To the left and right of the kaseda women walk, presumably family members, dressed in clothing appropriate for the ma'dandan; they hold onto the cloth. Two to parengnge' and two to indo' (the rice priests who perform the mangimbo and the massanduk) also wear ritual clothing. The sokkong bayu, the to parengnge' and the to indo' move around the kala'paran and the gorang counter-clockwise (cf. circling around the rante and the bala'kaan during the ma'batang of the dirapa'i in Tallunglipu where the women, under a white cloth, follow behind the bate lepong; see Chapter X.7. Men raise the mangaru, the war cry, and each time they do so, people in the procession scream and dash forward.

The next morning the to minaa and the to menani take turns in per-forming the massinggi', the eulogizing (described in the account of the la'pa' kasalle in Chapter II). Then follows the massurak tedong, a rite which exhibits many similarities to the Passomba Tedong. The metre and the melody, however, are different. The to menani[17] declaims the consecratory litany (menani: to sing). In Kesu' this was a function of the tongkonan Buntu Karunanga in Angin-Angin. The children and grandchildren of the to menani were also eligible to fill this position if they didn't belong to tongkonan Buntu Karunanga; the title, however, is bound to this tongkonan. Then the buffalo (a black one) is slaughtered. A to parengnge' enacts the mangimbo. A pig is also killed (called parepe') and a red rooster. All to parengnge' officiate. After completion of the offering, the feast is at an end.

The bua' padang is thus a major, but not all too extensive feast; one that is very well suited to an archaic economy. The cyclic character, too, cited above and also fitting into the archaic economy, became manifest once more in the report of an informant that one or two years later a merok-feast was held. This informant called the merok-feast a pembalikan to la'pa' or pembalikan bua'. This accentuates that there is a connection between the two feasts but doesn't make its nature clear; indeed, the bua' padang- and merok-feasts both belong to the deata-rituals, so that there is no question of any transfer from the one sphere to the other.

In any event the evidence all suggests that the celebration was ori-ginally a good bit simpler than it became in later years. In some terri-tories (Ma'kale, for example) there were even bua'-feasts that only lasted for a single day. Thus it seems that even the comparatively sober bua' padang-feast in Kesu' and elsewhere includes elements of the great bua'-ritual. Apparently, just as with the maro-ritual and the death feasts, all these celebrations have been subject to a process of ranking by escalation, the consequence of increasing wealth and compe-tition between local groups.

6. Menammu pare in the village of Ke'te, Kesu' (July 1983)

For the significance of this rite, see section 3, rite 12 above. I attend-ed this rite in Ke'te', a village that has been declared a monument because of its attractive setting and authentic buildings, on July 19, 1983. Closer examination, however, reveals that Ke'te' in other respects is not at all traditional: most of the residents are Christian, which left its mark on the rite which I witnessed. Although it is an Eastern ritual, the whole thing was to have been completed before noon, including the required offerings; yet in practice, what happened was altogether different. At 11 a.m. people began with the preparations; the site for the sacrifices was imposing, under the shade of an old banyan and an ancient sandal tree.

At 11 a.m. a bamboo-ao' was set up with the top pointing North (see Vol.I:272). It was an offering holder of slightly unusual appearance. Along the entire bamboo which was about 1.5 metres long, a fringe of daun pusuk was attached. On the lower part of the bamboo a karerang was suspended, a loosely plaited basket. One of the to indo' padang, the to ma'popemba'ka' ("he who sees to it that it (i.e. the rice) multiplies") was busy weaving strips of bamboo, one over, one under. For weaving, the trimmed inside and the green outside were used in alternation so that a crude diamond pattern emerged. This, they said, was going to be the floor of the galla' (= palanduan-duan).

A woman, the to ma'nasu pesung ("she who cooks the rice for the pesung") was busy boiling rice in an iron pot which stood on three stones. She was married to So' Lapu, one of the to indo' padang and also one of the functionaries on the present occasion. They are listed here below by function or title:
1. Daniël Datu Tiku, the sokkong bayu, a Christian. Thus the function of sokkong bayu existed still in Ke'te' although the holder of the function was not an adherent of the aluk to dolo. He allowed himself to be replaced by the to minaa during celebrations connected with old beliefs;
2. the to minaa; he replaced the absent sokkong bayu;
3. the to mangimbo ("he who utters the prayer"); he is also the bunga' lalan;
4. the to massanduk;
5. the to mantobok;
6. the to pabalian;
7. the to ma'popemba'ka';
8. the matua ulu;
9. the to ma'penuaka, whose function is explained in his title, "so that the roots grow well". This title, just as no. 7, is a local variation of standard to indo'-titles.
10. the to ma'pallin (see section 1, above); the functionary was absent;
11. the to massusuk ("the one who defines a border with a stick", i.e. determines the boundaries of a sawah; I have not come across this title for a rice priest anywhere else).
The functionaries wore simple clothing; most had on turbans with dangling ends.

11:45 - Two pigs were brought in, carried in a kamboti (a plaited bag). The to ma'pobemba'ka had still not finished his plaiting. The to ma'sanduk lit a cigarette from the pack I had brought her and asked me what brand it was.

11:55 - The galla' was ready; it was hung from the bamboo-ao' higher up than the karerang and decorated with pusuk. A belundak (see Fig. 11), boiled in the iron pot with other rice was removed and also hung on the bamboo. Next to the ao'-pole, moreover, were a pair of bamboo joints laid on the ground.

12:30 - The to minaa places the inflorescence of a betel plant on a torn strip of banana leaf and prays aloud. It is almost impossible to hear him because everyone keeps right on talking loudly. A langngan is fabricated against which eight bamboos are leaned with their opening facing East. The pigs are slaughtered and roasted by laying them against the langngan; before this, their blood was caught in a bamboo.
Meanwhile a number of to parengnge' had arrived. In Ke'te', the to parengnge' were 1. Arung (Daniël) Datu Tiku, 2. So' Pangala', 3. Indo' Samma (= Lai' Rannu), and 4. Pong Tondok. The sokkung bayu, as has been explained, could not come; another was also prevented from attending so that only two of the eminent functionaries were present. Of this pair, the female to parengnge' could certainly not be ignored; she kept giving instructions, and in a loud voice.

12:45 - The roasted pigs - not yet fully cooked - were cut into pieces. First the stomach portion was cut out and then the buttocks. No one could tell me why this was done. Then the intestines were removed, followed by other internal organs. Pieces were taken from these organs and other parts of the pig (from the intestines, the liver, the heart, the buku leso, the rump, the midriff) and put in a large bamboo. This bamboo, the far end of which had notches cut out of it, was meant exclusively for cooking meat that would be part of the offering (= pemanala, see Vol.I:206). The remaining meat that the assembled guests could consume would be stewed in a big iron pan. But this hadn't taken place yet.
Still more pieces were cut from the necks of the pigs for the to parengnge'. The rings of meat were thin because the pigs were so small. It leant an air of sadness to the rite; in the past two large pigs were slaughtered and, people said, there were a hundred people present. Since mass conversion to Christianity, however, the crowd of celebrants had dwindled; on the present occasion there were some twenty on hand. There were, however, also children present. The meat was constantly divided and redivided, and all the while the female to parengnge' kept making comments and issuing orders. As so often during rites in Tana Toraja, talk flew back and forth at a furious rate.

2:00 p.m. - The ma'pesung began: bamboo joints filled with blood from the sacrificed pigs were hung from the bamboo-ao'. A number of kaledo (see Fig. 11) were placed down: sirih, pinang, and pieces of meat were set on the pesung, and rice as well, served by the to ma'nasu pesung (first with a flat spoon which is afterwards scraped clean on a kind of ladle). The priest mumbled his incomprehensible prayer which lasted exactly two minutes. Then a group of boys rushed at the bamboo-ao' and stripped it bare of anything even vaguely edible. Then those present ate rice with pork served on a banana leaf.

3:00 p.m. - Everything was over. The kollong were collected for the to parengnge' who hadn't attended.

Manglullu', treading to release sowing rice, Ba'tan, Kesu'. See also pp.
90-91.
(Photo: Hetty Nooy-Palm, 1970.)

Harrowing with a team of buffaloes which are led, Kesu'. See also pp. 88–89 and Fig. 7. (Photo: Hetty Nooy-Palm, 1970.)

The harrow is turned, Kesu'. See also pp. 88-89 and Fig. 7.
(Photo: Hetty Nooy-Palm, 1970.)

Chapter V

RITUALS OF THE EAST RELATED
TO MAN'S LIFE CYCLE

"A hole was then in heaven dug,
The ground with an iron spade was turned,
And then this cord was therein placed,
His afterbirth was in it laid."

(The Chant:51)

1. Introduction[1]

Rites of passage associated with the East can be categorized in keeping
with the age of the principal celebrants:
- rites which take place at birth or during the period which follows immediately after; these are known as suru'na mellolo tau, "the cleaning
of the umbilical cord"; in this instance "cleaning" means the presentation of an offering to purify the atmosphere;
- rites which are connected with adolescence;
- marriage ceremonies, suru'na rampanan kapa'. Rampanan kapa': "that
which supports the kapa'" naturally also supports marriage (Vol.I:
34ff.). Suru', to clean, has the same meaning as above;
- burial of the burake-priest, the to minaa sando and the to menani,
the only death rituals which fall in the Eastern sphere.

2. Suru'na mellolo tau, rituals having to do with birth and the period immediately after

2.1. Pregnancy and birth

In the death chant quoted at the opening of this chapter, the life
history of the deceased is celebrated in song. The fragment cited mentions the fact that his umbilical cord and placenta were buried in
heaven. This implies that the deceased was of exalted origin. In practice, however, rites observed for upper class children do not vary in
ways worth mentioning from those enacted for children of lower standing. Before delivery an expectant mother must observe a number of
taboos; A.C. Kruyt reports these in detail (1923/24:127-30). Nobele,
too, devotes a number of pages to prohibitions and prescriptions connected with pregnancy and birth (1926:35-8). Those interested in more
complete information should consult Kruyt and Nobele; here I will
confine myself to a number of particularly important taboos.
  An expectant mother may not eat meat from animals slaughtered for
the funeral meal of a woman who died in childbed. Nor may she eat the
flesh of buffaloes or pigs who died in the act of bearing young. In

general people dislike women to enter a forge; for a pregnant woman such a visit would have grave consequences (what these consequences might be is not specified). An expectant mother may not strike a dog because the dog would then howl and that is said to mean that she will give birth to a child who cries a lot. A man whose wife is pregnant must also observe these taboos. Nor may he have his hair cut (since 1960 this prohibition has no longer been observed; at the time Sukarno was in power, men were forbidden to wear their hair long and thus the prohibition was prohibited). He may not cut another man's hair either without running the risk that during delivery his wife will loose too much blood. A future father may not enter a house where a child has died before teething, or else his own offspring will die shortly after birth. He may not kill any animal while his wife is pregnant, or the foetus will die in the womb. If he works in a smithy, then he must give up his work as soon as his wife conceives, or else their child will come into the world blind.

It is notable that a number of prohibitions are related to forges or to visits to a smith. A possible explanation might have to do with the manner in which man was created in the Upperworld: Puang Matua created the first humans from pure gold that he poured into his bellows. Man must therefore in no way give the impression that he wants to copy the creative act of the highest god (personal interpretation).

Before the child is born, mother and father observe certain rules. No festivity is held to celebrate the seventh month of pregnancy as on Java and Bali. After roughly seven months, however, the traditional (unlicensed) midwife, the to ma'pakianak, does come to examine the mother. She investigates whether the position of the unborn child is good. If not, then through massage the to ma'pakianak tries to improve it. As soon as labour pains begin, the midwife is fetched. She massages and "blows on" the mother-to-be. The woman in labour sits on a wooden trough or some other elevation, leaning with both hands on women who take positions in front of her. It also happens that the to ma'pakianak (or another woman) sits behind the pregnant woman, massaging her stomach with downwards pressure until the child comes out (according to Nobele, the midwife rubs the woman in labour's back and hands until the baby is born). As soon as the baby emerges, the women lift the mother up under her arms and the midwife rubs her stomach to facilitate emission of the afterbirth. If delivery is difficult, then everything in the house that is knotted or tied must be undone. The cover is removed from all storage places. The symbolism is unmistakable. Iron objects are also taken out of the house. The meaning of this act is perhaps less clear, unless once again there is a connection with smiths.

If delivery is overdue, then a to minaa is asked to come. The priest slaughters a chicken (the colour is not reported). Some of the meat is given to the deata to eat. The to minaa then asks people present in the house whether anyone of them has something against the pregnant woman, or has spoken angry words towards her, or may have had a dream that could be interpreted as inauspicious. Should someone answer one of these questions affirmatively, then it is thought that the cause of the difficult delivery has been removed. The father promises to sacrifice a pig to the deata if from this point on everything proceeds easily. This account derives from A.C. Kruyt. He fails to mention what happens if despite all such measures delivery goes wrong. He merely writes that people fear the screaming of the bombo of a woman who dies in childbirth. For the soul of the woman herself there appears to be no special anxiety.

If delivery is normal, people wait for the placenta to come out, too. Only then is the umbilical cord cut and tied. This used to take place with a fiber from a pineapple plant, but nowadays cotton thread is used. The cutting of the navel cord is done with a small bamboo knife, billa'. Crushed paria-leaves (Mormordica charantia, a climber with bitter, cucumber-shaped fruits) are placed on the navel.[2] The child is bathed (in water without any herbs) and wrapped in cotton cloth. (No cradle is known in Tana Toraja.) The baby is laid down on a mat, cushioned by a soft layer of textiles or a thin mattress. For the first twelve hours the newborn child nurses at the breast of another woman, not its mother, for people believe the mother needs rest.[3] In Tana Toraja it is unusual for a new mother to "roast" (be warmed) by the hearth fire, a common practice in many parts of Asia.

It is not always the midwife who cuts the umbilical cord, bathes and wraps the newborn child; other women may help as well. The navel cord and the placenta ("the younger sibling") are put into a small bag braided from tuyu-reed. Leaves from the paria are also placed in this kapipe, together with the leaves of a kind of groundnut, and yam and papaya leaves ("so that the child will not become ill when we eat vegetables"). These are all leaves eaten as vegetables. The midwife now stands on the steps of the house with her back turned to the dwelling. Someone - in the past, should birth take place in a leading family, this person was a slave - takes the small bag from her and buries it in the ground to the East of the house. Twelve sticks are set in the earth around the buried umbilical cord and afterbirth of a boy, six sticks are arranged similarly in the event of a girl. According to Nobele (1926: 37), a stone is placed on the spot where the kapipe is buried and three bamboos are implanted in the earth surrounding it (information concerning the Tallulembangna). When a boy is born, those who are in the house shout out three times, "Iyo iyo ya'u". The birth of a girl is heralded with "He-he-he, yoo-o" (this cry is also repeated three times, in the form of loud laughter).

When I asked wether there was a preference for boys or girls, I was told that people wanted their first born to be male but were keen that the next child would be a girl. Marriage in many parts of Tana Toraja tends to be uxorilocal: a young husband settles in the village of his bride. The couple's house stands on the compound of her parents, or in the immediate vicinity so that daughter and husband can care for her parents in their old age.

A newborn child is watched over zealously by its mother, grandmother (mother's mother) and, formerly, in upper-class Toraja families, by heriditary slaves as well.

2.2. Twins

The birth of twins of the same sex is considered a blessing. If the twins are a boy and girl, however, one is given to another family member to be raised. Two children of different sexes from a single womb are associated with incest. Should such twins be born to a mother who is of the puang-lineage, however, the event is seen as a blessing. One speaks then of "golden twins". The same rites are enacted at the birth of twins as at the birth of "ordinary" children.

2.3. Name-giving and first hair-cut

During the first ceremonial hair-cutting an agreement is usually reached about what name to give to the baby. In any event children are named before they are three months old. In front of their names boys acquire the prefix Laso'(k), penis, abbreviated So'; girls are given the prefix Lai', maidenhead. A boy or girl may be named after a grandparent who has recently died. Or people name a child to commemorate an important event which took place at about the time of the child's birth. Thus my informant was named Bua' Sarungallo because at the time he was born in Kesu' a great bua'-feast was being celebrated. Sometimes a child is named after an object. As they grow older, however, children often resent such names. One little boy originally called Stirring Spoon asked his parents if they would give him a different name. They complied with their six year old's whishes.

The "bringing outside" and the first hair-cut (ma'ku'ku) of a child are two ceremonies which are celebrated in rapid succession and which take up two days. They are enacted when the infant is between two and three months old. The mother, or other close relative, carries the baby outside the house. On this (first) day, the umpatassu' api dao mai banua is observed, "the bringing of fire from the house on the ground". As an offering, one performs the manglika' biang (see Merok: 158, and Van der Veen, unpublished a). The ma'ku'ku, first hair-cut, follows the next day. A large pig is slaughtered. A sacrifice is made to the deata: the ma'palangngan para. The offering is placed on a board located under the ridge of the roof on the North side of the house. The to minaa utters the prayer. Then the meat of the pig is distributed among the following persons:
1. whoever assisted at the birth (the to ma'pakianak, the midwife);
2. whoever cut the navel string (the to mangra'ta' lolo);
3. the one who bathed the baby after its birth (the to ma'dio');
4. the one who buried the afterbirth (the to manglamun toni);
5. the one who fed the baby during its first day (the to mataranak);
6. the to mangimbo ("he who recites the sacrificial prayer", the to minaa);
7. the to massanduk, "the one who serves the rice";
8. the the mantobok, "the one who stabs the pig to death";
9. the sipalakuan (the to mantobok's assistant).
Functions 6 through 9 are performed at many rites and are usually bound to specific tongkonan (Vol.I:100ff.).

Once the to minaa has recited the prayer, he daubs the baby's cheeks and forehead with blood from the sacrificed pig. Ribbons of twisted red and white thread are tied around the baby's wrists and ankles. In addition to these ritual acts, one should mention how mothers and grandmothers sing lullabies to the babies to make them grow prosperously (cf. the narration of certain myths which are believed to promote the growth of rice; see Chapter IV and Vol.I:162). As marriage is predominantly uxorilocal (a research in the village of Barana', Tikala, in 1949 made it clear that 75 % of the marriages were of this type) it is the maternal grandmother who has the strongest affiliation with her grandchildren during babyhood. The other grandparents, however, take a strong interest in their grandchildren too: they are present at the rituals which are held for these children. The mutual interest of the grandparents in their grandchildren becomes evident in the kinship term baisen, referring to parents of child's spouse (see Vol.I:42). The relation grandparents - grandchildren is an important one too (viz. the prevailing teknonymy). If a child has troubles with its parents, refuge is usually sought with the grandparents.

Times have changed. Indeed, modern medicine has entered the world of Tana Toraja, mother and child care along with the rest. Women deliver now in the hospital, if they find it necessary, and they can pay for it. When a new mother leaves the hospital, she is always presented with the umbilical cord and placenta, for these must be buried at home in traditional fashion. Whoever feels insecure in a hospital can always ask a traditional midwife to visit her there.

3. Practices which concern adolescents

There are basically three transitional rites for Toraja adolescents: the circumcision of males; the filing of the teeth of both young men and women; scarification by fire among boys. Today ritual circumcision as described here has become a rare event. Many Toraja have become Christians and even those who have not often have a preference for circumcision by a medical practitioner.

Circumcision was undertaken when adolescent males reach marriageable age. Informants have suggested this occurred at eighteen or so, which strikes me as rather late. A.C. Kruyt (1923/24:136), however, reported that circumcision preceded puberty, when the boys were between eight and nine years old. Someone (an unspecified agent) inserted a piece of wood between the tip of the penis and the foreskin and made a cut with a sharp knife of about half a centimetre. For boys from the puang-families, sandalwood was used, for to makaka wood from the banyan tree, for slaves, jambu-wood. Van der Veen stipulated that for the son of a puang wood from the Cordyline terminalis is inserted during circumcision as a "surface to cut on"; for to makaka-boys, sandalwood serves this purpose, for kaunan jambu-wood. The wood used during the circumcision of the son of a puang was decorated with incised figures (Van der Veen in A.C. Kruyt 1923/24:362, note 13 with illustration of a motif). On such an occasion, moreover, a buffalo, pig and chicken were sacrificed. Circumcision might not take place during the rice harvest.

Today there are still boys and girls who, upon reaching the age of puberty, have their teeth filed to points. An iron file is used, the finishing touches administered with a stone (a kind of whetstone?). No mention is made of any offerings.

Scars from fire (baruk) are inflicted by pressing burning "tinder" against a boy's arm; this "tinder" consists of the greyish tip of the main rib of the leaf of the sugar palm. This custom has fallen into neglect, especially near towns and cities. Submission to being burned is looked upon as a sign of courage. People also believe that the scars make it easier to pass through Puya; they are the "torches" which light the way to the realm of the dead.

People had little to tell me about the tattooing of girls, a process which Kennedy reports was formerly customary (1953:194). The term tobo was mentioned, but tobo refers as well to applying dyes, possibly even blood, to the face. Tattoos were said to have been applied at the

time a woman served as tumbang (or mangria barang) during the great
bua'-feast. The entire period of tumbang may be looked upon as a
separate rite for girls from the upper classes (see Chapters II and III;
and J. Kruyt 1921:45-77).

4. The marriage ritual (suru'na rampanan kapa')

4.1. Introduction

Available information about the significance of marriage in traditional
Toraja society is conflicting and confusing. Van der Veen, in 1950,
indicated that for thirty years already the marriage ceremony in Kesu'
had rarely been celebrated. According to him, people married after they
had been living together for some time and had conceived a child
(1950:292). The purpose of the marriage ceremony was actually to fix
the kapa'. A.C. Kruyt also reports that marriages came about rather
casually (1923/24:117-8). Yet, he introduces a condition which qualifies
such a general assessment: "If class and kinship give no cause for
objections, then parents allow their daughters (and sons? - personal
addition) free choice of partner". This makes it clear that parents not
only guard against a match between partners who are too closely
related, but that they also regard the class of a prospective husband
or wife for their child as important. This is true especially for girls. A
young woman may not marry "beneath her" (Vol.I:31). A youth's
parents also had a large say in his choice of marriage partner, at least
for members of the nobility, according to my informants. By 1970 young
men and women enjoyed far more latitude in their marriage selections
than they would have even one or two generations earlier. What I
learned about sexual relations was also far from consistent. Nobele
asserts that "in general no special importance is attached to virginity"
(1926:28); in the same article, however, he discloses what a heavy
penalty any woman of the puang-lineage could expect should she become
pregnant by a man of lower social standing (1926:29-30).
    Nobele's text suggests that above all women from higher classes could
not permit themselves much sexual freedom. What my informant W.
Papayungan had to say agrees with this conclusion: in the 1920s young
women from good families wore many copper ankle rings in Kesu' and
elsewhere. These ankle rings were not merely a status symbol; the
clinking sound they made was a warning to any man who wasn't free
that a girl of noble birth was approaching and that he had better take
to his heels to avoid finding himself, and the girl, in a compromising
situation.
    Although the marriage feast of the Toraja may be a less important
ritual than the extensive bua'- and burial feasts, for members of the
upper classes a wedding is still considered significant, an occasion on
which considerable effort and expense are expended. After all, wasn't
the marriage settled between Puang Matua and Arrang diBatu in the
upperworld the prototype for wedding ceremonies on earth?

4.2. The marriage ceremony (Sangalla')

The information below comes from Puang W.P. Sombolinggi, and concerns weddings in Sangalla'. The ceremony which he describes differs

little, however, from standard practice in Kesu' (see Van der Veen 1950). The leading roles in the ceremony - apart from the bride and groom - are performed by two to minaa: one of these priests serves as the bride's spokesman, the other as the groom's. Once a man and woman have gotten to know each other, the man informs his parents that he wants to marry Lai' X. If the parents support their son's intentions, sirih and pinang are brought to the family of the prospective bride. Those who bring this betel, pinang and gambir, do not belong to the young man's family. Now the girl's parents call their family together to discuss the proposal. At times they reject the suitor (no mention is made of possible grounds for such action), and in that case the sirih is sent back. Acceptance of the betel thus signifies approval of the groom's intentions.

Some time later an envoy is sent to the young woman's parents. He asks when the young man may call at the girl's house. Both families set a date, making sure it will be a favourable day. On the appointed day, the young man goes to the girl's house together with an escort of other boys or men - their age is immaterial. The group must consist of an even number (not counting the groom); an uneven number would bring bad luck. The group walks very slowly, one after another. Upon their arrival, they are received by the bride's family. In the meantime a pig has been slaughtered (no rules govern either the size or markings of the animal). A joint meal is enjoyed, at least in Kesu', and, although my informant didn't say so, it would seem likely the same would hold true in Sangalla'.

The bridegroom, his escort and his priest (to minaa) are seated in the front room of the bride's family's house, the Northernmost room (sali). The bride sits in the bedroom on the South side of the house, the sumbung. She sits together with the to minaa who is the spokesman for her and her family. This to minaa takes a place next to the wall which separates the sumbung from the sali. In the ornate style typical of priests, he inquires after the purpose of the men's "visit". "Have you come to take shelter from the rain?" On the other side of the wall, the second priest, the spokesman for the groom and his family, answers: "We have not come because it is raining, but because we wish to conform to the rules of the marriage ceremony".

Both priests now exchange several further verses. The groom's to minaa seizes the chance to ask: "Has this woman had good dreams, tell us about it?" The other priest replies: "She has already had good dreams, all the chickens have gathered". This last phrase involves an allusion to the (many) children that she will bear. In the dialogue which Van der Veen transcribed the sequence of remarks is roughly as follows:
- The bride's to minaa asks if the visitors have come on their way to the market.
- The groom's to minaa answers that, no, they are not going to the market.
- The bride's to minaa inquires if they have come in search of pure gold.
- The groom's priest replies that, no, they have not come looking for pure gold, but rather the golden motive for their coming was to achieve a marriage: "For this is the custom that Puang Matua established in the middle of heaven when he entered the boulder of basalt.[4] This is what the Lord whose head is crowned with grey ordained for good and all -

like a harrow (ultimately determines the flatness of the surface of the field) - when he embarked on marriage by entering into the huge wall of rock." (Van der Veen 1950:300). Afterwards the bride's spokesman, the to minaa, raises the subject of the kapa' which ends the exchange of remarks. Then the bride goes to the room where the groom sits. She takes her place beside him. A barasang is carried in, a finely plaited rattan basket in which there is food prepared by the bride's family, including some of the pig that has been slaughtered. Now the groom's family begins to eat. Bride and groom partake of food that is served to them in a langko'.[5]

Thereafter bride and groom go to sleep with each other. The man remains in his bride's home. Several times in succession his family then brings a barasang with food to the bride's family's house. The moment for the final rite arrives. Husband and wife seat themselves in the sumbung and a barasang with food, once again from the man's house, is set in front of them. Then the amount of the kapa' is discussed between the heads of the two families and their respective to minaa. Once an agreement has been reached about this fine for adultery, then the barasang is opened and people start to eat. This marks the end of the marriage ceremony.

For a detailed rendition of the marriage ceremony in puang-territories, see Nobele 1926:19-25; his account is primarily restricted to a marriage between puang-families. A.C. Kruyt (1923/24:118-20) also describes wedding procedures.

Today, since about 1970, weddings have become elaborate; especially the Toraja who live in Ujung Pandang, the capital of South Sulawesi, go to great lengths to celebrate in style. People try to abide by tradition, both in Ujung Pandang and in Tana Toraja; the to minaa, one spokesman for the bride, one for the groom, are never omitted. Even at Christian weddings, they are present.

5. *The death ritual of the to burake, to minaa sando, and the to menani; three priests who participate in the great bua'-feast*

The death ritual for the to burake, to minaa sando[6] and the to menani is described here because, in contrast to the ceremonies observed for all other dead, their burials fall in the sphere of the East (rambu tuka'). No death chants may be sung and the dancing that takes place belongs to rituals of the East: mangimbong, manganda', etc. Those who have a function in the ritual wear yellow clothing, for black may not be worn. The guest houses must be decorated with leaves that appear typically in rituals of the East: the leaves of the sugar palm and the red leaves of the blood-wort. The platform on which the meat is divided is not called bala'kaan (as during a ritual for the dead), but rather gorang bulaan, the golden gorang, a direct allusion to the festal scaffolding upon which a burake during his life performs so many official functions.

After death, the deceased lies with his head turned to the North and remains so until he is carried out of the house. Thus he does not have his head facing West or South as others who die do. He is not referred to as to mate, the dead one, either, but as to mara'pe (the one who is laid out; ra'pe means stretched out).

Just as with death rituals of the West, one can distinguish several grades or orders of ceremony for the interment of a to burake or to menani. It would seem that the lower rituals here have not wholly freed themselves from the sphere of the West. The simplest of all is called di-dedekan pangkung bai, a name also used for one low form of death ritual that falls in the Western sphere (see Chapter IX.1.3.). The dead to burake, to minaa sando or to menani is carried out through a hole in the house that is made by removing some boards from the West side or the floor of the sali-room (and thus not the East side). In this form of death ritual one or more pigs may be slaughtered and their carcases divided on the "golden" gorang.

The death rituals for these departed functionaries which are of a slightly higher order include the tallung bongi, limang bongi and the pitung bongi, terms also used for funerals in the Western sphere (see, respectively, the Chapters IX.2.2. and X.2. and X.3.). During these rituals, the dead to burake is carried from the house through the para (the triangular part of the front façade). To serve as an example of this order of celebration, I will describe the rites of the tallung bongi (three nights) held for such a functionary.

Day 1. A red rooster (sella') is killed, wrapped in bamboo leaves and cooked. The to maro' (mourners) consume the chicken, and the deceased also receives a portion. This marks the onset of the feast. Subsequently a buffalo is slaughtered. First, however, the pa'surak tedong takes place, as it does customarily in the course of higher death rituals. One does not go as far as singing the praises of the buffalo (Passomba Tedong) as on other rituals of the East, the merok-feast[7], for example, but at times the animal's family tree is traced aloud (pa'surak tedong). The killing of the buffalo is part of the unrandukan bua', the opening rite of the funeral. A live red rooster is placed on the breast of the deceased, tied with string from trousers which belonged to the dead man. The rooster is conveyed with the deceased to the tomb, where it is released. The rooster symbolizes that the dead man during his lifetime fulfilled the leading function in the great bua'-feast (B. Sarungallo; the symbolism was not further explained.

At the front of the house in which the deceased lies on view, a vast ladder with 12 rungs is built. The ladder reaches to the para. As soon as the buffalo has been killed, 24 to tumbang (the title in this context is not clear) - 12 boys, 12 girls - climb onto the ladder, one boy and one girl side by side on each rung. The young people sing a song that belongs to the death ritual of a to burake, to minaa sando or a to menani: ma'toburakei (the text could not be recorded). Then the boys and girls "kiss" each other, enacting the rite known as ma'pangalukan (the meaning of this word, however, is to invoke the deities). Exactly what the kissing involves is not clear; to be sure it will be acted out with restraint, for without doubt there is an interested public present. In front of the house a couple of baka bua (large baskets woven out of rattan) are put down filled with uncooked rice. Those who attend the feast contribute this rice. My informant added that the gift signified the following: umpokaa' tananan bua' rampe matampu', "the establishment of the bua'-feast that falls in the sphere of the West". It is in fact a curious expression, for the feast is rather considered to belong to the rituals of the East. My informant's words reflect the dialectical aspect of this ritual. Beside the baskets, a woman stands, a close relative of the deceased; as people come to fill the baskets with rice, she sprinkles them with grains of cooked rice that have been dyed yellow, a sign of appreciation but also a gesture expressing the hope of the host(ess) of the ritual, that he (she) will receive the blessing of the gods of the upperworld (or Puang Matua).

In the evening people dance the manimbong and the manganda'. To karondonan, people in a trance, appear. They lacerate themselves with knives and krisses. [8]

Day 2. In the morning the gorang bulaan is constructed on a plain (rante) [9] not far from the deceased's house. The to tumbang recommence with "kissing" on the ladder that leans against the para, the eran to tumbang. They take their positions by coming out through an opening which has been made in the para. After the pangalukan has been repeated, they climb down and go three times around the house in which the deceased lies on view, moving clockwise. Then they proceed to the gorang bulaan which they also circle round three times, similarly clockwise. Subsequently they sit down at rather a considerable distance from the "golden" gorang. Two buffaloes are led up to the gorang; after the passurak tedong they are slaughtered. Some pigs are killed also. The meat of the dead animals is divided among important figures and visitors. First, however, some scraps of buffalo are given to the deceased "to eat" (pemanala). Each of the to tumbang also receives a portion. Afterwards the to tumbang once again walk three times around the gorang and then three times around the house of mourning. At this point distribution of the meat occurs; as usual the to parengnge' get their share first.

The meat is cooked in a piong. The dead, the to mara'pe, is fed once more. A "colleague" of the deceased, a to burake, serves him this meal. Then the soul (bombo) of the dead priest is fed by the to mebalun (the death priest). The rite is known as bombo to mara'pe dito' barira, "the bombo of the to mara'pe receives food at the Western post". The to ma'kayo (= mebalun) puts down the meal on four pieces of banana leaf.

Underneath the offering meal, the to burake uses 12 tabang-leaves which he has first placed on the chest of the deceased. Once he has put down the food on the leaves, he sings a song with a certain melody, unnengnge'. The song, transcribed from the lips of the burake tambolang Tumba' of Mengkendek, goes as follows:

Kema'burakei tumba', Kema'bingsui manarang.	Thus the to burake sings, In this way the bingsu launches the singing.
Unrundunan aluk bua', Sangka'na pa'maruasan.	So are the rites of the bua'-feast observed in their set order; So was a feast organized that served as an example.
Dibanga' rika te aluk, Tang dipentutuan rika.	This feast isn't from just yesterday; This ritual wasn't there at the beginning.
Inang alukna nenekki,	These rites, it is selfevident, come from our ancestors,

Sangka'na panglalanki.	An example of the set sequence that must be followed.
Nene' e to dolo e,	Hey, you ancestors, Hey, ancestors of ours,
To bunga' panglalan e.	You who showed the way.
Inde-indeko sa'deki,	Come, sit here next to us (along the edge),
Unnisungko tingayoko.	Sit yourselves down before us,
Tarundunan aluk bua',	For we are beginning to carry out the bua'-rites,
Sangka'na pamaruasan.	For we are going to celebrate the feast that serves as an example.
Te alukna to mara'pe,	These are the rites of the dead,
Sangka' to situang tanduk.	This is the example (the sequence) of the horned lord[10],
Burakei tangnga langi',	The burake in the centre of heaven,
Bingsui to palullungan.	The bingsu, the one who enfolds,
Burakei randan langi',	The burake who came along the edge of the sky,
Bingsui ta'pian bombang.	The bingsu, the chaff (the foam?) of the wave.
Dakka Manurun di Rappang,	Dakka Manurun of Rappang,
Mari' Gallang ri Sa'dan,	Mari' Gallang of Sa'dan,
Aru'belo ri Sesean,	Aru'belo of Sesean,
Tumba' Pandung ri Endekan,	Tumba' Pandung of Enrekang[11],
Tumba' Pasalin ri Balombong,	Tumba' Pasalin of Balombong,
Tumba' Tana ri Buntao',	Tumba' Tana of Buntao',
Tumba' Borrong lan di La'bo',	Tumba' Borrong of La'bo',
Tumba' Tarima ri Kalosi,	Tumba' Tarima of Kalosi,
Tumba' Rangga ri Lempangan,	Tumba' Rangga of Lempangan,
Tumba' Mangallo ri Awa',	Tumba' Mangallo of Awa',
Tumba' Sanda lan di Pa'tong,	Tumba' Sanda of Pa'tong,
Silelean ko mairi',	Let us make it known,
Sikuanko sola nasang,	that we are throwing a feast for the
Allen padatu-datuko.	Lord.

Mitadoi kan pantoto,   Let us remember,
Mibengan kan mangilala.

Mangilalana nene'ta,   A remembrance handed down to us
Pantotona to dolota.   by our ancestors.

Angki mangilala tumbang,   So that quickly we organize a feast,
Pantoto ma'kaiangan.

Unrundunan aluk sando,   An original sando-feast[12],
Sangka' to situang tanduk.   An example set by the horned lord.

Den o Upa' dipoupa',   May Thou above grant us your
Paraya dipoparaya.   blessing,

Anna paria te suru',   So that the ritual may bring us
Pataranak te samaya.   prosperity and well-being,

Anta masakke mairi',   So that we all will live a long life.
Madarinding sola nasang.

After completion of this unnengnge', the to burake eats. Then the
priest, playing a clapper drum, goes three times around the house,
invoking the gods (ma'pangalukan). Now some of those who are present
fall into a trance. Then the manimbong and manganda' are performed.

Day 3. In the morning a buffalo which has been tied to the golden
gorang is slaughtered and dismembered. For the dead man, parts of the
nose, the tongue and the ears of the animal are cooked. From these ingredients some food is prepared. The priest's corpse is now carried out
through the para, through the Northern, most elevated part of the
house, symbolizing his immediate ascend to heaven. The to burake
offers the food to the mara'pe; it has been arranged on five pieces of
banana leaf.

Before the deceased is confined to a grave in the cliffs, many of the
male celebrants take part in a mock battle, in which they wield flexible
stalks (kambola). After burial, a pig is slaughtered beside the grave
(ma'palumpun to mara'pe: the burial of the to mara'pe).

Chapter VI

RITUALS OF EXORCISM: MARO AND BUGI'

"The maro-feast is as sour palm wine,
as milk that has been left standing all night,
as unhusked rice that has been soaked in water."
(The maro-song of Ne' Nora:56-7)

1. Introduction

Both the maro and bugi' are rituals of exorcism whose primary purpose
is to drive out evil, especially illnesses and plagues which threaten
men, animals and crops. Both are rituals of the East. Although
exorcism is at the core of both, they differ in character. These differences will be examined in the course of this chapter.

2. Maro

2.1. Name and goal of the ritual

The name maro means "mad", "crazy" but as such it is only used for
animals; maro-maro, to lack intelligence, to be an idiot, is applied to
people.[1] Thus the word maro alerts us to a connection between the
ritual and an animal; which animal will be discussed below (section
2.3.).

Just as it is possible to distinguish the maro from the bugi', one can
differentiate two kinds of maro-rituals. One form concentrates above all
on the expelling of illness and healing of the sick. The other is a
conversion ritual as part of a funeral ceremony. This second form also
is in essence celebrated in order to banish evil influences, dangers that
can threaten the community.

2.2. The maro-ritual for the sick

The Toraja believe that someone falls ill because he has committed a
transgression. A person can also become sick if one of the members of
his family has violated a taboo. It is usually the to minaa who must find
out by means of his divining rod (tille) who has sinned and how.[2] For
the art of divination as practiced among the Toraja (ma'biangi), see Van
der Veen 1929, and Vol.I:269ff. and 275. If the transgression is minor,
the to minaa makes a purificatory offering. This is in most instances
the ma'pallin: a black chicken and a bamboo are subsequently burned in
their entirety.

Among lesser offences, for example, is the use by a free man of a

dish, bowl or other eating utensil which belongs to a slave. Although
the free to makaka or to parengnge' has naturally done so by mistake,
he can fall ill.[3] Among grave transgressions, the worst is incest
between brother and sister. Epidemics can be unleashed through incest
to harrass man, animals and vegetation. For the purification rite that
must be observed, see Vol.I:31. Since the guilty brother and sister
were usually killed, they could not serve as the focal point of a ritual.
The most common cause of serious illness is said to be the violation of
one or another sexual taboo by the patient himself or by a family
member. The maro is then performed to achieve the sick person's cure.
     J. Kruyt provides a detailed account of the maro in Balusu
(1921:1ff.). The text below comes from B. Sarungallo's description of
the maro-ritual.

2.3. Descriptions of the maro-rites

Just as with other important rituals, with the maro one recognizes celebrations which differ in order of magnitude. How "high" a maro is
apparently depends on the status of the person who is sick. Should the
maro-ritual be a conversion ritual in the context of a funeral, then a
"lower" maro will follow a lower order of death feast, and a "higher"
maro a death feast of some standing. From the moment that the bate,
the "flag", is raised on its bamboo mast, there is little difference in
fact between the two varieties of maro, the healing exorcism and the
conversion ritual.
     According to B. Sarungallo, construction of a tadoran preceded the
ritual itself, followed by performance of the ma'suru'. The word suru',
to comb, is indicative of a purificatory sacrifice (see Merok:3). Perhaps
here Sarungallo is alluding to the randuk tumengkai suru', "the purificatory offering begins to take steps", a rite for the cleansing of the
atmosphere from the influence of death; "take steps" is a figurative way
to say that the offering starts to have effect. Thereafter the actual
maro gets under way. Below is a listing of various gradations of the
ritual: the names indicate the places where the central and concluding
rites take place.

1. Ma'bate bubun (bubun: well). A long period of preparation precedes
the feast. First the to parengnge' gather to discuss the cause of the
illness. The cause will invariably lie in one or another transgression.
During this meeting the dignitaries eat chicken and rice and drink palm
wine. Then Puang Matua is invoked. A decision is reached concerning
which tongkonan will be at the hub of the feast. A convenient time is
set. The to minaa or the paita ("the seer") takes the phase of the moon
and the position of the stars into consideration, without paying
particular attention to omens or portents.
     Some months later the first rite, the massape tabang ("tear off the
leaves of the tabang-plant"), takes place. Until this rite has been enacted, the maro may not be celebrated. A chicken is slaughtered and
piong are prepared in the house. This happens at about 7 in the
evening. Five pesung are gotten ready, using tabang-leaves to hold the
offering. The first pesung is for Puang Matua, the second for Indo'
Belo Tumbang, the patroness of medicine (below; and Merok:142-3), the
third for the deata of heaven, the fourth for the deata of the earth,
and the fifth for the spirits of the underworld.

On the second day members of the ramage come together, mangrim-pung. In the evening six piong are cooked, their contents to be used once again for preparing five pesung.

The membase (membase: to wash; see Woordenboek: v. base), a puri-ficatory rite, is staged on the third day. In the evening eight piong are made ready from a single chicken. Five pesung constitute the offering. From this point on the actual maro-feast begins. First comes the ma'gelong. Not everyone at the feast sings the gelong, only the men. At this stage no one becomes possessed yet. As a matter of fact, the patients are still inside the house. Not before the ma'gelong has given way to the ondo-dancing (ma'ondo or unnondo: to leap up and make dancing movements in a rapid tempo with bent knees), are the patients brought outside. All the gods who have received a pesung are called upon to work a remedy for the sick, i.e. to aid the recovery of all kinds of illnesses. Each patient is laid on the ground and covered with cloths until he or she gets warm and begins to sweat. The cover-ings do not need to be maa'-cloths, ordinary fabrics will do.

The celebrants sit in a circle around the patient(s), and then the patient's cloths are removed. The to ma'dampi (medicine-man) cuts his tongue and spits the blood that flows from his wound into his hand; with this mixture of blood and saliva he rubs the limbs, stomach and back of every patient. Then each sick person is thoroughly warmed with flaming bamboos; the medicine-man blows the flames in his or her direction. Another informant described a different version of this event: the patients were placed on a platform under which leaves were set on fire. It is the medicine-man who kindles the leaves with a torch which he waves under the platform.

If the sick person is a woman, and if she is up to it, then she dances on a kind of small bamboo table. Underneath the table bamboo torches are kept burning to warm her. Two sick women may dance at the same time, or a sick and a healthy woman together. The dancing really consists of rocking backwards and forwards. For sick men no such table is constructed. No explanation was given for this differentia-tion. Yet, in rituals of exorcism on the whole men seldom dance, it is more of a woman's activity. At times a sick woman dances on top of a drum, or performs gymnastic exercises on the instrument, "so that her body will grow strong again", as my informant (J. Tammu) explained. Afterwards the patient sits down once more. The medicine-man goes up to her and stabs her with a kris (here I must raise doubts about the accuracy of the account, for usually a sacral sword is used for such an act). Blood may flow, but in most instances it does not. (Van der Veen maintains that no blood should be lost during such ritual violence. At his request the medicine-man cut his finger slightly; the wound healed at once through the application of a tabang-leaf.) The sick woman can also be stabbed in the back. Alternatively she may be scored with a long sword wielded by the medicine-man.

At her request, the woman can be worked on in a special manner with a sacral sword. This technique of incision is known as tere, to make surface cuts, not to cut all the way through. A medicine-man goes to stand behind the sick woman; first they dance together. Then he places a sword that he holds at both ends with the edge of the blade pulled back against her stomach. While the man pivots on his axis the woman, as it were, is rotated on the sword.[4] The dance is called ma'lambang (see also the description below of the great maro ma'bate-feast in

Tikala). The deata help; they enter into the patient so that she isn't wounded (informant: J. Tammu). She is possessed. The deata come into the body of the woman in trance so that she, possessed by the gods, can inflict wounds on herself, or let them be inflicted, without incurring any serious injury.

Once the patients have been handled in this fashion, others attending the ritual also begin to dance. Various people fall into a trance. It is often the same people who succumb, those with a predisposition for trance. All those in a trance perform stunts reminiscent of fakirs: they climb a ladder with sharp knives for rungs (this ascent can be interpreted as an attempt to reach the upperworld - personal interpretation) or they sit on a spear or play the flute perched high on a bamboo pole. Not only do the deata see to it that no harm comes to the performers, but they even communicate what stunts should be acted out. Each person receives a special assignment. The spectators can tell from what happens what the deata have commanded. Only one deata is present in each of the people possessed.

Not everyone is allowed to attend a maro-ritual. The feast is taboo for people in mourning or persons who have recently attended a death feast. The chance would be too great that the persons in question had eaten meat at the death feast, or were obliged to eat maize or yam, and to wear black clothing - all of which are taboo at this deata ritual, and potential causes of injury from weapons applied. The deata, who want to protect maro-participants, do not wish to meet with any interference on their way, otherwise they'll turn around and go back to the upperworld. And such interference can come from elements that have to do with rituals of the West, rituals falling in the sphere of the aluk rampe matampu'.

The ma'bate bubun is primarily celebrated in the evening or through the night. On the evening of the first day, the singing and dancing begin and go until 1 a.m. The next evening everything is repeated, lasting this time until 5 a.m., with, to be sure, some intervals. Women submit to the manterei, the "surface" incisions administered by the medicine-man.

The to ma'dampi is also the man who gives out medicine consisting of his own blood caught in a leaf of the Dracaena terminalis. This is rubbed onto the patients. The medicine-man ignites a torch with which he drives away evil (i.e. the spirit making the person ill). Once again people go into a trance to the tune of the songs that are sung. The healing ritual attracts many visitors, in no small part because of the acrobatic high jinks and fakir stunts which must be performed. The ritual goes on until the patients are cured ("or dead", B. Sarungallo added gloomily).

As concluding rite, the ma'bate bubun[5] takes place. Three chickens are slaughtered and ten piong prepared. Five pesung are made from these foods. They are set out for the gods, on this occasion on the leaves of Dracaena terminalis. The five pesung are placed near a well (bubun). Celebrants form into a procession and proceed to the well in fixed order. In front walks the person who carries a long bamboo pole (bate), the end of which is wreathed with tabang-leaves. A sacral maa'-cloth hangs from the top. (According to Van der Veen this is a piece of red cotton cloth and not a maa'.) Next follow the patients who have been cured. After them come distinguished members of the community. Then the three medicine-men advance, those who have prepared food for them and for the sick in their wake. Three chickens are killed. Packets of glutinous rice (pokon) may possibly be prepared, to be enjoyed with palm wine and chicken. In addition to the three chickens mentioned above, others are brought along. If there are many chickens, then they are distributed, the medicine-men being the first to get their share.

2. Ma'bate uai (uai: water) is a variant of the maro-ritual which differs from the preceding description only in that the concluding rite takes place by the riverside. This time the banner in front of the procession is the bate uai ("the water flag"). For this artefact, see Fig. 15a. The procession is for all intents and purposes the same as the procession during the bate bubun. Before continuing on to the river, the celebrants pause at the well. The concluding rite consists of bathing in the river (= the water).

3. Ma'bate buntu. The concluding rite of the feast (the carrying out of the bate) is enacted on a hill (buntu). Before climbing the hill, celebrants bathe in the river and beside the well. From one chicken, ten piong are prepared. In other respects this ritual is the same as 1. and 2. The bate consists of a bamboo-tallang wreathed at the tip with

Fig. 15. Bate in Kesu' and Tikala.

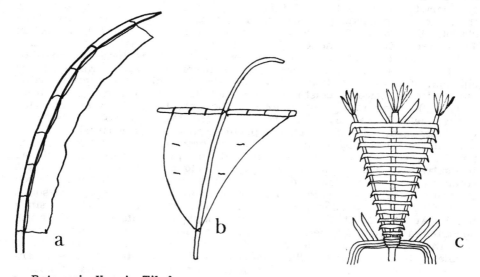

a. Bate uai, Kesu', Tikala.

b. Bate manurun, Kesu'.

c. Bate manurun, Tikala (for details, see Fig. 17, p. 136).

tabang-leaves. On both sides of the pole two old swords stick out. A maa'-cloth hangs from the top of the bate (according to Van der Veen an ordinary red cotton cloth).

4. Ma'bate manurun, the great maro-feast. Manurun means: descended from the heavens; bate: flag, or a bamboo from which a cloth hangs. Ma'bate manurun is the highest order of maro-ritual. In Kesu', for example, it may only be celebrated by the anak pare-pare nangka' (nobility; see Vol.I:48). The to parengnge' set the date for the feast. On the first day participants bathe at the well; on the second day they bathe by the river; the third day they climb the hill. On the fourth day the bate manurun is set up at the symbolic pasa' rambu tuka', "the market of the ascending smoke", i.e. the square where the rituals of the East take place. Because the bate manurun is a sacral object, it is erected on the Northeast of the festive grounds. At this stage of the ritual gellu'-dancers perform. Before they begin to dance, these women line up, one next to the other; on both sides of the line, in former days, there stood a slave. The dancers are decked out in festal finery: they wear a wreath of tarrung-fruits or a sa'pi' on their heads; manik ata chains and rara' (gilded cylinders) hang around their necks; they have on golden bracelets, and a waistband decorated with ancient coins. Krisses are stuck into their waistbands. A kandaure hangs down their backs. (For the outfits of these dancers, see Fig. 2 and Nooy-Palm 1969:173, fig. 4.) The gellu'-dancers do not go into a trance. Their ornamentation with its coins, tarrung-fruits and golden jewelry is appropriate to the sphere of this deata-feast. The bate is more sizable than for the preceding maro-rituals and it is draped with many maa'-cloths. The form of the bate in Kesu' differs somewhat from that in Tikala (see Fig. 15b and c). In Tikala it is a collossal "trident" which ends in a decoration of tabang-leaves; in Kesu' the bate is a bamboo which has its upper end bent into a decorative arch. Hundreds of chicken, and even at times pigs, are slaughtered for the great maro-feast. In procession celebrants proceed to the "market", the feast square, keeping in a definite order: the bate leads the way; the sick follow; behind them come the medicine-men; then the cooks; next the gellu'-dancers; and finally all the people who attend the ritual.

Upon arrival at the square, the bate is erected (at some Northeastern point). Three chickens are slaughtered and processed into ten piong. In contrast to usual practice, women now sing maro-songs. The sick are treated; people sit down to a meal. The chickens which have been brought along are divided. The women once more sing maro-songs (according to B. Sarungallo the men decide which of the women sings best). At this point the dancers perform again. Informant J. Tammu specifies a special sequence of song and dance: first, before people eat, the women dancers perform; then the unnondo takes place; after people have eaten, the gellu'-dancers (female) and the nondo-dancers (male) merge forces. During this last dance trance phenomena do occur, which will be discussed in more detail in the following section. Men may also sing maro-songs. When everyone is exhausted, then the principal part of the feast has ended. The bate is disassembled. The day after this ma'pasa', "going to the market", i.e. the feast square, the ma'palimbong takes place. Ma'palimbong means to let fill up with water; the expression is a way of saying that the feast reaches its end. A chicken is sacrificed in the tongkonan.

One of my informants presented a somewhat different account of the final phase of the feast, basing his remarks on the large number of chickens brought along. His version is reproduced below:

The chickens are divided among those in attendance and eaten. The sick are not overlooked. The medicine-men in particular are well remembered. The one who has precedence receives some twenty chickens. Then the rice priests get their share, followed by the sokkong bayu and the other to parengnge'. Previously, an offering of chicken has been made to the ancestors of the Southwest. Afterwards (the next day?) the rite of bathing at the well follows (mendio'). In the morning the ma'pakande Puang is enacted beside this well: a piong and a red rooster are offered to Puang Matua. At the ritual bathing place another offering is laid down on a tabang-leaf (ma'pesung). Finally, a live rooster and a piong are brought to a special place outside the village. There the rooster is slaughtered and then the bate is brought to the spot to be taken apart. (It can be assumed that this special place is located to the Northeast of the settlement.)

2.4. The maro-ritual to cure the sick as it originated in the upperworld

From the Passomba Tedong, the myth which tells of the origins of the cosmos, it is clear that the maro-ritual was established first in the upperworld (Merok:142-3). Puang Matua's child, Banno Bulaan, The Golden Rice-Water, fell ill. A messenger was sent to Indo' Belo Tumbang, the Mother who is the Ornament of Those Who Can Dance so Beautifully (leap is probably a better translation, for that is what tumbang literally means, not dance). This goddess is also called Indo' Bunga Sampa, Benevolent Mother Blossom. The goddess was sitting with the gods Puang Matua, Puang Bassi-Bassian and Puang Ambo-Amboan (these latter are alternate names in fact for Puang Matua), enjoying betel nut, when the messenger delivered the request (whose request is not said) that she cure the Golden Rice-Water. Indo' Belo Tumbang then made her wish known that Kambuno Langi', The Sunshade of Heaven, the first to minaa in the upperworld, should make an expiatory offering before she herself went to heal the patient. The priest then brought the offering in the front room of the Iron House in the upperworld. Thereafter the goddess cured The Golden Rice-Water by spitting well-chewed blood-wort leaves over her (Van der Veen 1979:38-9, and oral information). The goddess is the patroness of the maro-ritual. She sprayed the patient in the upperworld from her mouth in the same way the medicine-man does during the ritual on earth. Her name Indo' Belo Tumbang[6] alludes in part to the fact that she is considered to have the tumbang under her protection. These to tumbang are the women who go into a trance during the ritual and keep making leaps (tumbang) while they remain in this state. We should point out that the tumbang in the maro-ritual are not at all the same tumbang as those who officiate during the great bua'-feast. These latter tumbang never enter into a trance. Nevertheless, both sets of tumbang aspire to the same end: those who take part in the bua' kasalle-feast are set in a great tree in order to make contact with the upperworld; during their trance, the tumbang in the maro-feast leap up over and over and take a journey to heaven in their trance (see, among others, Van der Veen 1979:104-5, verse 341). For a comparison of the neurotic behaviour of the chickens in the upperworld with the antics of the tumbang in the maro-feast, see

Vol.I:209. Chickens, slaughtered in great number, are the principal sacrificial animals for the maro-feast. (Another name for the highest form
of the maro is maro datu or maro sangullelle.)

2.5. Characteristics of the maro-ritual

The reader will have noticed how often the maro-ritual has been referred to as a feast; indeed the ritual trappings are festal. It is a ritual
that demands intensive preparations. Chickens must be brought together and slaughtered, "a good hundred", food must be gotten ready,
etc. The verse cited at the beginning of this chapter alludes to these
efforts. The feast succeeds because of the common commitment of all
participants who believe in the power of the songs, of the drums, of
the trance, the sacral cloths, the swords, the tabang-leaves, and, "last
but not least", the bate. Should a large number of tourists attend the
maro-feast, if there is too much scepticism roundabout, then the feast
will not achieve its purpose. Then the Toraja say no one will be cured
and whoever cuts or punishes his or her body can incur serious
injuries.
   In the rituals examined in previous chapters, functionaries performed
who behaved with exemplary decorum (which does not detract from the
fact that on the "big day" of such rituals the prevailing mood,
reinforced in no small measure by palm wine, is lively and joyous). The
maro, and the bugi', too, are of different character. There is nothing
serene about them; tension often reigns. The trance which is central to
these rituals endows them with a savage, unrestrained quality. It is
true that in the beginning of such a ritual the to parengnge' or other
leaders of society together with the to minaa play a role, personages
who emanate authority and composure, yet as the maro develops the
element of possession grows more and more pronounced. At the moment
that the sick are to be treated, the eloquent to minaa reciting his
endless verses gives way to the taciturn, but hectically busy medicine-
man. The sick require his unflagging attention. And in addition to the
patients there are also the dancers and the singers of the maro-songs
whose music has healing powers and conveys the more sensitive
celebrants into a trance. Those who fall into a trance belong to different categories: those who in their fantasy make all kinds of journeys
through the air and those who, possessed by spirits, either do harm to
themselves if they don't let it be done to them by others, or else perform fakir-like feats.
   Many persons, possessed by trance, are leaping, dancing, or wobbl-
ing over the feast square, their hair loose, their sarongs in disarray.
In contrast the gellu'-dancers with their attractive attire add lustre to
the maro-feast; they do their best to please the deata. They wear
precious kandaure on their backs and a waistband of costly beads
draped about their hips. Their sarongs and jackets are white, and on
their heads they bear a wreath of yellow tarrung-fruits. Yellow and
white are the colours of the upperworld. The wreath is at times replaced by a triangular head ornament which represents para, the triangular upper front part of the tongkonan, that section of the roof
which symbolizes the upperworld (see Fig. 2a and b).
   Iron smiths also have a special relation to the maro-feast. The reason
for this relation has to do with part of their work: the fabrication of
weapons. It was impossible for me to inquire more deeply into the

special connection between smiths and the maro (but see Zerner 1981:89-113).

The dominant colour of the maro-feast is red, a colour associated with blood and life. The bate is red, the cloth that hangs from the bamboo which is carried out at the conclusion of the ritual. The tabang-leaves are red, and so is the saliva of the sirih-chewer, red as the blood which, despite the fact that on principle it may not flow, comes in gushes and spurts. The red bate-cloth and the sacral maa'-fabrics which adorn the bate manurun - and which often are also predominantly red in colour - are so powerful, so sacral, that they can ward off evil influences. The same can be said for the weapons displayed, male symbols (the counterparts of the textiles, female symbols). These la'bo' pinae or tonapa radiate a special force consistent with the healing aspects of the ritual.

The "pièce de résistance" in the maro-feast is the bate, celebrated in song:

"She is so red that she lights up the village,
she is so red that she lights up the village,
she is so red that her gleam embraces the settlement,
that she makes the compound glow."
(Van der Veen 1979:158-9, verse 15)

The red bate - red by virtue of the textiles fastened to the bamboo - is compared with the radiance of a glowing fire; it can make the village "hot" (Indonesian angat, a concept which involves intrinsic danger). Yet fire is not only threatening, it also is salutary: fire can purify. Indeed both fire and water are elements which have important, ritual cleansing properties. The sick are held over the fire.

"Water is consumed by fire,
moisture singed by the glowing coals,
spreading steadily with flaring flames."
(Van der Veen 1979:74-5, verse 150)

The tongkonan, centre of the ramage, is the centre of the maro-feast. According to J. Tammu, if there is a plan to celebrate a great bua'-feast after the maro, an anak dara is already set up in the house (cf. Vol.I:241). In such an anak dara Tammu sees a symbolic union between middle- and upperworld.

As in all rituals, in the maro rice has a role to play, often in the form of husked rice which has been popped, ra'tuk. Other important plants in the maro-feast have already been mentioned: the bamboo and the tabang.

2.6. Maro-songs

Maro-songs[7] begin in a calm tempo, which soon quickens in keeping with the text, for practically at once there is a first reference to possession ("De maro-zang van Ne' Nora'" and "De maro-zang van Sangayu", Van der Veen 1979:38-109 and 109-129 respectively).

It does not take long for the imagery to become wilder, more ecstatic, at times incomprehensible. The world is seen through a distorting lens: a river that flows uphill, that reverses against its own current, proas that travel upside down. This might be an allusion to the fact that man imagines everything in the upperworld as different, as the opposite to

life on earth. Yet it seems to me more likely that the metaphors allude
to the fact that the normal course of events has been disrupted. The
maro-ritual is to restore order. The sick must be made well; illness
caused by the violation of a taboo must be cured.

Together with proas sailing upside down, the maro-songs make
mention of boats equipped with iron swords (Van der Veen 1979:69,
verse 122). This is the kind of vessel that appears in the myth of Pano
Bulaan (Vol.I:173 and 175). In Dayak mythology (Bahau), a similar
proa is the legendary craft of headhunters. The free-flowing hair sung
of in the maro-songs is also possibly an allusion to headhunting, the
hair with which the proas were bound (Van der Veen 1979:70, verse
127). Indeed, village warriors also let their hair down after they had
taken a head (A.C. Kruyt 1923/24:269). The soaked rice mentioned in
the maro-ritual also brings the headhunters to mind (see the verse
quoted at the beginning of this chapter). This was the kind of rice
headhunters were given to eat.

It is by way of rivers streaming uphill that women in trance
ultimately arrive in the upperworld at the house where everything
stands in reverse. With the point of a rolled blood-wort leaf they prick
through the solar disc. Then the situation returns to normal, or at
least becomes less abnormal. For by the end of the maro-song that Van
der Veen has transcribed, those in a trance have not yet returned
completely to their ordinary state, not yet resumed quotidian reality.
Their journey has taken them too far away, their ecstasy has been too
exhausting. Those in a trance have been to a place far in the distance
and yet close at hand.

The role of the tumbang in the maro-songs is depicted in more detail
in the text which follows. The songs are sung by a chorus which has a
leader; the songs accompany the tumbang in their ecstatic voyage to
the upperworld. The texts of the songs reveal that the tumbang is a
woman (see Van der Veen 1979:52-3, verse 43). The instability, the
restless nature of these women is expressed in the maro-songs:

"I have now turned into wind,
I have been converted into a whirlwind,
she steers her way past the whirlwind,
on her course she flies past the wind.
She flies past and arrives in a celestial state,
she steers past and is thrown into rapture,
she pursues the state in which it is forbidden to tread the earth,
and whirls on possessed by a spirit."
                    (Van der Veen 1979:52-3, verses 44 and 45)

At the first note of music some women already fall into a trance; others
soon follow. It is usually the same who quickly succumb. Apparently,
this is - to an extent - a matter of heredity; a verse from one of the
songs points in this direction:
"... the descendants of those who are in ecstasy,
the progeny of those who may not tread the earth,
the offspring of those who are possessed by a spirit."
                    (Van der Veen 1979:46-7, verse 14)

The tumbang speaks of herself in the maro-songs in the first and the
third person; this conveys the impression that she is constantly taking
distance from herself:

"Then I am like a chiming bell,
like a small, round globule that shakes back and forth,
...
she is shaken back and forth by the experts,
she is moved back and forth by the skilful"
                    (Van der Veen 1979:46-7, verses 19 and 20)

Once a tumbang has fallen into a trance, she is, as it were,
"converted"[8] by the puang (Puang Matua?) and the deata:
"He converts her form,
he reforms her,
he induces her to go against the grain."
                    (Van der Veen 1979:54-5, verse 56)

Also, in the following verses, selected from Ne' Nora's maro-song
(verses 24f., 95 and 46f.):
"I slept for a moment during the day,
My drowsiness seized me.
The noble woman brought me in sleep ..."

"My insides quiver,
my heart was, as it were, clouded over,
my body shudders,
my hairs rise on end."

"I am tired while carrying on in a supermundane state,
I am worn out while being in rapture,
I am like someone stunned by betel-nut ..."

The tumbang see everything upside down: water running uphill, houses
reversed, and the like. The explanation is simple: looking down from
above, the way the tumbang does, she sees everything as if it had
been stood on its head. For many peoples (and not only the Toraja) the
upperworld is the earth in reverse, the mirror image of the world of
humanity. The real message of this reversal is that the world of mankind is in a state of chaos, the result of human sin and trespass. The
tumbang on her journey to the upperworld notices the differences
between the two worlds:
"I am really walking along the edge of the heavens,
I am really going alone one half of it,
I am already close to the halfway mark.
In the North were the earth is joined together,
where the lands swallow each other up,
where the edges of the welkin swallow each other,
from the chaff of the waves,
where the land is turned upside down,
and the waters flow the wrong way,
the waters flow upwards,
the stream and the rivers return upwards."
                    (Van der Veen 1979:94-5, verses 278-82)

The tumbang feels like she is floating (verse 82):
"All the time she is flying back and forth,
All the time just hovering,
She will only touch down on the land beyond."

She tries to reach the sky of which in a later verse it is said (verses 336-8):
"They say, the sky is far away,
they say, heaven is a long distance from here.
It is far, but yet it is near,
it is a long distance away, but yet it is close to us.
It is so far from here that (in the time it takes to reach it) one
can tip a sun hat just one time,
it is one step of a virgin away."

And then she reaches heaven (verse 114)[9]:
"The sky is spread yonder below is,
our feet keep tripping among the stars,
we tread the sun beneath us."

The tumbang, on her journey to the upperworld, climbs a ladder; she perseveres as far as the firmament, until she is admitted to the tiers of heaven (verses 327-33). Only then does the tumbang come back down to earth (verse 341):
"I am back from viewing the firmament,
from considering with care the heavens,
from attaining the peak of the realm above the earth."

In the language of the Toraja "firmament" and "heaven" are langi', "the realm above the earth" is sala padang. Sala padang means literally false or mistaken earth. Once more a phrase consistent with the notion of conversion. For the rest, heaven is exceptionally beautiful: the houses are splendid, etc. The tumbang, however, must return to earth and the journey back is dreadful, fraught with dangers:
"I am lowered down to a water pool,
there I am caught in a deep whirlpool ..."
etc.
"There below are eight heads,
there below are six fins,
seventeen tails.
He has Dracaena leaves for fins,
he has blood-wort leaves for quiles,
foam of many colours is his tail ..."
etc.
"He wakes me up while I am in a deep sleep,
when it is midnight,
when the darkness is fading,
when the darkness is attenuating ..."
etc.

                              (Van der Veen 1979:107, verses 359-64)

In the culture of the Toraja, women are associated with water. It is my impression, however, that in the maro-feast the tumbang is connected with the more gruesome aspects of water. She doesn't land back on earth but under the earth in the perilous pools where monsters lurk. Such a grisly creature also appears in the maro-song of Sangayu' (Van der Veen 1979:123, verse 66). It is the beast who finally revives the tumbang from her trance.
Whereas the karondonan and kandeatan are said to be possessed by

spirits, that is not true for the tumbang. At least if we rely on the maro-songs; she swerves back and forth over the earth on the way to heaven, but the spirits do not possess her; she does not lose her own identity. In the maro-ritual she is the counterpart of the women who bear the same name in the bua'-feast (although the number of girls or women who participate as tumbang in the bua'-feast is fixed at eight, the number of tumbang in the maro is not restricted).

Finally, B. Sarungallo maintains that there are eschatological elements in maro-songs. Certain passages would presage the future. When the first men landed on the moon, in 1969, according to Sarungallo, the Toraja were not surprised. This had been predicted long before in their maro-songs: people would walk the heavenly bodies. The songs also speak of wading through a sea of blood, an allusion, in Sarungallo's opinion, to the bloody wars fought in this century. Sarungallo's views may be interesting as an example of acculturation, as a modern Toraja's interpretation of ancient songs, but they do not contribute to our understanding of the maro-songs in their original context. For this purpose, the following is more significant: the tumbang's contact with heavenly bodies indicates the deep concern of the Toraja for relations with the upperworld; the sea of blood refers to headhunting, but at the same time also the the underworld.

2.7. The maro as conversion ritual during a burial

For a general discussion of conversion rituals, see Chapter VII. For Van der Veen, the maro as conversion ritual is known primarily on the slopes of Sesean, in the territories of Bori', Riu and Tikala (Merok:2). In these parts people cannot embark on other rituals of the East unless this special form of maro has been celebrated previously. The maro thus precedes the major bua'-feast. At times it is held immediately before the bua'-feast commences or may even be a component of the bua'-feast it-self (cf. Chapter II, rites 15 through 17). The ritual has a more or less established time and place, between a death feast on the one hand and a great bua'-feast on the other. The maro for curing the sick, however, is not necessarily confined to a time slot between a death feast and bua'-ritual. Nevertheless, even then the condition must be fulfilled that all recent dead within the bua'-community have been buried.

In Kesu' it is difficult to define the place which the maro-feast occupies. My informants agreed it was celebrated before a conversion ritual. Successive orders of maro correspond with the ranking of con-version rituals: maro bate uai comes before the ma'tadoran, ma'palang-ngan para and ma'tete' ao'; maro ma'bate precedes the manganta', and bate manurun the merok. It is my impression that the maro-feast is a purificatory ritual that must cleanse the community of any taint of death. We alluded to this idea at the outset of this chapter. The notion that the ritual concerns the purification of the human community as a whole was confirmed by my informant K. Kadang who said that the small bate uai was set up in order to convey all the dead in the community to another sphere. He added that the large triangular bate is erected after the demise of a to makaka (Kadang carried out his research primarily in Tikala). According to information acquired in Tandung (Kesu'), the bate uai is brought out for the to makaka direngnge', the bate manurun for the anak pare-pare nangka', whereas no bate is erected for the unfree when they die.

In the conversion ritual the form of the bate is thus related to the class of those who have died. Just as in every maro-ritual, the bate here, too, is decorated. While people are busy doing this, the gelong bate, the bate-song, is sung. For one such song, see Van der Veen's translation of the "Gelong bate" (1979:155-63). Everyone who falls in a trance at this maro-feast must place a piong of rice covered with a tabang-leaf at the foot of the bate. At the end of the maro-ritual, the bate is stripped of its ornaments (massossoran bate, the decline of the bate; sosso' means to become less). The cloths and swords are stored away. The denuded bamboo pole is left standing on the feast square (Van der Veen 1979:155). The bate has served its purpose: the dead have been transported to the sphere of the gods. (In adhering to Van der Veen's usage, I accept the bate as female: the bamboo-tallang from which the bate is made is considered to be feminine.) The bate is decorated with many cloths, sacral maa'-fabrics and ordinary textiles as well; these textiles are female attributes. The swords which are part of the decorations of the bate manurun are, to be sure, associated with men, with courage, with war and headhunting. The bunches of rice which at times crown the bate are a symbol of the upperworld, of abundance. The entire structure is considered holy.

Below follows an account of the "big day" during a maro as conversion ritual celebrated on the slopes of Sesean on November 2, 1966.

2.8. Bate umpabalik bandera to mate, held in Sereale village

Although this ritual is called a maro-feast, the word balik makes it clear that the feast should be categorized as a conversion ritual. The term designating the feast means literally: "The flag which reverses the banners of death" (bandera are the banners or textiles fastened to a bamboo pole which are placed in front of the festal huts during the second part of a death feast). The celebration is also at times spoken of as maro ma'bate, a great maro-feast during which a bamboo with a red flag is erected. This maro is observed to convey someone who has died to the Eastern sphere so that the deceased may be looked upon as a deata (Woordenboek: v. bate). The feast takes place some years after the dirapa'i has been held (see Chapter X.4.). First, family members come together to take counsel (ma'pulung) about when to celebrate this maro as a thanksgiving after the dirapa'i (information from W. Papayungan).

Members of participating tongkonan set up a bate consisting of gigantic bamboo poles. Although the bamboo poles are not heavy, their size makes the transport difficult enough to invoke the image of people struggling to move a megalith. A pig is slaughtered for each participating tongkonan on the day preceding commencement of the ritual proper. The drums begin to play and on the same day a number of smaller ceremonies take place, such as the ma'pallin, the expiatory offering that involves incineration of a black chicken and a piong of rice outside the village. A great many chickens are killed on this occasion, as at any maro-feast. The to minaa receive no mean share. Only during this maro, however, pigs are also slaughtered. For a maro to cure the sick, this is not the procedure. The next day, the "big day", the bate is carried forth to the feast plain (ma'pasa': to proceed to the market). At this particular maro-feast, six bate were set up on the

rante kala'paran, the terrain where, among other celebrations, the
great bua'-feast is held. Five bate stood near the enormous banyan tree
on the North side of the plain. One stood on its own, more to the East
(see Fig. 16).

Fig. 16. Location of the bate in Sereale village, Tikala.

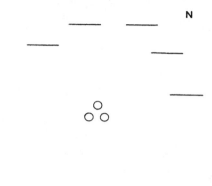

——— bate ('flag')

O bamboo with tabang-leaves

Between the various bate there was a group of bamboo poles, one pole
for each bate, bound together. The tips of these bamboos were
decorated with tabang-leaves. While men were dancing a circle around
one of the bate which had just been stood in place, they sang (ma'gelong). On their heads they wore wreaths of an unidentified leaf; the to
minaa who danced with them wore a wreath of tabang-leaves.[10]
     Afterwards the ma'pesung took place; one to minaa, at times two,
officiated at each bate. Offerings were placed on a tabang-leaf or
banana leaf. At the foot of each bate several such offerings were laid
on the ground. Each bate was composed of three bamboo poles fastened
together; the principal pole was entwined with a sarita-cloth. Various
cloths were used to wrap the other two bamboos of each bate and the
various horizontal bars that were part of the overall construction: maa',
sarita, old and new batiks, Rongkong cloths and Sumba fabrics, and
one or two new textiles. To the tip of the central bamboo a sword was
affixed, and swords were also attached, two or three on each side, to
the lowest horizontal bar (see Fig. 17). These weapons and the sacral
cloths indicate that the bate serves as a symbol to ward off evil influences, as do the tabang-leaves which crown the construction (see
Vol.I:225).
     During the erection of the bate, a festive crowd had collected on the
plain. Many men were wearing gold or gilded necklaces, manik ata (see

Fig. 17. Bate manurun, Tikala.

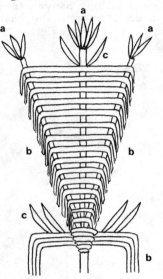

a. tabang-leaves

b. old sacral cloths alternated with newer textiles

c. old sacral swords

Nooy-Palm 1969:193 and plate VI, photo 2). The to minaa wore big tali bate', batik cloths, on their heads. Women and children were draped with old silver coins, Theresa-half-a-crowns and other currency from the time of the Dutch East Indies Company. To add to the festal excitement, gellu'-dancers performed; not only the human spectators, but the gods as well were considered to take delight in the performance. The gellu' danced in three groups. People expressed their pleasure by tucking money into the waistbands of the dancers. These bills were later skewered on the ribs of sugar-palm leaves which are part of the dancers' headgear. Among the dancers was a girl not yet one metre tall who bore some thousand rupiah (Dfl. 10) on her head. I was told this is a new custom, only popular since World War II. The gifts, to be sure, are for the most part display; the dancers get to keep only a small percentage.

Afterwards food was served. Everyone's humour improved, spirits ran high. The hosts were generous with palm wine, meat and rice cooked in banana leaves. Plentiful food and drink was to put everyone in a fine mood, the deata included. After the eating, the gellu'-dancers performed again, but when the drumming turned "wild", they withdrew. And then various persons fell into a trance. The drums continued to pound out a rapid beat. A few women pressed forward into the circle formed by a crowd. They held each other by the hand and swung around, their hair hanging free. Men joined them, flagellating themselves and others who were possessed with bunches of tabang-leaves. One man cut himself in the forearm with a sword: there was no visible wound, no blood flowed. Nonetheless tabang-leaves were quickly applied to the place where the sword had come down on his arm. Another man slashed his calf, also with a sword. A small wound began to bleed. Another had inflicted scratches on his forehead with a knife. A young woman turned karondonan and stepped into the circle. More women and men, all in all a good dozen, became possessed. One man seized a sword with the edge of the blade pointing towards him. He had an older woman lean her stomach against the edge and pivoted rapidly with her around (ma'lambang). He turned in place; the woman stood with her feet on his. The man's face, and the woman's were turned outwards. By whom were the possessed possessed? By devils (Indonesian: setan) according to some Christians, by the deata according to others.

It seemed that having a good time was very much part of the ritual; thus one possessed woman fought in single combat with a man who wasn't possessed. Each had a rice winnowing fan which was both weapon and shield. A roar arose each time the woman who tottered about like a sleepwalker struck her opponent a blow. Gradually the possessed awoke from their trance. I saw how three were restored to consciousness. They sat together under a cloth near the bate that stood off to the East. A medicine-man fanned them with tabang-leaves.

In the meantime the crowd had become so dense that it was all but impossible to see anything of the dancing. Those who weren't in a trance went around singing and jigging. Before the meal mentioned above was served, the to minaa had performed the ma'pesung at each bate. Then one by one the bate were stripped, a sign that the feast was nearing its conclusion. For the crowd's delight, calf-kicking was still staged. It was time to begin on the homeward journey to reach home before dark. Those who had to return to faraway Rantepao soon left the mountain village and its celebrants behind them. On the way people said that in the past the achievements of the karondonan were much more impressive and gruesome. For example, one possessed would cut off his head and then quickly set it back on the stump of his neck!

2.9. Epilogue

Maro-songs differ markedly from the orderly songs of creation and prayers which the to minaa in Kesu' recite at the great bua'- and merok-feasts. Corresponding creation myths told on the slopes of Sesean are of a more savage nature, as is evident in the "Overleve-ringen van den Beginne vanuit de Hemel" as remembered by the priest Ne' Mani' (Van der Veen 1976). And it is precisely in the Sesean region, not in Kesu', that maro is frequently observed.

The maro is a deata-feast: it belongs, like bugi', to the rituals of the East. It differs in character, however, from the bua' kasalle and the merok: the trance, the infliction of injuries (to others and to self), the manic dancing and the maro-songs with their murky passages imbue the maro with something demonic. People are filled with anxiety because of raging sickness or, in the event of a maro-feast as conversion ritual, because the sphere of death is hovering them. (For a more detailed de-scription of the phenomenon of trance among the Balinese, see Belo 1960; and for a more theoretical appraisal, Van Wulften Palthe 1940.)

Some general remarks on trance phenomena in Toraja-land seem appo-site. General collapse (limpness) at the onset and end of possession do occur, as well as "violent motor agitation during the trance" (the ter-minology is from Belo 1960:66). Auto-aggression in combination with arc-en-ciel (bending over backwards) does not take place, although other forms of "attack upon the self" can be observed. Those possessed inflict wounds on themselves either by stabbing or cutting themselves with knives or swords or coming into contact with the edge of a weapon. People also walk on glowing coals and embers. The possessed do not threaten others with their weapons, however, as happens in Bali when the kris dancers attack Rangda. From information provided by the Toraja it appears they assume that deata enter into the bodies of the possessed. On the other hand, we can infer from the maro-songs that the tumbang does not relinquish her own identity.

What do the Sa'dan-Toraja think about trance? They attach a positive value to it. To their way of thinking this form of rapture has beneficial effects. The presence of too many people (Caucasians and, possibly, Christian Toraja with scorn for trances) can nullify such beneficial effects, however.[11] This is the reason that scant publicity is given to such rituals, for as soon as scepticism rears its head, the maro will not longer succeed. A few Toraja, W. Papayungan for one, have doubts about the actuality of ritual trances. He believed deception was involved. During the ma'lambang, for example, the sword would be conveniently blunt. This still does not alter the fact that, according to Van der Veen, wounds can be inflicted if the sword slips, so that the action is not without danger. Van der Veen holds the opinion that possession is not sham and that freedom from wounds should be attributed to intense auto-suggestion which might cause a constriction of the blood vessels. In bringing a sword down on an arm or leg, the actor does not suddenly hold back the blow. W. Meyer, a German physician in Ujung Pandang, maintains that the trances are real and that there is no pretense involved by the possessed.

The maro aims for a return to normalcy, it aspires to driving out evil. Daily order has been disturbed; more serious yet: the community is threatened. By organizing a major ritual one tries to restore equilibrium. Upper- and lowerworld are invoked for their assistance. The tumbang in the trance not only reaches the upperworld; she plummets, too, into deep, and dangerous whirlpools. In the gelong unnondo (the song at a maro-feast which accompanies the nondo-dance), not only are the gods of heaven, of the edge of the firmament and of diverse regions on earth invited to descend to the place of celebration by way of the blood-wort plant[12], but also the gods of the underworld (to kebali'bi)[13] (Van der Veen 1979:112-3, verses 12-18).

The maro may be a deata-feast, but nevertheless it is close to the "left" and the West, allied to death rituals and headhunting. Many maro-rites take place in the evening or at night. Rites for the gods of the Northeast are held before noon: after that time, yet before dark, the rites for the ancestors (of the Southwest). When rites are enacted in the evening or at night, they are usually to purify the atmosphere of evil, of demonic powers. The sphere of the maro itself is demonic.

Maro and headhunting are both crisis rituals: the first is an answer to a crisis caused by sickness, the second to one called forth by a violent death. Are the two rituals related? How, for example, should we explicate passages in the maro-songs which refer to headhunting?

"They (= the fingers) are reddened with human blood,
they are dyed by the heads carried in the hand by a string."
(Van der Veen 1979:98-9, verse 301)

There does indeed exist a connection between headhunting and the healing maro-ritual. For his cure, someone seriously ill drinks from a captured head. Sick children are given broth to drink in which severed heads have been boiled (see Chapter XIII.4.). Severed heads emanated power. But the various forms of the maro have more objectives than simply restoring the sick to health; they are also celebrated to ward off disaster and to purify the territory of the community, either the village or the bua'-circle. And such important rituals as the maro datu or the maro sangullelle at which the great bate, the bate manurun is set up, also serve to promote human fertility, to ask the deata to bless the "three-eared" rice and all of the ramage's possessions. Just as all other rituals, the maro implores the upperworld to bestow its blessing on the entire adat-community.

3. Bugi'

3.1. The goal of the bugi'-ritual

Like the maro, the bugi' is a ritual of exorcism that can take many forms. It is especially intended to protect the community from disaster in the guise of diseases that strike as plagues or epidemics, smallpox, for example, or blast that ravages the rice crop. One can, indeed, distinguish bugi'-rituals which are designed to prevent epidemics which affect man from those which concern the well-being of the rice. In the latter case the land (padang) must be purified (ma'bugi' padang); such a bugi' is performed before the rice cycle commences.

3.2. The term bugi'

The bugi'-ritual probably derives its name from Bugi', Buginese. According to Van der Veen the bugi'-ritual either grew out of the maro, or it came (with small pox?) from Buginese areas, Luwu' included. He witnessed a similar ritual in Luwu' during which the female leader went into a trance. The bugi' resembles the maro in so many respects that it can hardly have come into existence on its own. Bugi'-songs are patently similar to the gelong maro. In maro-songs the sick who are the subjects of the ritual, are singled out by name; the to bugi' is referred to as "the one who, possessed by a bugi'-spirit, is treated"; as to narampa bugi', "the one who, ensnared by a bugi'-demon, is possessed" (Woordenboek: v. bugi' and Van der Veen 1979:50-1). This discloses that bugi'-patients also are treated during the maro-feast. The term bugi' and balanda are used to designate that which is considered to be abnormal, extraordinary or eccentric: e.g. "bugi' angga'raka inde, balanda tang tonganra'ka?", "am I a bugi' here, one who carries on for the hell of it, someone who acts like a Dutchman?" (from a bugi'-song). A Buginese or a Dutchman in this refrain will stand for an abnormal, exotic creature (Van der Veen 1979:163). To this we might add: creatures who can bring disease with them. In this connection the To Paragusi should be cited as well, "The Portuguese", an evil spirit which is also treated with veneration at the bugi'-feast (Woordenboek: v. Paragusi; and Vol.I:126ff.).

The principal god or spirit of the bugi'-ritual is Datu Maruru' or Puang Maruru', "The Righteous Lord" or "The Just Prince", as he is called especially in Kesu' and Ma'kale. By using this title of respect people wish to honour the Spirit of Smallpox and gain his favour. Elsewhere this spirit is known as Pong Mangambo', "The Sower", a name which is perhaps based on the resemblance which smallpox has to a

crop that has been sown. He resides at the edge of heaven in a house
thatched with blood-wort leaves (Crystal and Yamashita 1982:6). For
Datu Maruru' (alias Pong Mangambo') in this context, see further Vol.I:
127 and 189ff.

Oddly enough, despite their prominence in bugi'-methology, Datu
Maruru' and To Paragusi are scarcely mentioned in the bugi'-songs,
which abound in reference to the Buginese and to Dutchmen.

Van der Veen presents an example of a bugi'-song with an introduction (1979:163-85). The song bears a certain likeness to maro-songs:
here, too, mention is made of things placed in a reversed order. The
song, however, is somewhat more placid in tone, and the tumbang's
travels are omitted. The bugi'-song closes with an image of the ideal
village: houses draped with sacral cloths and sows everywhere on the
compound, a picture of prosperity. With this ending the mood of con-
juration yields to the wishful thinking, recurrent in so many folk tales
and songs. Bugi' involves more than exorcism; like the bua' and merok
it entails prayers for general well-being and affluence.

3.3. *Differences and similarities with the maro-feast*

Whereas informants maintain that in Kesu', the bugi', unlike the maro,
can never be a conversion ritual following a burial ceremony, in Mengkendek (the puang-states) it can be (Crystal and Yamashita 1982:6).
Nonetheless, in Kesu' the bugi' may not be celebrated until all the dead
in the village (or the adat-community, bua' or penanian) have been
buried. According to them bugi' is usually concerned with the warding
off of epidemics, i.e. it is preventive rather than curative. In the bugi'
possessed celebrants appear, but no tumbang. Nor are there gellu'-
dancers to add glamour. The bate is not erected for a bugi'-feast
either, although poles of bamboo-betung are set up. These are decorated with young sugar-palm leaves, the symbol of the Eastern sphere.
These bamboos either represent the four cardinal directions, or - like
the gorang and the bala'kaan - they are a material symbol through
which man tries to maintain relations with the upperworld. At the foot
of the bamboos offerings are set out for the bugi'-spirit or bugi'-
demon. Other artefacts familiar in the maro also play a role in the
bugi': the swords, for example, which are used on the sick. Indeed
trance phenomena also occur during the bugi'-ritual and people in this
state inflict injuries on themselves (B. Sarungallo denies that this takes
place in Kesu'). This can also be done by the to ma'dampi; these medicine-men are no less central to the bugi' than to the maro. Unlike the
maro, however, we are not told that the bugi' originated in the upperworld. It is also not celebrated as any kind of preparatory purification
ritual that must precede a bua'- or merok-feast. On the whole the bugi'
is less spectacular than the maro, in good part because there are no
bate, no colourful festal clothing, and no gellu'-dancers.

3.4. *Diverse forms of the bugi'*

Just as with the maro, one can distinguish a number of ranks or orders
of bugi'-feasts. Since my informant came from Kesu' where the bugi' is
seldom celebrated, I did not acquire a clear picture of the bugi' from
what he told me. What did emerge, however, was that the ritual was
not only held to protect or cure mankind from illness (epidemics) but

also to achieve the same for rice.

1. The bugi' messun was the lowest form of the bugi' reported to me. Messun is the name of the concluding rite performed when the sick have been cured. The term is used as well for the sacrificing of a chicken (or chickens) while the rice is still growing. The sacrifice is to put an end to any sickness that might be lurking in the crop. The term messun is also used for an offering of eggs in the event of (not further specified) illnesses (Woordenboek:631). Perhaps the basic meaning of messun is "a rite to make sickness go away" (information from Van der Veen).

The actual contents of the messun celebrated when the sick have been cured, are not perfectly clear to me. For the sacrifice involved, three chickens are killed, one black and two red; rice is made ready, both cooked and uncooked. To present the offering, a group of men go to a special place outside the village, proceding in silence. The designated time is 3 in the morning. The leader is the to pabalian (= helper), a kaunan (unfree). He issues instructions and he is the only one who speaks; the others should observe strict silence. Offerings are placed at four locations (the sequence, and position in relation to the points of the compass were not divulged). At the first location the offering set down consists of a pesung of banana leaf with uncoloured, cooked rice and bits of cooked chicken from one of the two red fowl that have been slaughtered. This offering is for the deata. At another spot meat from the black chicken is set down (also on a pesung of banana leaf) for the to matua. At two places offerings for Datu Maruru' are put down. On a kandean lau (a bowl made from half a gourd) tabang-leaves are spread out and covered with uncooked rice. On five pesung of tabang-leaves raw and cooked chicken (in alternation) are laid down together with yellow-coloured cooked rice (for an explanation of the combination of raw and cooked foodstuffs, see below). During the day which follows, the to pabalian leads the men and the sick who have been cured to the top of a hill where bugi'-songs are sung and people go into a trance. Afterwards a lavish meal is enjoyed with the main course consisting of chicken with rice. (The question arises: where is the medicine-man? Is he perhaps the to pabalian?)

2. Ma'parapa' bubun ("to calm the well down, make it peaceful"), is the second order of bugi'-feast. Chickens are slaughtered, both on the compound of the sick person(s) and beside the well. Bugi'-songs are performed near the well. What else happens is not clear, which also holds true for:

3. La'pa' dena', "the freeing of the paddy bird"[14], the final rite of which takes place on a hill.

4. La'pa' bugi', "to free oneself from the bugi'-demon" is the name of the next order of bugi'-ritual. Celebrants begin by going to the river (who the celebrants are is not clear; presumably patients, the to pabalian and trance dancers). Late in the afternoon people return to the compound and fence in the ricebarn (ma'kalambu alang). Inside the fence sit a man and a woman. The to pabalian leads the ritual. Three chickens are killed. All the man and woman do is sit; they may not talk with anyone; no one may see them eating. Their food is pushed in

under the "fence". They must finish everything and afterwards shove
the plates back outside the barrier. In answer to my question about
what the couple represented, I received the answer that they were
substitutes for "the people" (= inhabitants of the village). On the
second day the la'pa' bugi' takes place on the pasa' rambu' tuka', a
terrain reserved for deata-feasts. Three chickens are slaughtered for
the offering meal. For the festal dinner, which a host of people
consume, hundreds of chickens are slaughtered and large quantities of
pokon (see Fig. 11) are prepared. Some of the chickens are cooked.
Every guest receives six pokon or twelve pokon and a small bamboo
filled with palm wine. The uncooked chickens are placed on bingka'
(winnowing fans). These bingka' are of three kinds: large, small, and
wattled ones, which have the form of a small basket (bakku').[15] The
small baskets are handed out in the following order:
1. the indo' bugi', and
2. the ambe' bugi'; the two form a couple selected from among local villagers who are "clean", that is to say, who have no outstanding sacrificial obligations to their deceased relatives. The couple is subjected to
several taboos, among which food taboos (Crystal and Yamashita 1982:
15);
3. the anak pare-pare nangka';
4. the to parengnge';
5. the family heads.
The to pabalian who arranges the ceremony receives twenty white
chickens. Afterwards the bugi'-songs begin. People go into a trance
(karondonan) and beat themselves over the head with bamboo cylinders
containing palm wine. As a conclusion to the feast, maro-songs are
sung.
    For a detailed and absorbing description of the bugi'-feast in Meng-
kendek, see Crystal and Yamashita 1982.

3.5. The deata sojourn on earth: ma'bugi' padang

The bugi'-feast which I attented in Tallunglipu (Tikala, November 2,
1966) was said to belong to the suru' padang, "the purification of the
earth", a rite that is part of the agricultural ritual celebrated to ask
for the upperworld's blessing and to pray to the ancestors for a successful rice harvest. It is also held before the planting of rice begins.
One cannot celebrate the feast, however, if any corpse is still inside a
house in the village (or the adat-community). In Tallunglipu there were
no dead to obstruct the feast, but in neighbouring Parinding the ma'batang (cf. Chapter IX.2.2.) was being enacted at roughly the same time.
This village, however, fell under Bori', a (bua'-)community bordering
on Tikala. All eleven saroan which make up Tallunglipu participated in
the ma'bugi' padang. The ritual begins with the untanan rangking, "the
planting (= setting down) of the rangking-basket". This is a loosely
plaited offering holder made from the ribs of the sugar-palm leaf. In it,
for the gods, the to minaa places meat from a small rooster.
    About two weeks later, the ma'pasa' bugi' takes place. People hold a
"market" (see above), i.e. they go to celebrate the feast on a ritual
plain. The previous day, in the afternoon, the umpakande to matua will
have taken place, a sacrifice to the ancestors. The next morning first a
rooster is slaughtered, a sella', on the compound of the tongkonan
nearest to where the feast is to be held. After the offering has been

made, people proceed to the "market" (ma'pasa' bugi'); here the to minaa presents an offering to Datu (To Mangambo'), to the to matua, and to the deata. Datu, Lord Small Pox, is a man with two sides to his character. One of his two personalities eats only raw foods, the other only cooked. For his "raw" self, pindan is prepared on a plate: bits of raw chicken from the sacrificed sella', uncooked rice that has been dyed yellow and yellow rice flour made from uncooked pulu, glutinous rice. Yellow is the colour of the gods of the upperworld, so we may conclude that the Datu belongs to this sphere. The to minaa also lets the blood of the sacrificed sella' drip onto the pindan. Then the food is packed into three small joints of bamboo, three piong. These three piong are associated with the three gods, Gauntikembong, Pong Bang-gairante and Pong Tulakpadang. The piong are not put into the fire. A coconut is also set out for Pong Mangambo'. The to minaa cuts a piece off the top of the coconut from near the three "eyes". On the top he now places a raw egg, removing a bit from its shell.

Yet Lord Small Pox does not restrict his diet to raw food. Chicken and rice are also cooked for him. This food is served on tabang-leaves. I would, however, like to ask for a bit of extra attention for the raw food that the Datu eats: in general, "raw" is associated with the sphere of the dead, with the West. Is Lord Small Pox perhaps not considered to be completely a deata of the East? It is a question that cannot be answered for sure, but certainly Lord Small Pox is not a figure who confers blessings. His honorific name, "The sower who sows the golden disease" (= smallpox) might suggest that people regard this deity who spreads death and destruction as belonging to two worlds, East and West. According to a to minaa from Kesu', the to matua and the deata also receive cooked food at the same time as the Datu but for them the offering is placed on pieces of banana leaf and not on blood-wort leaves.

The offering for the ancestors lies to the West, for the deata in the middle, and for Datu to the East. The to minaa stands with his face turned to the North as he presents the offerings. For Datu a basket of loosely woven bamboo slats with hexagonal openings (pa'kalamata) is also set down. In this basket the divinity receives a rooster as a present. Pong Mangambo' is no easy master. He is said to grow angry if everything isn't carried out just as it should be and in keeping with his wishes. The place where this phase of the ritual was observed was decorated with seven young palm branches coloured yellow which were inserted in the earth. Between these branches a maa'-cloth was stretched (to the North of where the offerings were brought). On the East side of the altar other plants had been set into the ground: blood-wort leaves, a sandalwood branch, frangrant leaves, leaves from the dirak, a tree with white, fragrant blossoms.

After the ma'pesung and mangimbo, people eat: the food consists simply of rice and chicken, for during the maro and ma'bugi only rice and chicken or rooster may be eaten. Afterwards seven men began to sing, standing at the place where the offerings had been brought. They stepped back and forth as they sang. This row of singers and dancers kept growing. Already at the sound of the first voices, a woman became possessed by the deata. With her hair trailing free she collapsed and rolled downhill. Other women helped her up but she kept collapsing time and again. The women rubbed her wrists. But as soon as she had taken a few steps like a sleepwalker, she crumpled again.

After a while this woman woke from her trance, but not for long.

People began to get hot and looked for a shadier place to go on with the feast. The men began to sing (maro), bending far over forwards and then leaning backwards. Some carried small children three or four years old on their shoulders. The woman became karondonan again. Other women grabbed her and rubbed her wrists. Meanwhile she appears to have communicated what kinds of amusements the deata who had entered into her would like to attend. If these were performed, she would come to her sense. A sword was fetched which may only be used at such feasts. The medicine-man demonstrated how sharp it was by cutting himself in the arm - no blood flowed. The woman who was possessed leaned against the blade, bending far forward, practically double, so that it seemed the to ma'dampi was cutting her in half. When she stood upright again, however, not a drop of blood was visible, not a scratch of any kind. Then the woman let her back be scored with the sword and later her calves - she suffered no wounds.

Several other people, eight in all, young and old, let themselves be stabbed in the forehead with a small, sharp knife. They stood with their heads bent forwards and the blood spattered the ground - the knife was sharp. The medicine-man applied a tabang-leaf to their wounds so that they would stop bleeding. The events described here were interspersed with a circle dance during which first maro-, then ma'gelong- and finally nondo-songs were performed. The maro-songs usually induced trance phenomena, the other songs did not. The woman whose behaviour I have described was the only one I saw who entered into a deep trance; other women were possessed to a lesser extent. According to the patients whose foreheads had been cut, the wounds eased their headaches. More and more people bared their calves to the sword, but none of them started bleeding.

Next twelve men with bare stomachs stood in a row. The medicine-man first stuck himself with the sword in the lower part of his belly, his face twitching with pain. Then he passed along the row twice, giving each man a quick cut with the sword. The younger men really felt it; their faces showed how much it hurt. One youth let himself be rolled up in a mat. Three men squatted down one behind the other. The man in front held on to the mat. Men took turns leaping over the squatting man and the one who held the mat. The whole thing reminded me of a circus act. After it ended, people resumed the circle dance, men and women, and the singing of maro- and other songs. The medicine-man also became possessed, just as a Christian who had informed me before the feast began that he didn't want anything to do with such heathen nonsense. But the feast came to an end. The deata who had descended to earth had enjoyed themselves; their visit had served its purpose and those who had fallen into a trance were feeling "better".

The to minaa sprinkled the possessed with water from a kandean lau. There were leaves from the darinding in the water, the passakke (plants which confer a blessing, which have a "cooling" effect, thus neutralizing the "hot" sphere of the trance). He also added small potsherds and three yellow beads. The trance aspect of the ritual drew to its close.

In the afternoon, on the compound nearest to the feast terrain, the ma'pabalik was held with the to minaa sacrificing a rooster. The offering was processed into three piong. And in this way the bugi'-ritual ended.

Bate manurun, the bamboo pole with old swords and cloths during the ma'pasa'-rite of the maro-feast in Kandeapi (territory of Tikala). See also pp. 134-136 and Figs. 16 and 17.
(Photo: F. v.d. Kooi, 1937.)

Bate manurun, the bamboo pole with old swords and cloths during the ma'pasa'-rite of the maro-feast in Kandeapi (territory of Tikala). See also pp. 134-136 and Figs. 16 and 17. (Photo: F. v.d. Kooi, 1937.)

Two bate manurun erected during the ma'pasa'-rite of the maro-feast in Kandeapi (territory of Tikala). See also pp. 134-136. (Photo: F. v. d. Kooi, 1937.)

The meal which follows the sacrifice on the day of the ma'pasa'-rite of the maro-feast in Kandeapi (territory of Tikala). See also p. 136. (Photo: F. v.d. Kooi, 1937.)

Dancing at the maro-feast. Gellu'-dance on the day of the ma'pasa'-rite of the maro-feast in Kandeapi (territory of Tikala). See also p. 136. (Photo: F. v.d. Kooi, 1937.)

The medicine-man cuts a woman in a trance with a sword. Bugi' padang-feast at Tallunglipu. See also pp. 142-145. (Photo: Hetty Nooy-Palm, 1966.)

The medicine-man cuts a woman in a trance with a sword. Bugi' padang-feast at Tallunglipu. See also pp. 142-145. (Photo: Hetty Nooy-Palm, 1966.)

Chapter VII

CONVERSION RITUALS

"South he stands, a coconut palm,
A sugar palm, high over all.
Then westward does he pass from view,
He goes down where the sun descends.
There shall he to the heaven rise,
There in the all-enfolding dwell.
A deity shall there become,
The all-enfolding he shall be."

(The Chant:46)

1. Introduction

The term "conversion ritual" has a rather odd ring to it, yet I thought it best to abide by Toraja usage. Conversion ritual is the translation of pembalikan (actually aluk pembalikan, derived from ma'balik, to convert). In the interest of brevity the ritual is usually designated by the single word pembalikan.

During death feasts celebrants direct their prayers and sacrificial rites to the ancestors of the Southwest. In the conversion rituals which follow, offerings are no longer placed in this direction, but in the Northeast, the sphere of the deata. This is true also for the offerings presented to the deceased. As a basis for orientation, as central point, the tongkonan serves. The change of direction involved in a conversion ritual is expressed in the term pembalikan pesungna, "the offering meal is turned around". This implies that the deceased is conveyed from the sphere of death, the dangerous sphere which is considered polluted, to the sphere of life, the sphere of the East. Gods and ancestors are complementary powers. Both categories influence life on earth. Through the care of his descendants, the deceased, above all if he is of noble birth, is able to achieve a higher status, that of deata (Woordenboek:509, dibalikan pesungna; The Chant:6). The dead becomes a divinity able to pour out his blessings upon his offspring, a to mebali puang, someone who has become a lord in the upperworld. This holds true for the higher forms of burial. Yet a conversion ritual also takes place after lower death rituals. Underlying the conversion appended to all death rituals, even those of lower rank, is possibly the apprehension that otherwise the spirits of the dead would continue to stir about in the vicinity of the village. The village territory would remain impure and no other feast could subsequently be celebrated. Spirits aside, one can regard the conversion ritual as the expression of a wish to restore normal relations with the gods of the upperworld.

2. Different orders of conversion rituals

Among death rituals there is a hierarchy which is a function of the importance of the person who has died. This ranking order has been set out in Chapter I. The same order will be adhered to in describing death rituals in Chapter IX. It would seem unnecessary to repeat it here, for it is available for convenient reference.

2.1. Babo bo'bo', the conversion ritual after the dikaletekan tallu manuk

Dikaletekan tallu manuk is the death ritual for stillborn infants (cf. the Chapters I and IX). Babo bo'bo, the top layer of boiled rice, is usually not entirely cooked. It is not certain what actually occurs, whether such rice is prepared as an offering or that the term is merely a reference to the fact that the ritual concerns the burial of a stillborn child, a being who has not been able to attain adulthood (figuratively, a being not "cooked until done").

2.2. Piong sanglampa and pesung sangdaun, the conversion ritual after the disilli'

Sanglampa, one bamboo joint, is filled with rice and meat and prepared piong-style. A portion of the food from this piong (the rest is consumed) is placed on one small piece (sangdaun) of banana leaf as an offering (pesung). This is set out for the deata. Piong sanglampa and pesung sangdaun are always talked about in a single breath as the simplest form of offering.

2.3. Manglika' biang, the intertwining of the biang-reed, the conversion ritual after the didedekan pangkung bai and the bai tungga'

This, too, is one of the simple conversion rituals. It can also serve as pembalikan for the dikaletekan tallu manuk and disilli', but it is prescribed as conversion ritual for the didedekan pangkung bai and the bai tungga (see also Chapters I and IX). This biang is set up to the Northeast of the house. For the accompanying prayer see Merok:158, and Van der Veen, unpublished a.

2.4. Ma'tadoran manuk, the conversion ritual after the bai a'pa'

The tadoran is erected to the Northeast of the house. The name manuk indicates that a chicken is sacrificed.

2.5. Ma'tadoran bai, the conversion ritual after the sangbongi

This rite is the same as the ma'tadoran manuk except that a pig instead of a chicken is sacrificed. Some meat from the pig is put in a basket as part of the tadoran.

2.6. Ma'palangngan para, the conversion ritual after the tallung bongi

A sacrifice is made to the gods of the Northeast. A pig is slaughtered. Pieces of its meat are placed on the para (Woordenboek: v. para). According to Van der Veen another term for this ritual is ma'parekke

para. Rekke means northern; in this context a reference to the front of
the house.

Finally, B. Sarungallo maintains that the ma'tete ao' can also serve as
conversion ritual for the tallung bongi.

2.7. Manganta', the conversion ritual after several higher rituals

The manganta' is an extensive ritual. Manganta' means "accompanying".
Thus the panganta', the textiles and other accessories hung up in the
central room of a house of mourning during the ma'doya (the vigil
beside the dead) are called "escorts". Such cloths also have a role to
play in the manganta'. Death rituals for which the manganta' is the indicated pembalikan include the dipalimang bongi, dipapitung bongi, and
dirapa'i dilayu-layu. The name massura' tallang may be substituted for
manganta' as emerges from the description of this ritual in the village
of Tonga which follows below.

2.7.1. Celebration of the manganta'-ritual in Tonga, Kesu' (October 17, 1966)

The tongkonan Dado' Pong was the centre of this ceremony. For the
celebration of this ritual, the ramage of the deceased must ask the
permission of the government (the head of the district) and of the
sokkong bayu. Both the civil executive and the traditional adat leader
must concur. On the preceding day (October 16) the umpakande to
matua, an offering to the ancestors, was held. As a rule on such an
occasion a black chicken is slaughtered, but this time a small pig had
been killed. As an altar, a small mat of loosely woven bamboo did
service. It was roughly 20 cm² and rested on four bamboo struts each
of which was some 30 cm high. These vertical bamboos were filled with
tuak and the upper end was decorated with incisions. People also drink
their palm wine from bamboo cylinders but these are not decorated like
those for the gods. The altar is called palanduan-duan, and it is set up
on the West side of the tongkonan, the side of the "descending smoke",
rambu solo'. Literally palanduan-duan means: "that which resembles the
rack above the hearth, the place for firewood". More or less above the
shrine, under the eaves of the roof, there hung a calabash with palm
wine and a folded banana leaf containing rice, food from a bamboo
(piong) and betel.

On October 17 everything was in readiness for the manganta'. Mats
were spread out on the floor of the ricebarn. In three places on the
compound palm branches had been stood in the earth with their tops
bent towards each other so that those attending the feast had a shady
retreat where they could sit. At a spot also cast in shadow by palm
branches, Northeast of the tongkonan, the ceremony would take place.
Fig. 18 helps locate various objects used in the conversion ritual. The
pentingaran, a shrine consisting of four bamboo struts, was approximately 60 cm high. A pattern was cut into the top of each strut; this
gives the manganta' its other name, massura' tallang. Massura' tallang is
a cryptic expression for enacting a sacrifice to the gods on an altar of
bamboo (tallang) which has figures carved into its stiles (sura'). For
an illustration of this structure see J. Kruyt 1921:166, fig. 7. Leaning
against the struts on the front side of the altar are two smaller bamboos; one contains palm wine, the other water (see Fig. 19). The tuak
is for the deata to drink, the water is for them to wash their hands. In

Fig. 18. Ground-plan of tongkonan and compound during the manganta' celebrated in Kesu'.

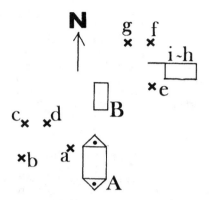

A   tongkonan Dado' Pong
B   ricebarn, place for the most eminent guests, men only
a   place for the umpakande to matua
b, c, d   places for other guests, men and women, in the shade of palm branches arched towards each other
e   site where the manganta' is observed under a canopy of palm branches
f   tadoran
g   place of the ma'lika' biang
h   place for pentingaran, see Fig. 19
i   the panganta', textiles hanging over a pole

the larger bamboo uprights there is also tuak. The gods apparently are every bit as thirsty as man. Thus the pentingaran closely resembles the palanduan-duan (see above) but the former has two floors of flattened bamboo slats and the latter only one. Moreover, the two shrines are set up at different locations in relation to the house. Pentingaran is literally the place where one looks upwards (metingara: to look upwards). On three sides the pentingaran was surrounded by a red cloth; young, green tabang-leaves (the leaves of these Dracaena terminalis are as a rule red) stuck up out of the tops of the bamboo uprights.

Five pigs were carried to the spot, each hanging by trussed feet from a bamboo pole. Their crying was dreadful. Before they were slaughtered, they were consecrated (disuru'). As Van der Veen has remarked, someone else attends to this consecration, not the to minaa who recites the prayer. During the act a sirih-leaf, a pinang-nut and a bit of lime are placed on the pig. The slaughter, singing of the hair and butchery of the meat are accomplished quickly and with skill.

Meanwhile palm wine had been brought in large bamboo containers. More and more guests arrived, and the space reserved for them became more and more crowded. The company was amiable. One had to be a bit patient, however, about eating. First the gods had to be fed: the to

Fig. 19. Pentingaran set up for the massura' tallang.

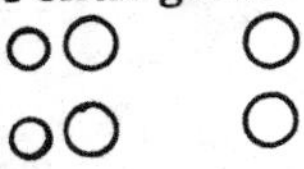

○ smaller bamboo joint, or suke
○ larger bamboo joint

There are two suke and four larger bamboo joints. The suke are fastened to the two larger front stiles. One of them is filled with water, the other with palm wine. One of the larger bamboo joints (tallang) also contains palm wine. The three remaining larger bamboo joints are filled with an infusion of darinding- and passakke-leaves. For these leaves, which confer blessings, see Vol.I:229.

minaa would utter the prayer. The rice was being cooked all this time and the meat of the pig prepared in piong. The offering couldn't be delayed too long, for although offerings to the ancestors should take place in the late afternoon when the sun is already drawing near the West, the gods receive their food earlier in the day. It was about noon when the gods were presented with their allotment of rice and pork served on a banana leaf. A serving was placed on both levels of the pentingaran. People told me that the offering on the upper level was for Puang Matua, that on the lower one for the deata.[1] From the pig, the gods receive a bit of the liver, the kidneys, the tail, the breast bone, the upper part of the neck and the kalumpani' (the lean meat in front of the rear legs). They also are given a small amount of fat. Only the first of the five pigs slaughtered was used sacrificially. After this ma'pesung, the to minaa uttered his prayer which I recorded. Unfortunately, the tape later turned out to be a failure. It was not the priest's fault. He wasn't in the least perturbed by the tape recorder, and held the microphone to his lips as if it was a daily habit. He was prompted - as usually is true - by another to minaa who sat on the ground. While singing the litany, a priest keeps his face constantly turned to the East, to the direction of the rising sun and of the gods.

After the gods had been honoured and fed, guests could satisfy themselves. There was laughter on all sides, conversation, conviviality; palm wine poured freely and it was easy to notice that people felt at ease. After the meal the meat was divided. There was first a public sale of meat, the proceeds from which would go to support a good cause; this custom, popular since World War II, is practised commonly nowadays throughout Indonesia at major feasts. The division of the meat at the manganta' will be discussed below. The enthusiastic and lively manner in which the meat is divided contrasts to the solemn mood during the prayer (mangimbo). For a small black dog that kept snatching tasty morsels of pork, it was also a good day.

The red cloths, the sirih-pouch and other artefacts draped over the shrine during the manganta' or massura' tallang possibly symbolize the deceased. The fact that the pentingaran is set up to the Northeast of the house and that the ritual is held at this spot indicate that now the deceased is considered one of the deata. During the death ritual the pole hung with cloths is suspended above the corpse itself. During the manganta'-ritual the bamboo instead runs East-West which symbolizes the new status of the deceased; he has acquired the status of a deata.

It is possible that the name manganta', "accompanying", expresses how the ritual escorts the dead person from the sphere of death to the sphere of the gods.[2]

Distribution of the meat is an event in which everyone is interested (see Fig. 20). First portions of cooked meat are set on a dulang (dish on a pedestal) for various functionaries:

1. the sokkong bayu, who functions as to mangimbo. At this ritual the to minaa recited the prayer and was rewarded with a portion of the meat;
2. the datu baine, who functions as to ma'sanduk;
3. the to mantobok, the one who stabs the pig to death, a function formerly fulfilled by a slave;
4. a petulak, an "assistant" or helper, someone who aids the first three functionaris.

The tongkonan to which these four functionaries belong are, respectively, Sallebayu, Aya', Tonga and Sangkombong (in the village of Tonga).

Fig. 20. The division of meat on the day of the manganta' in the village of Tonga, Kesu' (October 17, 1966).

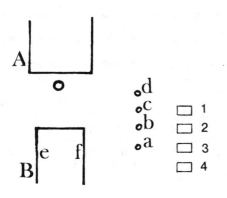

A   tongkonan
B   ricebarn
e   seat for the sokkong bayu
f   seat for the datu baine
a-d portions of meat and rice
     set out on the dulang
1-24 portions of meat and rice
     set down on banana leaves
o   place where the small pig is
     slaughtered for the umpa-
     kande to matua

It is not clear for whom the three extra pesung (25-27) are intended.

The four portions on banana leaves to the West of the dulang are also for the to parengnge'. The 24 pesung placed to the North of the dulang are allotted to all to parengnge', to tongkonan Kesu' and to members of the ramage which has organized the manganta'.

In the meantime the four remaining pigs have been parcelled out. The raw meat (with the raw meat remaining from the first pig) is divided as follows (the names of the recipients are called aloud in succession):

1. to indo' .. (followed by their personal names) - four priests in all (at the present ritual one position was vacant);

2. matua ulu[3] - there were two of these functionaries, one of whom, the to massanduk was assisted in his duties by the to pabalian, the to ma'nasu pesung (both kaunan) and the to sipalakuan, a member of the ramage giving the feast;

3. to minaa - four in number, the first of whom was the priest who officiated at the manganta';

4a. members of tongkonan Kesu', the mother-tongkonan of the district;

4b. the camat (the district head) - in the past one of the parengnge' of the district held this function and received this share; today the camat comes from elsewhere. Although he does not live in Tonga, he is still called parengnge'[4];

4c. the kepala desa, the village head;

4d. the juru tulis of the kecamatan, the clerk in the district office; not a resident of Tonga;

4e. the juru tulis of the kampung, the clerk in the village head's office;

5a. prominent villagers; these are members of the tongkonan Sallebayu, Aya, Tonga and Sangkombong;

5b. the local population, i.e. heads of families.

Those who have contributed a pig as a rule receive half of it back again (ikko'na: that part of a pig which after slaughter is returned to the one who raised the pig or the owner; the word literally means: the tail of the animal, but in this instance it extends as far as half-way along the body and includes the hindquarters). When a pig is sold, the ikko'na also reverts to the owner or to the one who raised the pig.

With the distribution of meat, the ritual ended.

2.8. Mangrara pare, a conversion ritual after the highest death rituals

The mangrara pare ("the sprinkling of the rice with blood") is the conversion ritual which is held combined with the dirapa'i rapasan sundun and dirapa'i sapu randanan death feasts. The central locations of the celebration are the sawahs and the drying place for the rice of someone who died some years previously and for whom one of the dirapa'i-rituals was enacted. Also during the mangrara pare offerings for the deceased are no longer placed in the Southwest, the direction of the ancestors (nene', to matua), but in the Northeast, the direction of the deata. This is referred to as "the turning around (conversion) of the pesung". In the prayer which has been reproduced in full at the end of this chapter, mention is made of a shrine of Puang Matua, one used in the spheres of the North and the East, the shrine (surasan tallang) consisting of four upright struts, decorated with carvings, and two floors of bamboo (see verses 32 and 39 of the Pangimbo mangrara pare). Surasan tallang is at once the name for the altar and for the offering placed on it. In fact it is the same shrine discussed in section

2.7. above.

B. Sarungallo explained to me that the mangrara pare consists of the following six components:
1. ma'kambunoi;
2. mangrakan;
3. ma'billa'i;
4. mamunu';
5. ma'pakande to matua;
6. allona:
    a. untanan poya-poya,
    b. untanan kalumbassik,
    c. ma'ke'te,
    d. ma'pesung pokon,
    e. umbaa puaro.

Numbers 2 and 3 of these rites are also part of the annual rice ritual. In that context they were discussed in Chapter IV. My informant described the successive components of the mangrara pare in brief as follows:

1. The to indo' brings an offering on the Northeast edge of the sawah dike. The name of the rite derives from kambuno, the fan-palm (Livistona rotundifolia): a branch from this palm tree is planted at the site of the offering. A pig and a chicken are sacrificed. A dog is killed as well, but its meat is not part of the offering. The dog is eaten by slaves. The blood of the sacrificial animals is sprinkled over the rice (The Chant:8). The paddy is still young. The major part of the ensuing rites takes place after harvest, so that between this and the following component of the ritual some months elapse.

2. The first bunches of paddy are reaped; a chicken and a dog are killed. The offering occurs at the sawah. Mangrakan means: stewing fruits that are not yet entirely ripe, e.g. immature rice in the ear. Van der Veen reports that first an offering is made at the sawah and then two or four bunches of rice are cut off; these are bound together with stalks of the danga-danga (a kind of gladiolus) and placed in the lantang bunu', a special hut which is built on the drying place of the rice, the pangrampa'. The next day an offering takes place beside the lantang bunu'. When the rice is brought to storage, the two or four ritually cut and bound bunches are the first to be placed in the ricebarn. They are set down in a corner by a daughter, granddaughter or sister of the deceased. These bunches may not be eaten, for they protect the rice in the barn. The two or four bunches may be regarded as a "rice mother".

3. From the earliest bunches of rice which are harvested an offering is made, the ma'billa'i, which takes place in the house. Then people are free to continue with the harvest. During the ma'billa'i three grains of rice are wrapped in the leaf of a kind of taro, together with a sharp chip of bamboo (= billa') and buried beneath the stone rice mortar. A pig is sacrificed on this occasion. The to ma'pesung pokon (see Chapter IV) remains behind on the pangrampa', the drying place for the rice, in the lantang bunu'. She has a special task in this ritual. She is also the to ma'nasu pesung during the merok-feast. The name to ma'pesung pokon comes from pokon (see Fig. 11). As long as the rice is still standing in the field this woman may not eat anything that comes from a death feast. Once the festivities end, she loses her title.

4. Mamunu': the binding of harvested ears of rice into bunches using a

band that has been stripped from bamboo. A chicken and pig are sacrificed on the sawah dike. The offering is placed on a banana leaf. The
text of this rite was not recorded.
5. The ma'pakande to matua follows customary procedures for sacrificing
a pig to the ancestors, the to matua.
6. Allona: the word is an indication that this is the "big day" of the
ritual.
a. Untanan poya-poya: here the central ceremony takes place. Two pigs
are sacrificed. Guests arrive, family members and villagers. Around the
sawah which is the centre of the rite, poya-poya are set up, young
sugar-palm leaves arranged in the form of a noose.[5] This is a sign that
a feast is being held (B. Sarungallo).
b. Untanan kalumbassik. The sawah is surrounded with bamboo arches,
kalumbassik, which probably serve as a sign to demarcate the sawah as
a consecrated location.
c. Ma'ke'te. For the ma'ke'te ("the rice cutting") twenty to thirty
people go to the sawah to cut rice and, singing, each returns with five
to ten bunches of rice.
d. Ma'pesung pokon. The to ma'pesung pokon fills a basket with objects
including a bottle made from a calabash, a passakke and a rabana (?).
In her hand she holds a piong which she uses as a staff. She walks at
the head of the group cutting the rice. Using the leaves of the plant
which confers a blessing for a sprinkler, she sprinkles the bunches of
rice with water from the calabash and then returns to her hut. Tagari
is burned so that the bunches (of rice?) are, as it were, adulated with
incense. In the meantime the to indo' has prepared the pesung and
performed the mangimbo. Other to indo' (rice priests) at this feast
include one who enacts the massanduk, another who acts as mantobok,
and the to pabalian, their helper. The rite is staged on the pangrampa', the drying place of the rice.
e. Umbaa puaro. Puaro is a brazier made from a cooking pot from which
the top has been hacked off. With this brazier the to ma'pesung pokon
walks around the sawah. Later the puaro is brought into the lantang
bunu', the hut on the drying place of the rice. In the puaro twigs from
the cemara are burned.

The feast which has been sketched here bears witness to a close connection between the deceased of high standing and the rice. Even
before the mangrara pare has been brought to completion, the dead man
can exercise his influence on the growth of the crop. He will be
consulted during the cultivation of rice. This role is depicted in the
fragment of the following death song:

> "He to the firmament shall rise
> Ascend to the all-enfolding.
> There he a deity shall be
> The all-enfolding shall become.
> We look for him to sow the rice
> When time it is to strew the seed.
> He shall the Pleiades become
> Become a yellow shining star
> There at the far rim of the sky
> There, at the zenith shall be changed."
>   (The Chant:71)

2.8.1. The prayer pronounced during the mangrara pare
The ripening of the crop is promoted by "the sprinkling of the rice
with blood". At the end of the feast, the rice is harvested and the
death ritual is conclusively "converted".
In contrast to the merok which is rather a feast for the entire rapu,
the mangrara pare is only attended by the immediate family of the deceased. The to minaa delivers the prayer which follows below. The
reader will not fail to notice that the deceased is not mentioned in this
offering prayer. It is rather a eulogy describing the deeds of Puang
Matua which includes a prayer for wealth in terms of buffaloes, children
and other possessions. The recording of the Toraja text and the original Dutch translation are both the work of Van der Veen. The prayer
is printed here in its entirety, for it has never been published before.

Pangimbo Mangrara Pare	The Prayer at the Sprinkling of the Rice with Blood
Inde dao, Puang Matua!	Him there on high, Puang Matua!
La kubungka' ba'ba manikna,	Let me throw open his door of bead-work,
la kukillang pentiroan bulaanna.	let me lift his golden window.
Iamo mamma' lan bilikna,	He who sleeps in his room,
matindo lan sondong bulaanna.	who slumbers in his golden chamber.
La kueranni surasan tallang,	Let me use as a ladder unto Him the offering on a shrine with incised figures,
kupelalanni karidisan pandung balo.	Let me use as a ladder unto Him the ribs of the sugar palm wrapped in kapok and smeared with blood.
Tongkon lan to' tabang tua,	He sits enthroned in the place of the ancient blood-wort[6],
dao to' kaluku siayun.	there above where the cononut palms sway to one another.
Umpate'dang sauan sibarrung, po'poran siayoka.	He established the double bellows, the ovens joined as if in a yoke.
Nanii tumampa tau, rumende to lino.	In them he created a man, he poured out the inhabitant of earth.
Tumampa nene'na pare, nene'na bai, nene'na tedong, manuk, nene'na bassi.	He created the first rice plant, the ancestor of the pigs, the forefather of the buffalo, the chicken, the first iron.
Nene'na kapa', nene'na ipo,	The first cotton plant, the first plant poison,

tangkean suru', nene'na uai,
nene'na api.

the procedures for sacrifice, the
first water, the first fire.

Sanda naborong-boronganni,
liling kanan lan ba'tangna
langi'.

He ordered everything in divisions,
in the middle of the heavens encircling it from the right.

Tamben simairi'omoko,

anggenna deata lan ba'tangna
langi',
lan ma'gulung-gulunganna to'
paonganan.

Form now one group among yourselves,
all you gods in the centre of the
skies,
in the sublimity of that which covers
the universe.

Deata karua lan rampe matallona
langi',
sanda karua daa ulunna langi'.

The eight gods on the East of the
firmament,
the plenary eight there in the North
of the firmament.

Sanda karua dio rampe matampu'na
langi',
sanda karua lo' pollo'na langi',

sanda karua lan tangngana langi'.

The plenary eight on the West of the
firmament,
the plenary eight yonder in the
South of the firmament,
the plenary eight in the middle of
the firmament.

Duang papa'na langi' dao,

tallu kasitodoranna.

The second layer of the firmament on
high,
the three layers on top of each
other.

Annanna dao, pitunna,
ma'lolosu langanna.

The sixth on high, the seventh,
forming the top, reaching upwards.

Ma'tampak daoanna,
ma'papa' merangna dao,
ungkambi' lindo masakke.

At the zenith of that which is high,
in the layer like honey on high[7]
having a benevolent countenance.

Sirodo tinting lan ba'tangna
langi',
tiemban payo-payomoko lan ba'-
tangna langi'.

Moving back and forward like a line
in the middle of the firmament,
rocking to and fro like a scarecrow
in the middle of the firmament.

Garagako sangke'deran,

tampako sanguangkaran.

Go, prepare for a collective leave
taking,
prepare for a common departure.

Pamanda'ko sape rundunmu,
paturukko lamba' beluakmu.

Bind the locks of your hair,
bend the hair on your head downwards.[8]

Pokinalloko sumpu memba'ka',

sumpu buntangan,

Take as provisions everything that
multiplies most,
that which is full to the very brim,

lo'dok kano-kano.

springing up like bits of sediment in the palm wine.[9]

Nakorok londong Puang Matua,

Puang Matua calls them, like a rooster collects the hens with his crowing,

natitian bayan To Kaubanan.

To Kaubanan summons them, like a parakeet releases its call.

Iamo umpasisuka' allo bongi,

He who determined the mutual measure of day and night,

umpasisangkararoan masiang malillin.

He who measured the dimensions of the light and dark as if with the shell of a coconut.

Lumepong bulan, tumari' allo,

He cut the moon like a circle,
He shaped the sun like a disc,

Undandan bintoen tasak,
umpa'turruk asi-asi malillin.

He placed the stars in rows,
He made the lights of darkness in multitudes.

Umpandan Lemba bulaan,

He made the Ursa Mayor lie down at full length,

ussedan londongna Lapandek,

He suspended the Cock of Lapandek (in the firmament),

manukna Pong Tulangdidi'.

the Chicken of Pong Tulangdidi'.

Umpatongkon Ma'dika,

He arranged the constellation Ma'dika,

umpaesung Lake tau,

He put down the constellation Lake tau,

umpatibian kila', rumende galugu.

He made the lightning flash, He moulded the thunder.

Nasonglo' uran dilangi',
nalao tana'tak didewata.

And so the rain fell from heaven,
so it came pouring down from the divine sphere.[10]

Susu mammi'na pare,
panoran kasallena tallu bulinna.

The sumptuous breast for the rice,
the vast udders for the three-ears.

Bungka'ko ba'ba manikmu,
Puang Matua,
bongsorangko eran bulaanmu.

You, open your door of beadwork,
Puang Matua,
lower your golden ladder.

Umpolalan malengko lentong,
umpolambanan ma'tundoran to mamaa.

Going along the twisted stiles,
crossing the place where the bearers are drawn up in rows.

Patirandukki indete padang tuo balo',
lipu tumbo kumuku'.

Let it then please you to start at the level of the earth, rich in blessings,
the place of the flourishing life.

Tirandukkiko te surasan tallang,

PLease, make a beginning beside this

karidisan pandung balo.

shrine with incised figures,
the ribs of the sugar palm wrapped
with kapok and smeared with blood.

Tundanko sangdeatammu lan kapa-
danganan
mutongkon dao te surasan tallang.

Awake all your fellow gods in
regions roundabout,
alight on this shrine with incised
figures.

Membanoko sarinna kanan,

ma'kaseroangko matanna kalimbuang.

Wash yourself with the cream of the
water that bubbles up out of the
earth,
purify yourself with that which
streams from the well.

Kumandemoko sanda mammi'na,

tumimbu'moko sanda marasa.

Eat then from all that is
sumptuous,
consume then all that is tasty.

Diongmo duku'na bai la mukande
tang sikundun,
sitondon burana tetean tampo

la mutimbu' tang sikalubamban.

Under here lies the meat of the pig,
savour it,
together with the harvest of the
walking of the sawah dike,
enjoy it without any hindrance.

Mangiru'-iru'ko tuak tang
lelangan,
pangrambinna to melo aluk,

pangdedekna to maballo bisara.

Drink time and again of the palm
wine in which no lizard lurks,
which is tapped from the sugar
palm of those who pay heed to the
proper adat,
which is beaten from those whose
adat ceremonies follow the true
order.

Pangnganmoko kalosi ponno
issinna,
bolu tang silenda ura'na,

kapu' ma'lumpa bumbungan.

Chew then the areca nut, full of
contents,
the betel, whose veins do not miss
each other,
lime, white as the foam of bubbling
milk.

La lumokkonmiraka lalanmu,

la tumetemiraka ta'gulingammo,
To Kaubanan?

Will you on your return follow the
same way,
will you also tred the path on the
way back that you took coming here,
To Kaubanan?

La mupakkanpa te surasan tallang
keampo, keanak,

mana' marapuan, mendaun sugi',

Requite then this offering on the
shrine with incised figures so that
we acquire grandchildren and
children,
numerous offspring from generation
to generation, a wealth of possessions countless as the leaves,

tumangke ianan, matua induk,
banu' karurungan.

that we may hold wealth in our
hands, and grow as old as the sugar
palm, long-lasting as the hard pith
of the sugar palm.

La kikandemo sesa dia'mu,

la kitimbu'mo ra'dak barokomu.

Let us now consume that which You
after satiation have left over,
let us now enjoy that which your
throat has left remaining.

La kipopali' manuk,

kiposissik tanda masiang.

Let it be for us like the intact scale
of a chicken, an omen of good
fortune,
let it be for us like a scale that
presages well.[11]

Kisanda ma'tali ulang,

pantan ma'ponto kale'ke'.

May we together wear a rope as a
bandeau,
each of us wear for an armband
a ring which once pierced the nose
of a buffalo.

Kamasakkean diparandanna,

rupanna tanda marendeng dipa-
sanda biringna.

May that which awaits us be fortunate,
may that which is destined on all
sides be every variety of the good.

Tongkonan Buntu Kalando, Sangalla'.
The tongkonan is the centre of all major rituals, thereby serving as a
link between the rituals of the East and West. See also Table 4, p. 322.
(Photo: Hetty Nooy-Palm, 1970.)

PART II
THE RITUALS OF THE WEST

Tau-tau, a nearly life-size effigy, representing a member of
the puang family. See also p. 301.
(Photo: Hetty Nooy-Palm, 1972.)

Chapter VIII

DEATH RITUALS:
INTRODUCTION AND GENERAL REVIEW

"We are as the phantoms of this world,
the apparitions of this region,
as the wind that blows along the house."

(Woordenboek:34)

1. Introduction

It is natural for man to puzzle over life and death. The Sa'dan-Toraja are no exception. Yet I am unaware of even a single myth which explains how mankind became mortal. A legend reported in brief by A.C. Kruyt merely describes the entrance into the world of the first death priest (see Vol.I:280). Death apparently is accepted as inescapable. This is even true in myths dealing with the problem of death, such as the tale of Lakipadada who in search of Tang Mate (= Not Death, Immortality) fails at the last moment (cf. Vol.I:149, Nobele 1926:121-7, and Tandilangi' 1967:23-33).

Toraja poetry expresses how ephemeral life is. Death and life are intertwined. Through ritual, prescribed by the ancestors and observed by the living, eminent dead attain the place they deserve in the hereafter. From there they can exercise a benevolent influence over their offspring (The Chant:9-10). Their care extends to man's primary food, the rice. Aluk to mate, the death ritual, accordingly is a focal point of Toraja culture. In Van der Veen's Woordenboek, the entry concerning ritual burial, some two and a half pages long, is a dense summary of relevant rites and functionaries. Of all major rituals, the death ritual offers the most resistance to the incursions of modern times. It is celebrated by Christians, too, although in modified form.

In connection with the diverse aspects of death rituals which also have their commercial side, the Reformed Mission League of the Netherlands Reformed Church has assumed a cautious stance in relation to their celebration ever since the early days of the League's activities. The now independent Toraja Church has continued to exercise similar prudence. Mission and church have confined themselves to providing certain guidelines to Christian Toraja with regard to burial procedures. Many pigs and buffaloes are frequently slaughtered during Christian funerals, too, in keeping with prevailing ideas concerning status and reciprocity. The Church has raised no objections to such practices worth mentioning, even though from time to time complaints resound against the costs which such exhibition of status entails. The corpses of Christians are also laid to rest in cliff-graves, just as happened with most of the dead in the past. Yet the core of the traditional mortuary ritual, the sacrifices to the gods and to the soul of the deceased, has been eliminated. This clarifies the Church's resistance to the making of a tau-tau, the effigy which represents the deceased. It is the soul's place of residence, the recipient of offerings. Nevertheless at Christian funerals tau-tau may still be encountered. Family members of the deceased argue that such an effigy is no more than an image of the dead, comparable to a portrait. In 1983 a serious conflict developed between Toraja Church leaders and rich Toraja Christians. These rich believers would not renounce the tau-tau as part of funeral rites. They argued emphatically that the mortuary effigies did not contain a soul. Instead the effigy was a status symbol and it was the "communists", they maintained, who wished to deprive them of this symbol. Yet as far as I can tell, the tau-tau is more than a mere portrait: it is also called bombo dikita, the soul of the dead (bombo) in visible form. From a Christian viewpoint, the Church's objections against the tau-tau are comprehensible. (See Koubi's statement: "En conclusion, pour les Toradja du Sud, l'effigie, qu'elle soit éphèmère ou durable, a un statut particulier: elle est bien plus qu'un objet rituel associé à la mort d'un noble, elle est, sinon le défunt, du moins son 'double visible', aussi, comme le mort fait-elle l'objet d'un culte: elle est parée, veillée, entourée, pleurée et transportée." (Koubi 1979:170). Concerning the tau-tau's soul, see Volkman 1979a:28.)

In the account which follows I deal only with the death ritual as observed for persons who during their lifetime were adherents of traditional religion.[1]

The basic elements of the death ritual are identical for all classes: the wrapping of the corpse, followed by lamentation, the death song and the slaughter of sacrificial animals. Ultimately entombment in a rock grave follows, i.e. in a cave consisting of one or more burial chambers which have been hewn out of the face of a cliff or from one of the massive boulders found in the plains. In some districts, however, in Sa'dan, for example, customary practice is to bury the dead in the earth. A small house is then erected on top of this grave. Certain components of the ritual vary in diverse regions of Tana Toraja. For adults, moreover, the ritual is different than for (small) children; for eminent persons it is more extensive than for common folk.

In a lecture delivered to the Ethnologenkring in 1948, Van Wouden pointed out that the death ritual as enacted in the three southern districts (Ma'kale, Sangalla' and Mengkendek) differed from that observed in more northern districts. The well-known great "death feast"[2] in the southern districts has evolved from a celebration for the entire community into one for separate family groups and has thus acquired a different character. There are only a few districts nowadays, those on the slopes of Mount Sesean, in Baruppu', and in Pangala' in the extreme north of Tana Toraja, where the second great death feast is celebrated annually by the whole community to honour all those who have died during the preceding year; in other places the second feast for each deceased is observed individually, at a time deemed appropriate by the family group concerned. Of course, one might object that it is often difficult to distinguish family group and community at large, but the objection does not alter the fact that there is a difference between the two and that is a real one. More contestable is Van Wouden's thesis that the privatization of the second death feast in the southern districts must be attributed to Buginese influence in these parts. In the first place, we find this same development also else-

where, for example, in Kesu', Tikala and Buntao', and in the second
place, the reference to the Buginese overlooks the fundamental fact that
in language and culture the Sa'dan-Toraja are closely related to the
Buginese, far more closely than they are to the Bare'e-Toraja.

This last observation, however, does not preclude occasional similarities between the Sa'dan and the Bare'e. Among the To Baruppu' ("the
people from Baruppu'")[3] and in Pangala', for example, there is a phase
of the death ritual which bears a strong resemblance to the second
burial carried out by the Bare'e-Toraja after the bones of the deceased
have been exhumed and cleaned. This, however, is not specifically a
Bare'e practice. It recurs as well in the tiwah of the Ngaju (see Stöhr
1965:31ff.) and in the ijambe of the Maäyan-Siung-Dayak who also lay
all their dead to rest at the same time during a general death ritual. As
among the Maäyan-Siung, the bones of To Baruppu' corpses are also
subjected to collective cleansing at an appointed time; for this purpose
they are dug up from their respective graves. I have been told this
practice is now a thing of the past, however, for the entire Baruppu'
population has converted to Christianity. In Pangala', on the other
hand, the digging up of corpses to rewrap them is still current practice
– as revealed in a film shot sometime around 1970. The remains of the
dead, packed in cloths and plastic sheeting were stripped by family
members and then wrapped again. Thereupon the remains were placed
in small, trough-shaped wooden boxes. (This film is in the archives of
the Ethnographical Museum Nusantara in Delft.) We mention this because
there is an unmistakable parallel between this second purification of
bodily remains and the renewal at set times of the apparel of the tau-
tau, the doll which represents the deceased (see the Chapters X.5.2.,
XI.1.3. and XII.2.).

After this brief detour to consider less common forms of death
rituals, it is advisable to return for a moment to the reported tendency
towards privatization of death rites. It is not confined to princely
funerals, but can also be noticed in districts without princes.

It appears this tendency might be connected with the trend towards a
"personality cult" evinced in the custom of massinggi' during such celebrations as a bua'-feast. A parallel can be observed during death
rituals when the to minaa honours the life and work of the deceased in
an eloquent laudation, and in the badong, the death chants glorifying
the dead person (cf. The Chant, songs IA through IID). The assumption seems obvious that increasing prosperity has created enhanced possibilities for ostentatious glorification of individuals, and through these
individuals of the luster of their families. Emphasis on the glory of the
family has almost by necessity entailed a progressive de-communalization
of death rituals.

There are many different forms of death rituals. The highest of these
are reserved for a puang, a to minaa sando and a burake tambolang.[4]
Death feasts of a slightly lower order are for (other) adat-chiefs and
their immediate family (at times also for a to minaa). Class is clearly a
determining factor in the choice of an appropriate death ritual, but
wealth is as well. A funeral such as the dirapa'i, for example, is extremely expensive. The burial of Lai' Kalua', Pong Maramba's widow (an
adat-chief related to eminent families in Kesu'), is said to have involved
an expenditure of Dfl. 200,000. At this death feast, held a short time
after the end of World War II, 200 buffaloes were killed. Lai' Kalua's
funeral did not conform in all respects to a traditional dirapa'i, for she

was a Christian, but it was celebrated in a grand manner, complete
with a mortuary effigy.

The highest order of dirapa'i, the rapasan sundun, calls for slaughtering at least 24 buffaloes; usually more are put to death. If Lai'
Kalua' had not converted to Christianity shortly before her demise,
her funeral would have fallen into this category. Both of the great
rituals discussed in Chapters XI and XII belong to this highest order of
the dirapa'i.

Almost equal to the preceding funeral is the dipapitung bongi, "that
which takes place in seven nights", referred to in abbreviated form as
pitung bongi, "seven nights". For this feast at least seven buffaloes
are killed. For the dipalimang bongi, "that which takes place in five
nights", the slaughter of five buffaloes is prescribed; for the dipatallung bongi or tallung bongi (three nights) a minimum of three
buffaloes is required; for the sangbongi (one night) a solitary buffalo
is sufficient (cf. the summary in Chapter I). Although the latter forms
of death ritual are somewhat less elaborate than the preceding ones,
even they are often rather expensive; the specified number of buffaloes, one, three, five or seven, is in reality a minimum which is usually
far exceeded.

The funerals of "common folk" contrast with the vast scale of burials
conducted for a rich puang or to makaka, yet they too are characterized by an inclination to put on a good show. It is my impression that
especially among lower class people the slaughter of a buffalo means
severe economic sacrifice, costing them more pain and trouble than the
felling of a precious saleko at the funeral of a parengnge'. People fear
not spending enough on the ritual so that others can make them feel
ashamed. For this reason poor villagers may feel compelled to pay more
for the burial of a family member than they can truly afford.

People make short work of the funeral of a small child: it would seem
such deaths are a painful experience which it is thought best to forget
as soon as possible. A different explanation for the simple ritual might
be based on the premise that someone who dies in his youth is not
feared as dangerous after death, less to be dreaded than someone who
perishes as an adult (the dead for whom a death ritual has not yet
been completed are still impure). Or, we could argue that the simple
funeral is considered sufficient because the youthful deceased can never
become an ancestor in the sense of a spirit capable after burial of
emanating a benevolent influence.

In the succeeding chapters diverse forms of funerals are presented,
beginning with the most simple ritual of all, the ceremony held for dead
babies. Descriptions pertain primarily to Kesu' (informants: Allo Rante
and B. Sarungallo). Reports of rituals in Sangalla' have also been included (informants: Puang Paliwan Tandilangi' and Puang W. Sombolinggi). Not only do ceremonies for the dead vary from region to region;
within one and the same district they can also differ. The latter is
primarily a function of the obligation to adhere to the death ritual
usually practised by the family of the decaesed's mother (Vol.I:26).

Variations within each of the forms of the death ritual are commonly
designated by the name of a particular village or region, at times even
by the name of a certain tongkonan. Thus in Kesu' people talk of the
aluk To Ba'tan (the ritual of people from the village of Ba'tan), the
aluk To Nonongan and the aluk To Sullukan. Especially the ritual of the
leading tongkonan Sullukan is deviant.

The death ritual has, of course, attracted the interest of social re-searchers. In their publications certain biases intrude as a consequence of the fact that they are better informed about practices in one or an-other specific region. A.C. Kruyt, however, gives a more general exposition of death rituals (1923/24:137-75). Keers (1939), too, does not confine herself to a partial presentation, but offers a survey of diverse forms of burial throughout the whole of Tana Toraja. Belksma describes burial and mourning customs in Rantepao' and Pangala' (1922) and in Tikala District (1923 and 1924). Crystal (1970), Nobele (1926: 38-58) and Tandilangi' (1969) provide rather extensive accounts of various forms of funerals in the puang-districts (Nobele's information concerns Ma'kale, Tandilangi's Sangalla', and Salombe's Sangalla' (1972) and Mengkendek (1977)). Crystal has reported what took place immedi-ately after the death of the puang of Sangalla' (Crystal 1972:26-32). Bodrogi (1970:21-38) describes several death rites as celebrated for a member of the puang-family of Ma'kale, including the carrying of the deceased to the grave. Holt has written about a burial in Kesu', in-cluding the dances performed at the time (Holt 1939:61-5, photos 52-63). Koubi's contribution to the literature consists of a brief account of several death rites in Kesu' (1975: 105-9) and of a book "Rambu Solo': La Fumée Descend" (1982) which, unfortunately, I have been unable to consult. Volkman has written about several death rites in Tikala (1979a:1-17). Wilcox's narrative concerning a princely funeral in puang-states contains information about a rite during the ritual which no one else has reported (1949:66-89). Jannel and Lontcho's book "Laissez venir ceux qui pleurent" (n.d.), a work designed to have popular appeal, deserves mention as well. It contains numerous fine photo-graphs. Koubi and Lontcho wrote the text. In addition there exist reports of death rituals published in a number of all but inaccessible sources. The death ritual is described in detail in Van der Veen, unpublished c. At present it is being typed out. The manuscript sec-tion of the Royal Institute of Linguistics and Anthropology in Leiden has a copy of the manuscript which I prepared concerning the aluk To Nonongan as it was explained to me by members of several of the most prominent local families and by an ex-slave who was familiar with the ritual.

2. General review

After someone dies, his family comes together to determine what ritual to observe. This is especially true for a person of some note. The date on which the ritual is to begin is also set at this time. In reaching the decisions necessary, not only family members and, first and foremost, the family head participate in the discussion, but also the village head, and, where a great funeral ceremony is anticipated, the district head as well. At times even the regent (bupati) must be consulted. Indeed, a permit is required for the number of buffaloes that will be slaughtered. Not even cock fights can be staged without government permission. A funeral is a complex undertaking for which many preparatory measures are necessary.

The Toraja, when speaking about death rites, will immediately indicate what they consider to be important: the order of magnitude of the ritual, the sequence of the rites - which are then enumerated (in practice people do not always abide by this sequence), the number and kinds of buffaloes to be slaughtered and their role in the ritual, the number of pigs to be assembled and butchered, the arrival of important personages and tourists, the various individuals with a part to play in the ritual (the more important the ceremony, the more functionaries), and, finally, the cock fights that are a feature of death rituals of a high order. To be sure the number of functionaries mounts in proportion to the eminence of the ritual to be observed. The artefacts to be used increase as well. Various of the relevant functionaries have already made an appearance in Vol.I, the death priests and the to minaa among them (Vol.I:280-2, 275-9). The to minaa officiates exclusively at important funeral celebrations, and then during later phases of the ritual. In contrast to the taciturn to mebalun his is highly articulate: part of his task consists of singing a biography of the deceased and reciting adat decrees and other traditions (Volkman 1979a). Many of the objects utilized during the deata ritual have already been mentioned in Vol.I. The most important of these are the tau-tau (Vol.I:261-3), the bala'kaan (Vol.I:76, 197ff., 272), the lakkean (lakkian, Vol.I:261) and the sarigan (Vol.I:261). Other artefacts will crop up in the course of the description of these rituals.

In Chapters IX and X the text is essentially a condensed account of what my Toraja informants considered the most important rites during a death ritual. They in fact provided little information concerning events at the time of death and shortly thereafter. In their eyes the death feast only commences once the deceased dies ritually, an action that is, to be sure, only part of rituals of a higher order when the bodily remains are carried from the Southern to the central room of the house. Below I wish to raise a number of subjects largely overlooked or slighted by my informants.

Looking after the dead entails considerable care and worry for his immediate household, somewhat less trouble for his family as a whole. For the poor it is desirable to conduct a burial as quickly as possible: the reception of guests means expenses and the meal eaten in honour of the dead therefore is restricted to chicken with rice. The dead is interred within 24 hours, for otherwise the stench would be unbearable: the poor do not possess the resources to stanch or mask the odor. the corpse is not swathed in yards and yards of material; a few pieces of cloth and a kain must do. All the death priest does is make the passing of the deceased known by knocking against the pigsty with a stick. There is not even a ceremonial vigil (ma'doya). What is never omitted, however, even in the most simple ritual, is the killing of a chicken directly after the moment of death and the slaughtering of a black chicken shortly after burial has been accomplished. This last sacrifice, ma'pallin, is extremely common in all sorts of rituals; it serves to avert evil (see Vol.I:247 and Merok:156-8). On the day of the burial and the following day as well, however simple the death ritual being observed, no one may work on the sawah.

The rich - and those, too, of limited means but who cannot be considered poor - face other prospects in the event of a family death. Money must be collected to pay for the death ritual, for the purchase of the buffaloes and pigs to be slaughtered, for the construction of guest houses and feasts - huts, for song and dance groups and for improvement of the road to the festive grounds. To cover these costs sawahs are sometimes mortgaged. Rivalries within the family group are also liable to influence the flow of events. They can be the reason that considerable time elapses between death and ritual burial; the interval has been known on occasion to last a generation!

Case A
A leading man from Kesu' told me that his grandfather died before he himself was born but that only 25 years later was his grandfather buried. It was as an adult that the grandson attended the funeral of the grandfather he had never known. The reason for the protracted delay was that the family could not agree about the inheritance.

Case B
A similar train of events took place in Buntao'. Here, too, it took about twenty years before the deceased nene', who belonged to the most eminent family in the district, was ritually buried. Once again dispute over inheritance was the retarding factor. During my stay in Buntao' in 1966 I was invited by family members to enter the room where the corpse of the nene' who had died some ten years previously was still kept. In keeping with Toraja custom, the corpse was concealed in a kind of enormous cocoon of layers of cloth and laid on a bed surrounded by a mosquito net. I spent the night in a neighbouring room. No one found this at all odd. The deceased had enjoyed little rest since her death: as a result of political agitation during the 1950s the family had been obliged to flee on several occasions and each time they had, temporarily, buried grandmother, a rather unorthodox procedure in Tana Toraja. As a rule the dead stays above ground: i.e. the corpse lies in state in the Southern room of the house until the death ritual officially begins.

Case C
Family dispute often figures unpleasantly also in death rituals of less consequence. A teacher in Kesu' wished to bury his father in a rather simple way. His sister, living in Ujung Pandang, when she learned of her father's death, had other ideas. Instead of one, she wanted to slaughter five buffaloes. She managed to get her way, to her brother's great displeasure. He had a large family to support. He didn't only resent the expense, however, but the continual delay of the funeral, a result of disagreement with his sister, annoyed him no end.

In general a period of one or more years separates the moment of death from the beginning of a "higher" death ritual. As soon as a person dies, however, a chicken is killed, for example, by striking it to death with a stick. This is called by the curious term of diremba'i, from mangremba', to chase away. Van der Veen explained this to me from the wish of the mourners to chase away the soul of the deceased. In Tikala the animal is not killed with a stick, but beaten to death on one of the hearthstones. In some regions (Nonongan) dibarira is practised; the chicken's neck is crushed between two bamboo slats (barira) of the enclosure surrounding the space beneath the house, the part of the dwelling which is associated with the underworld. No one may eat of this chicken; it is either tossed under the house or buried to its West.
   In his unpublished notes concerning the "three nights ritual", Van der Veen reports the killing of a pig known as ma'puli or ma'karu'-dusan[5] at about the same time that the chicken is killed. In recent

times this pig has been replaced by a buffalo, one more sign that the
Toraja are striving constantly to make every funeral more closely
resemble the next higher order of celebration. The meat of the
slaughtered animal may not be eaten.

At roughly the time the chicken and pig are slaughtered, the washing
of the dead commences. The corpse is then smeared with coconut oil,
dressed modestly and wrapped in white cloths. Lamenting begins. The
cloths are presented by family members who are not among the
deceased's closest relatives, a gift which will be reciprocated by the
immediate family when an appropriate occasion arises. Next the deceased
is bundled up in still more white cloths until the whole is stiff, a task
for the death priest who has, meanwhile, been informed of the need for
his services. A thick bandage plaited from strands of kapok is also
wrapped around the corpse. The bandage absorbs a great deal of
moisture from the dead body. Kapok belongs to the sphere of the dead.
Afterwards the deceased is swaddled in yet more cloths until he is
hidden in an enormous bolster which resembles a monstrous cocoon.
Subsequently, until the death ritual formally begins, the corpse is
placed on a platform in the Southern room of the house. It may or may
not be laid in a coffin (at times with a cover, at times not).[6] The
cadaveral fluid is drained via a bamboo which, inserted through the
thick bolster, ends in an earthenware pot which rests beneath the deceased.[7] Gases from the decaying corpse are released through a second
bamboo which is inserted in the upper side of the packaged corpse; the
far end of this bamboo sticks outside the house. A.C. Kruyt (1923/24:
143) reports that after some fourteen days the winding sheet and kapok
have hardened into a thick crust and there is hardly a trace any more
of an offensive odor.[8]

It is beyond dispute, however, that despite various measures, the
stench emitted by the putrefying corpse is far from agreeable. One
Toraja told me that as a youth he thoroughly disliked entering the
house where his grandfather's corpse lay on display. Outside the room
where the deceased was kept the scent was also unmistakable. Other
Toraja were less sensitive. "The deceased greets you", my informant
said when my face betrayed that I knew about the presence of a corpse
in the house. Certain weather may be responsible for prolonging the
period during which the corpse emits a stench well beyond two weeks.
The emanating odor is evidently considered a sign of welcome. As a
Toraja one lives with his dead, or must learn to live with them, but not
everyone shares the same thoughts on the subject! One girl confided
that she planned to emigrate because she had no desire to spend her
whole life as a penjaga mayat (Indonesian: a guardian of corpses).

The description just presented is confined to what happens immediately after the death of a to makaka. Among the very rich proceedings
are still more elaborate. Death is heralded by the firing of gunshots.
Once the corpse has been washed and annointed with coconut oil, it is
dressed in fancy clothing. A man is clothed in a jacket, trousers, and
a kain of fine material. He is girded with a golden kris and given a
sirih pouch with silver trimmings (sampa or sepu' sapekan). A gold
chain is draped around his neck, a manik ata. A folded headcloth is set
on his head, a tali sissik. A dead woman is attired in an attractive
jacket, and a checked sarong; she wears gold bracelets (komba), and
on her head a sa'pi' bulaan, a "golden" cap. After the corpse has been
clothed, it is placed in a sitting position against the West wall of the

Southern room of the house.[9] After a day or so, when as many people as possible have had an opportunity to view the deceased in state, the corpse is stretched out on the floor of the Southern room; it is stripped of regalia and jewels and wrapped in a white kain. (N.B. approximately 5 to 6 hours after death, rigor mortis sets in; this rigidity disappears after 24 hours so that only then can the body be laid out fully extended.)

At this point the wailing of female family members begins. We should keep in mind that all these acts are merely rites which take place prior to any formal death feast. The date for such a celebration remains to be established (for major rituals this always follows the rice harvest), and that may take some doing.

In the meantime the death priest and several close family members have already begun their vigil by the dead - which brings us to a brief description of their special position. Indeed, they more than anybody else come into close contact with the sphere of death. For a death priest such contact is virtually unbroken. Elsewhere I have pointed out how as a consequence in some districts he has become something of an "untouchable" (Vol.I:280ff.). His intercourse with other people is extremely limited except during a death ritual and the rites which precede a death feast. He must cultivate his own ricefield, no one assists him. Presumably his isolation makes the death priest into a man of few words: he usually goes his way in silence. The to mebalun has the most contact with his assistant, the to pabalian (= helper). The two take turns setting down food and tuak next to the deceased. A female slave prepares food for the dead, the to massanduk dalle, "she who spoons out the maize" (for the deceased). It is Van der Veen's contention (unpublished c) that she is the same figure as the to usso'boi rante, "she who enters the plain first". Another figure is the to (di)ma'peulli', "she who removes the maggots (from the corpse)", a function of symbolic significance also carried out by a female slave. Other informants insisted that the to ma'peulli' did in fact rid the corpse of worms (see also below under the prohibitions enforced by the Netherlands East Indies government).

The surviving spouse, widow or widower, has an especially hard time. This to balu is closest to the deceased which explains why he or she is subject to the variety of prohibitions and prescriptions listed below. In the past these were yet more strict, especially in the Tallu-lembangna. Already the first day after the death of a marriage partner, the survivor is forbidden to eat rice. Once the first phase of the death feast begins, a to balu of princely blood is shut up in a bamboo cage for five days and not let out for any reason whatsoever, not even to pass waste. During this period the to balu's diet consists only of (shredded?) coconut and ginger; tuak is served to drink (Nobele 1926:41).[10] It seems certain that leniency will have been observed in enforcing such impossible prescriptions. Puang Lasok Rinding's widow was not subject to such treatment, possibly in recognition of her age and poor health. Elsewhere, in Kesu', for example, rules were less harsh. An end, however, comes to all the to balu's trials which are especially arduous for a widow. What follows in the text is valid for the to balu in all districts of Tana Toraja.

Once the deceased has been transferred to the rock grave, the widow's hair is cut ceremonially. She sits to the West of the house of mourning with her face turned to the West, and her head covered with a sarong. After she lets the sarong slip down, the death priest cuts a lock of her hair three times in succession, severing but a little bit each time. This takes place while he cries: "Garri' morokkoka", "she is penitent". Her hair is then washed. Only afterwards may the to balu marry again. (According to Van der Veen, the death priest leads the to balu three times around the house of mourning, the third time calling out the words "Garri' morokkoka", "she is penitent"[11]; then he cuts some hair from her head.) This hair cut possibly symbolize severing connections with the sphere of death. No mention was made of whether a widower is also obliged to submit to such regulations. Less distance separates a widow from the sphere of death than a widower. The to balu (widow) is supported in her travail by the to ma'tongkonan, a female relative ("she who sits"; tongkon means to sit). This functionary participates as well in keeping watch over the deceased; she, too, observes the food taboos. In Kesu' one spoke of the to ma'pemali, yet this functionary is in fact a woman from the deceased's family who replaces the widow or widower if he or she has already died.

The question arises why at the time the Netherlands East Indies government and the Church did not take measures to place restrictions on such a highly evolved death ritual. The government contented itself with calling for the immediate burial of anyone who died from a contagious disease, and for the rest drafted regulations limiting the number of buffaloes to be slaughtered, and prohibitions against removing maggots from the corpse, against cock fights and headhunting. The Reformed Mission League supported these prohibitions (see Van Lijf 1951/52:362ff. and 1952/53:273). Throughout Tana Toraja there was also an ordinance in effect that anyone dying in a city had to be buried within 24 hours. People evaded this by-law by removing a corpse with all speed to a village in order to celebrate a fitting death ritual. At present haste is less of an issue since a corpse may be injected with formalin to prevent putrefaction. This has meant in turn, however, that when someone dies in the capital of South Sulawesi, Ujung Pandang, he is transported as rapidly as possible "upwards" (to the North) in order to be able to bury him in all splendour in the presence of his family (the cost of transporting a corpse some 360 km amounted to Dfl. 200 in 1978).

Even the rather concise account set down in the following chapters, pieced together from what my informants had to tell me, is sufficient to show how the living Toraja coexist with their dead and how much care and attention they devote to ritual burial. Such care begins at once after someone has drawn his last breath; the bodily remains lie there but the deceased's soul, the bombo, leaves its mortal casing to stalk at large. At the hours that the deceased was accustomed to eat, the bombo is served food and drink. As the death ritual advances further and further, the deceased, at first considered impure, belonging to the sphere of the West, is gradually introduced into the sphere of the East. The final step, the transition to the sphere of the East, the metamorphosis from bombo into deata is accomplished by means of a conversion ritual (cf. Chapter VII.2.).

Yet already prior to such a conversion ritual, the deceased is helped along the way to the East: this is brought about through death chants, badong, which accompany him on his journey through Puya to the firmament. It is done also through the singing of the to minaa, who celebrates the life history of the dead man, proclaiming his importance and his worthiness to become a deata. The same does not hold true, however, for the "ordinary" dead (Vol.I:123-4); such people after death do not become active ancestors.

Although the Toraja do their best to present the death ritual as a coherent whole, here, too, - as in all other Toraja rituals - we encounter paradoxes. The more a death ritual advances, the less impure the deceased becomes; he is clearly on his way towards attaining the status of deata. But the tau-tau, present in late stages of the ritual, also known as bombo dikita, "the soul of the dead which is visible", is evidence that the deceased is still among the living - even while he is making his way towards Puya.

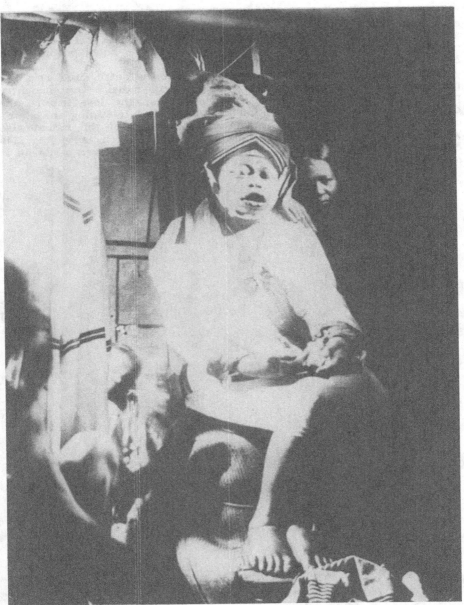

An eminent Toraja placed in the sali-room shortly after his death. As a
rule the corpse is set down in a seated position with his back bound to
bamboo poles. This dead man has not yet been dressed in his ceremonial apparel. The tali sissik, however, has already been set on his
head. The name of the deceased is unknown. (Sissik: folded like the
scales of a fish.) See also pp. 176-177.
(Photo: Royal Tropical Institute, Amsterdam.)

Tau-tau lampa with the head-gear of a manganda'-dancer, consisting of plumes made of parakeet feathers (bulu baan), of old coins sewed onto a maa'-cloth stretched between a real pair of horns, and of a sarita folded around the horns. The face is fashioned out of cloth with diamond-shaped eyes fastened to it. The tau-tau wears a dark jacket, a shoulder-cloth and a sarong; these last two items are of imported fabrics. The effigy's accessories consist of a kris and four necklaces: two rara', one manik ata and one with round yellow balls for beads (for these accessories see Nooy-Palm 1969:173). In front of the tau-tau there stands a chain of tuang-tuang. This conveys the status of the deceased. Also in front of the tau-tau a mat is visible, and in the foreground, to the left, a menhir (simbuang batu).
(Photo: Mrs. Ursula Schulz-Dornburg, 1984.)

Langngan, an object used both in rituals of the East and West. The langngan serves to support lengths of bamboo in which food for ritual meals is prepared. It is made out of various kinds of wood in different districts. The parts are sometimes knotted together with rattan. For langngan used in rituals of the East, the knot is tied so that it faces up and to the East; for rituals of the West, the knot must face downwards and towards the West. Langngan for Eastern rituals are set up to the East or Northeast of the tongkonan; those for Western rituals, to the West or Northwest. A fire is kindled beneath the langngan and lengths of bamboo-tallang filled with food are leaned against the "roasting spit". In rituals of the East the bamboos are so arranged that the openings point to the East; in rituals of the West they rest against the langngan with their openings in a Westerly direction. The bamboo-tallang is chosen because its walls are neither too thick nor too thin; the contents must be able to be roasted easily. Preparation of the ritual meals is the work of men. (Photo: Hetty Nooy-Palm, 1972.)

Chapter IX

SIMPLE DEATH RITUALS

"Come, let us sing the lament now,
That we may weave the mourning song."
(The Chant:47)

1. Rituals for children and poor people

The following descriptions come from Kesu'. No death priest participates in the burial of children. For adults he appears at rituals beginning with the didedekan pangkung bai (section 1.3.). Officially the to mebalun first enters proceedings at the time he is called upon to wrap the corpse (= mebalun).

1.1. Dikaletekan tallu manuk

The name of the burial ("as if striking a chicken's egg with the back of a cleaver") defies interpretation. My informants didn't even try. This ritual is for interring a baby either stillborn or dying soon after entry into the world. The tiny corpse of a stillborn infant is buried beneath the ricebarn or to the East of the house[1] together with the umbilical cord and a hen's egg (tallu manuk). The corpse is laid out in a basket from rushes (kapipe). The manner of burial is reminiscent of the deposition of the afterbirth. The father carries the corpse in his sarong; he is also the one to place it in the ground. He sticks a few shafts of bamboo in the ground encircling the grave, and ties their ends together.

1.2. Disilli' [2]

When a baby dies before cutting teeth, the body is placed that same evening in a hole hollowed out of an antolong-tree (also known as kayu mate, "dead wood"). The child's father, trailed by the mother, carries the corpse to the tree in a cloth. Deposition takes place at roughly 6:30 p.m. The cavity in the tree is covered over with ijuk, hairy fibres which grow in the axils of the sugar palm. Next to the tree a dog and a pig are slaughtered. Their flesh may not be brought home (what happens with it is not specified further, but it would seem likely that it is consumed on the spot; this is what happens during the disilli' for adults).

Dipelolok kayu and dipeantolong are two alternate names for this form of deposition. As at the preceding ceremony, here, too, no death priest or other functionary takes part. The ceremony is also called disilli' bai because a pig is killed as part of the proceedings. At the disilli' tedong a buffalo is killed; this is celebrated when the dead infant has prominent parents. Also for adults who are buried according to the disilli'-ritual, a dog and pig are put to death. Again, the flesh of these animals must not be taken home but is eaten at the scene of the ceremony. (It is my assumption that for adults a rock grave is used, for one can scarcely cram a corpse of that size into a hollowed out tree trunk.) The meat is cooked in bamboo without the addition of any rice. On the day that a disilli'-funeral is observed, no one in the village is allowed to work.

No further explication of deposition in a tree trunk was forthcoming. The child's string of life is severed, the tree continues to grow (personal interpretation). The Toraja suggest that a bird will settle on one of the branches of the tree and then soar with the child's soul to the upperworld.

1.3. Didedekan pangkung bai

This death ritual is typical for poor persons without close relatives ("for him/her, i.e. the deceased, the pigsty is struck"). Death is announced by the death priest who beats against the deceased's pigsty three times with a piece of wood. This is the only action he takes. Perhaps striking the pigsty is to signify that a pig is to be fetched that will be slaughtered for the deceased. Nothing further was reported about this form of burial. Presumably after being washed and rubbed with coconut oil the corpse is wrapped in a number of cloths - natural in colour, or grey - and unceremoniously conveyed to the grave. (My information comes from persons of considerable status who have an inclination not to elaborate concerning rituals which, in their eyes, are of slight significance.)

In the rituals which follow below, although the diremba'i or dibarira is not mentioned explicitly, the rite is never omitted (see Chapter VIII).

1.4. Bai tungga'

This, too, is a rite for the poor ("one pig"). After the corpse has been washed and annointed with coconut oil, it is trussed in a sarong. A pig is slaughtered on the compound of the house of mourning. The meat is put in a bamboo. Yams are eaten, and tuak is drunk. The rite for which the pig is slaughtered is the ma'doya, "keeping watch beside the dead" (for the details of this rite, see the following subsection). No one mentioned at what time burial should take place. Four men transport the deceased to the grave in the rocks. The rite is held within two days of demise. On the day after the burial, the ma'pallin takes place. Work on the sawah is not permitted on this day.

1.5. Bai a'pa'

A minimum of four pigs are slaughtered; their number may run up to as many as ten. The dead is bathed, rubbed with oil and wrapped in a cloth. Family members come together to confer about when funeral rites can begin. Their wish is to start as soon as possible. Once agreement has been reached, on the appointed day a pig is fetched which is slaughtered during the afternoon. This formally marks the beginning of the ma'doya, the vigil beside the dead. The rite, however, is less a death watch than a condolence visit paid by family and friends. The dead rests in the room which lies in the South of the house. Conveyance to another room is not part of this ritual. Ma'doya literally means "to pay a visit in order to sit with the immediate family beside the dead" (only the women do so). People bring some sweet potatoes, maize, bananas and palm wine with them, gifts for the deceased's close relatives. Some of these gifts are offered to the dead as well. The women who pay the visit are dressed partly or entirely in black and usually have a black cloth draped over their heads. Visitors bring the lantang pangngan with them, a bamboo construction in which sirih/ pinang has been placed for the deceased.

The women go upstairs into the house and sit down beside the dead. The men remain below on the compound and sit on the floor beneath the ricebarn. The to balu, the widow or widower, has already taken up a position to the West of the corpse.[3] From the very onset of the ritual, members of the deceased's immediate family are subject to the maro' (marao'), a period during which they are forbidden to eat rice; they consume maize and yams instead. Rice is associated with the sphere of the East and the upperworld. At a later stage of the death ritual, one does eat rice again, but not during this initial mourning period during which friends, too, may choose to abstain. The meat of the pig slaughtered for the maro'-rite is cooked in bamboo and eaten together with yams.

A pig is killed again the next morning; the rite is called mantunu (the killing of an animal for someone who has died). The beast is divided in the usual manner (see Vol.I:208-9). The pig's head, however, is preserved. One carries the deceased - the same day - to the rock grave; the pig's head is hacked into small pieces, cooked in a bamboo and eaten in the vicinity of the grave. Then people return to the deceased's house. Here another pig is slaughtered and again consumed with yams. The ma'pallin takes place. After the dead has been carried to the rock grave, the clothing of his immediate family is dyed black. This rite is the ma'bolong. It may seem surprising that this hasn't already occurred earlier, but custom dictates otherwise.

On the third day of the ritual, the kumande takes place, the repeal of the prohibition against eating rice for those observing strict mourning. A pig is slaughtered and its meat eaten with rice. Immediately beforehand the mangrondan bota is enacted, "letting grains of rice fall down". People let some rice and bits of pork fall through gaps in the floor; this serves as food for the dead.[4] The underlying idea is that the dead person's soul still lingers under the house (despite burial in the rock tomb!).

On the fourth day a chicken is killed somewhat to the South of the house of the deceased. The chicken is prepared in bamboo and eaten with rice. Two pesung are made: some rice and chicken are set down as food for the dead. The remaining food is taken home and eaten there. The rite is known as untoe sero which literally means "grasping that which is pure" or "grasping the state of purity". It is the final offering presented to the deceased (see below). A pig is also slaughtered at the rock grave. The rite signifies that the burial is complete, the family has fulfilled its obligations as it should. Actually, the membase has the same significance. This "washing of the hands" has taken place two or three days after the preceding rite. A chicken is killed and cooked with rice in bamboo (all in all three piong are prepared). The rite is held in front of the house of mourning. A small shrine is erected made of a piece of bamboo to which a (braided?) leaf of the sugar palm has been fastened. Here, on a pesung, food prepared in the piong is offered to Puang Matua.

2. Rituals at which at least one buffalo is slaughtered

2.1. The sangbongi or dipasang bongi

The sangbongi ("one night") or dipasang bongi, "that which takes place in one night", resembles, in its ritual aspects, the preceding celebration, the bai a'pa'. During the mantunu, however, a buffalo is slaughtered; when the body is carried to the rock grave a pig is killed; and during the untoe sero another pig is killed. In addition to the buffalo (a pudu'), a total of four pigs may be slaughtered. Badong, death chants, are sung for the deceased (see Van der Veen's introduction to the elegies which he has transcribed and translated, The Chant:7-18). During rituals lower than the sangbongi no such badong may be performed. Indeed, in some adat communities badong may only be sung at a ritual equal to or higher than the tallung bongi. (The name bongi refers to the Western sphere; bongi = night = dark.)

2.2. The tallung bongi

During the tallung bongi ("three nights") at least three buffaloes and sixteen pigs are slaughtered. Here, too, the ma'doya, the vigil beside the dead, takes place.

As soon as death occurs, after the corpse is washed and smeared with coconut oil, it is wrapped in a cloth and laid out with the head to the West. Then the to mebalun, "the wrapper of the dead", i.e. the death priest, and the to pabalian, his assistant, are summoned. When the to mebalun beats his drum (gandang), the head of the deceased is turned towards the South. Up until now the deceased has been referred to as "the sick one" (to makula'); hereafter he is definitely "dead" and the death ritual may begin. On the same day, after noon, one buffalo is slaughtered, the pa'karu'dusan.[5] The word derives from ru'du, to die. The buffalo is killed on the day that the deceased ritually dies.

The immediate family members of the deceased may not eat any meat from this buffalo, for the animal "follows after the dead". The buffalo and the deceased are considered to have died at the same time. The crowd rushes upon the dead buffalo[6] and hacks it to pieces. Thus the animal meets a different end from most buffaloes at a death feast; its meat is not divided along traditional lines. The buffalo belongs to the deceased. During the ma'puli (another name for this rite in puang-states and in Baruppu'), a pig is also slaughtered. Again, the death priest and his helper claim their share - as always as much as they want. Then the deceased receives something to eat. Next the death priest and his helper have their meal and only then is it the turn of the to parengnge'. If there isn't enough to go around, then another buffalo is killed. The maro' begins, the prohibition against eating rice for close family members. They may only consume maize and yams.

The to ma'kuasa enters upon the scene. This is a functionary in the death ritual who looks after the deceased and abides by strict taboos.[7] As soon as the death ritual commences, for seven days he is not allowed to eat cooked food. He can be recognized by the red turban on his head. Usually the to ma'kuasa is one of the deceased's family, yet not a son. In Kesu' this functionary is said to be a slave, but my Kesu' informants were silent on this point (Woordenboek: v. koeasa). In keeping with the aluk to Sullukan (ritual as observed by members of tongkonan Sullukan) in La'bo, Kesu', the to ma'kuasa is not a slave, but a family member, keeping watch over the deceased. In addition to this functionary, the to balu (widow or widower) and the to ma'pemali, a female relative, also observe strict mourning for the dead and remain at the side of the corpse. When necessary the to ma'pemali can replace the widow or widower and carry out his of her duties (to ma'pemali = to ma'tongkonan, see Woordenboek: v. pemali and tongkon). Another functionary (family member?) obliged to conform to certain rules is the to dibulle tangnga ("she who is carried in the middle"). And, finally, there is the to massanduk dalle, "she who serves the cooked maize from the pot" (i.e. the maize intended for the deceased), a slave.

After two nights have passed, the day arrives for the ma'batang ("to carry out the most important part of the death ritual", see Woordenboek: v. batang). A not further specified individual is requested by the to minaa to slaughter a chicken and a dog early in the morning. The chicken is killed because the deata must be asked for permission to fell a tree (kaniala', a kapok tree). Then the dog is slaughtered, signifying that the tree has been cut down "to serve the dead". The tree is brought to the deceased's compound. After a pig has been slaughtered, a bier (sarigan) is fashioned out of the kapok trunk. The rite is called mesarigan ("to prepare a bier"). The ma'doya tangnga, the middlemost ma'doya, also takes place on this day. Following this it is customary for the to minaa to sing about the life of the deceased (ma'kakarun) in order to help him on his way through Puya to achieve the status of deata. The singing also guides the buffaloes of the deceased towards Puya. The longer the procession of buffaloes, the more respect the deceased will enjoy in Puya and this is one of the reasons why relatives try to kill as many buffaloes as possible at a death feast. To be sure a large number of slaughtered animals also enhances respect for the deceased and his family on earth.

On this day men also go to the rante to make the bala'kaan, the platform that is the centre of the division of meat. This is accomplished without any accompanying rite. The bala'kaan used for this ritual has four posts. Yet another pig is slaughtered for the panganta' (derived from the word which means to accompany, see Woordenboek: v. anta'). Kains, sarongs, woven textiles and a sirih-pouch are suspended from a bamboo which is specially brought into position above the deceased. The fabrics may represent the clothing and accessories of the deceased. The rite is called ma'palangngan panganta' (langngan: the length of bamboo-aur from which the fabrics hang, one on top of another). They hang in the same direction as the corpse is laid out (see Fig. 21). The kains and other textiles are used again later during the manganta', a conversion ritual (see Chapter VII.2.7.).

Later on this same day a pig is killed for the ma'bambangan (the word means "to die"). The rite is described in the first section of Chapter XI which recounts the events of November 5, 1969 at the funeral of Sa'pang. Before this pig is slaughtered, another pig is killed

Fig. 21. Diagrammatic sketch of a dead nobleman lying in state in his tongkonan (by Johannis Lobo).

The corpse in its wrappings (A) rests on a low scaffold (B) that is decorated with cloths (nature and design not specified). The outside covering of the corpse is a red fabric to which a row of krisses has been attached. At the head end (C) gold and silver coins have been fastened to the wrapping. The widow sits close by (D). The following objects are on display at the head end of the corpse: a dulang (wooden bowl on one foot), the dead man's "plate" (E); a cup (F); and sirih/pinang in a bowl (G). The rectangular line drawn around the corpse represents a mosquito net (not always present). Three bamboo poles and four kandaure are rigged up above the deceased. From the poles hang, respectively, a (modern) pair of trousers, a (modern) jacket, and (sketched in black and white squares) various kains. The diagram apparently depicts the ma'palangngan panganta' (see also Chapters IX.2.2. and X.2.).

for a different component of the ritual, ma'tau-tau. From bamboo a tau-tau lampa is made, an effigy which must portray the deceased but which differs in form and purpose from the tau-tau set up beside the rock grave. The tau-tau lampa is discussed further in Chapter X.

After a meal, roughly at noon, the ma'batang takes place. It is considered the principal rite of the feast and is enacted, for the most part, on the rante, the square outside the village that is the setting for a major portion of the death rituals. The simbuang batu (menhirs) are erected on this square. A buffalo is slaughtered and its flesh divided. Actually the sokkong bayu should distribute the meat, but as a rule he looks for a substitute from among his family members. The chosen figure is assisted by five other meat dividers, the panggau bamba. These are all experts with the necessary experience in this

work. Next everyone returns again to the deceased's house where once
more a pig is slaughtered, this time for the ma'doya tampak ("the final
rite of the death watch"). The to mebalun and to pabalian claim their
share of the pig after the death priest has presented food to the dead
(the meal for the deceased consists of maize and some meat from the
slaughtered animal). What remains is divided further (among whom is
not reported). On this occasion merely a single pig is killed.

On the fourth day of this death ritual, the ma'palao takes place: the
buffaloes are led to the rante. Before their departure, the pa'palao or
tulak tallang is slaughtered (the names of this buffalo derive from
palao, to transport the earthly remains of the deceased in a procession
to the rante, and from tulak, prop or stay, in this instance the support of the tallang-bamboo).[8] The to mebalun and the to pabalian take
their share of the buffalo meat. Some is given, too, to the deceased.
Afterwards the corpse is placed on top of the sarigan. Celebrants then
proceed to the rante, with functionaries in sedan chairs up front. In
Kesu' the following order is maintained:

5	4	3	2	1
tau-tau	bier (sarigan)	to ma'pemali (or to balu)	to dibulle tangnga	to massanduk dalle

Upon arrival at the rante, the sarigan is set down. The to ma'pemali,
the to dibulle tangnga and the to massanduk dalle step down from the
sedan chairs in which they have been conveyed to the feast plain. The
tau-tau lampa are disassembled and the parts remain behind on the
rante together with the sedan chairs of the functionaries. Meanwhile
those present take their places under palm branches that have been put
up. Female functionaries sit in a special place. The first order of
business to follow is the slaughter of the remaining buffaloes. A special
part of the flesh, the taa baine, is handed out among the women who
have come along with the procession. What remains is placed on the
bala'kaan. After these women have accepted their share, they go back
to the deceased's house, led by the to ma'pemali, followed by the to
dibulle tangnga and in turn by the to massanduk dalle.

In the meantime the remaining meat is hoisted onto the bala'kaan for
division. First to receive shares are the villages adjoining the village in
which the deceased's house stands. This is a token of honour for these
villages, "with which one is married", as the Toraja put it. This distribution of meat is known as ma'kande padang, "giving food to the earth"
(see Fig. 22). Next ensues the usual division of meat among the to parengnge'. Once distribution has been completed, the deceased is carried
(meaa) to the liang (the grave cut in the rock). The ma'pallin follows
and afterwards a pig is slaughtered. Once more the to mebalun and the
to pabalian take their share of the animal, but this is the last time.
The meaa or ma'peliang, the bearing of the corpse to the rock grave,
entails bringing all the deceased's accessories to the grave and hanging
them there: his sun hat, sirih-pouch, etc. These objects may not be
kept in the house which the deceased inhabited during his lifetime.
Slaughtering a dog is also part of the meaa-rite (dog meat in the past
was food for slaves; I am not sure whether nowadays others partake as
well). At this point everyone returns to the death house. The next day
the ma'bolong takes place; clothing is turned black. The to mebalun's

Fig. 22. Distribution of the meat from a slaughtered buffalo during the ma'kande padang.

a. Division outwards from Ba'tan

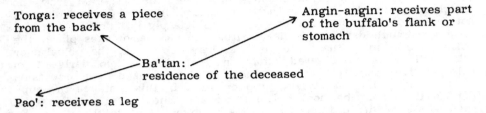

Tonga: receives a piece
from the back

Angin-angin: receives part
of the buffalo's flank or
stomach

Ba'tan:
residence of the deceased

Pao': receives a leg

b. Division outwards from Tonga

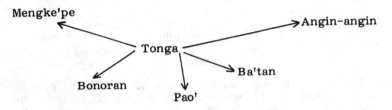

Mengke'pe

Angin-angin

Tonga

Bonoran

Pao'

Ba'tan

All villages adjoining the place where a person has died receive some meat. The villages of b. constitute the complex Tikunna Malenong, "that which surrounds the Malenong rock". Until 1920 Bonoran and Tonga were joined as one.

role here is described in Chapter XI. Upon conclusion of the ma'bolong, the to mebalun and to pabalian receive their payment. Their part in the ritual has been played out.

The next evening, or one of the subsequent ones, the prohibition against family members' eating rice or cooked food is lifted: food is served on three successive evenings.

On the first evening the to massanduk initiates the eating of rice: "as the first to eat rice", "kumande bunga'". A pig is slaughtered. On the second evening the to dibulle tangnga and the to ma'kuasa eat rice once again: "as those in the middle to eat rice", "kumande tangnga". Another pig is killed. On the third evening the to ma'pemali eats rice, followed by all the rest. A pig's head is cooked and the meat served to all to maro'. The next morning a pig is once more slaughtered close to the house and the deceased is given food. (My informants were not clear about this event: is food brought to the rock grave? They were probably alluding to the umbaa kande; see also Chapter X.) The mangrondan bota precedes the following rite (or occurs practically at the same time); after grains of rice have been allowed to fall, all to maro' receive rice and, on occasion, tuak. The rite is known as kumande tampak, "to eat rice as the last". Afterwards a pig's head is cooked for the ussolan bombo, "accompanying the soul of the deceased". One of the family members escorts the soul on its way out. He acts as if he lets the dead person climb onto his back. He plays a special tune on a flute and walks to the South, abandoning the village. Outside the settlement he pauses to let the deceased come down off his back. Returning to the house, the escort announces, "I have already left" (my informant laughed heartily while describing this part of the death ritual; he thought it diverting rather than imposing). Once more the untoe sero follows, "the grasping of what is pure". This is the last offering made to the deceased. A pig is slaughtered at the mouth of the rock grave. The sacrifice frees celebrants from the prescriptions of mourning; people are purified, loosed from the sphere of death (Woordenboek: v. toë). The rite signifies that everything has gone properly and reached its due end (B. Sarungallo).

After this rite, the membase (= to wash oneself, or to wash one's hands) is enacted. A chicken is slaughtered, thereby ridding the house of any and all impurity. In front of the house a tadoran is erected, which is equivalent to observing a conversion ritual. There is some confusion here, however, for the tallung bongi should involve a higher order of conversion ritual, not the ma'tadoran but rather the ma'palang-ngan para (cf. Chapter VII.2.6.). For the role of the widow or widower at this point, see Chapter VIII.2.

Deposition of a baby who died before cutting teeth; the corpse is laid in a hollow cut from an antolong-tree (Kesu'). This death ceremony is also called liang pia, "rock grave for a child". See also pp. 183-184. (Photo: Hetty Nooy-Palm, 1969.)

Lantang pangngan, literally: "guest house for sirih/pinang". The construction consists of bamboo and has a function to fulfil in the death ritual. On the evening of the ma'doya, the watch over the dead, the lantang pangngan is carried in procession to the deceased's house. After the dead is consigned to the rock grave, the "guest house" is set down in front of, or close beside the burial site. For those who die at an early age, the pangngan is merely a forked branch with sirih/pinang attached. See also p. 185.
(Photo: J.W.A. Willems, 1938.)

Chapter X

DEATH RITUALS OF A HIGHER ORDER

"The ladder was set up for him,
They opened up the door for him,
The sleeping mat spread out for him
Head cushions there put down for him.
And then the door they shut on him,
His hat they hung, the steps removed."

(The Chant:34)

1. Introduction

Although the ceremonies in the preceding chapter may strike us as
rather complex, the Toraja themselves consider these to be among their
more straightforward rituals. The death feasts described in this chapter
are of a higher order: they require intense effort and cost a great deal
of money. It soon becomes evident that such death feasts are essentially
elaborations of rituals of a lower order. Certain rites are repeated a
number of times: keeping watch beside the dead, for example, and the
intoning of death chants. In addition several new rites are inserted and
new artefacts introduced. The number of buffaloes that are killed in-
creases and there are more buffaloes which fulfil special functions in
the ritual. More time and energy are invested in decorations. Everything is on a grander and more costly scale. In essence, however,
higher rituals are but an extension of lower ones, further embroidery
on the same pattern, an involutionary development.[1] Rites and actions
observed between death and commencement of the death ritual are, at
best cursorily reported in the text below; for a fuller discussion see
Chapter IX.

The schematic account of these feasts in sections 2-4 are followed by
more detailed descriptions of certain components such as: ma'tomatua
(section 5), ma'tombi and ma'batang (sections 6 and 7) and ma'parando
(section 8).

2. Limang bongi, the five nights ritual

During the limang bongi (or dipalimang bongi, that which lasts for five
nights), the ma'doya occurs no less than five times. Every day family
members pay a condolence call, bringing gifts with them (for the
ma'doya, see Chapter IX.1.5.). For this ritual a minimum of five black
buffaloes and eighteen black pigs are slaughtered. Actually, these
numbers only refer to the death feast proper. Prior to commencement of
the ritual, the deceased is considered "sick", to makula', which means

feverish or hot. "Hot" refers to the dangerous state of a person who died recently, and for whom the proper death rites have not been carried out. Only once the dead person dies ritually is he treated as described in Chapter VIII; the shroud around the bodily remains is then wrapped with a thick layer of kapok. The dead is lamented; the to mebalun who has wrapped the corpse has also the task of providing the corpse with food. The deceased remains exposed in the Southern room until the moment of his official death, i.e. when the death ritual proper commences. The moment is announced by the striking of a gong. The corpse is now carried off to the central room of the house and placed with the head turned towards the South. This orientation symbolizes the change of status from someone who is "sick" to someone who is "dead", from a to makula' to a to mate. At roughly the same time the pa'karu'-dusan is put to death, a black buffalo (pudu'). The sumbung penaa (see Vol.I:197) is sacrificed as well. On this day the first ma'doya takes place. A pig is killed as an offering (it is not clear whether family members supply this pig, but I assume so). The third day is extremely busy; a variety of rites is held. The bala'kaan is constructed (mebala'kaan). For the tallung bongi-ritual an old bala'kaan still stand-ing on the rante may be repaired; that is considered enough. For the limang bongi a new one must always be built.[2] Preparations are made moreover for hauling the monolith (see Vol.I:263-9). Beforehand a black pig and a buffalo are killed.

The ma'doya, the mourning visit by family members, is repeated. The to minaa sings aloud the events of the deceased's life (ma'kakarun, see Chapters VIII and IX.2.2.). As the fourth rite, on the fourth day the ma'palangngan panganta' is observed, the hanging of cloths above the corpse (see Fig. 21).

Then wood is fetched for building the bier (mesarigan), usually from the kapok tree (kaniala') but in Ma'kale also from the kamiri. A chicken and a dog are slaughtered for this rite.[3] A special effigy-maker pre-pares an effigy which, people say, resembles the dead. After all these activities, the family comes together again for the subsequent ma'doya; a pig is killed.

The ma'batang tombi follows: preparations for carrying out and dis-playing textiles that figure in the ritual. The tombi, which are first displayed in front of the house and afterwards on the rante, play a part in the ma'batang-rite which I mentioned earlier (Chapter IX.2.2.). Two buffaloes and a pig are sacrificed. Nor is the ma'doya skipped on this day; the offering involved is once more a pig.

On the fifth day the mantunu[4] is staged, the killing of the buffaloes on the rante. Meat from the animals is sent to adjacent villages. As part of the rite three important buffaloes are slaughtered: the parepe' (a pig is killed together with this buffalo), the tulak bala'kaan, and the batu bangla' (for the first two, see Vol.I:197-8; I have no further information, however, about the batu bangla'). Subsequently, the ma'peliang or meaa occurs. The ma'pallin follows, and afterwards cloth-ing is dyed black. The soul of the deceased is then led outside the village (ussolan bombo, see Chapter IX.2.2.). The to maro' are now allowed to eat rice again (kumande). Before the final kumande, the mangrondan bota takes place.

3. Pitung bongi (or dipapitung bongi)

Although this form of burial appears in the sequence of rituals prior to
the dirapa'i, here there is no question of a sequence of grandeur, for
the ritual of the seven nights is considered equivalent to the dirapa'i.
People often choose not to celebrate the pitung bongi, for it requires
extraordinary effort - a great deal has to happen in only a short time.

As so often is true, this great ritual may "officially" commence a
considerable time after the person honoured has died. Preparations may
last a long while; they include the construction of guest accommodations, the collection of the buffaloes which family members must contribute, and the hiring of badong-singers and dancers. It is possible that
the deceased is conveyed to another tongkonan before the feast begins,
if this new location is more convenient or preferable for logistic reasons
(a better water supply, for example, or more room for guest houses).

The formal part of the death ritual begins with the "waking" of the
deceased by the striking of a gong. The same afternoon, at roughly
two, the bodily remains are conveyed from the Southern room to the
central room. The corpse then is situated with its head to the South.
During this first day, at about the same time that the corpse is relo-
cated in the central room, the pa'karu'dusan is slaughtered. The first
ma'doya also takes place, as part of which a pig is killed about five in
the afternoon. From this point on, every night until the deceased is
entombed, badong are sung. On the second day of the ritual the
ma'doya repeats; two pigs are killed this time. During the ma'doya on
the third day, a buffalo and a pig are sacrificed.

Three rites are enacted on the fourth day:
- the ma'palangngan panganta', during which a pig is sacrificed (for
this rite, in which textiles figure prominently, see the description of
the tallung bongi, Chapter IX.2.2. and Fig. 21);
- the manglelleng sarigan, the hewing of wood for the bier. The offering that is made consists of a chicken and a little bit of dog's blood.
Some drops of blood are allowed to trickle from the ears of a small dog.
The animal's ears are held straight up and the blood is rubbed into a
cloth that has been brought especially for this ritual purpose. The to
mebalun takes possession of the dog afterwards; its subsequent fate is
not reported;
- the ma'doya; a buffalo and a pig are killed.

On the fifth day celebrants take part in four ceremonies:
- the ma'tau-tau, the fabrication of the wooden effigy that represents
the deceased; a pig is sacrificed;
- the massabu sarigan, the consecration of the wooden bier; a pig is
the requisite offering;
- the melantang, the construction of a kind of shrine where everything
needed for preparing sirih/pinang is deposited, an offering that can be
considered as a gift for the deceased but which probably should be
interpreted as a sacrifice which accompanies the building of the guest
accommodations (lantang);
- the mebala'kaan, the making of the bala'kaan; a pig is slaughtered.

Various rites occupy the sixth day as well:
- the ma'palao, the deceased is carried in a procession to the rante or
pantunuan. Here a buffalo is slaughtered. A pig is also sacrificed

during this rite, but where was not specified;
- the ma'doya tangnga; the name suggests this should be the ma'doya which falls in the middle of the series of observances of this rite (tangnga: middle), but this is not at all true in reality; a pig is slaughtered;
- the ma'kakarun (see Chapters VIII and IX.2.2.).

On the seventh day there are two important rites:
- the mantunu, the buffaloes are put to death on the pantunuan. Among the animals killed are the tulak bala'kaan, the batu bangla and the parepe'. The last-named is sacrificed in the afternoon. Now the buffalo is also slaughtered that is intended for the taa baine. Buffalo meat is sent to surrounding settlements, "the giving of food to adjacent villages" (see Chapter IX.2.2. and Fig. 22);
- the ma'doya tampak, the last of the ma'doya-rites (tampak: end); a pig is slaughtered.

On the eighth day the meaa takes place and the dead is conveyed to his final resting place. A black chicken is sacrificed (ma'pallin), and then a pig. The ritual proceeds to the peangka', the slaughter of buffaloes for the division of meat. The flesh of these animals is distributed among notables who are present. (N.B. This is not the same rite as "the giving of food to adjacent villages".) After the return from the rock grave, the membase sali follows; this rite, the purification of the central room of the house, is carried out by a female slave (who is known in her function as to membase sali). Finally the ma'bolong, the dying of clothes black, is performed. During each of these actions, a pig is killed as an offering.

Once the ma'bolong has been completed, the rites of the mangrondan bota, "the eating of rice" (kumande) begin. In such a major ritual, the first, second and final kumande are clearly differentiated; accompanying each in turn, a pig is sacrificed. Afterwards the ussolan bombo, escorting the dead man's soul beyond village precincts, is acted out.
   The following functionaries officiate during the pitung bongi:
1. the to mebalun, the death priest;
2. the to pabalian, the death priest's helper;
3. the to umbaa gandang, the one who brings the drum;
(these first three functionaries are all male; the numbers 4, 6 and 7 are female; number 5 may be either)
4. the to ma'pemali;
5. the to maro' (= to mariu);
6. the to massanduk dalle, "she who serves the maize from the pot" (for those in mourning), a slave (see Chapter IX.2.2.);
7. the to ma'mariri, a woman as well. Her function is not clear to me; ma'mariri means to dip clothing in water with tumeric to dye it yellow;
8. the to ma'kuasa, a man (see Chapter IX.2.2.);
9. three women, the to silali', whose function will be discussed in Chapter XI.1.2. (the silali'-ceremony). These are the to dipandanni bassi, "she who is set down like iron", the to dilali', "she whose shoulders are burdened with care", the leading functionary in the ritual, and the to umbuang sampin, "she who throws away the cloth" (sampin);
10. the to membase sali, a female slave;

11. the to untoe dulang, "he who holds the dulang (a plate on a pedestal)"; a man with an obscure role;
12. there is a twelfth official whose task remains something of a mystery to me.

Upon conclusion of the death feast, a conversion ritual is celebrated but not according to any fixed schedule. In Kesu' a conversion ritual of this order is called manganta', but in Sangalla' people speak of the ma'gandang, the beating of a drum, a rite during which a chicken and dog are sacrificed at the rock grave (for this conversion ritual, see Chapter VII.2.7.).

4. Dirapa'i, that which is enacted with an interval

The dirapa'i is a death ritual with an intermission (rapa', to be still, to stop speaking or to cease doing something). There are different echelons of dirapa'i which the Toraja distinguish:
a. dirapa'i dilayu-layu (the rapa'i that induces wilting = layu). During such a ritual in 1940 no less than nine buffaloes had to be slaughtered;
b. rapasan sundun, the complete rapa'i-ritual, the celebration of which in 1940 required the sacrificing of at least twenty-four buffaloes;
c. sapu randanan, in actuality an elaborate version of the rapasan sundun.[5]
For the dirapa'i dilayu-layu, in addition to the number of cited buffaloes, thirty-six pigs must be killed. During a rapasan sundun, by 1966, the number of pigs that had to be executed in addition to the quota of buffaloes had declined to thirty-six; previously often far more were required.

Below I list the rites of the rapasan sundun succinctly, for they are presented at greater length in following chapters. First the ma'karu'-dusan is held, the slaughter of the special buffalo known as the pa'-karu'dusan. The animal is killed "because a person has died".

On the first day the buffalo called the sumbung penaa ("the follower of the breath, the appendage of the soul", see Vol.I:197) is also slaughtered. The ma'doya is observed as well, entailing sacrifice of a pig. Four functionaries in all perform their offices on this first day:
1. the to ma'pemali;
2. the to ma'kuasa;
3. the to mebalun;
4. the to pabalian, the to mebalun's assistant.
The ma'bambangan is the first rite of the second day. A pig is slaughtered. During the ma'doya tangnga, also observed on the second day, a buffalo and a pig are sacrificed, The to minaa thereupon chronicles the deceased's life in song (ma'kakarun). The following functionaries put in an appearance:
5. the to massanduk dalle;
6. the to ma'nasu to mebalun, "she who cooks for the death priest", a female slave;
7. the to sipalakuan, an "assistant".
On the third day the ma'batang is celebrated; a buffalo is slaughtered. This day the buffalo especially for women is also sacrificed (taa baine, the part for women). Two women carry the meat, and a third distributes it among the women who are present. Next a supply of firewood

is made ready (ma'patama kayu). Meat is dispatched to adjoining villages. This day is the last time that a watch is kept over the dead (ma'doya tampak); a pig is killed. A number of additional functionaries carry out appointed tasks:

8. the to silali':
a. the to dipandanni bassi, "she who is set down like iron";
b. the to dilali', "she whose shoulders are burdened with care";
c. the to umbuang sampin, also called to mangria sampin, "she in whose lap the cloths are thrown" (cf. above and Chapter XII);
9. the to untoe bia', three men bearing torches who stand beside the deceased, one at the head, one at the feet, one in the middle;
10. the to untoe ue, "those who hold the rattan in which the rapasan (see below) comes to rest".

Commentary is needed about groups 8, 9 and 10. The to silali' are women who either belong to the deceased's family or to the slave class. They officiate during the silali'-rite. The to untoe bia' and the to untoe ue are functionaries needed whenever a rapasan[6] is used, a coffin that resembles a rice mortar. The rapasan is kept in a cave from which it is brought down especially for the ceremony; it is returned to the cave when it has served its function. On the night following the ma'doya tampak, the bodily remains are laid in the rapasan. The three to untoe bia' each wave a burning torch over the roll of cloth in which the dead man has been wrapped. This happens at the moment that the three to untoe ue, two to makaka and a slave, lift the corpse into the rapasan. Similarly, two of the to untoe bia' are free men, one a slave. Once the torches have been extinguished, the to untoe ue, "they who hold the rattan", wind strips of rattan around the coffin and lift it three times in succession. The to untoe bia' help them. The slaves hold the rattan strips at the foot end of the deceased. The to massanduk dalle and another woman, the to dibulle tangnga, also have a role to play in this rite; their actions are described at greater length in Chapter XI. Once the corpse has lain for some time in the rapasan, it is lifted out again. The deceased in all his wrappings is now suspended from the ba' or teng, a beam running parallel to the ridge beam about half-way between the floor and the roof. The corpse comes to hang on the Western ba'. After a time the deceased is placed once more in the rapasan (according to Van der Veen, the bodily remains in the rapasan are hung from the beam).

At this point an interval follows which may last a "year" or more. Throughout this period, which is not in any event the same as a calendar year, the deceased stays in the death house. The widow or widower and the to ma'pemali keep watch over him (their vigil is not called ma'doya). Later the ritual is resumed. It begins anew with the ma'pasusu, which entails sacrifice of a buffalo. The ma'pasusu will be described in Chapter XI.1.2. On the same day the ma'bolong[7] is enacted as well, with the slaughter of a pig.

On the days which follow various rites take place:
- the ma'pakande, the sacrifice consists of a pig;
- the ma'mentang, with, once again, the offering of a pig; and
- the ma'tutu' ba'bai, during which a pig is sacrificed, too. Ma'tutu' means "to close the door (ba'ba)". The rapasan, left open up to this moment, now acquires a lid of woven rattan. The following rites are then observed:

- the manglossokan, "freeing oneself from the death ritual", a pig is slaughtered;
- the ma'kayu, the hauling of wood needed for the bier and for the "house of the corpse" (lakkean or lakkian); a dog is sacrificed;
- the ma'tundan, "to awake". A pig is sacrificed to demonstrate that the celebrants are in earnest about continuing with the ritual - the dead is "awakened";
- the manglelleng sarigan, the cutting down of trees to secure wood for the bier; a chicken and a dog comprise the offering;
- the mebala'kaan, a buffalo and a pig are sacrificed;
- the melakkean (melakkian), "to make a small death house", i.e. to construct a platform in the form of a Toraja house in which the corpse is placed throughout the second phase of the death feast; this lakkian is situated on the rante (Vol.I:261);
- the melantang, "to make the feast huts" (guest accommodations); a buffalo and a pig are killed;
- the ma'palangngan ba'; a pig is sacrificed[8];
- the ma'popengkalao do mai ba'; a pig is the offering[8];
- the ma'palangngan sarigan, "to lift the corpse in the sarigan"; a pig is sacrificed (Woordenboek:272). This implies that the bodily remains are laid out on the bier inside the house of mourning. Yet this introduces an additional bit of confusion for the corpse is not carried outside the house on the bier, but rather a number of men lift it in its winding sheet and bring it into the open air. Personally, I've never seen a bier inside a Toraja house. Presumably this rite is first enacted later, for example after the massabu sarigan (see below);
- the mangaro, to take the corpse out of the rapasan; a pig is sacrificed;
- the ma'doya; the offering is a pig;
- the ma'balun, "to wrap the corpse", the bodily remains are wrapped anew, the task of the death priest;
- the ma'palangngan ba'; a pig is sacrificed[8];
- the mangrambu bulisak, "to chase away, to remove the splinters"; a pig is killed;
- the mangrera, feeding the dead; the offering is a pig;
- the ma'doya; a pig is sacrificed;
- the manglelleng tau-tau, wood for the tau-tau is felled; offering of a chicken and a dog;
- the ma'tau-tau, a pig is sacrificed for the carving of the tau-tau;
- the manglassak tau-tau, the mortuary effigy is given sexual parts; a pig is sacrificed;
- the ma'popengkalao, "the bringing down" (of the corpse): the bodily remains are removed from the house of mourning to the ricebarn; the offering consists of a pig;
- the massabu sarigan; a pig is sacrificed;
- the ma'doya dio alang, ma'doya three days in a row; a pig is slaughtered on each day;
- the massabu tau-tau, the consecration of the tau-tau by the to minaa; for the accompanying invocation see Koubi 1979:167. This invocation also takes place at the ma'tau-tau. A pig is sacrificed;
- the unlelleng kayu digaraga osing ditampan balun, "to cut wood to make charcoal for smelting the trappings of the shroud"; the trappings are of gold and silver leaf; a chicken serves as offering;
- the untanan pasa', "to establish a market place", i.e. the feast

terrain; a pig is sacrificed;
- the sembangan baratu, cock fights; on the day the cock fights are to
begin, a huge pig or buffalo is slaughtered. (These fights are forbidden by the Indonesian government, but at times cock fights are tole-
rated during major rituals.);
- the ma'pasa' tedong, the decorated buffaloes are led in procession to
the slaughtering place (rante) and circle three times around the bala'-
kaan; then the buffaloes fight against each other; a pig is sacrificed;
- the ma'tambuli rante, "to make a hole in the rante"; the hole is presumably for the simbuang (= menhir) which is to be erected; a buffalo
comprises the offering;
- the mesimbuang, the erecting of the menhir; this huge stone has
already been dragged to the rante (cf. Vol.I:263-9); it is set on end
now and a pig is sacrificed;
- the ma'palao, a buffalo is sacrificed; a procession bearing the corpse
proceeds to the rante; everyone chases after a young pig that has been
released, trying to catch it;
- the ma'doya dio rante, for three successive days the death watch is
observed on the rante; a pig is sacrificed each day;
  the ma'palumbang (lumbang: the killing of a buffalo for a great death
feast); a buffalo is sacrificed;
- the mantunu, a buffalo is sacrificed and divided among the women
attending;
- on the day before the meaa, a buffalo is sacrificed (parepe' or tandi
rapasan);
- the meaa, the carrying of the dead to the rock grave. Two pigs are
killed as an offering, the first as soon as the corpse is removed from
the lakkian (cf. above), the second beside the grave.

The ma'bolong takes place next. Then follow:
- the kumande bunga', a pig is sacrificed;
- kumande tangnga, the offering consists of a pig;
- umbaa kande, "to bring food" (to the deceased at the rock grave), a
pig is sacrificed;
- kumande tampak, preceded by the mangrondan bota, the offering consisting of two pigs; each kumande is followed by the act of letting
grains of rice fall through gaps in the floor (see below). During the
night after the kumande tampak has been performed, the bombo, the
soul of the deceased, is led out of the village;
- untoe sero, "to grasp the state of purity", a purification rite which
entails sacrifice of a pig (and payment to the to mebalun);
- membase, "to wash the hands" in the sense of purify. The two rites
of purification are enacted one right after the other. Apparently they
decontaminate celebrants from the sphere of death (cf. Chapter
IX.2.2.).

Because most of these rites have already been described and discussed
earlier in this book, I have confined myself to their mere enumeration.
Van der Veen was so kind as to provide the following explanation for
the kumande rites and the escorting of the deceased's soul beyond the
settlement. Since his account is more elaborate than information which I
received from my Kesu' sources, I include it here. The kumande tangnga, "the eating of rice by the middle group" is a rite marking the
point at which a number of functionaries in the death ritual no longer

observe certain rules of mourning, especially the prohibition against eating rice. Another group composed of family and relatives has already resumed consumption of rice with observance of the preceding kumande bunga', loosely translatable as "the eating of rice by those who go in front". The kumande tampak, "the eating of rice by the last group" closes the mourning period for the to ma'pemali, the to ma'kuasa and the to balu, the widow or widower (yet the to balu is not released from funeral prohibitions altogether; several rites remain for him or her to undergo, cf. Chapter VIII.2.). Those who now eat rice again let some grains fall through a chink in the floor, together with scraps of pork (mangrondan or urrondonan bota, "to let rice fall below"). Late in the afternoon or in the evening, the dead man's soul is then led outside the village. Different members of the family go for this rite to a spot beyond the village to the South of the settlement (this version differs from that of Sarungallo; cf. Chapter IX).[9] From this point on the deceased and his surviving relatives part company. The soul of the dead embarks on his journey to Puya, his relatives return to the village. This in fact brings an end to the death ritual.

A deceased of some eminence arrives in the kingdom of the dead in the company of a herd of buffaloes, the buffalo herder, the tombi and other regalia. The dead in Puya await him like an important guest; the newcomer is provided with sirih/pinang. In some regions the living know about Puya through the tales of the to pululondongan, shamans. According to their reports, the kingdom of the dead is no different from the world of the living: there are rich and poor in the hereafter, humble huts and fancy houses, grey, black and dappled buffaloes. There is little talk of any inversion of reality, except for occasional death chants which make mention of doors which close in a way that is opposite to how doors shut on earth. The to pululondongan are intermediaries between the living and the dead. They appear to enter into a trance; muttering the names of dead people, they create the impression that they themselves are sojourning in the kingdom of death. The shaman, encircled during his seance by the relatives of the deceased, can pass messages from the living to the dead and from the dead to the living. He can even convey small gifts, like sirih/pinang and cigarettes. These gifts are ultimately entrusted to the shaman himself (Tangdilintin 1981:48). It is possible for the deceased's family to learn through dreams or from the shaman that the dead person is not satisfied with the gifts; the dead can also express his displeasure with the number of buffaloes slaughtered in his honour during the death ritual. It is possible that the family was unable to sacrifice sufficient buffaloes at the time of the feast. They can atone for their shortcomings later. A ceremony can be organized during which a buffalo is tethered to the bala'kaan and the to minaa declares that this animal is one which is still being "sent on" to the deceased (dipa'pea: to send).

Some time after the deceased has been buried in the rock grave, the ma'tomatua (ma'nene', mangeka') is observed. The deceased still is located in the Southwest. The rite is to reinforce bonds with the ancestors.

5. Ma'tomatua

5.1. Introduction

Ma'tomatua (or ma'nene' or mangeka') signifies the making of an offering
to the ancestors of the Southwest. The rite is held after a death ritual
equal to or higher in order than the tallung bongi. It is uncertain
whether it is also observed for slaves. The ritual can only be enacted
after the rice has already been stored. The family deliberates concerning which tongkonan should be selected as the assembly place and point
of departure for celebrating the ma'tomatua. This meeting apparently is
accompanied by an offering, for one speaks of "the place where the
sirih/pinang (the offering) is set down", "nanai umpopengkalao pangngan".[10] The tongkonan chosen will at a later stage serve as the centre
of the merok-feast which the ramage celebrates. The family (or a large
number of family members?) then proceeds with the to minaa to the
grave. Here a pig is slaughtered.[11] The parts of the slaughtered animal
that must be used during the pemanala are kept apart (see Vol.I:206).
The remaining meat (most of the pig) is cooked in bamboos and eaten
later by family members. No mention was made of whether the to minaa
receives a share as well, but I assume so. Afterwards (close to the
tongkonan?) a small altar is constructed, a palanduan-duan or palan-
doan-doan (for this altar, see Chapter VII). The offering which the to
minaa brings is called pa'palaku-lakuan (from malaku: to request), or
pa'palako-lakoan. Betel and pinang are placed on the altar together with
some scraps of cooked pork.[12] Next the to minaa takes a piece of
bamboo and fills it with water. Another bamboo he fills with tuak so
that the to matua can drink. At sacrifices to the gods and the ancestors, water is meant to enable them to wash their hands before proceeding to eat. The to minaa now delivers a prayer over the altar. Van
der Veen generously made the text of this prayer, in Toraja and in
Dutch translation, available for publication. His rather free rendering
of the original raises problems here and there but I have chosen to
adopt his text integrally. To be sure, Van der Veen's thorough knowledge of Toraja language and culture placed him in a unique position to
interpret the meaning of a prayer often remarkable for its obscurity. J.
Tammu, Van der Veen's assistant, has given an explanation of the
accompanying ceremony (see section 5.2.).

5.2. The meaning of the ma'tomatua

In the prayer spoken over the setting down of the sirih/pinang, the to
minaa invites all ancestors to share in the offering which their living
descendants have prepared for them. In his invitation, the to minaa
states that he doesn't consider any ancestor higher or more worthy of
respect than the others, for their offspring, those making the offering,
come from villages in the environs of those places where the ancestors
themselves formerly lived. That is why the ancestors are served in the
same fashion with sirih/pinang; none is more revered than the others.
Then the full group of ancestors is called upon to enjoy the sirih/
pinang offered to them, sirih/pinang which has been specially selected.
The words of verses 5 and 6 of the text in section 5.3.1. indicate this
is sirih/pinang of the best quality.
  In his prayer over the offering, the to minaa states that he has

served all the ancestors round about with betel and areca. Subsequently he rises to proclaim powerful words of blessing over the various
dishes which have been served, tasty complements to succulent pork.
The left-overs set out for the ancestors are eaten together by all the
descendants who have brought the offering.

In the prayer uttered upon parting, emphasis falls upon confirmation
of conformity to the "sacral union" (= basse, see Vol.I:79), a promise
made under oath. And furthermore stress is placed on the ancestors'
continuing to confer blessings on their descendants, as the descendants
forge ahead in life, keeping their word in appreciation for the offering
which consisted of such delicious things to eat. All will go well as long
as the ancestors continue to bestow their watchfulness and care.

The meaning of the last eight lines of the mangimbo sisarak is that
the ancestors, in return for the sacrificial meal which is served to
them, will abide by their commitment to protect the lives of their
progeny.

Before celebrants move on to celebrate a merok-feast, two rites must
first be observed: the mangrara pare, already discussed in Chapter
VII, and the massampinni (literally: "to provide with cotton cloths").
There are two parts to the massampinni: a. the ma'bungka' alang
(literally: "to open the ricebarn"), to perform the first act of cultivation on the sawah, celebrated with the offering of a pig; and b. the
massampinni itself, held the following day, entailing the sacrifice of a
buffalo and a pig.

During this rite the clothing of the tau-tau, the wooden effigies that
portray the dead, is changed. They receive new garments. The deceased themselves also are provided with new apparel: clothing is
placed in their graves beside them. The to minaa delivers the same
prayer as earlier during the ma'tomatua. The small altar (palanduan-
duan) is used once again.

5.3. Prayers from the ma'tomatua

5.3.1. Pangimbo umpatorro pangngan [13]
The to minaa offers the sirih while singing the following litany:

Pangimbo umpatorro pangngan	The prayer over the laying down of the sirih/pinang
Kamu te to diponene',	You regarded as ancestors,
Kamu te dipotomatua,	You considered as forefathers.
Tae'komi dipatayang lamba'[14]	None of you will, like a fig tree, be exalted higher
Lan kapuran pangngan.[15]	While the sirih/pinang is sprinkled with lime,
Tae'komi la dipalangso barana'	None of you will be raised on high like a banyan tree
Lan pelambaran[16] dibaolu.	While the betel leaves are handed out.
Belanna iatu taruk bulaanmi	Because your golden progeny are people
To ma'rara tiku[17],	Who come from encircling regions,

Ia tu lolosu kandauremu[18]
To ma'lomba' leleali.

Your noble offspring are people
Whose blood comes from nearby.

Unno'ko' mokomi ma'pangngan,

Sit here now to chew the betel
quid,

Unnesung mokomi ma'pangngan,

Sit yourselves down to chew the
betel quid,

Ma'damerak-merak.

Staining the mouth red.

Diongmo bolu tang silenda
ura'na[19]
Kalosi ponno issinna.

The betel that lies there is betel
whose veins touch each other,
The areca nuts are plump with meaty
fruit.

Kapu' ma'lumpa bumbungan

Lime, white as the surging foam
on milk,

Sambako dikakkiri' gallang

Tobacco, rolled and cut fine as thin
ankle rings,

Gatta dipapada limbu.

Gambier, regular in shape.

Anno'ko mokomi ma'pangngan-
pangngan
Unnesung mokomi ma'damerak-
merak.

Sit down now to chew the betel quid
on and on,
Sit down to make your mouths red.

5.3.2. Pangimbo pesung

The prayer over the offering meal

Kamu te to diponene'

You here who we regard as
forefathers,

Kamu te do dipotomatua

You here who we regard as
ancestors,

Mangka mokomi kupaliling bon-
tong lan kapuran pangngan
Limbu balana mokomi kukambio

I have circled around you like a
stockade around a buffalo stable,
I have gone around you, like
their enclosure surrounds them,

santung lan pelambaran dibaolu[20],

plucking the stringed instruments
while the betel leaves were handed
out.

Bangunmo' la ma'pakatua'[21] induk
te kande mammi'mi,

Already I have stood up to ensure
lasting well-being, inviolable like
the wood of the sugar palm over the
tasty meal,

Diongmo' la ma'pabami' karurungan[22] te timbu' marasammi.

Already I have seated myself here to
pronounce a powerful blessing,
indestructible as the hard wood of
the old sugar palm, over this
wonderful meal.

Burana tetean tampo[23],
Lumpana pananda uai.[24]

The yield of the sawahs,
the welling up of that surrounded by
embankments.

Sitondon duku'na bai,
Sisola issinna to ma'bulu
bonde'[25]

In tastiness suited to pork,
together with the meat of he who has
hairs like the herbaceous cotton
plant.

Anna uainna salle balubu,

Litena mayang kalando burena.

And that which is in the great
martavan (big jar of foreign origin),
the moisture of the spadix with
the long sheath.

Iate sesa isimmi,

sola ra'dak barokomi,

What remains from between your
teeth,
with that left over from your throat,

La napatobang dikollong taruk
bulaanmi,
La naparonno' dibaroko lolosu[26]
kandauremi.

May it be thrown into the throat of
your golden progeny,
may it slide down inside the neck of
your noble issue.

5.3.3. Pangimbo sisarak

The prayer spoken upon parting
from each other

Mangkamokan ma'patobang
dikollong, sesa isimmi,

Already we have let the surplus
from your teeth slide down inside
the neck,

Pura mokan ma'paronno'
dibaroko ra'dak barokomi.

already we have plunged the left-
overs from your throat down ours.

Apala diong pakan te sanda
malambi' lako batang dikalemi[27],
Diong pakan sanda medete'[28]
lako tondon to batangmi.[29]

But we are still seated here to re-
mind you of the old promise,
we are seated here still to bring
up our agreement.

La unggaraga piki' sisulu'
basse[30],

Let us make an agreement, confirm-
ing it on both sides with a promise
made under oath,

La untampa piki' sisangkala
pindan.[31]

let us enter into a bond mutually
binding it with a sacral promise.

Belanna tang lumokkonpa
lalanna to diponene',

Because those who are regarded as
our ancestors, shall not turn back
on their way,

Tang lumu'pi'pa pa'gulinganna
to dipotorro to matua.

Because those who are regarded as
ancestors shall not turn back on
their path which has been travelled
back and forth.

Susi duka taruk bulaanmi
Tang lumokkonpa lalanna.[32]

So likewise your golden progeny,
they shall not turn back on their
way.

Ten te lolosu kandauremi

Also your descendants, shining like
a kandaure,

Tang lumu'pi'pa pa'gulinganna.

they shall not turn back on their

path which has been travelled back
and forth.

La urriakomi[33] penaa ma'bulu
podong

Will you with your heart, that is
like thin bamboo, full of earth
mounds of flying termites,

Lako taruk bulaanmi.

Extend your care over your golden
progeny,

La ussaladankomi sunga'
mentangke[34] a'rari

Will you with your spirit, which is
like a branch on which the flying
termites nestle,

Lako lolosu kandauremi.

Bear protectively on your hands,
your descendants shining like a kandaure.

Da mipatoe langga',
Da mipadeken loga'-loga'.

Will you not maintain it laxly,
will you not be weak in abiding by
it.

Susi duka te taruk bulaanmi,
Ten te lolosu kandauremi,

So, too, your golden progeny,
likewise your descendants, shining
like a kandaure,

Tang la tikkondo'[35] tingtingmo
lako kande mammi'mi,

Do not relax like a line which snaps
free, (the union with) your tasty
food,

Tang la matombe' la'pa-la'pa[36]
lako timbu' marassammi.

Never move up and down like a
sweeping bamboo, (the union with)
your delicious meal.

Ke manda'i buntu rengnge'mi[37]

As long as the mountain which you
have to carry remains steadfast,

Ke bintinni patondon[38] sari-
rimi.[39]

As long as the responsibility which
rests on your shoulders is firmly
borne.

6. Ma'tombi, a rite from the limang bongi held in Sangalla', 1966

In this and the immediately following section, the carrying out and display of sacral textiles and other regalia is described. The first account
applies to Sangalla', the second to Tikala. The rite is recounted in
Chapter XI.1.2. as a component of the ma'batang. The exact significance of the manipulation of textiles is not clear; sacral cloths belong to
the female section of society. The rite is customary only as part of
death feasts of a high order. The artefacts emphasize the status of the
ceremony. During burial of members of the puang's family, these same
cloths (tombi), which give the rite its name (ma'tombi), do service. (In
Kesu' carrying out flags and other regalia occurs during the ma'batang.)

The deceased honoured by this rite was Lai' Ranggina, a younger
sister of puang Batualu, who was a first cousin of the puang of Sangalla'. She lay in state in tongkonan Buntu which was built on a high
place. Buntu, indeed, means hill. After a steep climb which offered

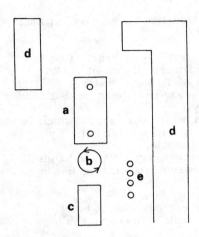

Fig. 23. Groundplan of tongkonan
Buntu.

a. tongkonan Buntu
b. badong-dancers
c. ricebarns
d. guest accommodations
e. female dancers

splendid views, we reached the house of mourning. (One of the Toraja
women accompanying me, a woman of standing, refused to make the
ascent and remained behind in Tokesan. She knew she was supposed to
supply a buffalo for the ritual and did not intend to do so.) Our arrival coincided with the day for welcoming guests. The ricebarns were
in readiness. Guest accommodations had been constructed, too (for a
diagram of the area, see Fig. 23).

One of the high points of the day was preparation of the belo tedong
("the buffalo's finery")[40], an ornament which called to mind the triangular facade of a tongkonan (see Fig. 24).

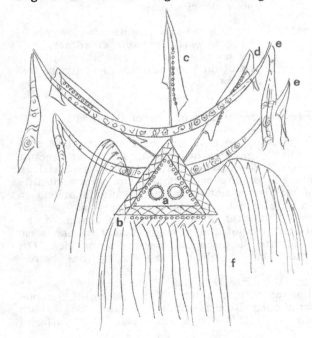

Fig. 24. Belo tedong.

a. komba (bracelets)
b. pollo' dodo
c. tombi
d. bandera
e. (kain) sarita
f. daun pusuk
This type of belo tedong
is reserved for members
of the puang-family.

Various pieces of inherited property appeared as part of the ornamentation: sarita-cloths, tombi, bandera of red cloth decorated with coins (bandera, borrowed from the Portuguese, has become the Indonesian word for flag), pollo' dodo (the band of cloth which runs along the lower hem of a woman's sarong decorated with woven figures and trimmed old coins), and komba (bracelets added as a decorative touch at a point on the belo tedong corresponding roughly to the place on the façade of the tongkonan where the barre allo - sun motif - appears). The wife of the puang of Sangalla', having arrived after us, became fully engaged in giving directions for fitting out the belo tedong. (Somewhat later in the morning, the puang was expected.) The to ma'kuasa, recognizable by the red ribbon he wore about his head, was also freely offering advice. He was a relative of the dead woman.

The manik tedong (literally: "the buffalo's beads") was brought forward and suspended from the lower - left - side of the belo tedong. The manik tedong (see Fig. 25) is a string decorated with large pieces of citrus rind (here from a kind of shaddock) alternating with bamboo cylinders having figures cut into their surface, and with fruits of the egg-plant (tarrung).

Fig. 25. Manik tedong.

Guests then began to arrive hard on each other's heels. Members of the deceased's family descended each time from the house of mourning to greet new arrivals. Young women and men served coffee or tea and cakes. The to mebalun then made his entrance, dressed in white, or rather in greyish yellow. He beat upon a drum, a signal for all helpers to return to their places. Before refreshments were passed around, the ma'bating (wailing beside the dead) resounded.

Afterwards a group of girls advanced into the compound wearing dancing apparel; they were accompanied by a youth who played the gandang (drum). In all there were nine dancers in black sarongs with white blouses wearing a belt of beads (sassang) with fringes also of beads. The dancers also had ropes of beads about their necks. The group leader wore a kandaure which dangled from her back. Each of the girls had a paper ornament on her head consisting of a red turban or toque decorated with small white figures and crowned with a triangular ornament which also evoked the façade of a Toraja house. Tunes sung during the dancing were said to be sailo'.[41]

A steady increase in the rate of activities all happening at the same time, made close observation difficult. Three bandera (flags) were fastened to the belo tedong and then a kris (gayang) as well. This kris was of Balinese model with a man-like figure for a handle. It was bound with a red cloth. The buffalo was led forward, the parepe', who would be sacrificed the next day. The manik tedong, extracted from the belo tedong, was draped about the animal's neck. The ma'badong followed: the song for the dead sung by a group of people who formed into a circle. As soon as the song resounded, five men began to dance around the belo tedong (see Fig. 26).[42] They moved counter-clockwise. Before one circuit was completed, four more men joined them and they all danced three, four, five times around the belo tedong, their ranks joined during the last circuit by two women. The men wore a sambu' (kain) and had a machete on the left hip; the women had on a headcloth and carried a betel-pouch over the right shoulder.

Fig. 26. Dancing around the belo tedong.

The first time 5 men danced around the belo tedong, the second time nine men, the third time 9 men, the fourth time 9 men and two women and the fifth time 9 men and two women. The dancers moved counter-clockwise.

In the meantime the massailo' had also started, so that the death song of commemoration and the dancers' singing mingled in the air. The girls formed rank and began to dance (Fig. 27). After some time their leader, the one with the kandaure, finished the dance by climbing onto a drum.

The tombi were now carried forward. These banners, originating from the tongkonan of Kalaya, were set in place in front of the house on its right side, behind the belo tedong. The circle of ma'badong-dancers kept enlarging and people began making leaps. The to mebalun came along, clothed in white. Children kept crowding in until the puang told them to move back.

As the ma'badong drew to a close, the dancers hoisted the entire belo tedong and formed a procession. They were followed by someone who led the parepe'. The buffalo wore the manik tedong and had a maa'-cloth thrown over its back. With yelling and shouting, the procession neared the pantunuan (for the arrangement of animals see Fig. 28).

Fig. 27. Arrangement of female massailo'-dancers.

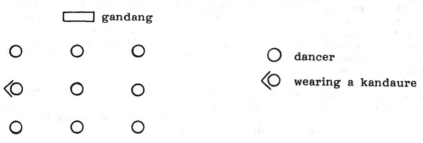

Fig. 28. Pantunuan in Sangalla'.

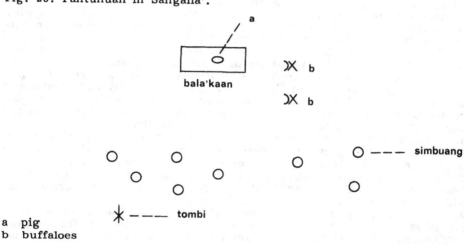

a pig
b buffaloes

The pig that was sacrificed here came as a gift from a to parengnge'. According to rule, the animal was divided; pieces of meat from the bala'kaan were brought around to important functionaries in the customary fashion. The name of each recipient of flesh was called out in turn. Now the tombi were removed from their poles. After they were folded up and cleared away, the women returned home.

Division of the parepe' (which would be put to death the next day) adhered to the following pattern: the stomach was for tongkonan Kasean, the rest for the to parengnge' (from the village or tongkonan Buntu?) with the exception of the head which was for tongkonan Kalaya. One of the to parengnge' from tongkonan Kasean has the task of stabbing the animal to death. A certain reciprocal relation exists among these three adjacent tongkonan:

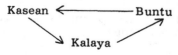

According to reports, on the day of the mebalun, the day preceding
the ma'tombi, eight pigs had been slaughtered and shared out among
the residents. One of the eight to parengnge' mounted the bala'kaan
and supervised division of the meat. (If we accept a contradictory version, only one pig and one buffalo were killed at this mebalun.)

The day after the ma'tombi, both the massailo' and the ma'badong
would again take place.

An account of the dipalimang bongi as reported in Sangalla' follows
below in shortened form. It deviates in certain respects from the
account rendered above. The previous version of the ma'tombi also
differs in ways from what is registered below.
1. The ma'karu'dusan is the initial rite. A pig and buffalo (a pudu')
are the offering. The to mebalun presides.
2. Allo datuna ("the day of the lord"). The to mebalun leads the rite
during which a pig is killed on the compound.
3. The mebalun. The death priest leads the rite, once more wrapping
the corpse in a cloth. A pig and a buffalo serve as offerings. On this
and the following day guests are received.
4. The day after the mebalun is devoted to the ma'tombi as just
described in the text. All kinds of important ornaments are brought
forth, some with sacral significance, such as the ancient maa'-cloths. I
have already commented on the kain sarita, tombi, gayang, komba and
belo tedong. The belo tedong is prepared by family members of the deceased or by the pa'tondokan (those who belong to the village). On the
bala'kaan a pig is divided up; two buffaloes are slaughtered.
5. The mantunu (the slaughter of animals for the deceased). Three
buffaloes and two pigs are killed; the to mebalun leads the rite. The
parepe' is also sacrificed on this day and divided among the members of
the to balu (widow or widower). Division of the meat takes place on the
bala'kaan. The belo tedong is dismantled. The cloths and ornaments,
which form part of it, are put in safekeeping.
6. The meaa (ma'peliang). The dead is brought to the grave where a
pig is killed at the base of the rock. On the compound in front of the
tongkonan, two buffaloes are slaughtered. A portion of the meat from
these beasts is put in a pan and brought to the grave.
7. After three days, white clothing (and other implements in use) is
given a blacking. This mourning hue is worn by the family (by the
ramage and the rampean).[43] A pig is killed.
8. One week later clothes are dyed black a second time (ma'pakatua =
ma'bolong in Kesu'). A pig is slaughtered then, too.
9. After an interval of three days, then the kandean dalle is observed
(kandean means plate, dalle is maize; those dressed in mourning may
only eat maize). Another pig is slain.
10. The ma'lolo (= kumande in Kesu') release the people from the prohibition against eating rice. One or two pigs are killed. (Ma'lolo signifies: to be correct, to be in the proper state.)
11. Three days later the ma'karoen is held. A black chicken is sacrificed to the West of the house of mourning (ma'karoen-roen: to be busy
in the gloaming). This rite may be the same as ma'pallin in Kesu' (cf.
Merok:156-8 and Vol.I:247).
12. In three days time the ma'bai pudu' takes place; a black pig is
slaughtered (the colour of mourning).
13. Roughly an entire rice-season of suspended funeral activity passes.

Then the ma'gandang initiates the conversion ritual of the dead and marks the end of prescribing mourning. A sella' (a cock with specific markings, see Vol.I:210) is offered to the gods. This rite is called the ma'rambu tali. For the first time the to minaa is in charge.

14. In the afternoon the manta'da (= to request, to implore) is enacted. A boar (todi) is killed near the rock grave in remembrance of the deceased.

15. The next morning the la'pa' gandang is performed ("letting go of the drum" in the sense of ending, concluding the death ritual). An offering of two pigs is made. The to minaa officiates. The rite takes place in front of the house. The segments of one of the sacrificed pigs are placed next to the sandal tree on a small altar (pa'palanduan = pa'-paparukan). This shrine, with its two levels, has already been described in detail during an earlier account of the manganta' (see Chapter VII, section 2.7.1.). Rites 13-15 listed here apparently are part of a conversion ritual, even though this was not said to me explicitly. A sella', to be sure, is always sacrificed to the deata of the East (see Vol.I:210).

7. Ma'batang tombi in Parinding village in the kecamatan of Tikala' (Bori' subdistrict)

Tongkonan Kombong and the rante provided the central setting for this celebration on November 7, 1966. The ma'batang was a component rite for the dirapa'i held for Ne' Parra.

On the previous day, the ma'puli took place. Many guests had been received; on the compound four buffaloes and thirty-odd pigs has been slaughtered. All that remained of the feast were apart from three massive stones upon which an enormous roasting pan still rested: ashes, charcoal and exhaustion. For three nights without ceasing people had chanted the badong.

Fig. 29. Arrangement of the tombi etc. in front of the tongkonan.

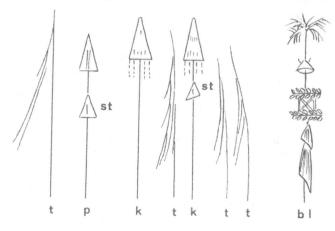

t	tombi
p	payung
k	kandaure
b l	bate lepong
st	betel pouch

t   p   k   t k   t   t   b l

In front of tongkonan Kombong, the house of the dead woman, four tombi (banners), an umbrella, two kandaure and a single bate lepong (see below) were set up (Fig. 29). The kandaure were fastened to bamboo staffs; their shape was that of a half-opened umbrella. Beneath an actual umbrella and also beneath one of the kandaure, hung a betel pouch. To the left, aligned with the kandaure, umbrella and tombi in front of the tongkonan, stood the bate lepong. This effigy, an image of the dead person, had the appearance of a scarecrow (see Fig. 30). It consisted of a bamboo staff topped with a hat, also of bamboo; horizontally mounted on this staff were two other, shorter lengths of bamboo decorated with ferns; these represented shoulders and pelvis. A kain sarita was bound crosswise to the central pole; red-white cloths were attached lengthwise. Beneath the lower horizontal bamboo section a black dodo (woman's sarong), complete with female undergarment was fastened. The bate lepong was affixed to a simbuang kayu consisting of the trunk of a banana tree. Report had it that on previous days the horns of slaughtered buffaloes had been fastened to this simbuang kayu. Traditionally the simbuang also serves as a symbolic pole to which buffaloes are bound while being slaughtered. In actuality, short sturdy pegs in the ground serve this purpose.

We went to dine; after the meal a small pig was slain and roasted as a suckling. Constant blows fell upon the gong (= bombongan, "to give vent to mourning"). In the interim the rapasan (temporary coffin) was brought out. It had the form of an issong (rice mortar, see Fig. 31).

Fig. 30. Bate lepong ("the round banner"); an effigy used in the ma'batang and ma'tombi rites.

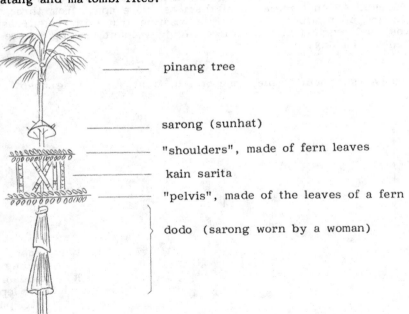

pinang tree

sarong (sunhat)

"shoulders", made of fern leaves

kain sarita

"pelvis", made of the leaves of a fern

dodo (sarong worn by a woman)

Fig. 31. Issong, coffin in the shape of a rice mortar (Tikala; elsewhere erong or rapasan). The "coffin" is conveyed by carrying it on bamboo.

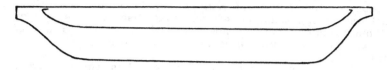

As the sun set, or somewhat later, the roll of cloth in which the deceased was swathed would be placed in the rapasan where it would remain for five days before being suspended in the West part of the sali-room in the house. (No mention was made of whether the coffin would be hung up as well.)

A procession formed. The bate lepong, the kandaure and other portable ornaments were lifted up. The mourning women grouped themselves behind these objects, taking their place underneath a long, white cloth. Male members of the family and visitors followed them without stepping under the cloth. Following the narrow sawah path, up and downhill, the celebrants approached the rante. Here, ready for slaughter, buffaloes stood among the simbuang batu (see Vol.I:265, 267). Seven to minaa mounted the bala'kaan which was supported by six living trees, mostly sandalwood.[45] Each to minaa took a turn reciting. This consumed, all in all, a good two hours. No one was able to tell me exactly what the to minaa were saying. People, in fact, hardly paid attention. Women passed the time by rolling thread from pineapple fibre, just as western women under similar conditions might sit knitting. In closing, one of the to minaa scattered meat for the ancestors (this offering is called dikiki'). Small boys were quick to gather these up. This meat came from animals previously slaughtered.

At this point family members conferred about the buffaloes to be slain. Some of the animals served to repay an old debt, the donor fulfilling his promise to return borrowed buffaloes during a death feast. Buffaloes for such a purpose must, it goes without saying, meet certain standards. It appears that people often worry themselves beforehand about whether an animal will be acceptable or not. Before I had arrived at Parinding, an old man had walked beside me whose son preceded us leading a young buffalo steer; he was to redeem a pledge at the death feast with the buffalo, he explained, "at least if they'll take him".

An old cow scratched herself against the simbuang batu, not at all suspecting the lot which awaited her.[46] Before the killing began people walked counter-clockwise around the rante, bearing the bate lepong.

Shouts announced that slayings were severed with machetes at roughly the same instant. On the point of the death the animals stood nearly free, one foot tied to a small pole. Once mortal wounds were inflicted they still staggered, or even bolted for a short stretch before their hooves gave way. Their blood splattered against the simbuang batu. The crowd was excited. Small boys rushed forward to scoop up blood in sharp, pointed pieces of bamboo. At death rituals this is their usual task; the blood is cooked, and then consumed.

8. Ma'parando in Sangalla'[47]

This rite was an important part of the death ritual held for Ne' Pare of tongkonan Lengkua' in the village of Randangbatu (October 3, 1969). The entire ritual was a dipalimang bongi; the adat observed was that of Tu Manete. Although Randangbatu is now situated in Kesu', as far as adat usage is concerned the village must be considered part of the puang-territories.

The ma'parando is only enacted if the deceased has (great) great grandchildren[48]; consequently, it is not often performed. The ceremony coincides with the day of the mantunu, the slaughter of the buffaloes on the pantunuan. Three buffaloes are killed on this occasion: the parepe', the tulak bala'kaan (Vol.I:197), and the batu bangla' (the function of this buffalo is unknown to me). By the time we arrived, two had already been slaughtered. The third, with a mortal gash, was still alive. It was a gruesome, unreal sight. He stood there with severed windpipe, yet on his feet, calm, dignified. There was no question of intentional cruelty. He was so powerful, according to one spectator, because someone with hostile motives had practiced witchcraft. Another man, however, said it was a question of pure physical prowess: just as there are men who are strong and men who are less strong, buffaloes, too, differ. The animal was led away, somehow able to walk under its own power, to be shot. Sometimes a soldier is present to dispatch such exceptions with a bullet from his weapon. Boys pounced on the last slaughtered buffalo to catch its blood with their bamboo containers.

The return march to the death house began. Along the way I noticed the belo tedong on the ground. It diverged somewhat in appearance from the belo tedong fabricated after death for someone from the puang-lineage (see Fig. 24). Its ornamentation consisted of two vertical stalks of bamboo tamped full at their upper ends with tabang-leaves (Cordyline terminalis); inbetween a palm leaf (pusuk) had been tied fast. The belo tedong had been used for decoration of the parepe' (Fig. 32).

Fig. 32. Belo tedong at the ma'parando in Sangalla'.

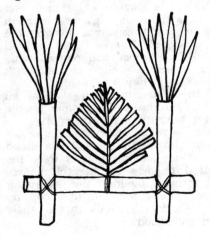

We reached the compound where the tongkonan stood within which the
dead rested and where, round about, the ricebarns were decked out
with old, costly maa'-cloths. One of these old cloths was so vast that it
could be suspended from the floor of the alang (ricebarn). The cloth
was worth some twenty buffaloes and many generations old. Its colour
was a dark, wine red and its pattern resembled a Persian carpet.
Elephants appeared in the design.

The deceased had lived long enough to see her great grandchildren.
The core of the ma'parando is thankfulness for such longevity. The two
oldest great grandchildren, dressed in black, wore adornments. The
girl received a yellow kandaure to put on as finery; a man helped her
plait it shut along the front. In addition she was given a golden gayang
(kris) to wear and a paper mitre, red and white, was placed on her
head. The young man also wore a fine kandaure which a woman had
plaited shut in front. On his head he wore a black, flannel cap; sun-
glasses added a finishing touch to his outfit. Only two great grandchildren were dressed in kandaure; the other ones had to make do with
paper hats.

Badong were sung. A few hours later the great grandchildren were
supposed to be carried on the shoulders of fullgrown men three times
about the house in which the deceased lay at rest. This was to occur
between three and four p.m. Behind the men bearing the children,
others were to follow with torches. The sole musical accompaniment of
the event would be recitation of the song for the dead. Unfortunately,
it was not possible to attent this part of the ceremony.

Wilcox has written about the ma'parando at length (Wilcox 1949:85ff.).
The rite which he witnessed was the ma'parando in honour of the
departed mother of the puang of Sangalla'. He recounts how the corpse
was conveyed to the pantunuan and how there the daughter of the
deceased, who had kept a vigil over the dead for a full three years,
then descended from the bier, and climbed onto the shoulders of a man
(a slave, Wilcox maintains). Preceded by torchbearers and deluged with
shouts from the assembled crowd, the daughter was then carried three
times around the bier. Afterwards, three great grandchildren, a boy
and two girls, were similarly carried three times about the remains of
their great grandmother. The puang walked before them, holding up a
torch. The encirclement always meant motion in a counter-clockwise
direction.

The ceremony took place under a full moon. Wilcox makes some
mention of the clothing worn. Granddaughters appeared in golden
jewelry and triangular head ornaments. The solitary grandson had on a
turban of satin adorned with feathers and golden brooches. The
daughter had drawn a sarong of purple and reddish brown, apparently
a textile of Buginese origin, about her head and shoulders. The puang
wore white.

To return to the ma'parando at which I was present - at eight o'clock
in the next morning, the roll of cloth in which the dead was bundled,
red material with golden figures on the outside, was carried down out
of the death house. On its front end the barre allo, the sun motif, was
the most prominent decoration. Women with black cloths over their
heads sat down beside the shroud and began to wail. Men began to
dance around them, singing their song for the deceased. More women,
heads covered by cloths, later joined the group.

It began to rain: it was said that the dead would be brought to the grave the same morning.

In Kesu' the ma'parando is not celebrated except in the region neighbouring on Sangalla' where the village was situated that provided the
setting for the rite which I saw.

The tombi, kandaure, bate lepong and issong arranged in front of the
death house. See also pp. 213-215 and Figs. 29, 30 and 31.
(Photo: Hetty Nooy-Palm, 1966.)

Simbuang and bate lepong, Parinding, Bori' (Tikala). See also p. 215.
(Photo: Hetty Nooy-Palm, 1966.)

Ma'bating (lamentation) over the dead during ma'parando in Sangalla'.
Great grandchildren of the deceased are wearing triangular head orna-
ments. See also p. 217.
(Photo: Hetty Nooy-Palm, 1969.)

Death feast at Kondongan (Tikala). Pantunuan with lakke-lakkean, death feast for Ne' Arung-langi', former District Head of Tikala. The corpse in its wrapping resembles a cylinder. (Photo: F. v.d. Kooi, 1937.)

Pantunuan, the place where, during the second part of the death ritual, the buffaloes are slaughtered. This photo was taken at the death feast for Ne' Arunglangi', former District Head of Tikala. The pantunuan lies in the village of Kondongan, Tikala District. (Photo: F. v.d. Kooi, 1937.)

Chapter XI

SA'PANG'S FUNERAL

"He sits now with his ancestors,
His seat is with his forefathers.
South he stands, a coconut palm,
A sugar palm, high over all.
Then westward does he pass from view,
He goes down where the sun descends."

(The Chant:46)

1. The first part of the death ritual for Sa'pang at Tandung, Kesu'

1.1. Background and preparations

The deceased, a rich farmer of high esteem from Tandung, Kesu', one of the anak pare-pare nangka', already gave indications before his death (June 13, 1969) how and in what style he wished his death feast to be celebrated.[1] It goes without saying that adat experts also had a voice in settling matters. The burial would in all likelihood be one of the last times that a notable from this area would be interred according to customs dictated by ancient Toraja belief, for in Kesu', especially, many people have converted to Christianity. As usual the ritual for the dead would follow the death ritual observed traditionally by the mother's side of the deceased's family (aluk susu). For Sa'pang this meant the ritual of the people of Tonga (aluk To Tonga).[2] Given Sa'-pang's status, it was agreed to celebrate a dirapa'i, the highest order of dirapa'i in fact, the sapu randanan (cf. Chapter X.4.).

My informants, including S.B. Sarungallo, proceeded at once to discuss the crucial matter of the slaughtering of buffaloes and how it would be organized:

a. children of the deceased would sacrifice a number of buffaloes in accordance with their share in the inheritance (see below, section 2);

b. those who assisted with preparing and performing the ritual must have buffaloes killed for them;

c. the persons expected to contribute buffaloes in reciprocation of gifts made by Sa'pang during his lifetime in honour of celebrations organized by them or their families.

In addition particular attention was lavished beforehand on certain aspects of the ritual which were regarded as high points:

- the leading in of the buffaloes;
- the reception of guests;
- dances;
- division of the meat;
- cock fights.

Hereafter a resume of the components was drawn up. Since these have just passed in review (Chapter X.4.), I won't repeat them here. It turned out, moreover, that in practice people departed from the prescribed sequence (see below).

The account begins with events surrounding Sa'pang's death and rests on informants' reports. The aluk pia was the only part of the death ritual which I actually attended (see below, section 1.2.).

As soon as Sa'pang died, a gong was beaten.[3] Women started to pound paddy. At Sa'pang's death, as is customary, this pounding was done in a special way which announced that a dirapa'i-ceremony would be held for him. Were an "ordinary" death ritual planned, one of a lower order, rice may not be pounded "off and on", i.e. not with blows in the depression of the mortar alternating with blows on the edge. Then a simpler rythm is employed. On this occasion though, the sound was different.

Once Sa'pang's death had been made known, relatives and acquaintances came to pay their respects. Several of the dead man's sons had washed the corpse in the meantime. Sa'pang's cloths were taken out, washed and dried. It is usual for the dead to be on view for some time, dressed in his finest apparel, even, on occasion, wearing gloves (cf. Chapter VIII.2.). Sa'pang was decked out in a military jacket, not a traditional costume. A headcloth, folded in a special way (disissik), however, was draped round his head as usual. Then he was set on a chair. For three days important villagers had the opportunity to pay their last respects. The District Head came, too. Then the dead man was stripped of his finery. The corpse was stretched out to its full length and wrapped in pondan-cloth, a fabric made from pineapple fibres, which is suitably strong for this purpose. It surprised me to learn that the death priest did not wrap the body but "others" did, presumably close male relatives. The sepu', betel pouch, was hung beside the dead. At his feet, a plate, or more than one, was placed. Sirih/pinang and palm wine were also present. After some time (the number of days is not specified) the body was wrapped anew. I wasn't told who performed this act (the to mebalun or "others"?). A kind of decoration was affixed to the outer layer of the wrapping. This consisted of strips of pondan-cloth, woven together with the same simple technique, one over, one under, used to weave mats. Moisture was drained from the corpse through bamboos. Every night the to mebalun fed the dead. A bier was prepared from split bamboos. The bier would be used a few times early during the ritual to transport the corpse (see below; it remains unclear to me where Sa'pang was on view in a seated position; presumably this should have taken place in the sumbung-room; see Vol.I:233).

Meanwhile other preparations were under way. The number of buffaloes which family members were expected to contribute - a number related closely to their inheritance - was determined. The guest accommodations had to be built. In the past slaves could do this work as a service, but nowadays for the most part wage labourers must be hired. It cost about Dfl. 200 to build a guest house in 1969. Members of the former slave class and villagers do perform other services, however, on a volunteer basis.

Since a film team was expected and people were counting on a large group of tourists, a road had to be made. The elaborateness of such preparations and the fact that one son at work in Irian Jaya (New

Guinea) had not yet returned, were responsible for several successive postponements of the date fixed to begin the feast. To put all in readiness 240 people were occupied for an entire month (200 on the road; 40 girls and women pounding rice). Workers received food, drink and materials for smoking.

1.2. Aluk pia, first part of the death ritual

Originally, the first part of the ritual for the dead was scheduled for September 25; delay in completion of the lantang (guest houses) and other complications resulted in postpoing opening ceremonies a few times until the date was finally set for November 4. Acting on the advice of Bua' Sarungallo, I decided to depart for Tandung already on November 3 (Bua' Sarungallo filled, by virtue of his role as the camat's deputy, an important function in the organization of the feast). Tandung, the scene of the death ritual, is situated on the level summit of a hill. Guest quarters were the first objects to catch the eye; they resembled Toraja houses cut in two. Each apart lantang had the form of a tongkonan split across its width in the middle. The proportions of the guest house were rather exaggerated in comparison to those of a Toraja house. The roof came far forward and jutted out above. The rear wall, and on occasion a side wall as well, rested on bamboos which sometimes extended several metres over the abyss of the adjoining ravine. The façade of the guest house nestled on the ground. Bamboo, compactly tied together, was the material used to construct these feast abodes. Flattened bamboo served for floors; walls were made up of bamboo strips and painted, sometimes, with an appropriate image: the quarters provided for the Red Cross had the emblem of the organization on one wall, for example, and the lodgings of the Chairman of Parkindo[4] bore at the summit of its façade the painting of a Christmas tree decorated with a candle. A prize was offered for the best-decorated guest lodge. Every building had a ground floor and an upper storey. Each had a hearth of the type customary in permanent houses: a massive basin of earth in which the cooking pan balances on three stones. A rack filled with firewood invariably hung above the hearth so that residents of the lantang could prepare meals. (For the situation of the guest accommodations in relation to other buildings, see Fig. 44 below.)

Several buildings were put up. The largest ones stood somewhat apart. These were accorded to members of the Indonesian government (one separate house), to foreign visitors (a second, large square building), and to an Indonesian film team come to record the event.

For other distinguished guests, space beneath the ricebarns was reserved. In the evening it was possible to screen these areas off by hanging up oblong lengths of cloth, either of cotton or of pondan, a fabric made from pineapple fibres. Close family relations, the sons of the deceased and their families included, could also take up residence in the guest accommodations. At the centre of festivities were two tongkonan and their ricebarns: Batu, the tongkonan of the sokkong bayu of Tandung, with six ricebarns, and Tandung, also with six alang. It was in tongkonan Tandung, where Sa'pang now lay in his death roll, that he drew his last breath.

People were still occupied with preparations for the feast proper. Some were affixing star-shaped figures of gold-leaf to the strips of red flannel hanging from the horns of the kabongo' on the ricebarn opposite the house of mourning. Others were rehearsing for the ma'katia, a song which takes its name from katia, a tune sung during mortuary feasts, but borrowed from the Buginese since c. 1935. The singing is accompanied by a dance (cf. Holt 1939:56, 58, 110, 116).[5]

Late in the afternoon all preparations were completed so that as darkness fell badong could be chanted. For a death song typical of those performed here, see section 3 below.

Tuesday, November 4, 1969
On this first day of Sa'pang's funeral, the feast was ushered in by blows on the gong (bombongan) which is only played when major ceremonies for the dead are celebrated. Two buffaloes are slaughtered on this day: the ma'karu'dusan and the sumbung penaa (for the latter, see Vol.I:197-8). The ma'doya, the vigil over the dead, commences, too. The evening before the ceremony of the ma'karu'dusan, a banana is cooked and given to eat to the deceased and to the to ma'pemali who has been allowed to eat cooked food until now, but not any more afterwards.

At roughly noon the façade of tongkonan Tandung was decorated with eight golden krisses. The red flannel was stripped from the buffalo horns on the ricebarn and draped over the horns of the kabongo' on the tongkonan itself. A bit later in the day the portrait of Sa'pang was hung on the outside front wall as well. After a little while a kandaure (cf. Vol.I:255ff.) and various tombi (cf. Vol.I:257, 261) were hung out near the Northwest corner of the death house. (The kandaure had a proper name: Pa'sarrin: to sweep together.) The tombi were attached to a staff. They included a square batiked cloth (tali bate), 70 x 70 cm, a tali etan (a black rectangular headcloth), a pio uki' (cf. Vol.I:257), a tombi saratu' (literally: the 100 tombi), a piece of crocheting resembling an old-fashioned bedspread, probably its original inspiration, and a sarita (Vol.I:267). Long white streamers were hung out along entrance paths to the village as well.

During the previous night Sa'pang had been brought up to the sali-room. Until then he had remained in the space under the house on the bed where he died, wrapped in layers of cloth. This is not customary; formerly the deceased used first to lie in state in the sumbung-room before conveyance to the sali. Once in the sali-room, however, the dead was set down as customary: against the Southern wall with his head to the West (Fig. 33A). The wall of the sali had no ornamentation. Actually it is incorrect at this point to speak of "the dead": until the ceremony about which I will presently give an account, the deceased is rather "the sick one", to makula', a euphemism usually applied to persons of eminence prior to their ritual "death".

The time had now arrived for turning "the sick one". The to meba-lun, the wrapper of the dead, held onto the shroud enclosing the deceased at the head end, and with the help of a number of men, quickly spun it around (Fig. 33B). These men are not fixed functionaries; during this phase of the ritual there are not yet any to maro[6], no mourners forbidden to eat cooked rice. The to mebalun, however, does perform officially. Other mourners would fulfil formal roles at a later stage of the ritual. (These functionaries, the to untoe aluk, "those who cling to the ritual", may also come close to the dead.)

Not only is the corpse trussed up in many pondan-cloths, but the entire bale, which assumes the proportions of a giant cocoon, is sewed

Fig. 33. Groundplan A and B of tongkonan Tandung and the position of the deceased before and after the turning of the death roll.

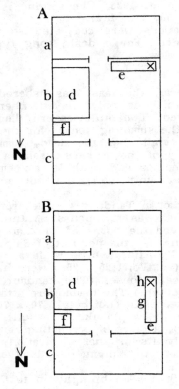

A. The position of the deceased before he is turned.
There is no indication of the places where the to ma'pemali and to balu sit, for, indeed, the deceased has not yet ritually "died".

B. The position of the deceased after he is turned.
a   sumbung
b   sali
c   tangdo'
d   hearth
e   deceased
x   the head of the deceased
f   stairs
g   place where the to ma'pemali sits, facing West
h   place where the to balu sits, facing the head of the deceased

together. This is accomplished by covering the whole with an elongated piece of fabric and stitching it to itself along its length. At both ends a circular piece of cloth is sewn in place. This is usually the job of the to mebalun.

Before the bulky roll containing the deceased was placed on the floor, it was tossed up and down a number of times to the accompaniment of a brief song. What I could hear sounded like "Hojjomilelelele", perhaps translatable as "We ask permission to lift you", or "Come, let's hoist him". The dead man's head was now swung to the South. The living must never sleep with their head in this direction, except for the to balu (widow or widower). Sa'pang was no longer "sick", but dead, a to mate or to menulusau'.

The serre' datu, "the cat who is a prince" (see Vol.I:215ff.) should have been present at the turning of the deceased, but was nowhere to be found. At last the animal was discovered, captured, and tossed from the palanduan, the rack for firewood above the hearth, down to the cooking place below, a gesture integral to the rite, representing what people call the cat's suicide because its master has died (mentuyo serre' mate puangna, literally: "the self-destruction of the cat because its master had died"). The cat, however, had more to endure: the animal was grabbed by the head and told three times that the master of the house had passed away. This was too much for the beast, so that as soon as it was safe on the ground once more, it took to its heels. (It was said that the final "annunciation" did not at all belong to the ceremony; the self-destruction of the cat was the essential point. It is possible that the presence of a foreign reporter from "National Geographic" provided inducement to elaborate affairs somewhat.) To kill the cat is never part of the intention of the rite.

At this juncture the women began wailing (umbating). The deceased's oldest daughter led off. She, like each of the lamenters, had her own, very personal style.[7] She leaned with her head and shoulders upon the winding sheet; a vast cloth woven from undyed pineapple fibres covered her. She launched into venting her grief; another woman, with a different style, somewhat less-convincing, although this is perhaps indecorous to suggest, followed. Her wailing was interrupted by sobs. One shouldn't conceive of the wailing as something artificial or contrived. This idea occurs because the wailing begins almost automatically after the wrapping of the deceased; for "the sick one" no one expresses desolation. The wrapping is indeed looked upon as the moment of death; only then does the dead man leave his relatives behind for good. Realization of this leavetaking is put into words in the laments which female kin sing, too. Certain phrases, special expressions, recur time and again but each woman transforms them into highly personal sentiment. The dirges are an individual manifestation of the mourning of women. Men avail themselves of another, similarly individual style; they sing retteng - songs which are often satirical (see The Chant:16-9).

One of the outstanding dignitaries of Toraja society, a man active in the field of poetry, told me how he once composed a threnody in female style; when he later recited it to a woman, she at once burst into tears (text not available).

From the moment that the deceased "dies", his close relatives may no longer eat rice. They have become, as I alluded to previously, to maro' or to maroo' (to marao'). Henceforth the to ma'pemali may eat only raw food. Others, too, who enter the death house, may really not have rice, with the exception of the to mebalun. In the immediate vicinity of the deceased, in addition to the death priest, were the to balu and the to ma'pemali as well. As customary, their hair hung loose. They wore a black sarong knotted under the arms. No jacket may be worn. The to balu sat facing the head end of the death roll. When she sleeps, her head, the same as the deceased's, is turned towards the South. Her back is turned towards her dead partner's earthly remains. Sa'pang had more than one widow, for he was married seven times. Only one widow (the oldest?, the first married?) stayed constantly beside him.

According to plan, the turning of the deceased, his "death", should more or less coincide with the slaughtering of the two buffaloes known as the karu'dusan (or puli) and the sumbung penaa. In this instance the sacrifices took place between 12 and 1 p.m., shortly after the turning of the deceased. Ru'du' signifies "to die"; it is applicable in particular to human death. Puli means "die along with". Sumbung penaa is a way of saying, "appendage of the soul". These are the first two buffaloes put to death in the course of this form of ritual for the dead (the karu'dusan is also slain during rituals of lower order; see Chapter IX.2.2.).

The animals are killed right in front of the death house. The slaughter is carried out in a special way. The beast is tied fast by one forefoot (above the hoof), its head is lifted with the help of the rattan nose-ring, and then the throat is slashed with a la'bo' (machete). The two buffaloes, neither yet fully mature, met a swift end. Only after they had been hacked into pieces was there a beginning made of distributing meat. Until then the head of the panggau bamba (dividers of the meat) dressed in adat costume with a pleated headcloth had called aloud for patience. In prior times a mass rushed upon the buffaloes and cut them apart alive. This practice, forbidden by the Netherlands Indies government, remains unlawful. The crowd is restrained at some distance from the slaughtering spot. First the butchers must separate the animals into large sections. If this part of the work were left to the crowd, the tumult might rapidly prove dangerous. Even now the disorder which follows is bad enough. At a given signal the crowd rushes in, everyone competing to cut off as much choice meat from the carcass as he can. In the shortest imaginable time the buffaloes are stripped of every edible scrap; even the heads which on other occasions are left intact share this fate.

Close family members, as reported earlier in this book, are excluded from partaking of the meat of these two animals. Nor does the dead eat of the flesh of these buffaloes, although he was served meat from the pigs also slaughtered during the rite. Parts of a pig (dipemanala, see Vol.I:206) were placed down on a piece of banana leaf; this food is given to the dead.

The ma'katia, previously rehearsed, took place. Fourteen dancers drew up in front of the tongkonan and began to dance while they sang. They wore white jackets and sarongs and small, round black sunhats. Nor was a "ballet master" missing.

From this day on the "watch beside the dead" took place (ma'doya). A kain sekomandi[8] was fastened to the South and West walls of the saliroom; a betel pouch of the kind popular among the Buginese dangled against the cloth. Sa'pang had worn this pouch during religious ceremonies. The to mebalun was entrusted with feeding the deceased.

The ricebarns and guest accommodations were lit with electric bulbs and kerosine pressure lamps. In front of the death house the ma'badong took place, performed by professionals from various villages. After they formed a great circle in a special way, the dancers, singing the death chant, executed certain steps, and moved around as illustrated in Figs. 34 and 35 (see also Holt 1939: photo's 11-13).

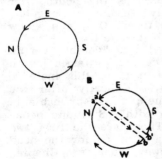

Fig. 34. Choreography of the badong-dancers.

A. The direction in which the badong-dancers move during their performance.

B. The formation in which the dancers arrange themselves to begin the dance. The dancers form two rows, a-b and a'-b' (see broken line). In turn, one after another, the dancers proceed to b or b'. From here, with b and b' as starting-points, two half-circles are formed which afterwards join in a whole circle. Once the circle is completed, the dance begins.

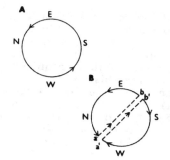

Fig. 35. Badong-dancers breaking the circle at
the end of the dance.

A. The direction in which the badong-dancers
advance during their performance.

B. The way in which the badong-dancers dis-
solve their formation after dancing. Each
dancer stops (one after another) upon reaching either a or a' and proceeds in single file -
see the broken line - to points b and b'.

They alternated this performance of a rather modern death chant with
the touching badong to dolo (death chants) of the ancients, handed
down from earlier days. (For the badong, see The Chant:1-16 and
19-73.) In recompence for their performance, the dancers would receive
a buffalo.[9]

On the evening of this first day, the to minaa should eulogize the
dead in a litany (ma'kukua) which is sung in a manner reminiscent of
the crowing of a rooster. He consults with members of the family about
a name for the deceased (see below). I did not attend this ma'kukua.

Wednesday, November 5, 1969
This day was regarded as the highlight of the feast; today many guests
(family members) would arrive. During the morning rice was pounded in
two long rice mortars (issong) according to the special rhythm - first
on the rim, then in the basin - commonly employed for the dirapa'i.
People may not pound rice in this way during their workaday existence.
In the event of a death feast of lower order, this rhythm is excluded
and those pounding the rice strike only in the basin of the issong. The
women who pounded the rice worked to the North of the two ricebarns
which stood Northeast of the tongkonan. There was nothing extraordinary about their dress.

Now the slaughter of the buffaloes, brought to the scene primarily by
members of the deceased's family, would take place. First a handsome
pudu' bull and a balian, a gelding with enormous horns, were led
forward. All buffaloes were registered in a notebook (just as pigs were,
too) with an evaluation added. Other buffaloes, 25 in all, followed in
succession.[10]

The executioner delivered his first blow to victim number one.
Although on the previous day the slaughter had gone smoothly, this
time there was a hitch. The pudu', his throat cut, remained trotting
about the slaughtering place. It was a sickening spectacle. With blood
streaming from his wound, throat gurgling, the bull refused to fall.
The crowd watched, without excitement, but mildly surprised. For fully
twenty minutes the gallant bull rambled around and around until, once
a command was given for a second blow with the machete, the colossus
sank in a heap. The unfortunate incident was attributed to magic (see
also the description of the ma'parando in Sangalla', Chapter X.8.).

In Toraja language the name for those who kill buffaloes is pa'tinggoro. Their work requires special skill, for one should topple a buffalo
with a single stroke delivered while the animal is standing. In reward,

the executioner receives the portion of the neck on either side of the
wound. It is therefore in his own interest to do his job as quickly and
efficiently as possible; the deeper his blade sinks in, the more extensive his payment. In addition, to do a poor job brings shame. The
chance of failure is, however, always present. Expert skill is required
for administering the first blow. The man chosen for this feat can be
enfeebled by the magic of a jealous colleague who wished for the opportunity himself. Such magical powers pass from father to son, as so
often is true with magic. A western, psychological interpretation of the
failure of a pa'tinggoro would raise the possibility that the man's aware-
ness of the potential practice of magic against him makes him sufficient-
ly nervous to impair his performance.

The remaining buffaloes met their death, happily, without prolonged
suffering. The meat from all was divided according to traditional rules.

The ma'palangngan panganta' also occurred this day. A bamboo staff
was suspended over the dead, parallel with the corpse. Cloths were
thrown over the bamboo; the Northern-most cloth was an old pio uki', a
long loin cloth. The cloths remain hanging until the ma'bolong (see
below).[11] According to B. Sarungallo, the cloths from the bamboo are
later (during the second phase of the death ritual?) used to wrap the
deceased. At the ma'palangngan a pig is sacrificed; the to mebalun officiates.

A second important rite, the ma'bambangan was observed the same
day. Ma'bambangan means "make fall", "to fell", but also, "die" (used
for persons of high rank). My Toraja informants suggested that the
word ma'bambangan was connected to the ritual death of the deceased,
who previously was "sick". The rite requires some explanation. One of
the objects which play a role in it is the sissarean. This is a bamboo
structure, resembling a fence in some ways. It stood leaning against
the Southern wall of the sali-room against the kain sekomandi fastened
there. The sissarean consisted of three horizontal bamboo rods to which
three other parallel bamboo rods, somewhat shorter, were attached to
make a grid (see Fig. 36). The whole brings to mind an ampang bilik
(Vol.I:241ff.). Woven through the openings of the sissarean was a loin-
cloth (pio uki'). The word sissarean means something to lean against;
the object thus symbolizes a backrest for the deceased. The "backrest"
during the ma'bambangan was rotated a quarter turn so that its side

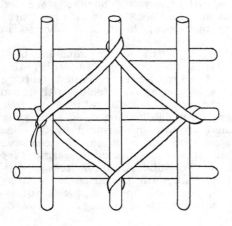

Fig. 36. The sissarean with
a pio wrapped around it.
(Sa'pang's funeral, Kesu', 1969)

lies flush with the ground. Perhaps, if I may venture an interpretation, this position is to convey the idea that the deceased has laid down, i.e. has "died".

On the afternoon of the ma'batang, the sissarean is dismantled and the bamboo parts, one by one, are thrown away by the to mebalun. As he does so, he calls aloud, in order of age, the name of the deceased's children. Should there be many children from various mothers, then he speaks only the name of each woman's oldest child. The meaning of this rite is that just as their dead father, these children in their turn will attain prosperity and be buried according to the dirapa'i (information B. Sarungallo). One bamboo rod is discarded with the words: tanda ambe' and one with the phrase: tanda indo' (tanda: sign, ambe': father; indo': mother). It seems plausible that this is meant as an act of homage to the family on the father's and the mother's side successively. People furthermore showed me an axe, also reclining against the West wall of the sali-room. This axe was used exclusively to chop the wood needed for the dead man's bier. A pig was sacrificed to "accompany the destruction of the backrest" and, just as the pigs slaughtered during the preceding rites, the carcass was roasted on the langngan to the West of the tongkonan. The death priest presided over the offering.

Throughout the day, as well as on the day before, the gong was struck. Everyone may have a go, the act has no special ritual content. The arrival of guests, however, is always announced by sounding the gong. On this day people came pouring in, for this was the big day of the first part of the death feast. The guests, family members included[12], came in groups, each of which represented a particular family.[13] Preceding each batch of arrivals were the buffaloes brought along as contributions to the feast, followed by pigs. People brought firewood and tuak as well, but no rice. Servants, in previous days slaves, carried the wood, palm wine and pigs. Next in each group came male relatives, either in adat costume or in modern cloths, but in the latter event usually wearing a sambu' (sarong for men) over one shoulder. The men filed in one after another, as did the women who followed them. These wore a black adat costume (see Nooy-Palm 1969: fig. 2 and plate X.1). Sunhats were worn as prescribed by tradition. Some women had on a pote, a mourning hood (see Fig. 47), others had merely tied a plain black cloth around their heads.

Some groups appeared more magnificent than others. At the vanguard stalked extremely rare buffaloes, like the costly saleko, for example. The special attraction of one group consisted of dancers mounted on hobby horses (Javanese: kuda kepang). Their performance won wide approval. Each group was escorted to its place by the same individual, an adopted son of the deceased's, according to what I was told. He, just as other male members of the family and many other important men at the feast, was dressed in adat finery. His apparel consisted of trousers with a special cut, a seppa tallu buku (three-piece trousers), a jacket, old-fashioned in style, bayu pasangan, and the sambu' that goes together with it. He wore a tali bate headcloth. This should be batiked material from Java, yet one fellow had improvised with a tablecloth, pink roses on a white background, folded on his head. Several prominent participants in the festivities also sported betel-pouches of traditional Buginese model, sepu' sapekan, worn where Scots in formal dress carry their sporran. Even youths who were members of the family

or who filled some ritual role had on jackets and, on occasion, trousers
of the same material as that worn by the older men: kain pondan.

A man and woman in adat costume welcomed guests of honour in the
large feast house. The man, So' Mala, (a great grandson of Sa'pang's
mother, the child of a different marriage, however, from that which
produced Sa'pang himself), wore black trousers and a black shirt of
shiny material, a tali bate on his head, and a golden kris. The woman
wore a kandaure on her back and a red ribbon tied around her hair
which was parted down the middle. The guests were invited to slat
themselves on the mats. Boys and girls offered them tea and cakes.[14]
Time and again the servers formed themselves into the same row, the
girls with teapots beautifully ornamented in silver and gold and with
covered platters, the boys carrying woven boxes in fine colours and
betel dishes. They had a busy time of it! Back and forth, youths and
girls travelled about the hall at least twenty times that day. What
further added to their workload was constant change of dress. At first
in white, the girls then appeared later in rose and then again in blue
before reverting to colours already exhibited before. Attired in traditional Toraja garments, their appearance was adorable, striking contrast
with the slaughter place littered with buffalo heads and other gory
remnants of sacrifices. Broken animal eyes looked upon a world which
no longer resembled any place on earth. Spilled blood, still bright red
in the morning, had already dried to purple, an arresting image of
life's transiency.

Pigs in number also met their end this day. Certain fat swine had
been left to wander free, trotting among festivities with their own easy,
characteristic gait until the knife claimed them. Now their heads nestled
with the severed heads of buffaloes.

At night there was a reprise of chanting and dancing the death song.
Retteng also were performed, elegies delivered in remembrance of the
deceased by old men, each rendering his own verses. At the conclusion
of every song, the entire body of men joined in a refrain (for the retteng see The Chant:16-9). The deceased's good qualities were praised,
including his prowess with women. At the mention of this gift of his,
one old woman, mentally disturbed, had pointed comment to make. Her
crude remarks clashed with the elevated style of the retteng.

I have been told that at death feasts young people sing also londi or
londe (Indonesian: pantun). These quatrains are sung alternately by
young men and women. This happens at night and provides an opportunity for sexual intercourse.

During the night a watch was maintained at the side of the dead.
Women wore mourning outfits woven from undyed pineapple fibre (for
this particular mourning colour, see Nooy-Palm and Schefold [forth-
coming]). The small to ma'pemali, Sa'pang's eight year old daughter,
had kept her vigil beside him from the instant of his demise. (For her
devotion, she was to receive a sawah.)

Thursday, November 6, 1969
Visitors continued to turn up during the day but there was no longer
the throng of the day before. In the morning the rapasan was hauled
from a cave in the vicinity. The box was laid on the ground on the
Western side of tongkonan Tandung. Oblong, the rapasan bears a
likeness to a rice mortar; the dead is placed in it at nightfall (see also
Chapter X). The rapasan had coloured wood-carvings. Its ornamentation

consisted primarily of doti langi' (a familiar incised motif, cf. Kadang 1960: figs. 17 and 23; Pakan 1973, see doti langi') and circles. Black, white and yellow tints were used.

The ma'katia (see above) was held again. Buffalo fights were staged in the afternoon. Bulls were pitted against each other, pairs carefully matched for colour and size. The animals, however, were not so full of fight; of the eight bouts arranged, only two aroused some suspense. Rounding up the bulls after they had been turned loose turned out to be the most difficult thing of all. Just before releasing the buffaloes to fight, their escorts performed a kind of war dance. Most men turned and ran once the buffaloes began to charge each other, but one or two exceptional characters just carried on with their dancing.

Thereafter the ma'batang and the taa baine occupied the afternoon hours. Before the ma'batang may be observed, however, the death roll must be enclosed in a cloth that is sewn tight. I presume this task had been performed because by now a procession formed in front of the house. Men (belonging to the to maro') lifted the tombi, kandaure and other banners which stood Northwest of the tongkonan; female relatives and other women of importance in the ritual took their place beneath an old red cloth (maa'), which was stretched on top of a long strip of material woven from pondan. Men in the lead, all moved off in a procession along the Western access road to the village. While the procession made its way towards the rante, the mortal remains of the deceased stayed inside the tongkonan.

Upon arrival at the rante, the staffs to which the kandaure and other banners were attached, and also a spear (doke) were implanted in the ground (see Figs. 37 and 38). The women assumed their proper place. There were ten women, a stand-in for the to ma'pemali among them. The small girl could not herself make the trip, for, weakened from eating only uncooked food, she could no longer endure walking under the scorching sun. Also present were two women who would play roles in the two rites scheduled for the coming evening. The to ma'pemali's replacement went to sit under a shelter of bamboo poles bedecked with the pondan fabric and the maa'-cloth (the shelter was called a duba-duba).

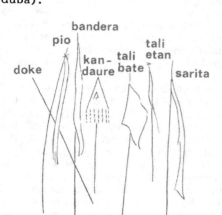

Fig. 37. Banners and kandaure displayed during the ma'batang (Sa'pang's funeral, Kesu', 1969).

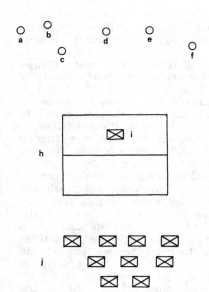

Fig. 38. Places of women and regalia during the ma'batang (Sa'pang's funeral, Kesu', 1969).
a. pio (loin cloth)
b. doke (spear)
c. bandera (flag)
d. kandaure (beaded ornament)
e. tali bate' (ancient batik headcloth from Java)
f. tali etan, black headband, the name for a cloth used during dirapa'i-rituals
g. sarita, a sacral cloth (see Vol.I: 257-9)
h. the lean-to over which the duba-duba is draped
i. the place where the substitute for the to ma'pemali sat
j. the places where the nine women sat

A bala'kaan had already been erected. This stood some distance to the North of the assembled women. It was a provisional bala'kaan propped on four bamboo piles. The permanent one would be constructed later (see below). It was not the to minaa who would climb to the platform, for at this point in the ritual he had not yet assumed his function; rather the death priest would officiate during offerings there.

Buffaloes would also be slaughtered during the ma'batang. This was contrary to usual practice. Departure from the rule can perhaps be explained by the greater number of guests present the previous day who had to be provided with food, and with a spectacle.

First the buffalo was to be slain that the women who had joined the procession were to share; this rite, the taa baine, is distinct from the ma'batang. Men brought the meat to the group of women (in contrast to B. Sarungallo's summary of the dirapa'i-ritual in which two women are supposed to serve the others). The animal was already butchered and pieces distributed when the leader of the panggau bamba (the meat dividers) arrived. He lashed the ground several times with his sambu' (man's sarong) in displeasure and shouted angrily that the division of the meat had been wrong.

The next buffalo to be slaughtered, siilang bua[15] by name, stood tied to an areca palm (kalosi) which had been felled and driven into the ground at the rante without ceremonial ado. This tree was referred to as simbuang kayu (see Fig. 39).[16] A spear was fetched, part of the inventory of possessions of a tongkonan with a special relation to the death house (sibali banua, see Vol.I:204-5). The weapon would be used in the next rite, the tekkenan doke, "the holding of the lance". It is the prerogative of one of the adat chiefs to be allowed to hold the spear (doke). The spear is handed to him by an important member of the tongkonan to which it belongs. For the time that he participates in this rite, the adat chief acquires the designation to tumekkan doke, "the one who holds the lance". He pretends to pierce the silang bua. In the past the buffalo was indeed lanced to death, but nowadays the spot

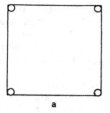

Fig. 39. Ma'batang of the dirapa'i in Tandung.

a. temporary bala'kaan
b. simbuang consisting of the trunks of felled areca-palms stuck into the earth
c. buffalo tethered to the simbuang (which way the animal faces is immaterial). The buffalo is the siilang bua

where the weapon should strike home is simply marked with lime and the spear is laid briefly across its back. The buffalo is dispatched with a cleaver.

The head of the buffalo "stabbed to death" in Tandung would be sent to the sokkung bayu (information from B. Sarungallo), and thus not to the tongkonan with which the adat chief who held the spear has a special relation. Subsequently other buffaloes were also killed. Division of the meat then proceeded, now under the capable supervision of the head of the panggau bamba. The rain magicians received their portion, too. The role of these figures deserves comment. Already before the ritual commenced, the rains had started in earnest. For two solid weeks preceding November 4 there were downpours in Kesu'. I was worried that rain would make it impossible to reach the site of the scheduled ritual. When I made my fears known, I was reassured that someone would be asked to help who had the power to dispel rain. My rather doubting grin in response was answered with calm assurance, "Wait and see". Indeed from the moment that the to ma'pamanta' set to work, no rain fell. There were four such magicians: one to fend off rain from each of the four principal points of the compass (a division of two to control rain in the North and two in the South is also possible). Farmers in daily life, for their services these anti-rain doctors received 3.5 Rupiah/day[17] with meals and smoking materials thrown in extra. They also received large shares of meat. They continued to ply their magic until the cock fights had been completed. For one day during the cock fights they let it rain heavily, aggrieved by an omission in their payment. To ma'pamanta' acquire their powers from their fathers who in turn had inherited their skills from their fathers. The magicians do not perform in public; they practice their arts secretly, otherwise they must fail.

The women began to grumble that it was taking such a long time to divide the meat. Among them was the wife of the sokkong bayu of Tandung. She was first in everything, even in leaving. Men pulled the staffs from which cloths were hanging out of the ground. They uprooted the spear as well. The women packed up the cloths and set out for the death house.

The silali' was the next rite, enacted in tongkonan Tandung. The most important object in this rite is an old sword, la'bo' to dolo or la'bo' penai, a weapon which descended from heaven together with the to manurun (the primeval ancestor). The sword may only be used during the death ritual of a brave man, someone whose life story is celebrated in song during the feast. Such a weapon is given to the deceased so that he can make himself known when he comes to stand in front of Pong Lalondong (the judge of the kingdom of the dead). The gift of the sword is, of course, symbolic. Only persons of high standing can take such a sword with them to Puya. This makes Pong Lalondong's work easier. At once he can classify such a dead man as one of the group of courageous nobility. Every prominent family has one or more ancient swords in its possession. Special capabilities are attributed to these la'bo' penai: they can ward off rain, or make a woman pregnant who has previously been barren. Although the sword is a weapon, it is not considered altogether masculine: "female" swords are also known; a male and female sword can function as a pair (Zerner 1981:103). In addition to the sword, women also play a vital role in the rite. Below a description of the silali' follows which was provided by B. Sarungallo, for I was not able to attend the rite myself.

The women who perform in the rite belong to the to untoe aluk, "those who uphold the ritual". These are the to ma'pemali, the to dibulle tangnga and the to massanduk dalle. They are also known, in this rite, by other names: to silali', to dipandanni bassi, and to ma'-peulli'.[18] The women sit close to each other on the ground to the East of the death roll. They reach out their right arms, the palm of the hand turned up, and rest them on the death roll. The la'bo' penai is laid across their palms, with the handle towards the deceased's head. The to mebalun places the following ingredients on the weapon:
a. bits of meat from buffaloes slaughtered during the ma'batang;
b. scraps of pork;
c. pounded maize that has been cooked;
d. cooked banana cut into small pieces;
e. pieces of tubers that have been boiled (Dioscorea alata L.; Toraja: andoa' or dua').
At this point the functionary known as the to ma'dipeulli' removes the pieces of meat from the sword very carefully so that nothing drops on the ground. That would bring misfortune (I forgot to inquire whom such misfortune would strike and whether the death priest recited a litany while setting out the ingredients).

In answer to my question why women held the sword in their hands, I was told that this symbolized the significance of women in the death ritual (actually of woman: aluk susu!). I am tempted to addd that the sword might have another significance in addition to what has already been described. It might be the symbol of the deceased himself. It would then represent the dead man in his childhood, born on women's arms, women who belong to the family but also the servants who surround the offspring of eminent Toraja families with such good care from early infancy on (see Chapter V.2.1.). The first phase of the dirapa'i-ritual literally means the ritual of the child, or the ritual of childhood.

The evening after the silali'-ceremony, the following rite, ma'patama kayu, took place. The rapasan had already been raised and lay on the ground, West of the death roll (see Fig. 40). The cloths which had previously hung from the bamboo pole above the dead had been re-

Fig. 40. Groundplan of tongkonan Tandung: the rite of lifting the deceased into the rapasan.

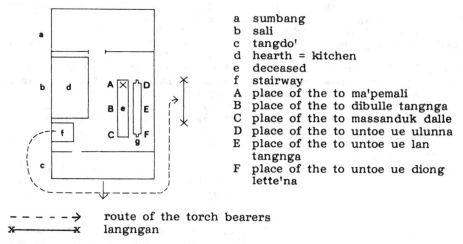

a   sumbang
b   sali
c   tangdo'
d   hearth = kitchen
e   deceased
f   stairway
A   place of the to ma'pemali
B   place of the to dibulle tangnga
C   place of the to massanduk dalle
D   place of the to untoe ue ulunna
E   place of the to untoe ue lan
    tangnga
F   place of the to untoe ue diong
    lette'na

- - - - - →   route of the torch bearers
x————x   langngan

Before the ceremony began, the rapasan was carried inside the stairway (f). Actually the coffin should be brought into the house through the ba'ba sade (for this doorway, see Vol.I:245).

moved. The to massanduk dalle, the to dibulle tangnga and the to ma'pemali stood upright East of the deceased. Three men, the to untoe ue diong lette'na ("he who holds fast to the rattan at the foot end"), the to untoe ue lan tangnga ("he who holds fast to the rattan in the middle") and the to untoe ue ulunna ("he who holds fast to the rattan at the head end") now took place in front of - that is to the West of - the rapasan. The three men lifted up the death roll by the rattan straps; then they heaved it up high before letting it sink again somewhat. Three times they repeated this up and down movement, calling out while they did so a short refrain which sounded like "hojjomilelelele" (see above). After the third cry, the dead man was laid in the rapasan. This "coffin" is also the symbol so well known in Asian cultures, the ship of souls, the vessel that carries the dead to the land of souls:
        "He lay there in his curved prau,
    He rested in his golden boat."
                    (The Chant:32)

Hereafter the ma'bia' began. The three men bolted down the stairs outside after first enjoining everyone else to remain above until their return. Shortly afterwards they came back, with as much haste as when they had taken leave. Each man bore a large torch (bia') which was kindled at the hearth fire. Simultaneously the three then passed their torches three times over the dead man stretched in the rapasan, moving always from West to East. The flame was practically overwhelming in the small space. Luckily the men were soon gone again downstairs. Later, when I descended to look around, the extinguished torches lay across the langngan to the West of the death house where earlier the sacrificial

pig had been roasted. It was brought to my attention that on an ordinary day, only one torch may be carried from the house, never three
at one time. After the torch-bearers had relinquished their flaming
sticks outside, the to mebalun inside enacted the offering. The light
was so dim that it was almost impossible to discern what the death
priest was doing; only a small oil lamp illuminated the room. The to
mebalun placed a number of pesung at the North end of the death roll.
On each leaf he put three kernels of maize and some meat which had
not been prepared in a piong. How the meat was cooked, I am unaware.
At the Northeast side of the coffin he doled out some maize onto a
scrap of banana leaf. On another scrap of leaf nearby he piled cooked
rice; into each of the bowls clustered about he distributed maize and
meat from the sacrificed pig (see Fig. 41). No prayer was spoken.

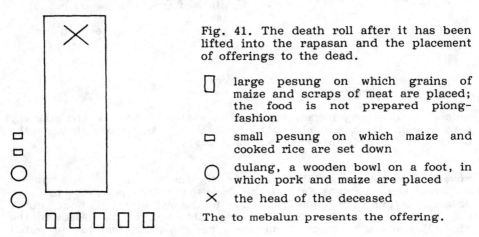

Fig. 41. The death roll after it has been
lifted into the rapasan and the placement
of offerings to the dead.

☐   large pesung on which grains of
    maize and scraps of meat are placed;
    the food is not prepared piong-
    fashion

☐   small pesung on which maize and
    cooked rice are set down

◯   dulang, a wooden bowl on a foot, in
    which pork and maize are placed

✕   the head of the deceased

The to mebalun presents the offering.

It was possible to learn something about the principals who participated
in the rite. The untoe ue diong lette'na belonged to the slave class; the
to untoe ue lan tangnga was a family member whose kinship with the
deceased could not definitely be traced. (According to report this
torch-bearer was also a kaunan.) The untoe ue ulunna was one of the
dead man's grandsons. (The untoe ue occupy themselves with all activities that have to do with the rapasan.) The to massanduk dalle and the
to dibulle tangnga alike also belonged, my informants said, to that class
once specified as kaunan, kaunan garonto', hereditary slaves.

Friday, November 7, 1969
Today the ma'pasusu was staged, in my absence. A pot was placed
underneath the dead; through a hole in the bottom of the rapasan a
bamboo was inserted so that the visible end rested in the pot. The pot
has the form of a woman's breast (susu). In this way, symbolically,
moisture was drained from the body (ma'pasusu means to drain away
milk). The corpse is thus rendered "dry". During the rite, a buffalo
was killed (information by Thana Lebang).

On Friday afternoon the cock fights (sisaong or paramisi; the last
word is derived from the Indonesian permisi, permission) commenced
which had so far been delayed by rain. (Those who held back the rain

had left the village.) Special, formal permission had been granted to
hold these fights. A fighting arena (ala-ala) was built. A buffalo was
sacrificed for the cock fights (unsembang suke baratu).[19] An announcement was made that combat might begin and fights could be
staged until November 13. There was a considerable lapse of time, however, before two owners with their birds ventured into the arena. Even
then there wasn't much spirit for the sport. Five bouts were all that
took place that afternoon.

After so hesitant a start, who could have dreamed that beginning
with the coming Sunday about eighty pairs of cocks would fight in the
arena each day before crowds of spectators that doubled the number of
visitors present at the very height of the ritual for the dead. Yet the
future had been legible long before in the form of the countless cocks
on view in baskets in the village. From November 7 and 8 on, a torrent
of people arrived in Tandung, most men carrying a fighting cock under
their arm. It is forbidden to address such travellers on their journey,
for talk will bring them bad luck. Even before fighting actually began,
owners were busy with their birds. At regular intervals the cocks were
taken from their enclosures (salokko'), watered and caressed. Of still
greater importance than the colour and marking of feathers, are certain
characteristics of the scales on the cocks' feet. In preparation for
battle, long sharp blades are fastened to the birds' spurs; these knives
(tadi, see Vol.I:212) are first rubbed with lemon juice. It is usual to
match cocks of different colours against each other. Every man who
steps into the arena is kept company by a helper.

From Saturday on the family no longer provided guests with meals.
From far and near people came to set up stalls to sell food, smoking
materials and similar commodities. The presence of such a pasa' (pasar,
market) is in keeping with the ritual for the dead. The entire feast
terrain of rituals is indeed referred to as pasa'. From such pasa' where
rituals have been celebrated over and over again standard markets do
develop. A buffalo is killed in the name of establishing the pasar
(untanan pasa') the existence of which is related to the attendance of
so many noblemen and to the vast scale of the feast.

Saturday, November 8, 1969
In the morning the ma'bolong unfolded, the final rite of the first stage
of Sa'pang's funeral. The to mebalun, trailed by the to ma'pemali, the
to massanduk dalle and the to dibulle tangnga, made his way to the
West entrance of the village where they drew up in formation to carry
out the ceremony. (For the significance of the clothes of the participants, see Nooy-Palm and Schefold, forthcoming.) With them they had
brought a kurin (an earthenware cooking pot with a round bottom), a
rectangular little tray made from the spathe of the spadix of the sugar
palm, several items of clothing woven from pineapple fibre, some black
mud from the sawah, leaves of the bilante (Homalanthus populnea) and
a bamboo container. In addition the to mebalun carried a bunch of
bamboo torches in his right hand and a chicken in his left. He killed
the chicken, removed the breast and cooked it until tender in bamboo,
piong-style. Rice was prepared in the same fashion. The food was then
set out on a banana leaf as an offering. The rest of the chicken was
for the to mebalun.

Meanwhile the clothing, piece by piece, was dyed black in the tray.
First mud was poured into the tray and mixed with the liquid in which

the bilante-leaves had been boiled in the kurin. Herein the small to
ma'pemali dipped the garments under the guidance of the other women.
Since it was still early, the girl apparently didn't suffer from exposure
to the sun. She was also allowed to leave the tongkonan where until
now she had kept watch over the dead. (It is my impression, however,
that she was not always inside the death house; see below.)

At about noon, the to minaa began to sing about Sa'pang's life. In
this song the dead man acquired a new name: Lalong Masallo', or,
freely translated, The Generous. While singing, the to minaa stood in
front of the ricebarn facing the death house. He fanned himself with a
sun hat held in one hand. (The song was not recorded.)

In the afternoon I left the village. On the way I passed many men
ascending to Tandung with their fighting cocks. This reminded me of
the role of the cock as supreme judge, and of the deceased who in the
hereafter, in Puya, would confront Pong Lalondong, the Highest Judge
of the kingdom of the dead (londong: rooster).

Before the bodily remains were suspended from the ba' (= teng), the
ma'mentang took place, a rite designed to purify the death room. Some
weeks later as a rule the corpse would be fastened to the Western ba'.

"That he may then sleep
Fanned by the wind."
(A strophe from a death song)

Because of my early departure, I was unable to witness the rite of the
suspension of the corpse from the ba' (= teng) (see Chapter X). After
a time, the corpse is laid again in the rapasan which is then sealed
with a cover of woven rattan (ma'tutu' ba'bai, "closing the door").

At the end of November, the definitive bala'kaan was constructed.
Wood was also chopped for making the tau-tau. This was work for two
men, one of whom had been trained as a sculptor on Bali. In reward
for their pains, the craftsmen of the tau-tau would receive a buffalo.

An interval separates the first and second parts of the dirapa'i.
During this period, however, several rites do take place, one of the
most important of which is the tulak tangnga, "the middel prop". On
this occasion, the deceased's family sacrifices a pig. Not only does the
rite commemorate the half-way point of the interval, but, in point of
fact, the half-way point of the dirapa'i as a whole. The cock fights
described above should actually also take place during the pause, and
not during the first part of the funeral (cf. Puang Paliwan Tandilangi's
comment, Chapter XII). The holding of the ritual market and of the
ma'tutu' ba'bai should similarly be enacted during the central rest
period. One may also regard the ma'mentang as a rite which belongs to
the interval as well, a rite for the purification of the room where the
dead has been kept. After the ma'mentang has been completed, the
second half of the death ritual can begin. As a sign of the recommence-
ment, the deceased once again receives food to eat (ma'pakande); the
offering consists of a pig.

1.3. The second part of the death ritual for Sa'pang

Because the second part of Sa'pang's funeral took place unexpectedly,
many family members, friends and interested parties, to their considerable indignation, could not be notified in time. This turn of events
was precipitated by the sudden arrival of Sa'pang's son from Irian Jaya

who had managed a leave from his duties and was unwilling to tarry in anticipation of the advent of other family members. Although I can't say whether he ever formulated the thought in these words, this son apparently felt that most relatives had been satisfied by attending the first part of the death ritual. When family arrived on May 10 in anticipation of still being able to share in some part of the observances, they discovered that the ma'palao, one of the last rites, had already taken place on May 8.

These circumstances did something to cast a pall over the celebration, as did continuous rain - despite the dedicated activities of the rain prevention magicians. The second part of the dirapa'i, designated as sapu randan (= figuratively, illustrious, unsurpassed; see above), should be festive indeed, but to my mind the second part of Sa'pang's funeral did not achieve the level of conviviality intended.

Events prevented me from attending the second part of Sa'pang's burial. B. Sarungallo was so kind, however, to make notes for me. He prepared a summary of the rites which took place. His information has been complemented where I felt it was necessary with commentary from an unpublished manuscript of Van der Veen, and from a written account of death rituals in Nonongan. It remains unfortunate, however, that I can not offer an eye-witness account, for the text which follows now necessarily has the nature of a reconstruction.

Below appear the rites for the second part of the death ritual as reported by Bua' Sarungallo. A comparison with the rites of the rapasan sundun as previously presented (Chapter X.4.) reveals deviation in their sequence. As a matter of fact, the same holds true for the rites of the aluk pia.

Shortly before the first part of the dirapa'i comes to its end, the name of the deceased is changed. The new name is selected by family members and the to minaa, who "shouts" it aloud. The new name is cited in the badong (see above). Personally, I did not observe any such "shouting" of a new name.

The deceased is removed from the teng and laid on the floor (ma'-parokko sali; rokko: to bring down, sali: floor). Afterwards the second part of the death feast can begin and as a sign of its beginning the deceased once more is given food. First, however, he is "awakened" (ma'tundan, "waking of the dead", the first rite): the cover is taken from the rapasan and a pig is slaughtered. It is usual that the "waking" is accompanied by a great deal of noise made by banging on all sorts of objects.

The 2nd rite is the mekayu, "the gathering of wood", i.e. the firewood needed for the second part of the death ritual.[20] This used to be a job for slaves; at least six men take part. Before the men go for the wood, a pig is killed for an offering which is made by the to mebulun and his helper, the to pabalian. The meat is divided among the to mekayu (those who fetch the wood).

Next followed the mesarigan (rite 3). Wood is needed for the sarigan. A tree has to be cut down for this purpose. Close to this tree the to minaa - thus not the to mebalun - conducts a minor rite. A chicken and a dog are slaughtered. The meat of the chicken is prepared in three piong and offered to the deata. One piong is for Puang Matua and is set down next to the tree. A second piong is placed about one metre from the tree; it is for the deata. The third piong is consecrated to the

ancestors of the Southwest, the nene'; in contrast to the previous two
piong, which were placed to the North of the tree, this piong is placed
to the South. The dog's meat is not included in an offering, but distributed to anyone with an appetite for it. (It is Van der Veen's idea that
the dog is put to death where it can keep the cat at bay which lurks
there to assail the dead - oral information.)

After the rite sketched above, the tree for the sarigan is felled. A
kaniala' or kemiri tree is selected for the purpose. Two or three men
bring the tree to earth. Wood is cut to measure and brought to the
compound of the death house. The hewers are assisted by several
others to drag the trunk back to the village, either family members,
villagers or (former) slaves. In recompense, they receive buffalo meat
or pork.

Ma'tampa bulaan, the forging of gold or silver trimmings for the death
roll is the name of rite 4. The wood which the smith needs, he chops
himself. A cock is sacrificed at the base of the tree which the smith
chooses to bring down. The bird's flesh is prepared in three piong (cf.
above, description of the massarigan). Then the ax bites into the
trunk. A (former) slave converts the wood into charcoal.

Manglelleng tau-tau (rite 5). The craftsman who makes the mortuary
effigy chooses a tree for his purpose himself (this woodcarver is called
pande tau-tau). Teken, who learned his art on Bali, created the image
of Sa'pang. Just before cutting down the nangka'-tree which usually
furnishes wood for mortuary effigies, celebrants offer a chicken to the
deata (spirits). The to minaa sets some cooked rice with chicken meat
and bits of betel leaf or betel fruit spinkled with lime on a number of
banana leaves at the base of the nangka'-tree. The to minaa then takes
a small bamboo with water and, pouring some drops on the food and
leaves, invites the gods to come enjoy the offerings after first washing
their hands. Finally, sprinkling the banana leaves with palm wine from
a bamboo container, the to minaa speaks a few words while presenting
the sacrifical food to the spirits. What the to minaa says, is not reported (Van der Veen, unpublished manuscript).

Melantang (rite 6). The guest accommodations (lantang) on the rante
are repaired. Usually, some new buildings are put up in addition.

Mebala'kaan (rite 7). The bala'kaan is constructed. It is roughly six
metres high and rests on six piles made of a variety of wood that is not
too hard (kaniala' or kapok). It is erected at the centre of the rante.
Before its construction, however, a buffalo (the parepe') must step
over the wood for the piles.

Mangriu batu (rite 8). The monolith is dragged to where it will be
raised. Relatives of the deceased go to search for a suitable stone
several days in advance. The stone designated is bound fast with
bamboos; the grips or handles which men grasp to haul the stone are
also of bamboo. The males of the village then make themselves ready to
drag the stone (see photos in Vol.I). Rice, buffalo and pig meat, and
tuak await them as payment. While the stone is being moved, the men
sing continuously; their voices form a kind of choir. Song is intended
to make the stone light. At the rante the stone must be raised upright.
It took tens of days to manoeuvre the stone for Sa'pang to a certain
point nearby. Still another day's exertions were necessary to bring it
to its ultimate destination. To raise the stone upright a pit must first
be excavated some two metres deep. Digging cannot begin, however,
without initially asking permission from Ampu Padang, Lord(s) of the

Earth. (One can also interpret the name as a plural and translate Ampu Padang as "the spirits of the earth".)

It is the to minaa who officiates during the ma'tambuli padang (the digging of the hole; rite 9). He addresses his invocation to the spirits of the earth. It is expected that the menhir will remain standing there forever. A pig is killed for an offering. Once the stone has been tipped onto its end, it is no batu (stone) any longer, but a simbuang. During the ma'palao (see below), the parepe' is fastened to the simbuang or tethered close by. The hauling of the stone into place is ramai, an Indonesian term which describes an ambiance that is cheerful, bustling, communal. People who do the hauling spatter each other with mud until all are caked with it. Onlookers are also pelted with lumps of earth and clods of turf (see Vol.I:263-9). Sa'pang's simbuang was named Belo Langi', Ornament of the Sky.

Mangaro (rite 10). The deceased is taken from the rapasan and laid on the floor of the sali-room. Up until now he has remained in the rapasan which was kept in the Western part of the room. The following persons kept watch over the dead:
1. the to ma'pemali;
2. the to massanduk dalle, "she who serves the maize";
3. the to ma'kampa to mate, "the guardian of the deceased" (= the to dibulle tangnga);
4. several family members and (former) slaves of the deceased.
Functionaries 1-3 also participated in the aluk pia. Together these figures maintained a vigil for Sa'pang, the ma'doya.

The ma'balun ("to wrap", rite 11) follows; the term describes what happens during the rite: the outside of the death roll is provided with new layers of cloth. This is accomplished by men who are skilled at it, not by the to mebalun. The death priest himself, however, sews the death roll shut; for a corpse from the class of free farmers he uses an iron or copper needle. (And for the noble Sa'pang?) Finally, when the death roll has been encased in red, the winding sheet is studded with figures cut from gold leaf (this cutting is the task of the pande bulaan, the goldsmith). A wide variety of figures is possible: a favourable motif for a dead woman of high rank is the doti, a cross (see Kadang 1960: figs.17 and 22). The ends of the death roll are usually adorned with the barre allo-motif (see Vol.I:239 and Kadang 1960:fig.77).

Ma'palangngan ba' (= to suspend the dead body from the ba'; rite 12). The dead is hung touching the Western wall of the house. B. Sarungallo comments that this symbolizes the deceased's departure from the house in which he has lived for so long. West, however, is also the direction of Puya. The rapasan, the "coffin", is now returned to the rock chamber where it stays when not in use.

Ma'popengkalao[21] or ma'popengkalao do mai ba' (rite 13): the bodily remains are taken down from the wall to await the moment when they will be placed on the sarigan to be brought to the ricebarn.

Ma'pasulluk (rite 14). All the special buffaloes to be slaughtered during the second part of the death feast, are "introduced" to the deceased (exactly how this takes place was not reported). These decorated buffaloes all are given a name and poems are composed about them. The finest beast, contributed by the head of Tandung village, received the name Ballo Matogon, Comely and Decorous in Appearance. For an instance of verses honouring buffaloes, see Vol.I:192. Should a buffalo die before his time to be slaughtered has come, his natural

death counts as fulfillment of the donor's obligation; no additional
buffalo needs to be supplied. (Van der Veen claims that the ma'pasulluk
is a rite of the dirapa'i-ritual during which the buffalo known as the
tandi rapasan is tethered in the space beneath the death house; see
Woordenboek: v. soelloek.)

Mangrambu bulisak (rite 15). This means "to blacken the wood chips
with smoke"; a pig is slaughtered. This is the name of the rite during
the dirapa'i when wood is made ready for the sarigan.

Ma'palangngan sarigan (= to lift the dead onto the bier; rite 16). At
about seven in the evening the deceased is carried from the death
house through the ba'ba sade and born in a procession around the
compound. (Who carries the corpse and in what fashion were not reported. Is it placed on a temporary bier? In what direction does the
procession move?) Then the corpse is brought to the ricebarn where,
out front, the sarigan (portable bier) stands ready. The death roll is
set down on the sarigan which is alligned with the ridge of the ricebarn
roof, running North-South. The dead lies with his head to the South.
The dead person's family may fix whatever time they wish for this rite.

Mangrera (rite 17). A pig is killed whose meat serves as food for the
deceased (pemanala; cf. Vol.I:206).

Ma'doya (rite 18; see also Chapter IX.2.2.). This time family members
keep their watch over the dead after he has been conveyed to the ricebarn.

Ma'tau-tau (rite 19), the making of the tau-tau. The tau-tau is made
ready before the deceased is placed on the floor under the ricebarn.
The craftsman who made the effigy is paid with buffalo meat, paddy
and cash.

Massabu sarigan (rite 20). The consecration of the sarigan, the portable bier for the deceased. I was not informed what offering was made.

Manglassak tau-tau (rite 21). The wooden mortuary effigy is fitted
out with sexual parts to leave no room for confusion. Then the doll is
set up in front of the ricebarn where the death roll is laid out.

Massabu tau-tau (rite 22). The consecration of the tau-tau by the to
mebalun. The soul of the deceased can now enter the tau-tau. Oddly
enough, when questioned on this point followers of Aluk To Dolo denied
to me, as vehemently as Christian Toraja do, that the soul takes up
residence in the effigy; see above. (N.B. The consecration of tau-tau
and sarigan will indeed have preceded lifting the corpse onto the bier.)

The rites beginning with the ma'palangngan sarigan up to and including the consecration of the mortuary effigy occupy about two days.

Ma'popengkalao rokko alang (rite 23). The death roll is placed on the
floor beneath the ricebarn.

Ma'pasa' tedong (rite 24). The buffaloes to be slaughtered are led
around in a procession after being harnessed and decorated. Small
cylinders (kasosok) are placed over their horns; these may be pure
gold, or else silver or tin covered with gold leaf, and they may be
ornamented with parakeet feathers and wisps of human hair known as
patotti or pana'-pana' (see Fig. 2).[22] Those who lead the buffaloes also
are dressed in festal garments. The to minaa walks in front. The lead
buffalo is the parepe' with a maa'-cloth over its back. Once the decoration of the buffaloes has been completed the procession leaves the
compound and goes to the rante. The string of buffaloes circles the
bala'kaan three times, moving counter-clockwise. Once the parade ends,
at a signal from the to minaa the crowd takes up safe places to watch

the buffalo fights about to begin (see further the description of the first part of Sa'pang's funeral).

Massembang bulo (rite 25). This rite only takes place if the deceased was a brave man of high rank (women seldom are eligible). For details, see my account of the second phase of the funeral held for Puang Lasok Rinding of Sangalla' (Chapter XII.2.). What follows now is a brief description excerpted from an unpublished manuscript of Van der Veen, supplemented with information from Nonongan. For enacting the rite a number of slaves wear the costume of war dancers (to ma'randing). Only the leader is dressed differently, in a bayu lamba' (Woordenboek: v. lamba') and with tabang-leaves as head decoration. He goes in front, carrying a sarita-cloth with him. The war dancers follow him. They go to a place where a lot of bamboo-bulo grows. With drawn swords the to ma'randing swoop down upon the bamboo as if doing battle. They must sever each bamboo with a single stroke. After the bamboos have been stacked and tied, they return to the death house, each to ma'randing with a bundle of bamboo over his shoulder. The leader is in the van again, holding fast to the tip of the sarita-cloth. The sarita trails behind, attached in turn to each bundle of bamboo. The to ma'randing walk single file, shouting the headhunters' cry (sumapuko). When the procession has returned to the compound of the death house, the bamboos are chopped into smaller sections about 15 cm long (tuang-tuang). These are threaded together on a rope, three pieces at a time. Between each group of three an imitation sword is suspended, made of wood and about 20 cm long. (In Nonongan sirih-pouches of pondan-fabric are also part of the ornamentation.) Once the chain has been threaded completely, it is hung up onto the death house: it stretches from the Western side door to the ricebarn opposite delimiting the compound. When the corpse is conveyed to the rante, the tuang-tuang travels along as well (see below). When the body has been laid in the grave, the tuang-tuang is brought back and draped about the deceased's finest ricebarn. Should the chain break, a pig must be sacrificed; only the to ma'randing may make, or repair the chain.

After these important preparations and rites have been accomplished, a day of great significance arrives, the ma'palao or massonglo' (rite 26); these words mean, respectively: "to bear the dead in a procession to the slaughtering place of the buffaloes" and "to descend in a parade to the feast plain". The day before guests poured in from all sides and occupied their lantang. On the big day the deceased is carried from the ricebarn to the rante and there placed on the lakkean (tower for the corpse). First the corpse is lifted from the floor under the ricebarn and let down on the sarigan. Then a roof is placed on the bier, a miniature of the roof of an ordinary house. The sarigan is decked out with fancy, coloured wood carvings and rests on six struts so that it can be put down whenever necessary. Sturdy bamboos are mounted beneath the bier so that it can be held aloft by a large number of bearers. The sarigan is decorated, too, with cloths and golden krisses.

Sedan chairs are made for the to massanduk dalle, the to dibulle tangnga and the to ma'pemali. These litters look like a tent. They are fitted with black cloth which conceals the person seated inside from public view. The top of each "tent" is crowned with a kandaure mounted on a bamboo frame. (No mention is made of a sedan chair for the to ma'pemali; she is not carried along in the procession. This, however, happens at the time that she replaces the to balu.)

People don't leave right away for the rante. They first sing the death songs while surrounding the bier which still rests on the ground. (Such badong are sung as well during the transit to the rante; they involve a special tune appropriate to this phase of the ritual; see The Chant:73.)

The procession procedes with great pomp. Usually it does not go directly to the rante but first passes along several of the deceased's sawahs; only in the event of bad weather is such a detour omitted. As far as the order of the procession is concerned[23]: the buffaloes which are to be slaughtered go in front; the parepe' first of all, with a maa'-cloth over its back. This buffalo is considered to be the mount that will carry the deceased to Puya (which explains the buffalo's name, roughly equivalent to "he who is close by", i.e. close by the deceased; repe': close together). The sacral cloth is to be regarded as the buffalo's saddle blanket. After the buffaloes follow half a dozen war dancers, to ma'randing with the tuang-tuang. While shouting war cries (sumapuko), they execute a dance which consists of a repeating pattern of three steps forward, three steps back (see Holt 1939:69-70). Then come men who bear the tombi (flags and banners) and other regalia (see below). They are followed by two men who carry a gong which is struck as it moves along. Next advance the three sedan chairs draped with black cloth in which ride the to massanduk dalle, the to dibulle tangnga and the to ma'pemali. (The place of the to balu remains obscure. Where was she?) Now I could understand the origins of the name of the second functionary, for she was indeed carried in the middle. "She who serves the maize" now has a different name; in her present function she is referred to as to usso'boi rante, "she who (as the first) digs a hole in the slaughtering place of the buffaloes" (Woordenboek: v. so'bo; cf. the to usso'boi rante in the great bua'-feast, Chapter II). There is no explanation for either function or name; it is possible that this female slave has to avert the evil influences which emanate from this sacral location.

The three sedan chairs are shaken roughly back and forth during the march; this happens to the bier as well, the handsomely decorated sarigan which follows.

Behind the sarigan comes the tau-tau in full dress and ornamentation, the living image of the dead.[24] The sedan chair of the tau-tau is surrounded with a red cloth to which various golden krisses are fastened. To the left and right of the tau-tau parasols stand open. In addition to relatives, hundreds of other persons follow the procession – friends, acquaintances, villagers, and, nowadays, tourists, too. On the rante everything is in readiness for the ma'palao. The menhir, hauled for the dead, has meanwhile been stood on end. Next to this mammouth rock and the other simbuang batu which have remained standing from previous death feasts, tree trunks have been planted (see below). The lakkean, the colossal tower for the corpse, has also been completed; it has a vast saddleback roof which arches up at both ends. Since the tower rests on high piles, a ladder is needed in order to be able to carry the death roll up to its place in the space beneath the roof. Below this space is a floor which serves to accommodate the tau-tau.

When the procession reaches the rante, it does not enter onto the feast square right away. First it circles around the area three times, then it proceeds onto it. Everyone stops; first of all the corpse is

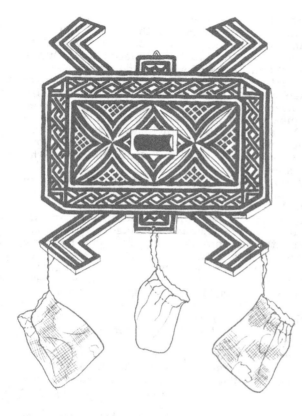

Fig. 42. Bungkang-bung-kang, "that which re-sembles a crab", an object made of wood that is carried in the funeral procession during a death ritual of a high order. The small figure hangs from a rattan cord fastened to the end of a bamboo pole (see, too, Vol.I:Ch.VI, note 21).

This bungkang-bungkang is made for a man's death feast. The hook-shaped protruberances represent the crab's feet, the rec-tangular ones the crab's head and tail. Models of sirih-pouches are attached to two feet and the tail. The wood itself is decor-ated with carved motifs. The primary motif, a rosette, is the pa'bua kapa', the cotton fruit.

A small wooden cylinder which portrays the death roll is inserted in the middle of the plank.

The item here reproduced comes from Kesu'.

Drawing by Suzanne Taub.

Fig. 43. Bungkang-bung-kang made for a woman of high rank. Here the principal woodcarving con-sists of two doti langi' ("spots of heaven"), cross motifs with a star or a lozenge in between. The elevation in the centre represents the corpse in its thick winding sheet.

The artefact was prepared in Kesu'.

Drawing by Suzanne Taub.

hoisted onto the waiting tower. Then the three women step down from their sedan chairs and climb up the lofty ladder of the lakkean. The to usso'boi rante (= to massanduk) leads the way, followed by the to dibulle tangnga and the to ma'pemali. The tau-tau is placed beneath the lakkean on a special platform. Then the staffs to which the tombi are fastened are stuck into the earth to the West of the tower. In part these are the same tombi which already were used during the aluk pia; some regalia, however, have been added: the bungkang-bungkang (see Figs. 42 and 43), two tombi busa (white penants), one tombi tali tarrun (a dark blue, square cloth), and a tombi which was described as "ordinary". Next to the death house four "ordinary" tombi and one bandera were set up. The path leading from the death house to the rante was also marked with a streamer.

The tuang-tuang is rigged up: one end is attached to the tower of the corpse, the other to the bala'kaan.

Meanwhile the buffaloes which will be slaughtered ritually have been tethered to pantok, short stakes driven into the ground. Yet, they are not tethered just anywhere. Next to the simbuang erected on the occasion of Sa'pang's death, stands the parepe' (= tandi rapasan, usually a bullock). Beside the huge stone, the trunk of an induk-tree stands upright, connected by a rope with the menhir. This trunk is designated as simbuang induk. Similarly, beside a second menhir, a simbuang lambiri (the trunk of a pseudo aren palm) is rigged upright; next to it a spotted buffalo stands tied with a rope. Beside another menhir is the trunk of a pinang-tree (simbuang kalosi) together with an "ordinary" buffalo, possibly a bonga. Beside yet another menhir stands a simbuang buangin with a buffalo not further specified. Another buffalo is tethered to a monolith joined to a simbuang pattung (for pattung, see Vol.I: 144, 229). The huge stones stand more or less in a row. In Nonongan, tombi are also hung out in the immediate vicinity of the menhirs, one for each of these massive stones. Whether this took place at Sa'pang's funeral, I am unsure.

For the comfort of spectators who arrive in ever greater numbers as the moment for the mantunu approaches, branches from the induk-palm are stuck into the ground to cast soothing shade. Once the bodily remains have been placed on the lakkean, the ma'doya dio rante takes place, the watch over the dead on the slaughtering grounds.

The next event cited was the mantaa tuo (mantaa: division of meat; tuo: living). The to mebalun fetches a small pig which he releases in front of the tower where the corpse has been placed. Those present do their best to capture the pig, which, I am afraid, emerges from the fray more dead than alive. The significance of the rite is not clear.

The following rite is the ma'palumbang, literally: "the piling of bunches of rice" (the name is not clear). A buffalo is slaughtered; part of the meat is processed according to the rule of pemanala: something from all portions of the animal is set aside (see Vol.I:206). This assortment of parts is offered to the to mebalun and to the to ma'kuasa. The considerable bulk of the buffalo which remains is divided (among whom is not stipulated).

The next day is the mantunu, the slaughter of so many assembled buffaloes. The parepe', however, is preserved to meet its death the following day. The mantunu is a hectic occasion with crowds on the feast plain pressing forward to see the bloody spectacle and receive part of the meat.

Finally, the next day, the mantunu parepe' takes place; and the mount of the deceased perishes. The buffalo's head was sent to tongkonan Batu, the sibali banua (see Vol.I:204-5) of tongkonan Tandung.[25] There is a special relation (sibali) between these houses which are situated in different villages. In addition buffalo meat is conferred on those who performed certain tasks with respect to the deceased. Meanwhile all on the rante has calmed down distinctly. The day of the mantunu is nowadays considered the acme of the feast; afterwards many guests depart for home although a group always remains to accompany the deceased to his final resting place.

The last journey, the meaa or ma'peliang, follows on the day that the dead man's mount is killed. That morning the corpse is removed from the lakkean and laid once more on the sarigan. For one last time, the deceased receives food. Then he is escorted to his grave. No specification was made of the sequence of events. Sa'pang's bodily remains were buried in a patane, a boulder in which a grave had been hewn (see Vol.I:260). The tomb is sealed with a shutter. In the past a burial house was constructed over the spot, one that could be of rather sizable dimensions, commensurate with a small ricebarn. The tau-tau is stationed under the floor of this grave. Sometimes the mortuary effigy is placed astride a mount (usually a horse, not a buffalo) made from wood. Contemporary patane are built of bricks joined with mortar and painted white. The sarigan remains in the neighbourhood of the grave.

Once the rite has reached its end, those who have paid this final honour to the dead, go home, unless, of course, they are staying for the following activity, one which draws new visitors (and participants): the inevitable cock fights.

Afterwards came the kumande bunga', the kumande tangnga, the umbaa kande, and the kumande tampak (see Chapters IX.2.2. and X.2.-4.). The ensuing rite, the membase sali, involved the offering of a pig. Membase sali means: the purification of the sali-room.

At this juncture the rite is enacted during which the bombo, Sa'pang's soul, is escorted out of the village. On the following day the untoe sero is held, and on the fifth day after burial, the membase. A pig is sacrificed for both of these last rites (previously described in Chapter X.4.).

1.4. Description of the feast terrain

During a major funeral, guest houses are erected all around the compound of the death house. These lantang also stretch along the road which leads to the rante. Guest accommodations are also frequently constructed round about this "square" itself. All in all the string of houses suggests a veritable village. This is why one speaks of tondok to mate, the village of the deceased. Also, the tongkonan where the dead is laid out is abandoned by its inhabitants, for the sphere of death - and, perhaps, the stench - are an obstacle to continued residence. Although people deny it, the following description demonstrates that throughout the duration of the death ritual, the vast house is not truly lived in.

Family members and guests received lodging according to their rank and class. Closeness of kinship to the deceased and mutual relations among family members were also taken into consideration in assigning accommodation. Preferably the children of one mother were housed in adjoining lantang. Here we must keep in mind that Sa'pang had eight wives, seven of whom were still alive at the time of his funeral. One of the widows, presumably the one with seniority, functioned as official to balu. The others remained either in the tongkonan or in lantang; see Fig. 44.

It is of interest, too, that the ricebarns were also furnished as guest houses, especially for eminent visitors coming from the outside world.

Fig. 44. Groundplan of Sa'pang's funeral held in Tandung, Kesu'.

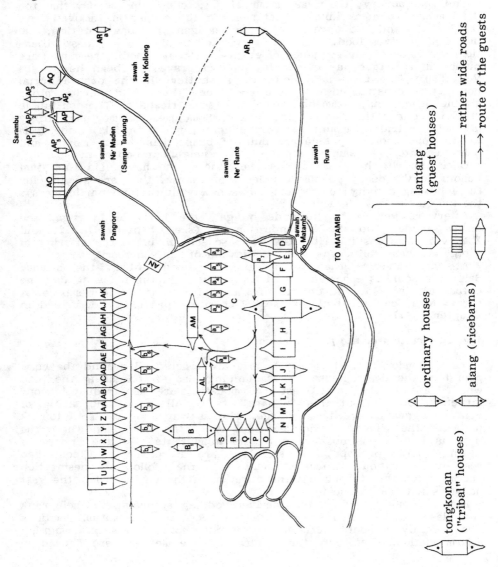

A. Tongkonan Tandung, Sa'pang's death house.
a1-9 The ricebarns belong to this tongkonan; some have names:
a1   alang Patongkong Kayu
a2   alang To Matua
a3   alang Ba'ba Sa'de
a6   alang Amboran

B. Tongkonan Batu with its ricebarns b1-6. These barns are nameless. Ne' Marini (his actual name is So' Toriu) together with his wife Lai' Peniro (this woman, a daughter of the deceased, is also known as Ne' Marini in keeping with the teknonymous practice of Tana Toraja) live here.

C. Compound of tongkonan Tandung. Here the pa'karu'dusan, the sumbung penaa and many other buffaloes were slaughtered. Here, too, on the first evening of the aluk pia, the to minaa burned the fragrant wood of the casuarine. This compound was used intensively for rites during the first phases of the death ritual.

D. Lantang (guest accommodation). This shelter was divided in two. The Western portion was occupied for a time by Yusup Samma', one of Sa'pang's grandsons, and by his mother, the first wife of Sa'pang's son So' Midi. A half-brother of Yusup, the son of his father by another mother, lodged in the Eastern part of the house. The upper story of this lantang, also divided down the middle of its length, was at the disposition of these same occupants.

E, F, and G. Guest quarters for the headman of the village of Tandung (Indonesian: kepala kampung), Sampe Tandung (alias Ne' Suda, see Table 3), one of Sa'pang's sons. In connection with his position, three guest houses were at his disposal where he could accommodate guests arriving somewhat late.

H and I. Here another son, So' Midi, father of Jusup Samma', stayed together with his present wife, their children, and several guests who were unknown to me.

J. Accommodation of the mother of the to ma'pemali. It is my impression that the to ma'pemali stayed here as well from time to time.

K. Lai' Lamba, one of So' Midi's and Sampe Tandung's younger sisters, for a time inhabited this lantang. Twice married, she spent some time here now and again with three children from her first husband, So' Tinggi. So' Tinggi' himself and his second wife also lodged in this shelter.

L. Lai' Lamba's second residence where she settled in with her second husband and her remaining offspring. The two guest houses, K and L, shared one kitchen. (When I expressed astonishment at this arrangement, people assured me it caused no problems whatsoever.)

M. The guest house accorded to Sa'pang's son, So' Rampa, a younger brother of So' Midi. He held an office in West Irian which prevented him from attending the first part of the ritual for the dead. As his

Table 1. Sa'pang's mother's first marriage.

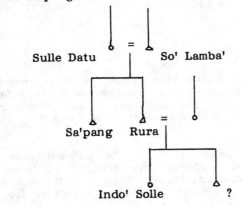

Table 2. Sa'pang's mother's second marriage.

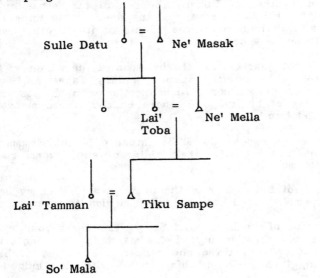

stand-in, his father-in-law then lived in this guest lodge.

N. This shelter was the temporary home of So' Tampang, a brother of So' Rampa, So' Midi, etc.

Guest houses D through M were thus occupied by a single family group, except for lantang J where the mother of the to ma'pemali resided. The to ma'pemali's duties bound her to the vicinity of the house of mourning and therefore also bound her mother, who had to cook for her.

The most eminent woman of the family group assigned to lantang D through M was Lai' Rante, Sa'pang's third wife. Sampe Tandung, her oldest son, was the head of this family group. Whenever a meeting was called, he represented this group of relatives in their dealings with outsiders and he also served as a link between them and the to ma'-pemali's mother. He was, word had it, the to ma'kuasa, but this contradicts the description which Van der Veen gives of this personage in his Woordenboek (v. koeasa): "Ma'kuasa, the official who during the ritual for the dead looks after the deceased and observes strict mourning taboos; for the first week after the commencement of the feast he may not eat any cooked food; the to ma'kuasa functions in rituals from the order of the dipatallung bongi up to and including the dirapa'i; in Kesu' this figure is a slave unless the ritual follows the aluk Sullukan ...".

O. The lantang of So' Lebu', Sa'pang's youngest son by his pre-deceased wife Lai' Panatta' (see Table 3.VI).

P and Q. Guest accommodations for So' Massarrang, the size of whose family required extensive quarters. He is Sa'pang's oldest son by the late Lai' Panatta'.

R. Among those staying here were the children of Ne' Marini's oldest daughter Lai' Parekan, herself dead. (For Ne' Marini, see B above.) She was one of four siblings, grandchildren of Sa'pang now fully mature and married. In this lodge there were thus also Sa'pang's great grandchildern.

S. Here Ne' Marini's son So' Belo stayed with his six children.

N.B. A cottage was erected between B and B1 where Lai' Tallo, the youngest child of Ne' Marini, resided. The cottage is not on the map.

T. Habitation of Palete and his family, somewhat more distant relatives of the deceased.

U. The accommodation of So' Kamban, Sa'pang's third cousin (sampu tallun).

V. Guest house of Ne' Losong, anak disarak (foster child) of Sa'pang.

W. Another foster child, So' Bato', stayed here.

X. Here So' Rone lodged, a relative equally as far removed from

Table 3. Sa'pang's marriages.

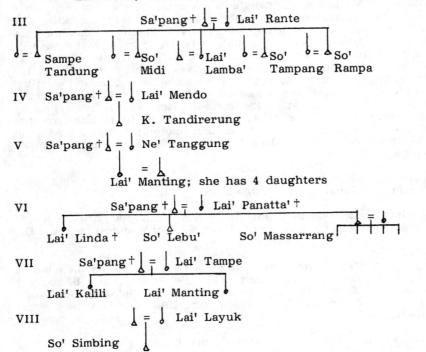

I   Sa'pang † △ = ○ Lai' Toban

Ne' Marini △ = ○ Lai' Peniro

Four children were born from this marriage; the oldest, Lai' Parekan, is no longer living.

II   Sa'pang † △ = ○ Lai' Dengan

Lai' Koko; she has 5 children (2 sons and 3 daughters)

III   Sa'pang † △ = ○ Lai' Rante

○ = △ Sampe Tandung   ○ = △ So' Midi   △ = ○ Lai' Lamba'   ○ = △ So' Tampang   ○ = △ So' Rampa

IV   Sa'pang † △ = ○ Lai' Mendo

K. Tandirerung

V   Sa'pang † △ = ○ Ne' Tanggung

= △

Lai' Manting; she has 4 daughters

VI   Sa'pang † △ = ○ Lai' Panatta' †

Lai' Linda †   So' Lebu'   So' Massarrang

VII   Sa'pang † △ = ○ Lai' Tampe

Lai' Kalili   Lai' Manting

VIII   △ = ○ Lai' Layuk

So' Simbing   △

In addition still remain:

IX   Sa'pang, the deceased's grandchild from his marriage with Lai' Toban (see Table 3.I)

X   Sampe Toding, adopted (disanga anak) in maturity for the support he gave Sa'pang during legal proceedings

XI   Four children raised from an early age in Sa'pang's house; in most instances these are children of members of the family and fall under the category anak disarak (anak passarak):

     1. Lai' Tokko

     2. ?, my informant could not recall the child's name

     3. Si Bato'

     4. Lai' Rore'

Sa'pang as Palete is.

a1. In this large ricebarn furnished to accommodate guests, W. Papayungan, an eminent Toraja originally from Kalambe, Tikala, resided. He has family in both Tikala and Kesu' territories. Although his kinship with Sa'pang was rather tenuous, his status commanded sufficient consideration for him to be assigned to spacious quarters.

a2. This ricebarn was provided for an ambe' tondok from Tandung, a distant relative of Sa'pang's. Family friendship was in this instance also insignificant. What mattered was that this villager was a descendant of the village founder (pangala tondok).

a3. Here the camat of Kesu' stayed, the contemporary district head.

a4. This ricebarn sheltered Pong Massaga' from Marante, a son of the important tongkonan Sullukan.

a5 and a6. Another ambe' tondok remained here. (Tandung is divided into two, each part with one ambe' tondok.)

a7. Lodging of Bua' Sarungallo and his family. Although no immediate kin of the deceased, Sarungallo was stationed in this imposing guest accommodation because, according to tradition, it was to be occupied by those belonging to tongkonan Salle Bayu (the tongkonan of Sarungallo) and also because he was the deputy of the camat of Sanggalangi' who was away in Macassar on business.

a8. This ricebarn housed the members of an eminent family from Buntao'.

a9. Already dilapidated, this ricebarn had no guests.

b1 and b2. Here resided members of the foremost family from Sa'dan.

b3. This ricebarn was reserved for soldiers in the Indonesian army who provided security at the feast.

b4. It is unknown to me who stayed here.

b5. Temporary abode for a member of a leading ramage from Nanggala, So' Kamban; no kin of the deceased.

b6. In this ricebarn lodged, among others, an eminent man from Anginangin (Tadongkon), Rante. Whether he was a relative of Sa'pang is uncertain.

Y. Guest quarters for Indo' Solle', Sa'pang's niece (see Table 1).

Z. The lantang where So' Simbuang resided, a son from Sa'pang's marriage with Lai' Layuk.

AA and AB. The lantang of Sampe Toding, an anak disarak of Sa'pang.

AC and AD. The guest houses of K. Tandirerung, a medical practitioner, one of the deceased's children (see Table 3.IV).

AE. Lai' Kalili, one of Sa'pang's daughters, stayed here (see Table 3.VII).

AF and AG. Lodges where Lai' Manting, one of Sa'pang's daughters from his marriage with Ne' Tanggung, stayed with her four daughters.

AH. F.K. Sarungallo's guest quarters. He had a leading role on the ritual as chairman of the impartial committee which supervised the number and quality of the buffaloes which Sa'pang's children would slaughter during the death feast.

AJ and AK. Both these accommodations were put at the disposal of Lai' Koko, a daughter of the dead man from his second marriage (see Table 3.II).

AL. The great feast hall for reception of guests. Arrivals were welcomed here and provided with materials for smoking, with betel and with refreshments.

AM. Lodgings of Professor H.Th. Chabot and Rev. H. den Dop.

AN. Cockfight arena.

AO. The lantang for unexpected guests and for those who welcomed arriving visitors (these were either relatives of the deceased or young people who offered their services).

AP. The house of the village head (not a traditional tongkonan). The vicinity of this house is called Sarambu. Throughout the feast the village head stayed in buildings E, F and G, for these were situated closer to the feast terrain.

AP1, AP2 and AP3. The village head, Sampe Tandung's ricebarns.

AP4 and AP5. The village head of Tandung's buffalo stables.

AQ. Headquarters for the Indonesian film crew from Jakarta.

ARa. The buffalo stable of Lai' Lamba'.

ARb. The buffalo stable of So' Midi.

2. The contribution of buffaloes by Sa'pang's children and the proposed division of the deceased's sawahs

Sa'pang's funeral can serve as an illustrative example for how the contribution of buffaloes by a dead person's children is of decisive importance in determining their shares in the inheritance. Offspring inherit in direct proportion to the buffaloes which they supply for slaughter at the feast. Yet not every child may provide buffaloes at his

or her own discretion; contributions are set by an impartial committee
consisting of family members, and, on occasion, of third parties as
well. Every child of the deceased is told how many buffaloes he or she
is expected to supply. The class of the child's mother is taken into
consideration, as well as the nature of the relations maintained between
the child in question and the dead parent, the services which the child
may have performed during the parent's lifetime, etc. No difference is
made between sons and daughters. Adopted children (whether of the
category anak disanga, or the category anak disarak or anak sangtepo
- see Vol.I:37ff.) also share in the inheritance; they receive less, however, than the deceased's natural children. Specification of the expected contribution in buffaloes is made about a month prior to the first
rite of the death feast.

Drawing up an acceptable division is no easy matter and those concerned do not always agree with the committee's decisions. In the event
of controversy the court must arbitrate, especially should the deceased
have no children and the inheritance be destined for division among
cousins. Pusaka (the Indonesian word for heirlooms) are usually preserved by the family titleholders; they may possibly also be divided if
they are things which the deceased wore during feasts, such as krisses
or sirih-pouches. Some goods are set aside to accompany the dead. A
surviving partner does not share in the inheritance, for she or he has
possessions of his or her own. Christians, too, adhere to the division
of their inheritance along these lines.

Below follows a summary of the distribution of Sa'pang's sawahs
among his children, grandchildren and adopted children as listed in
Table 3. The summary begins with a specification of the buffaloes which
these children and adopted children were required to contribute for the
death ritual:

I   This group of children[26] had to supply 7 buffaloes, including 1
       especially fine, 3 fine and 3 less fine;
II   These children[27] had to contribute 5 buffaloes, 1 especially fine, 1
       fine, and 3 less fine;
III   Together these children had to bring in 20 buffaloes, 1 especially
       fine, 10 fine and 9 less fine;
IV   This son was assigned to provide 3 buffaloes, 1 fine and 2 less
       fine;
V   This child had to contribute 2 buffaloes, 1 fine, 1 less fine;
VI   These children were called upon for 7 buffaloes, 1 especially fine,
       3 fine, 3 less fine;
VII   These children were asked for 2 buffaloes, both less fine speci-
       mens;
VIII   This child had to supply 3 less fine buffaloes;
IX   This child had to bring in 6 buffaloes, 1 fine, 5 less fine (this
       contribution was part of the tekken to mate, to be discussed
       below);
X   The adopted Sampe Toding (disanga anak) had to contribute 3 fine
       buffaloes;
XI   Each of these four adopted children had to supply 1 less fine
       buffalo.

That three children (see Tables 3.VII and 3.VIII) were only called upon
to provide less fine buffaloes may be connected to the status of their
mothers.

Fig. 45. The division of Sa'pang's sawahs.

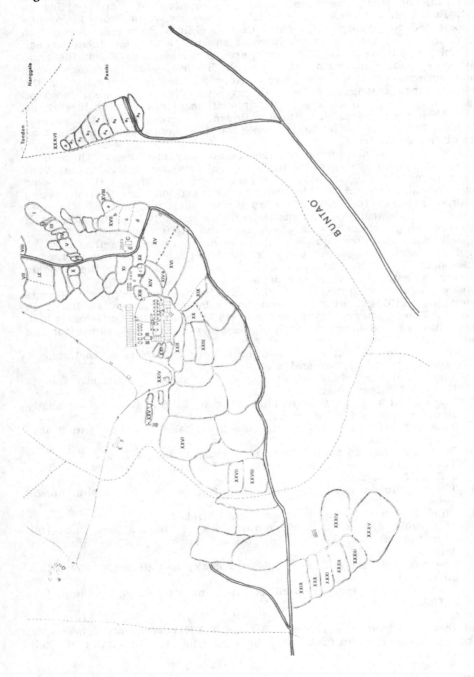

Below follows the division of Sa'pang's sawahs in the immediate vicinity of Tandung (see Fig. 45). The proposed distribution - which reveals the degree of complexity that can be involved in settling questions of inheritance - took into consideration the contribution of buffaloes specified above. Sawahs are designated by a Roman numeral followed by their proper names.

I. Tangdisso was already consigned (diba'gi) to Sampe Tandung and So' Midi.

II. Tangngana no. 1 and III. Ullan were allotted to Sampe Tandung and to So' Midi. So' Midi's mother contributed 3 buffaloes in support of her son, for sawahs I and II were estimated as worth 8 buffaloes. (The value of a sawah is estimated on a basis of its yield in bunches of rice (sangkutu') and then this level of productivity is converted into a number of buffaloes.)

IV. Mana'. This sawah was to be split into three, one third each for Sampe Tandung, Lai' Lamba' and So' Rampa (the son who lived in Irian Jaya).

V. Pangrante no. 1. During his lifetime Sa'pang gave this sawah to the to ma'pemali and her sister. After the second part of the death ritual, the to ma'pemali received yet another sawah for her services.

VI. Pongmaki. This rice field was considered to belong still to the deceased, i.e. it was not yet assessed and its eventual owner would be determined only after completion of the second phase of the death ritual.

VII. Rante Pindan. This field was for Ne' Marini.

VIII. To Nangka'. This field continued as a possession of the deceased (cf. VI. above).

IX. To Duri. Also remained property of the deceased,

X. ? This sawah belonged to Ne' Marini who acquired it from his father when he married.

XI. Sarambu was still Sa'pang's property.

XII. Lambanan was for K. Tandirerung.

XIII. Pangroro still belonged to the deceased.

XIV. Ne' Maden. This sawah was already given to Sampe Tandung.

XV. Ne' Kolong still belonged to the deceased.

XVI. Pangrante no. 2 (a second field by this name). Before Sa'pang's death half of this sawah was already designated as Lai' Linda's. It now belongs to her child So' Tulak. The other half is So' Lebu's.

XVII. To Pongko'. During Sa'pang's lifetime, this sawah had already been transferred to four of his children: Ne' Marini, So' Rampa, So' Tampang and Lai' Lamba.

XVIII. Kamiri was divided between Ne' Marini and So' Rampa.

XIX. Rura still belonged to the deceased.

XX. To' Kani was to be given to Lai' Koko.

XXI. Buka. Ne' Marini acquired this sawah.

XXII. Busso still remained in the hands of the deceased.

XXIII. Tangngana no. 2 (a second field by this name) was allotted to Lai' Koko.

XXIV. Saruan belonged still to the deceased.

XXV. Pangroro no. 2 (the second field by this name), also still the property of the deceased.

XXVI. To' Indu' was accorded to So' Sarrang (whose mother, now dead, was Lai' Panatta').

XXVII and XXVIII. Tallulangi' was for Lai' Manting.
XXIX through XXXIV. A complex called Pasang Bale. This complex belongs to Ne' Marini. It was not clear whether Sa'pang left him these sawahs before he died or afterwards.
XXXV. Pangrante no. 3. A sawah not yet conferred on an heir, thus remaining the deceased's posssession.
XXXVI. a1 through a8: a complex called Lansa' was also not split up as part of Sa'pang's inheritance before the second part of his death feast. A, B, C, D, E, F. houses.

The division of Sa'pang's inheritance was in fact not yet concluded as late as 1983, for Sa'pang's oldest son did not agree with the proposed terms.

However complex division of the inheritance in Kesu' may seem, prior to World War II it was yet more complicated as the result of a custom known as mangrinding (literally: "the erection of a wall"). This custom meant that even distant relatives had the prerogative of slaughtering buffaloes for the deceased which entitled them to claim a share in the inheritance. The mangrinding could have unpleasant consequences for children of the deceased when they were not in a position to contribute a large number of buffaloes. At present the division of a dead person's property involves shares proportionate to the number of his children.

3. The badong sung at Tandung

The badong are usually sung by people dancing in a large circle who move slowly in a clockwise direction. They indeed shuffle sidewards, for with their heads and bodies they face towards the centre of the circle. For how the circle is formed, see Figs. 34 and 35 and the accompanying captions. More details concerning dance and choreography are contained in Holt 1939:52-4 and 115, ills. 41 and 44, and in The Chant:11-3. The ma'badong usually occurs in the evening. The later the hour, the larger the circle. The badong reproduced below is an instance of a short death chant from Kesu'. Various kinds of elegies are known.[28] Each kind has a number of variations which can differ from region to region. There is, for example, the badong to songlo', the death chant sung by the men who carry the corpse on its bier to the rante; this is the only badong which does not involve formation of a circle. The badong performed at elite funerals is the badong diosso'mo. Its contents proclaim the eminence of the deceased. His birth is extraordinary, like the moon. After his death he goes to heaven to become part of a constellation in the sky. The soul of the deceased has returned to the gods, has become a divinity, membali puang (the term bombo never appears in the death chants).

The song tells the life story of the deceased: after his wondrous birth, the placenta and umbilical cord were buried just as is customary for ordinary mortals. Thanks to lullabies, the baby thrives; the man celebrated in song becomes rich, the owner of many buffaloes; women admire him. His praises are sung in a manner very reminiscent of the eulogies delivered at the bua' kasalle-feast. Nonetheless, old, he falls ill. The adat chiefs, here referred to as to bara'[29], came together with the to makaka: "They made the cleansing rites for him, rites for his confession willing"[30] (The Chant:31). Yet, to no avail: "But it was Ne'

Sara[31] who won; He wears the dried areca leaf" (The Chant:31). Now other rites are held for him: "He lay there in his proa decorated with carving, he rested in his golden boat"[32] (The Chant:32). The tombi are hung out for him, the deceased is brought to the ricebarn. The sacral banners are unfurled for him when he is carried to the rante. Then he is taken from there to be buried in the rock grave. In this genre of death chant, a rather detailed account is given of what takes place at an elite burial.

Now the soul of the dead embarks on a journey to the South; he laments. "His weeping is the morning rain, his sobbing is the drizzle fine"[33] (The Chant:35). The soul carries onward through Duri and Enrekang and the people there say:

"We called him, but he answered not,
We shouted, but he spoke no word."
"The sole of his foot answered us,
His heel it was that made reply."
(The Chant:35)

He reaches the kingdom of the dead. Usually Puya is described as follows in the badong: the soul stepped over a ditch and two trenches, reached the country situated to the South by way of the mountain Bamba Puang or by way of palm trees on high where the Great Bear and the Seven Sisters (Pleiades) "embrace" him:

"We look for him to sow the rice...!" (see Chapter IV)

The songs for the most part end by asking a blessing: children, wealth and buffaloes.

The journey undertaken by the soul of the deceased is recounted in more detail in the badong, but then the South is no longer the soul's destination, but its point of departure. Pongko' is then cited as the soul's goal, the mythical island that was the source of man, the pendant of Puya that also lies to the Southwest, but under the surface of the earth.

Below follows an example of a badong (death chant) from Kesu', transcribed by B. Sarungallo (Dutch translation by Van der Veen).

Makarorrongmi te tondok Ma'kantu'lung-tu'lungmi.	Silent is this village, it is lonesome.
Male natampe nene'ki Naboko' mendadiangki.	Our grandfather has abandoned us, He who begot us, has left us behind.
Nene' lalumba minai Anna sandako pakemo	Grandfather, wither goest Thou, That You, all dressed up,
Umbai lalu tamamo Banua tang merambu?	Perhaps has entered The house from which no smoke climbs?
Umbai disalli' leko',	It will after all be bolted in a reversed way,

Ditaruntun salian.	Locked in the contrary manner.
Ma'mallo'-mallo' Ilan batu dilobang.	He is merely still sighing In the gouged out rock.
Tiromi tu tau tongan Tu to natampa deata.	Have a look at this extraordinary person Who was created by the gods.
Malulun padang naola, Umpasilongsean riu,	The grass of the fields was trampled when he walked across it, Everywhere he made the grass hang limp,
Umpanampu' padang. Ma'ti tombang naorongi.	And made the blades of grass grow parched. The pond which he traversed dried up.
Umpakarangkean tasik, Unlambi'mo kalo' lamban,	The sea he made into dry land, He reached the ditch and crossed over, he went over the trenches.
Unlamban pasala-sala, Lamban lian peambongan.	He crossed to the far side, to the place where one gathers ambong-vegetables, The far side, where one collects Solanum Minahassa.
Sambali' petanantian Nabala dambu ma'dandan,	On the other side of the jambu-trees standing in rows,
Nasapa' mengkidi-kidi. Unlambi'mo pasa' langkan,	The stars stand between him and us. He arrived at the market of hen-harriers,
Tammuanna manuk-manuk. Umpobaluk-baluk bungin,	The place where birds are sold. He used sand as merchandise,
Umpobalanta karangan. Bendan kalukumi lolo',	He made use of gravel as trade goods. He stands there in the South as a coconut palm,
La ma'induk tumayangmi. La naola langngan langi'.	He rises up above everything in the form of a sugar palm. Now he is going to ascend to the firmament.
Natete langngan batara, Dadi deatami dao,	He walks the pathway to heaven, He becomes a divinity there above,
Kombongmi to palullungan, La ditulakmira langngan,	He becomes the one who enwraps all, He will be revered there on high,

La dipenombaimira,	He will be the object of veneration,
Anna bengki' tua' sanda,	So that he will bestow his favour on us,
Palisu sanda mairi',	So that our inheritance will be great,
Anta masakke mairi',	So that we will live long,
Madarinding sola nasang.	So that we will be blessed with health.

4. The recitation during division of sacrificial meat among descendants (mantaa bati')

This custom is observed as part of death rituals of high order in Kesu'. It is also called ka'panan balang, "holding the lung in the fist", a poetic reference to that part of the distribution of the meat during which the to minaa addresses the ancestors of the West, at the same time throwing morsels of meat set aside for them from the bala'kaan. In his address he mentions the relations of the deceased to the various ancestors of the people in the region, citing the names of the founders of the more important tongkonan. This is a precaution against any ancestor's taking offense if his name should not be called. First to be acknowledged are the heavenly beings who according to popular belief came down from the firmament in olden days bringing with them the adat institutions and rules for sacrifice; speaking of them the to minaa faces South. Turning to the North, he then tells of the sources which cause water "rich in blessings" to flow. Next he speaks of the way of pure gold which - and he looks West as he continues - came out of the West. Finally, pivoting towards the East, the to minaa addresses the Datu of Palopo (Luwu') who is to be thanked for the fertility of rice (see Vol.I:114).

Below, there follows a translation of the text recited by So' Sere, to minaa of Angin-angin, Kesu', during a mantaa bati'-ceremony. The text was written down by the former assistant of Van der Veen, J. Tammu, and translated into Dutch by Van der Veen. I must add that the poetical language of the text is often confusing and the translation sometimes uncertain.

Limbong lan rante kalua'	In great numbers on the wide plain are gathered
Bati' tikunna kasalle baitti',	the descendants from all around, great and small,
Metua' ponno lako to nalambi' sumpu matua,	To beg for a complete blessing from him who had reached the extreme of old age,
to nabamba to tumampana.	from him who was struck down by his Creator.
Makalima'na tasik lan tandung kalonangan mana' sariunna sitangnga silolok[34],	In full force, all are there, infinitely many gathered on the vast field, the descendants from those of average means to the very wealthiest,

Meparaa pantan lako to nalambi',
sumpu suka'na,

to nasambak to manggaraganna.

Patanan rampa'komi talinga
duammi,
palidan maya-mayakomi suling
patomalimmi.

Apa laennaraka te la mitananni
talinga duammi,
tanda senga'raka te la mipali-
danni suling patomalimmi?

La urrundunan bulorakan
panganna rara'na to diponene',

inde bala'kaan duku' dio aluk
mangka tipondok.

La umpasitete malaa'rakan pa'palumpun bulaanna to dipotomatua,
inde lempo bumarran dio sangka'
dipamangka salaga.[35]

Angki potangkean suru' kinallo
lalanna,

dio ka'panan balang sau'
engkokna padang.[36]

Angki potetangan lindo sara'ka'
bokong lambananna raeng ate
tedong,
sau' mendalelona lipu
daenan.[37]

Apa iamo nanii bunga' to mellao
langi' rampan di lino,

iamo nanii mendemme' kapadang-
anna tipamulanna to turun
dibintuen.

La kidemme'mo ka'panan balang
lalanna sukaran aluk,

To beseech benevolence in all respects from him who had attained
the highest degree of age,
him cast down by Him who had given
him form.

Will you please be still and
prick up both ears,
strain both your hearing ducts to
listen well.

Because are they strangers to whom
you should prick up your ears,
are they outsiders for whom you
strain your hearing ducts?

Let us straight from beginning
to end follow the splendid traditions instituted by those whom we
regard as our ancestors, here on the
platform for meat follow the adat
regulations of old.

Let us in orderly fashion turn ourselves from head to toe towards the
golden traditions of those whom we
regard as our ancestors, here on the
scaffolding which reeks of flesh,
with respect to the ritual observed
according to what for once and for
ever is set, just like a harrow.

Let us apply the nourishment for
their journey Southwards to the
tail of the earth,
use it as an offering when the
meat is being apportioned.

Let us take the provisions for their
trip South to the wagging part of
the earth in order to make the
peace-offering, the liver cut from a
buffalo.

Because this is the place where
the first of those who descended
from heaven touched earth,
that is the place where the first
one who came down from the stars
set foot on earth.

Let us stretch out our hands to the
assigning of the flesh, for the way
of the offering ritual,

la kikala'pamo raengan ate
tedong lambananna pantiran
kanna bisara.[38]

let us cut the liver of the buffalo
for the sake of the path of establishing the scope of the adat provisions.

Apa la napopentoean manda' anak
nakombong diong lisunna pala',
lumbang ma'tengko tiranduk.

May he pass it on to the children
whom he brought to life in the
centre of his handpalms to clutch
fast, crouching over while driving
the plough into the earth.

La napopelese-lesean bongsu
natakko bumbungan diong se'-
ponna kanuku malotong,
lukku ma'ayoka panoto.[39]

He will make it a support for the
young ones, those whom he made
take shape in the grooves of the
black nails, in bent posture driving
a plough which runs straight.

Anna kesonda penduan pentallun
kinallo lalanna te to nalambi'
sumpu matua, to nabamba to
tumampana.

May it be twice, three times a replacement for the nourishment for
the journey of this one who had
reached the extreme of old age,
struck down by his Creator.

Anna kesolan passangayokan[40]
bokong lambananna te do nadete'
sumpu suka'na,
to nasambak to manggaraganna.

May it be double the provisions
for the path of this one who had
arrived at the highest degree of
age, he who was cast down by
Him who had given him form.

Anna unnola ma'borong tallu
sukaran aluk,
umpolalan samma' kadaangna
kannan dibisara.[41]

May they observe the triple sacrificial ritual,
may they respect the boundaries of the areas determined in
the adat provisions.

E tongkonanna Tangdilino', lan
di Banua Puan!
La kidemme' ka'panan balang.

Hey, House of Tangdilino' in
Banua Puan!
We want to take up the holding of
the lungs in the fist.

Esungan kapayunganna Datu
Muane!
La kikala'pa raengan ate tedong.

Seat of the protective power of
Datu Muane!
We want to cut the buffalo liver
ourselves.

Denmo upa' nasakendek-kendekna
mendaun sugi',
napopentoean manda' taruk
tallangna,

May they grow ever richer in number like the leaves of the trees,
may they hand it down to their progeny, numerous as shoots of the
bamboo tallang, for them to cling
fast to,

nasalangngan-langnganna men-
tangke ianan.[42]

may their possessions grow up
like the branches on the trees.

E tongkonanna Puang ri Kesu' e,
to mangka deata, mangka to lino!
La kidemme' ka'panan balang.

Hey, House of Puang ri Kesu', first
god and later man!
We want to take up the allotting
of meat.

Apa la to sumio' sukaran aluk
matampu' matallo,
to napasilele patiran kannan
dibisara pollo'na ulunna uai.[43]

For this determines the sacrificial
ritual of the West and the East,
all around it sanctions the bounds
of the domain of the adat provisions
of the South and the North.

Iamo dinii untaa tuak sukaran
aluk,
dipasilele ba'bana lembang,
napada torro paria.[44]

That is the place where the scope of
the domain of the sacrificial ritual
is determined by the handing out of
palm wine, which has been distributed all around at the entrances of
the territory, where everyone
remains to his well-being.

Iamo dinii ussio' panaran
kannan dibisara,
dipasitutu' ma'ti ditari', pada
unnisung pataranak.[45]

It is the place where is determined
the scope of the domain of the adat
institutions, spread throughout the
demarcated territory, bringing a
blessing to everyone.

La napopentoean manda' anak
nakombong diong lisunna pala',
la napopelese-lesean bongsu
natakko bumbungan diong
se'ponna kanuku malotong, paka-
paka to napoampo.[46]

May he pass it on to the children
whom he brought to life in the
centre of his handpalms to clutch
fast,
May he will make it a support for
the young ones whom he made
take shape in the grooves of the
black nails, all the more so for those
whom he has as grandchildren.

E tongkonanna Manaek lan di
Nonongan,
esungan kapayunganna Datu
Baine!

Hey, House of Manaek in
Nonongan,
Seat of the protective might of
Datu Baine!

La kidemme' ka'panan balang,

la kikala'pa raengan ate tedong.

We want to stretch out our hands to
the assigning of the flesh,
we want to take up the cutting of
the buffalo liver.

E lalanna tagari sanguyun tama
rampe matallo!
La kidemme' ka'panan balang,

la kikala'pa raengan ate tedong.

Hey, path of the bundle of fragrant
grass in the East!
We want to stretch out our hands to
the assigning of the flesh,
we want to take up the cutting of
the buffalo liver.

E lalanna kalimbuang boba rekke
ulunna salu,

The path of the overflowing spring
to the North, the source of the

iamo lempang tama uma ma'kam-buno lumu'[47],

napokendek lompona padang.

river,
it diverts its course towards the sawah which has a sunshade of duck-weed,
through which rises the fat of the land.

Iamo tinombu tama pananda uai,

napolangnganna lupa' panaungan.

It veers aside into the dammed up water,
through which the season's yield shoots up.

E lalanna tutungan bia' e![48]

La kidemme' ka'panan balang.

Hey, path of the kindling of the torch!
We want to stretch out our hands to holding the lungs in the fist.

Lambananna kangkanan ballo marorrong,

la kikala'pa raengan ate tedong.

The path of holding the brightly burning torch in the palm of the hand,
we want to take up the cutting out of the buffalo's liver.

E lalanna bulaan matasak,
lambananna nane' tang karauan.

Hey! The way of the undiluted gold!
The path of the gold without alloy,

Apa iamo natampa gayang to men-daun sugi' narangnganan bunga rangka'na,

nasakendek-kendekna mendaun sugi'.

From this he who is rich as the leaves on the trees forges a golden kris which he applies to augment the fruit of his hands, and so he becomes ever richer increasing (his wealth) as the leaves of the trees.

Iamo naparende sarapang to men-tangke ianan, nasalangnganna.

He who has possessions as branches on the trees, melts it in order to make a great kris of gold, and so (these branches) ever grow.

Guest houses. First part of Sa'pang's funeral, Tandung, 1969. See also pp. 251-257. (Photo: Hetty Nooy-Palm, 1969.)

Badong-dancers at Sa'pang's funeral, Tandung, 1969. See also pp. 230-231.
(Photo: Hetty Nooy-Palm, 1969.)

The pounding of rice during the dirapa'i-ritual, Tandung,
1969. See also p. 231.
(Photo: Hetty Nooy-Palm, 1969.)

The temporary resting place for the deceased during the first part of Sa'pang's funeral in Tandung. The coffin is known as rapasan or erong and is shaped like a rice mortar. It is decorated with coloured motifs: doti langi' ("spots of heaven"), a cross which symbolizes abundance; circles, representing discs made out of shells; and tumpal-motifs. See also pp. 234-235. (Photo: Hetty Nooy-Palm, 1969.)

The to mebalun, the death priest, with torches in his right hand and a chicken in his left, is on his way to the ma'bolong-ceremony. Behind him follow the women who take part in this rite. See also pp. 241-242. (Photo: Hetty Nooy-Palm, 1969.)

Chapter XII

A PRINCELY BURIAL

"Come let us weave the lament now.
The mourning song, in sequence right.
Look at that exceptional man
Who was created by the gods.
The field's grasses has he trod down,
The pond he walked across dried up.
Then he this region southward passed,
Went, like the season, out of sight."

(The Chant:68)

1. The first part of the death ritual for Puang Lasok Rinding of Sangalla': the ma'batang or dipantunuan pia

1.1. Introduction

Puang Lasok Rinding died on August 31, 1968. He was an exceptional individual, learned in the history and adat of the Sa'dan Toraja, especially of the puang-territories, the Tallulembangna. His portly figure radiated authority. Considering the man's vast store of knowledge, his children regretted that during their father's lifetime they failed to record more of his words. With his demise, those interested in knowledge of the past suffered a serious loss.

Puang Lasok Rinding first glimpsed the light of day in tongkonan Batu Suaya, probably in November 1881.[1] Son of Puang Batu's (Palodang XI) second wife, his only sibling was Puang Lai' Sa'pang, a younger sister. He never had what we would call a formal education, for the first school in Sangalla' opened in 1917. His tuition was limited to those opportunities which a young nobleman of his time could make use of; his education, thus, was based on the principles of puang-ship, kapuangan. He spent years during his youth in the Buginese kingdom of Sidenreng to develop martial skills; his sojourn there also enabled him to learn Buginese, the language of the Toraja's neighbours. The trip to Sidenreng was not without dangers; he had to traverse a region which at that time was anything but safe. The path to the Buginese kingdom led through woods and densely thicketed mountain hillsides where robber bands had their hideaways. Upon his return a few years later to Sangalla', his father informed him that it was time to marry. Obediently he entered into marriage. Later he contracted additional marriages. When Puang Lasok Rinding passed away, only one wife survived him. He had five children, four grandchildren.

In 1903 when his father died, Puang Lasok Rinding succeeded him as Palodang XII; he was the forty-third descendant of his celestial

ancestor, Tamborolangi'.[2] As usual his consecration took place seated
on a special stone in Rante Allo. For the oath sworn during his in-
auguration as prince, see Van der Veen 1979:17-36 where the author
discusses the Tangdona Sulle Gayangna Bullu Matua (the swearing of
the oath by the majestic successor to Bullu Matua, the ancestor of the
puang-dynasty of Ma'kale). In this investiture service, the glorious
descent of the prince is recapitulated; his lofty status is elucidated and
not only his rights, but his duties are stipulated as well.

In 1906 the Dutch brought the Toraja territories under their control.
The puang's biography reports that he commanded his war lords, Pong
Sipa among them, to stop the Dutch. Resistance is said to have been
offered in the fortresses of Buntu Bebo and Sinaji. Sangalla', however,
was vanquished. The defeated made their surrender at Batumababu.
The puang himself met with the Dutch in Lalliu where he was given to
understand that should he demonstrate cooperativeness his reign would
be permitted to continue. Palodang XII agreed. Until his death he was
respected as the adat chief of the realm of Sangalla', To Sereala'
Penanianna, the twenty-four districts.

During the Japanese occupation, as well as throughout the days of
the N.I.T. (Negara Indonesia Timur)[3], the puang continued in his
function. Under the Japanese, he was a member of the Sjikai Gün (pro-
vincial house of representatives). For the brief period after the war
when the Netherlands held power, he was member of the Tongkonan
Ada' of Tana Toraja (for this period, see Van Lijf 1952-53:261ff.).
About 1955 royal titles and power were abolished in Tana Toraja. Let it
be said, however, that Lasok Rinding's personal authority did not disappear with his right to rule. For his subjects, the puang remained to
manglaa, the keeper of his people.

The last days of the puang's life were blighted by frequent illness.
As early as 1966 he told me upon my leavetaking that I was seeing him
alive for the last time. Whenever a man of note in Sangalla' falls so
seriously ill that his recovery is regarded as unlikely, people turn to
Puang Matua[4], making an offer to the god with the request that he heal
the invalid, or, if that cannot be, that he adopt the man's soul. The
dying person is laid upon a mattress in the middle room of the house.
Those present sit facing him. The doomed man's legs are extended in
front of the mattress with the knees raised to prevent the patient from
dying on the ground. People refer to this as disalilentek, "providing
the feet with an under-layer".[5] At the same time people grab hold of
anything with which they can make noise and cacaphony erupts. Drums
sound, gongs peal, guns fire to spread the news that the prince is
dying. Thereafter a pig is slain. Portions are used for an offering
which together with glutinous rice is placed in a barasang (basket
braided from fine rattan). The basket is suspended under the knees
of the deceased, and people who file past recite the following litany:

Inde To Matua Induk,	Thou Old Man here, old as the pith of the sugar palm,
Inde Kalo' Bisaranna,	the way (literally: trench) of the adat regulations for him here,
Dirundunanmo Alukmu,	the whole course of the adat institutions is for you observed,
Inde To Matua Induk,	the Old Man here, old as the pith of

Inde Banu' karurungan,

the sugar palm,
he here, old as the hard pith of the sugar palm,

Dirundunanmo Alukna,

the whole course of his adat institutions is observed,

Inde Kalo' Bisaranna,

and the way of the adat regulations for him here,

Dirundunanmo pakenden,

the continuation of the way is pursued,

Kenden male kenden lao.

which is in motion, which goes forth.

Kenden tama pole pole,

In his turn he may ascend and enter.

Kendenta lako Puang Matua,
To dao

This ascent is to Puang Matua on high,

To manggaranganta, Sampung[6] tummampata,

To our Form-giver above, ...[6] our Creator.

Lo' Indo' Ambena, To nene' mendeatanna,

His mother and father in the South are ancestors who became gods,

Angki masakke natampe,

so that he be blessed in his departure,

Madarinding nabokoi.

leave us behind in well-being.

The litany is repeated three times to ensure that the dead will receive a proper welcome in Puya and that surviving family members left behind will receive a blessing from their ancestors residing in this land of the souls.

Delicacies made of glutinous rice are placed in the mouth of the dying man (the deceased?); this is called dipamomo. As soon as death occurs, all noise ceases as a sign that mourning has begun. Then the ma'dio' (bathing) takes place. A pig is sacrificed for this rite, a large, fat creature, for it must provide food for all those who, in response to the announcement of pending death, have gathered in the meantime.

After the offering has been presented and the corpse has been washed and has had a massage to purge the intestines, the deceased is clothed in finery and equipped with regalia. He is seated precisely as if he yet lived (Nobele 1926:40).

Sitting in state continues for some time to afford as many family members and well-wishers as possible a chance to view the deceased for a final time. Discussions concerning a death feast then take place between relatives and government officials of the princedom (i.e. Sangalla'). Afterwards the dead is stripped of his attire and wrapped in cloth so that he comes to resemble a massive bale or roll. When a man has died this work is done by men, for a woman, women see to the wrapping. The women of the family furnish the necessary cloth. With a bamboo, moisture is drained from the body. The deceased is brought to the Southern room; he is alluded to as to makula' ("the sick one"). Until the first part of the feast begins, no one is allowed to make any further offering.

At this point further unofficial talks are staged among family members, leading functionaries of the former princedom (the To A'pa' among them; see Vol.I:82ff.) and officials of the present government administration. Instead of the family, functionaries on either side have the last word in determining when the burial ritual will begin and how it will proceed. Certain essential arrangements are gradually concluded by the immediate family, by the earlier mentioned functionaries from Sangalla', and by eminent local figures:

a. The naming of the deceased. After his demise, the puang who lived in the tongkonan layuk (the leading tongkonan in Sangalla', the tongkonan of the ruler) is spoken of as Dipamate Puang Palodang (in Ma'kale: Dipamate Puang Bullu; in Mengkendek: Dipamate Puang Pa Etong).

b. The order of the ritual, as well as the number of buffaloes and pigs, minimally, to be slaughtered. Also established is how many animals family members, the Administration of Sangalla', old style, and the people will undertake to supply.

c. The date for commencement of the first part of the feast.

d. The terrain (in this instance various terrains) where the death ritual will be staged. It was decided that rites would be held on two plains situated close to each other, Buntu Kalando and Lobe. Accordingly, after passing away, the puang was conveyed from tongkonan Kaero to tongkonan Buntu Kalando (the house bears the same name as the land which surrounds it). The tongkonan, considered the country house of the prince, originally consisted of a western-style building. After the prince's death, however, a decision was reached to tear it down and replace it with a traditional tongkonan[7] (see photo p. 166). The second plain, the pantunuan (the word rante is not used in puangstates), lies to the West of Buntu Kalando (see Fig. 46). In the area around tongkonan Kaero the water supply was inadequate, the land steep and the house itself hard to reach, all reasons contributing to the choice of Buntu Kalando and Lobe as the setting for the death feast.

e. Along the edges of both these terrains guest houses had to be built. Construction gets under way once the date is set for beginning the first part of the ritual. Should the two plains not offer space enough, then accommodations could also be put up along the road connecting Buntu Kalando with Lobe.

f. Other details which could be of importance for the death feast were also regulated.

The information above concerning procedures related to the ritual derives from Tandilangi' 1968-69.

Certain functionaries have a task in the death ritual, and even before the deceased passes away:

1. The to ma'parandan, someone in the deceased's family of the same class whose task it is to feed "the sick one" (in Kesu' this functionary is called the to ma'pemali).

2. The to balu, the widow or widower (cf. Chapter VIII).

3. The to ma'kuasa, at an elite death ritual in Sangalla' these are three men (one kaunan, two to makaka) who may not eat any cooked food, especially rice, until after the ma'bolong is celebrated.

4. The to ma'patallan, this functionary only takes part if the deceased has no parents or siblings.

5. The to ma'karu'dui, a woman and two men who keep a vigil at the time of the deceased's ritual demise.
6. The to ma'peulli', a kaunan-woman, "she who takes the maggots out of the corpse". At present the name has only symbolic value (see Chapter XI, note 18).
7. The to mangria sampin, "she in whose lap the cloths are thrown" (see below).
8. The to ma'paduku api, a kaunan who must tend the fire next to the deceased during the rites.
9. The to membase sali, a kaunan, who must "wash" the floor (of the death house), i.e. keep it clean (or purify it symbolically).
10. The to massari to balu, "she who supports the widow".
11. The to ma'lunu, a slave (kaunan tai manuk) whose task at death feasts used to be to stab buffaloes and pigs.
12. The to ma'kayo, the death priest. This priest is assisted by the to ma'lunu.
With the exception of the to ma'kuasa, these functionaries remain active during the second part of the ritual as well (Tandilangi' 1968-69).

Fig. 46. Feast terrains; first part of the death ritual

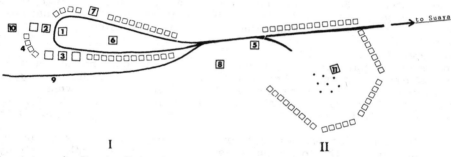

I

Feast terrain Buntu Kalando

II

Feast terrain Lobe

1   tongkonan Buntu Kalando
2   ordinary (non-traditional) house
3   central ricebarn of three opposite the tongkonan; this alang
     figured in the death ritual
4   four guest houses
5   restaurant
6   hall for reception of guests
7   hall for reception of guests
8   bala'kaan (provisional)
9   road
10   building for those who serve refreshments to arriving guests (tea,
     coffee, etc.)
11   cock fight arena
.˙. simbuang batu (menhirs)
☐   other guest houses

The first part of the death ritual in Sangalla' was designated as ma'batang (see Chapter XI.1.2.) or as aluk pia, the ritual for children, or even as dipantunuan pia ("that which happens on the small slaughtering grounds"). These names indicate that a kind of preliminary feast is involved, a simpler version of what will later be repeated in more elaborate fashion.

In the meantime the dead prince had been transferred to the central room of tongkonan Buntu Kalando.

1.2. Ma'batang and ma'karu'dusan, October 5-7, 1970

Monday, October 5, 1970
This was the day of the ma'batang. Since this and the following day were considered important, guests had already begun to pour in. Many commodities were delivered, for hospitality to so many guests requires vast organization. All in all shelters accommodated between two and four thousand people. Mattresses and food, especially rice, were brought in by truck. Workmen were busy putting the final touches to the guest houses which had to be erected at two locations. One smaller building was set aside for an exhibition of Toraja artefacts and implements. A vast lodge for foreign visitors stood in feast terrain I (Buntu Kalando, see Fig. 46), just as had been done at Sa'pang's burial in Tandung.

On September 30, I was told, the to minaa had come together to recite for hours on end. In their recitation it was emphasized that certain adat rules related to the ritual should not be violated.

Tuesday, October 6, 1970
I observed preparation of feast decorations which would be hung out on the ma'tombi banua as a sign that a ritual of a high order was being celebrated. The decorations consisted of a red fabric to which pollo' dodo (Nooy-Palm 1969:175, fig. 4) were sewn with thread made of pineapple fibre. It is not permissible to use cotton thread for this purpose. [8]

A kain sarita was brought out for me to inspect, just as a Sumbakain which one of the to ma'kuasa would wear as a headcloth. The only surviving wife of the late puang had been forbidden since the previous day to wear a jacket any longer, in keeping with mourning regulations for a widow. From November 7 she would have to forgo rice and subsist on uncooked food. As soon as the dead would be brought to the central room of the house and have his head turned to the South, his widow would take up her place seated next to him, face also to the South, her head covered with a mourning hood. [9] No one would be allowed to speak with her. She would only be allowed to leave the house to pass waste.

In the evening the sound of the ma'marakka could be heard coming from the death house. Ma'marakka is the name of a tune, a dirge performed at great death feasts. The ensemble, consisting of a flute player and two singers, serves to console the dead's descendants. The melodies are deeply plaintive to western ears.

Wednesday, October 7, 1970
Today the ma'karu'dusan was held. At about 6 in the morning the to ma'kayo (death priest) arrived with two drums over his shoulder. These drums were hung under the façade of the death house at its Northeastern side. The following rite was the throwing of a dead cock (a

sella') over the ridge of the roof. The death priest hurled the bird in an East-West trajectory; it cleared the roof of the death house easily, as if this sort of things were a daily occurrence. Considering the height of the house, it was no mean feat. The cock followed the soul of the deceased to the hereafter; it was "an appendage of the soul", like the buffalo described below who was to meet such a gruesome end. The next order of business was to lead the buffalo called the sumbung penaa under the South side of tongkonan Buntu Kalando. There the animal stood with its head facing South. He was tied with a long cord which both the to minaa and the to ma'kayo, facing West, held in their hands. The to minaa recited names from the puang's family tree.

As in Kesu', close members of the family may not eat of the flesh of the sumbung penaa (a pudu'). The beast died horribly. In Kesu' (1969) the buffalo whose carcass was to be shared out among a competing throng was killed before aspirants fell upon it; here, however - according to the eye-witness account of a member of the team of film-makers from Makassar - first the beast's legs were broken and then, while still alive, he was hacked to bits (just as happens on Flores). Men flail away with their cleavers in hope of securing a chunk of meat, without minding the risk of being wounded in the melee. Somehow, I was assured, mishaps seldom happen. Nobele (1926:42) also reports such butchery among the Sa'dan Toraja during death rituals.

Hereafter the deceased was conveyed from the central room to the front (Northern) room of the house and laid out with his head to the South. (This differs from procedures in Kesu' where the dead is carried from the Southern to the central room. Perhaps the difference is connected to the fact that it was the funeral of a prince which was being celebrated.) I was not present when the deceased was moved. From outside, through a small window, I caught a glimpse of people singing and dancing the badong in the front room while the corpse in its death roll was lifted up and down several times before being laid out in a North-South direction. Tandilangi' does indeed maintain that people dance around the corpse while intoning the badong. According to J. Tammu the deceased is hoisted into the air and tossed aloft to the accompaniment of song.

As when the dead still lay in the other room, here, too, betel, pinang and other accessories were set out at his feet. There was no or-namentation. Women (muffled in a cloth) began to wail, their faces pressed to the bier. By way of exception photographs were permitted because they served scientific purposes. In the afternoon, at about three, seven buffaloes were killed. The karu'dusan was the first, pierced with two thrusts of a spear. Family members may not eat of this buffalo. The other buffaloes were dispatched with a blow from a cleaver. Their meat was divided according to adat, except for one buffalo that was shared among Moslem family members. This animal was killed in keeping with Islamic law. Before darkness fell, the division of meat had been finished. The slaughtered buffaloes had been contributed by the children and other relatives of the deceased.

In the evening a small pig was slaughtered and prepared on the com-pound near the Northwest side of the house. A langngan (roasting spit) was used. Parts of the sacrificed pig were served to the deceased. The to ma'kayo also took some meat, wrapped in a banana lead, and laid it on the drums. The rite sketched here is known as rimpisan bia'.[10]

In the evening, after dinner, the ma'katia and massailo' took place

(for these dances, see Chapter XI.1.2.). The performers, nine in all,
were younger than 15. They wore a black jacket and coloured sarong.
On their heads they had a red toque decorated with a triangle in the
form of the façade of a Toraja house. This triangle was made of bamboo
and coloured paper, red, white and gold. In actuality this is the head
ornament of a gellu'-dancer and is associated with the sphere of the
East, yet one should not forget that this was the death ritual of a
prince, a man close to the gods of the upperworld. Gold earrings and a
red sash completed the dancers' outfit. During their formal appearance
on the big day of the death feast, the ma'tombi, they also strapped on
a waistband of beads with beaded fringes.

Not long before midnight the ma'badong to dolo began which lasted
far into the morning hours. The death songs were sung in alternation
with the singing of retteng.

1.3. Allo torro; Thursday, October 8, 1970

As the name indicates, this is a day of rest (allo: day, torro: rest,
stay). No special activities are scheduled. Rehearsals for the ma'katia
and massailo' were held, and another group of dancers practised as
well. In the afternoon I was allowed to enter the room in the death
house. Those who had eaten rice were forbidden to step on the floor
mat, the mat which had belonged to the deceased. Four women sat in
the room with sarongs pulled up under their armpits; they, like the
puang's widow, might wear no jacket or blouse. One slept to the West
of the corpse. The widow had withdrawn into a conical, tent-like
structure covered with white cloth. Contrary to what I had been led to
believe, she talked and others talked to her.

The death roll was covered with a red cloth to which coins, including
old V.O.C.'s, were attached. A doll was propped up against the rear
wall of the chamber, at the head end of the deceased. The doll wore a
headcloth. This was the pa'patonangan (tau-tau lampa) of puang Lasok
Rinding, not the definitive mortuary effigy which would be fabricated
later (see Chapter X.4.). The effigy had a face on which mouth, nose
and eyes were indicated (details were veiled in darkness). Its clothing
consisted of a white shirt and a kain. On its head was an old cloth
fastened to a frame of interwoven bamboo slats. As an ornament, the
effigy wore a rara' around his neck (Meyer 1972:798 (photo)).

1.4. Mebalun; Friday, October 9, 1970

At about 9 in the morning the ceremony of unwrapping the corpse
(mangrondon) began. On the compound, Northwest of the death house,
a pig was killed and prepared to eat. Together with the buffalo killed
later that day, the pig was part of the offering for the mebalun (to
wrap). At noon, people actually began to undo the winding sheet. When
the corpse was stripped it was brought into a squatting posture (it was
said that the legs were broken to achieve this; through the treatment
the corpse had received it was probably by then mummified). Then the
bodily remains, now in a crouch, were bound and swathed in cloth once
more. Wrapping took practically the entire day. Beautiful cloths were
also used; ornaments were given to the dead and wrapped with him
under successive layers of cloth. Wrapping is arduous, it must be done
properly so that finally the packaged corpse resembles a smooth cy-

linder, so sturdily constructed that, should the need arise, it can stand by itself. Sewing the winding sheet closed is the chore of the ma'kayo. Deciding which cloths should be used at various stages of the wrapping is the collective responsibility of the tomangria sampin. Nobele (1926:43) specifies that a golden needle draws the thread which stiches up the shroud of descendants of the puang-lineage.

After all else, a red fabric is laid across the wrapped corpse (according to reports). Some twenty foreign tourists were in attendance. It was deemed preferable that none of them enter the room where the dead man lay; otherwise, it was feared, everyone would come to stare out of curiosity. Yunus Somba explained to me that most dead people are swathed in a foetal position and only puang are trussed in a squatting posture. In the afternoon, about four, after completion of the wrapping of Lasok Rinding, a buffalo was killed to the Northeast of feast terrain I (see Fig. 46). The beast should actually have been slaughtered on the compound. That this was done elsewhere was presumably because the arrival of guests made it important to keep the compound clean. Neither the pig slaughtered earlier in the day, nor this buffalo was divided according to adat usage. Meat was simply given out to those present and to the residents of the village where the death house stood.

Once the puang had been swathed anew, the bamboo tau-tau was broken into pieces. The fabrics which the effigy had worn were hurled into the lap of the to mangria sampin. All day long additional guests were welcomed: some of the arrivals were Moslem family members from Duri. Those who lived in Sangalla' brought firewood; water was also transported in large bamboos. The main torrent of guests, however, would only pour in the next day and the day thereafter.

During the afternoon, wood was assembled for building the bala'kaan. Gathering this wood is called manobon. As yet there was no bala'kaan erected on the pantunuan. Its construction would occur in the course of the second phase of the death ritual. For now, a scaffold for division of meat was set up in another location (see Fig. 46). The remainder of the afternoon and evening were taken up by the ma'katia, massailo' and ma'badong. After dark the rimpisan bia' took place again.

1.5. Ma'tombi banua; Saturday, October 10, 1970

During the morning of the fourth day of the first part of the death ritual, at about ten, the ma'tombi banua began. The name of the rite implies that the fabrics are displayed in and on the house, the tongkonan which is the centre of this phase of the death feast. Yunus Somba interprets the ceremony as showing respect for the spirit of the house. As a sign that a ritual of high order was being celebrated, a special red cloth was fixed to the front façade. The cloth was so long that part of it could be draped over the corpse as well.[11]

Earlier, in front of the house (see Vol.I:233, fig. VIII.1) a scaffold was attached to the tulak somba; here were on display a golden kris, a kris more modest in execution, two old swords, two old cloths (maa'), two kandaure and Puang Lasok Rinding's portrait. A small table stood in front of the scaffold. Here other heirlooms belonging to the dynasty of Sangalla' were set out in a dark rattan basket (barasang).

One of the most important regalia, the flag Bate Manurun (Vol.I:151, 258) was unfurled above the kris and swords; this flag, presented to the son of Lakipadada, was rectangular. It bore as an emblem a dark brown Garuda, the mythical Hindu bird. This Garuda, on a red field, was portrayed as an anthropomorphic figure with a bird's head. It was impossible to estimate the age of this important piece. The "flag" was presumably batik. It was on display only during special occasions. One of the deceased's grandsons explained that the Bate Manurun seemed to change colour, which was of significance. It also had a (repaired) tear which, according to the same grandson, bode well for the family. He asked me if I'd noticed. When I saw the flag on the third day it appeared identical to when I'd first laid eyes on it, the first day.

The provisional bala'kaan was then built on the spot previously mentioned (see Fig. 46). The platform was about 8 m high and stood on 6 piles. The two central supports were made from the trunks of palm trees: the kalosi (Areca catechu, pinang-tree) and the ampiri (lambiri, the pseudo sugar palm). The number of piles is yet another sign that the ritual was of a high order. For feasts of lesser allure, only four struts suffice. According to Puang Paliwan Tandilangi', the platform may not be situated on the pantunuan; only later, when the second part of the death ritual is held, is the final bala'kaan constructed on this slaughtering grounds (Tandilangi' 1968-69).

Towards noon the parepe' (a pudu') and several other buffaloes were paraded about. All wore ornaments on their horns, a strip of red cloth covered with goldleaf. The parepe' could be distinguished, however, by the ancient maa'-cloth over its back. After the procession, the parepe' was tethered to the bala'kaan; his death would not occur until the next day. In the afternoon the belo tedong was also brought to feast terrain I. This construction may not enter the compound of the death house throughout the first phase of the feast. It was colossal, much larger than the belo tedong which was carried along during the ma'tombi which I attended in 1966. The principle of construction was the same, however, with as prominent components the triangle resembling the triangular peak of the tongkonan, the kain sarita etc. The whole thing was mounted on a kind of bier which rose and fell in motion.

In addition to the buffaloes mentioned above, a pig was slaughtered, the urrara bala'kaan ("the drenching of the bala'kaan with blood"); it was an offering for this platform on which division of the meat would take place. The pig's carcass was duly distributed on the bala'kaan according to adat precepts, the process supervised by the to minaa. The to parengnge' were the first to receive their portion, together with other functionaries belonging to the tongkonan in the village where the death house stood. Next government officials were given shares of flesh. The to ma'lunu took bits from certain buffaloes which he set before the deceased (pantiti'). For the division of the meat as a whole, in which the panggau bamba (meat dividers) also have their say, see Vol.I:202-4.

Throughout this day new formations of guests continued to arrive, bearing gifts: buffaloes, pigs, firewood and tuak. One group bore a fat pig in a lettoan, a sedan chair decorated with tabang-leaves. The pig lolled at ease behind a triangular decoration (resembling part of the belo tedong). It took ten men to carry the animal. Apparently because of its likeness to the belo tedong, this bier should not have been carried onto feast terrain I, yet it happened. Later Puang Tandilangi' told me that the lettoan was altogether out of keeping with the proper observance of a death feast.

Each group of arrivals was first welcomed in a special reception lodge. Young family members of the deceased, boys and girls, met them, offering betel and materials for smoking, converging, as in Tandung, from opposite directions to extend hospitality. These young people wore white. Those who led, a youth and a young woman, had on a kandaure. This ornament of beads was, as usual in Sangalla', elegantly braided in front (Meyer 1972:794 (photo)). Family members were also attired in white. This choice seems to have been connected to the claim that members of the puang's lineage have white blood. Affinal kin also wore white. The colour prevailed until the ma'bolong (see below). Other, more distant relatives, came in groups dressed in the distinguished black adat clothing of the Toraja. Relatives from Buginese regions wore their own, extremely colourful costumes and accessories.

To the left of the entrance to the welcome hall stood a young woman, to the right a young man, both wearing a kandaure. After guests had been offered betel and tobacco and had been seated for some time, they were shown to their guest accommodations where mattresses and mats lay in readiness. Here young attendants treated them to tea and cakes. The line of youths with teapots and platters with baked goods covered with neat cloths of lace doing the rounds were every bit as festive in appearance as the throngs of guests entering the compound one after another. In advance of most groups of guests, as a sort of escort, ceremonially adorned buffaloes ambled along, the property of the puang's relatives.

During the afternoon there had been buffalo fights. The beasts, however, except for the pair that led off, were not particularly fierce. Far more energetic was the foot boxing that developed into a sort of mass spectacle. The entire pantunuan teemed with youths and men unleashing kicks; their faces were rigid with tight-lipped rage. A fallen man often received an extra kick from someone with whom he had nothing at all to do. Aggression latent in the culture erupted visibly. The same was true for the cock fights. Both diversions had probably been arranged in honour of a distinghuished guest, the French ambassador. Otherwise foot boxing only occurs after the harvest. The arrival of a troop of to ma'randing at the pantunuan was also spectacular: these dancers only perform during major rituals for the dead.

The parepe' stood tied to the bala'kaan until late in the afternoon. In the evening the ma'katia and ma'badong repeated. Chanting continued until the wee hours. As on the previous night, a pig was slaughtered and roasted (rimpisan bia').

1.6. Mantunu; Sunday, October 11, 1970

On this day, as part of the death ritual, buffaloes were slaughtered (= mantunu; pantunuan, the slaughtering place of the buffaloes, derives from mantunu). In Puang Tandilangi's eyes this is the climax of the first part of the death ritual. Yet more important guests arrived with their retinue and gifts, buffaloes included. Their reception followed standard procedure and they were escorted either to the guest house on feast terrain Buntu Kalando or to one of the accommodations which had been built encircling feast terrain Lobe.

During the morning decorations were hung out once again on the front wall of the death house, including the portrait of the dead puang.

A short while after noon the buffaloes destined for slaughter were

brought to the plain where the bala'kaan stood. The parepe', the most
important buffalo, and a second buffalo, the tulak bala'kaan, "the
support of the bala'kaan", were bound fast underneath the platform. In
addition to this tulak bala'kaan, other buffaloes would be sacrificed: the
bumbunna, the "helpers" or secondaries. These are the simbuang
kalosi, the simbuang buangin, the simbuang ampiri and the simbuang
pattung.[12] The animals are named after the tree trunks to which they
are tied (see Vol.I:230 and 263-9). Before the killing begins, the meat
of the bai to balu, the pig that is sacrificed by the widow (or
widower), is divided on the bala'kaan. The meat of this pig is
distributed among all of the to balu's tongkonan. Then, one by one,
the buffaloes are put to death and divided: first the parepe', then the
tulak bala'kaan, then the rest. According to Puang Tandilangi' afterwards the identity of the puang's successor should be called aloud.
Yet, for political reasons, this important component of the death feast
was omitted (for a long while already the traditional kingdom had
become an administrative unit which leaves no room for any autochthonic
form of rule).
   After the slaughter of the buffaloes tethered to the tree trunks, their
flesh was divided. The head of the simbuang kalosi went to the tongkonan layuk (= tongkonan Kaero). The head of the simbuang ampiri to
Kadinge', that of the patung to yet another influential tongkonan.
During the distribution of certain pieces of buffalo meat, all the names
of the most important titleholders in Sangalla' were called out. The remaining portions of meat went to those in the villages who had helped
build the guest houses. Should the tananan basse be present[13] at the
feast, then they receive the hind leg of a buffalo. At Puang Lasok
Rinding's burial this took place. The to minaa threw an entire hind leg
down from the bala'kaan. Not all the buffaloes brought by guests were
killed, yet the leg of a buffalo or pig that has been slaughtered is
given as evidence that the deceased's family acknowledges its debt to
the donors, a debt to be repaid when the donor's family must celebrate
a death feast.
   As usual the ma'katia, massailo' and badong were sung on the evening
of this day. The badong went on until deep in the night. Yet another
special rite took place, between seven-thirty and eight. The death
priest sat down next to the window in the Northeast wall of the front
room of the death house. He had with him some six lengths of bamboo,
60-80 cm long. After he recited a brief litany, the bamboos were thrown
out the window, one after another, each at a different angle but all
roughly in a Northeastern direction. After all the bamboos lay outside,
the death priest went and studied their configuration; then they were
picked up and collected again. A special meaning is attached to the
pattern of fallen bamboos. Each symbolized a particular group. The relation of the bamboos to each other foretells whether the future of the
separate groups will be prosperous or not. According to my informant
Y. Somba, should a bamboo fall far from the rest, that means that the
person or persons represented by the bamboo will journey far away (his
interpretation admits the possibility that each shaft of bamboo symbolizes an individual rather than a group). Nobele reports that eight
bamboos are thrown out the window. These stand for: the deceased's
brothers and sisters, his children, his grandchildren, his great grandchildren, his nephews and nieces. A separate bamboo is reserved for
the children who keep the vigil over the deceased, the to ma'parandan.

In addition one bamboo is for the kaunan (a certain category, such as house slaves or all kaunan?). Furthermore another bamboo represents the cushions of the deceased (Nobele 1926:43-4). Nobele also reports that previously (after the death roll was stitched up) the eight bamboos had been covered with maa'-cloths, other fabrics and kandaure. The bamboos were laid over the crossbeams of the death house.

1.7. Ma'parempe'; Monday, October 12, 1970

Ma'parempe' means "to bring to an end"; on this day a number of closing rites are enacted. Two animals should be slaughtered, a buffalo and a pig. Close to noon the pig was killed. Between twelve and one, a rite took place known as the meaa. The name denotes the carrying of the corpse to the grave. Yet, during this first stage of the death ritual, the deceased is not conveyed to his final resting place so that the meaa at this point is a symbolic entombment of the corpse. This explains the killing of the parepe', the buffalo which in Kesu' is killed at the end of the second part of the death ritual; the parepe' is the mount who bears the dead to Puya. In Sangalla', as part of the meaa, the buffalo mentioned above is killed during the afternoon. Before the beast was felled with a sword, it was first pricked by a spear which only caused a superficial wound. This is a vestige of the ancient custom of spearing the buffalo to death. Still another pig was slaughtered. Puang Tandilangi' maintains more dancing around the corpse follows, while badong are chanted. Then the deceased is placed crosswise in the central part of the house, that is with his head to the West, and encircled by a mosquito net. He is, as it were, buried for the time being (dipandan, lan rapasan). Despite the word rapasan, however, the bodily remains are not placed in a "rice mortar". A coffin is never used during the burial of a puang. On this day the to ma'kayo beats the drum on three occasions, once before, once during and once after the storage of the Bate Manurun, the flag with the Garuda. The animals killed for offerings were not divided according to adat usage, but those who were present received pieces of meat.

On the evening of this day, no death chants may be sung any longer. Family members and many who have a function in the death ritual are actually obliged to continue the maro' until near the end of the second part of the feast. If they find this is asking too much of themselves, they may, after first slaughtering a pig, eat rice. They must bring food to the deceased (ma'pakande).

From this day onwards, cock fights were staged on the pantunuan. At first these were heavily attended, but enthusiasm cooled after the local administration imposed a tax of 250 Rps. (Dfl. 2.5) and an admission price of 25 Rps. These fights were to last for eight days, but they ended earlier. It is interesting to note in this context that according to Tandilangi' such cock fights do not belong to the true adat.

1.8. Ma'bolong; Friday, October 16, 1970

Today another rite belonging to those which bring the first part of the death feast to a close was observed, the ma'bolong. A pig was slaughtered for this ceremony and prepared for an offering. A number of additional pigs were killed as well. Up to this point the deceased's close relatives wore clothes that were not necessarily dark; during the ma'bolong their garments are made black as a sign that mourning is now to begin. In the Tallulembangna the relevant rules of mourning apparel differ from those followed elsewhere in Tana Toraja. In Sangalla' ma'bolong takes place on the compound of the death house. To that end a pot is needed that rests on three stones, i.e. a real cooking pot; consequently the pig to be sacrificed is called the dikaroan dapo (dapo: kitchen, karoan: to dig up some earth). The meaning of the whole is that one fashions a kitchen which serves for the ma'bolong.

Near the bala'kaan a buffalo is slaughtered; it was the last to be killed during this part of the feast. Then the bala'kaan was torn down. The meat of the dead buffalo was brought to the compound of tongkonan Buntu Kalando and divided there, not according to adat, but among everyone who had gathered around the "kitchen" mentioned above. From now on the three ma'kuasa may eat rice again. All who have taken part in the maro' have made their apparel black. Women wear the pote, a mourning cap (see Fig. 47).

Ma'pakatua[14]
Three days after the ma'bolong, this rite is held, during which clothes are blackened once more. No animals, however, are sacrificed.

Fig. 47. Pote, a hood of black cotton, used in mourning. A black tassel adorns the point. The bottom of the lower edge is macramé alternating with bands of card weaving. Beads are knotted into the macramé. These are brown, redbrown, yellowbrown, white, blue and green. Long, plaited fringes hang from the cap.
Such pote are nowadays no longer worn. In the past women put them on who observed the mourning prohibition against eating rice. Men used to wear a fillet of braided threads that was also called pote. This headband had a tassel with beads at the end. In some districts (Bittuang, Pali, Balepe', Balla, Simbuang) men wore a cloth on their heads.
This pote is part of the collection of the Royal Tropical Institute in Amsterdam (Inventory no. 1641-1).
Drawing by Suzanne Taub.

1.9. Ma'poli'[15]

After three more days, the ma'poli' is held, a further repetition of the preceding rite. The mourners' clothing is again made black. Two or three bananas were thrown into the kitchen of Buntu Kalando. They were processed into an offering which was brought by the death priest (just as the previous offerings). This rite also takes place in the context of the final ceremonies of the first part of the ritual. Those with a task to perform in the ritual remain in the vicinity of the death house until conclusion of the second part of the death feast.

Family members use the time between the first and second part of the death ritual to locate buffaloes with which they hope to make an impressive show when the buffaloes are paraded in procession during renewal of the feast.

1.10. Ma'pasurruk

The account below has been extracted from Tandilangi' (1968-69), for I was not in attendance. No date had been set for the ma'pasurruk (= to pass under something) when I was obliged to leave. The rite is connected to the tandi rapasan, "the buffalo that props up the rapasan", that puts itself beneath something, or passes below something.[16] The word has only symbolic significance; moreover in the death ritual of a puang no coffin is in use. The rite obliges the feast-givers to go in search of a handsome black pudu', one with well-formed horns. Once such a buffalo has been found, then the to minaa "hands him over" to the deceased, "inviting" the souls of other dead while he does so to see to it that the deceased meets with no obstacles during his journey through the realm of the dead (see Vol.I:121). This request takes the form of a litany (not recorded).

At this point people wait until the second part of the death ritual can begin. Also during this interim period, no rituals of the East may be celebrated.

1.11. Commentary concerning the first part of the death ritual

A death ritual with an interval never used to be observed in the Tallu-lembangna (the puang-states), one informant assured me. The emergence of this new form of burial can be explained as follows: in Tana Toraja people practise the rituals observed by their mother's side of the family; consequently, for several members of the puang-lineage whose mother's family came from Kesu' a death ritual with a rest period is indicated. Later this practice became more and more widespread because people were unwilling for Kesu' to outshine them.

Originally the ritual for members of the puang's dynasty and for the puang himself was the pitung bongi. Nobele writes, however, that in the past an interval was also conceivable during great death rituals in puang-areas (Nobele 1926:38). Costs for family members were less than in Kesu' because villages under the puang's dominion contributed to meeting expenses. In modern times tourism has led to a combination of the feast with commercial interests. No longer did every foreign (white) visitor receive food. A restaurant was open and payment was expected for meals and lodging. Far more tourists were present than at the death ritual I attended in Kesu'. Other novelties included the use of petromax lamps and loudspeakers.

Although the broad outline of the ritual for the dead in Sangalla' resembled the dirapa'i as observed traditionally in Kesu', certain differences were apparent. There was no rapasan (erong), for example. My informant Y. Somba told me that prior to the ritual, the deceased is kept for a while in an old coffin (duni). There is, furthermore, no announcement to a cat that his master has died. Nor in Sangalla' is the ma'bia' held. Nor is the ma'doya (the keeping watch over the dead) mentioned as a special rite. The parepe', furthermore, is in Sangalla' killed during the first phase of the death feast. In Kesu', on the other hand, there are neither a belo tedong nor a tau-tau lampa.

Explanation of the death ritual
The preceding description is concerned with what is only a small, preliminary ritual; this is indicated by its name, aluk pia, the ritual of
children. The dead is even compared to a child. The deceased is
wrapped in foetal position and the jigging with the death roll (to mara-
nak) is, according to my informant Y. Somba, an allusion to the
rocking of a baby to make him fall asleep. One plays also with the
child, as the ma'katia makes evident. The dead then falls asleep, only
to be awakened (ma'tundan) by a blast of cacaphonious sound, when
the second part of the death ritual begins (see, too, Sa'pang's funeral
at Kesu', Chapter XI.1.3.).

2. The second part of the death ritual for Puang Lasok Rinding of Sangalla'

2.1. Background and preparations

Some of the family would have preferred to begin the second part of
the death ritual at once after the end of the first part. Others, however, probably for reasons of prestige, demurred. Celebration of a
single, continuous death feast would have meant a considerable saving
of expenses. Nevertheless, the ritual was carried out in traditional
style with an interval. This pause lasted two years. Financial circumstances may help account for its duration, together with the
diminished enthusiasm of those who had already provided services
during the first part. The intermission is looked upon as a rest period.
The leading rite observed during the intermission is the mangriu' batu,
the hauling of a monolith. During the pause, the death priest goes on
tending the deceased who receives eat and drink every day. The to
balu remains at the deceased's side, as well as the to maro', those who
observe the taboo against eating rice.
   A variety of preparations are necessary before the second part of the
death ritual can begin: the repair of guest houses or construction of
new ones, the fabrication of the tau-tau and of the bier (sarigan; in
Sangalla': saringan). The bier is provided with a roof which arches up
at both ends in imitation of a Toraja house. The death roll is to be
conveyed in this bier from tongkonan Buntu Kalando to feast terrain II
(Lobe). The roof of the sarigan is covered with a precious maa'-cloth.
This particular maa' had a special name, Rangga Ulu. Rangga means
"having branches", ulu: head; rangga ulu is the name of a two-headed
snake in Toraja folklore. It is possible that the name has to do with
certain motifs which appear on the ancient cloth.
   Somewhat later, several additional constructions were made ready
which the procession bearing the corpse would carry along with it, including sedan chairs for the widow and for the to ma'parandan. These
sedan chairs resemble black tents. Usually the to balu's sedan chair is
decorated on top with a kandaure. The belo tedong is also assembled at
this time. As a rule it is completed only a short while before the procession departs for the pantunuan. Any onlooker who witnesses the
level of activity involved will worry that preparations never can be
ready on time. Yet seldom is anything left unfinished when the moment

to begin arrives.

2.2. *Rites*

Just as during the first part of the death ritual rites took place at two
sides, tongkonan Bantu Kalando with its compound and ricebarns (feast
terrain I), and Lobe (feast terrain II). A third site, moreover, was
added: the rock complex Suaya where puang have been buried since
olden days. This complex lies some distance away from feast terrain II,
see Fig. 48.

Fig. 48. Feast terrains; second part of the death ritual

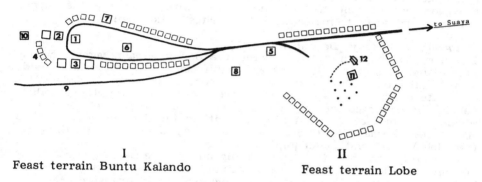

I
Feast terrain Buntu Kalando

II
Feast terrain Lobe

1   tongkonan Buntu Kalando
2   ordinary (non-traditional) house
3   the central ricebarn of three opposite the tongkonan; this alang
    figures in the death ritual
4   four guest houses
5   restaurant
6   hall for reception of guests
7   hall for reception of guests
8   bala'kaan
9   road
10 building for those who serve refreshments to arriving guests (tea,
    coffee, etc.)
11 cock fight arena
12 lakkean
.˙. simbuang batu (menhirs) and simbuang kayu (tree trunks)
_ _ _ tuang-tuang

People decided to let the second part of the death ritual begin at the
fixed date even though persistent drought meant that providing guests
with water might prove difficult. In addition government officials
pleaded for postponement to allow certain dignitaries the opportunity of
attending the proceedings, but the organizers stuck to their original
plan.
    As the first measure to embark on the second part of the death

ritual, according to schedule on November 4, 1972, the ma'tundan was held as early as November 4, 1972. The waking (tundan) of the deceased puts an end to the dirapa'i, the observance of a rest period. Since I was not yet on the spot (I arrived December 4), I must rely for the account below on facts culled from Nobele (1926), Tandilangi' (1968-69) and Van der Veen. From these sources it emerges that formerly, when the ritual still used to be held at tongkonan Kaero, a place which could only be reached with difficulty, very early in the morning the to ma'kayo beat two special drums and a gong which hung on the North-eastern side of the tongkonan in which the deceased lay at rest. A pig was then slaughtered, while the same afternoon a buffalo was killed as an offering. The deceased received some pieces of meat from both beasts. As soon as this rite had been concluded, the ma'badong can take place with regularity. I have no idea how often this happened. Provisionally everyone had his hands full with various preparations, working hard so that on December 4 the rites could begin.

Mangrondon; Monday, December 4, 1972
The name of the rite means to wrap the bodily remains again. Nobele writes that this has only symbolic significance, for just the outside layer of the bale which contains the corpse is changed (Nobele 1926: 47). Afterwards the death roll is covered with red material. This flannel fabric consisted of one rectangular piece and two circular ones which were sewn together. A pig is sacrificed for this rite and its head impaled on a bamboo staff erected on the compound of the death house (see Nobele 1926 and Tandilangi' 1968-69).

At roughly the same time as the mangrondon, the massembang bulo or ussembang bulo takes place, "the felling with a single stroke of the bamboo-bulo". From this bamboo the tuang-tuang is prepared, the collosal chain so many metres long (cf. Chapter XI.1.3.). It consists of a very long cord of fibres from the sugar palm threaded with bamboo "beads". These "beads", 30 cm long, alternate with groups of three or more bamboo rods some 60 cm long. They hang vertically from the cord. Among the "beads", moreover, hang imitation swords of wood, miniatures and sirih-pouches woven from pondan (pineapple fibres). It is the verticle sticks of bamboo, however, the tuang-tuang, which give the decoration its name.

As soon as it is ready, the tuang-tuang is hung up encircling the house where the bodily remains lay in state; the chain roughly follows the perimeter of the compound. When, during a later phase of the ritual, the deceased is carried to the pantunuan, the tuang-tuang goes along as well and is once more put up on display. After the deceased is brought to the grave, the bamboos are draped around his main ricebarn.

This chain is made for dead of high status, usually for men, seldom for women. One therefore only sees this decoration at the dirapa'i-ritual. To make the tuang-tuang, seven men went to a grove of bamboo. They were dressed as to ma'randing. Four of these war dancers had on a pio uki'. Before they left they performed a war dance to the East of tongkonan Buntu Kalando. One of those who belonged to the group wore other clothing: he had on a long jacket (bayu lamba') and a cap, known as the tanduk tabang (horns from tabang-leaves). This headgear was made from the sheath of a variety of palm leaf. A piece of wood was fastened to it on top and around this wood a kain sarita was pleated. To the tip of the wood, tabang-leaves were attached. This man's specific role (in Nonongan he is known as the to ma'tali tabang, "he who wears a headdress of tabang-leaves") was not clear to me. The to ma'randing had an additional attribute, a brass bell, a gorong-gorong. In a line the men then proceeded in the direction of Lobe where the bamboo grove was situated nearby. The leader, dressed in the costume of a to ma'randing, sang the following litany (translation by Van der Veen):

Sembang bulo

Ha, haha, haé!
Narondonnina' mani lapa manik-
mu é!
Natiba'tikkina' mani barang-
barang bulaanmu é!
Apaa.
La kusembangko tangsala sem-
bang é!
La kutina'ko tangsala tina' é!

Ha, haha, haé.
Your Worship's fine hairs could well
fall on me,
the golden sheath at your lower end
could leap at me.
But.
I want to fell you properly,

I want to strike you a true blow.

Ha, haha, haé!
Inang alukna nene'ku é!

La kurundunan tana' é!

Untanan batu to dolo, sitete
batu katonan.

Ha, haha, haé!
The adat of my ancestors
forever
will I follow as an established
institution,
fitting like a stone of the forefathers ring rows like those of
boundary stones.

Ha, haha, haé!
Da'mu ma'baine kura' é!
Da'mu ma'dodo' tiamballungko é!

Ke ma'baine kura'ko é!

Ke ma'dodo' tiamballungko é!

Toppo'ko dao kalandona
buntu é!
Daoko layukna batara é!
Anna tunuko to manglaa
tedong é!
Anna sumpunko to mangkambi'
karambau é!

Ha, haha, haé!
Don't behave like a lustful woman,
don't carry on like a swaying
woman.
When you behave like a lustful
woman,
when you carry on like a swaying
woman,
Then you will reach the top of a
high mountain,
in the zenith of the firmament,
that you will be set on fire by the
buffalo herders,
you will be burned by the
buffalo herders.

Ha, haha, haé!
Talingannamo pararrak é!

Matannamo to bulaan é!

Ha, haha, haé!
His ears are then ... (of the de-
ceased?)[17]
His eyes are then like gold (?)[18]

Ha, haha, haé!
Dao tangngana langi' é!
Dao esungan ma'gulung-gulung-
anna batara é!

Ha, haha, haé!
In the zenith of the firmament,
atop the seat of the most
exalted of the firmament.

Ha, haha, haé!
Anna su'pikko nene' to doloku é!
Untananko dio mata kairinna é!

Ha, haha, haé!
Then my ancestors defile you
and place you on their left side.

Ha, haha, haé!
Iamoto anna tarekko rampanan
kapa' sipele-pele é!

Ha, haha, haé!
In this way we decide on a marriage
for you, one which stupefies the
parties on both sides.

Ha, haha, haé!
Alukna nene'ku é!

Tonna garaga aluk sipiak tallang
lan di Sura' é!

Tonna tampa sangka' sisese siar-
rusan é!

Lan tiparitikna uai é!

Ha, haha, haé!
That is the adat decree of my
ancestors,
when they established the adat
rules in Sura' which are to each
other as the two halfs of a split
bamboo[19],
when they created the regulations
for rituals which are of two differ-
ent kinds in the high order of
dignity,
at the place where one let the water
flow away.

Ha, haha, haé!
Nasembangan ia bulo makamban
batang di kalena é!
Nagaragan ia tau-tau lampa
tondon to batangna é!

Ha, haha, haé!
They cut down the stems of the bulo
in front of them,
they fabricated the bamboo images
for their persons.

Ha, haha, haé!
Anna palolongi pole matallo
matampu' é!
Anna patiamboran pinamasakki
ulunna pollo'na uai é!

Ha, haha, haé!
And spreading these East and West,

they stretched them out like beads
considered valuable, extending to
the source and to the outlet of the
rivers.

Ha, haha, haé!
Da'mu ma'baine kura' é!
Da'mu ma'dodo' tiamballung é!
La kusembangko tangsala sembang é!
La kutina'ko tangsala tina' é!

[What follows here is largely a repe-
tition of the preceding. As final
verse, the following then appears:]

Ha, haha, haé!
Iake ma'baine kura'ko é!
Ke ma'dodo' tiamballungko é!
Toppo'ko dao kalandona buntu é!
Daoko layukna tanete é!
Natunuko to manglaa tedong é!
Nasumpunko to mangkambi'
karambau é!
Sangadinna ia kada sala é!
Maimokomi é!
Sembangmi é!

May words out of place remain
excluded.
Cut them, é!

After he had concluded his litany, the leader felled a bamboo with a single blow (the act which gives the rite its name, see above and Woordenboek: v. sembang). In so doing he faced North.[20] Still additional bamboos were then cut. Afterwards a chicken is sacrificed, a sella'. Rice is cooked, too, as an offering to the gods (for the arrangement of the functionaries and the artefacts during the massembang bulo, see Fig. 49).

Fig. 49. The massembang bulo; arrangement of celebrants and articles:
a the bamboo which is felled
b the to ma'randing, face to the North, sword in hand
c karerang
d langngan, aligned North-South

People went searching for a dog because as part of the rite blood should be made to flow from a dog's ear (presumably the vestige of a former sacrifice). Voices called for the trusty pet of the school teacher from a nearby village, but the animal could not be found. Meanwhile the sacrificed sella' was roasted over a fire and its flesh prepared piong-style. The bamboo used for the piong were severed in dipatuo-fashion; should they be cut dipamate instead, they may not be filled with rice (for explanation, see Fig. 50). The piong were intended for the deata (exactly which gods was not specified). Later they were leaned against a langngan set up running North-South so that, remarkably, their openings faced West, a position which is not customary with such offerings to the gods. The meat of the chicken was placed in a sacrificial basket (karerang). At the sport where the bamboo was ceremonially felled as described above, one of the to ma'randing made an offering. The altar used was a tadoran. Subsequently, the to ma'randing prepared the tuang-tuang on the compound of the tongkonan in which the puang's bodily remains lay in state.[21] The mounting of the bamboo chain proceeded as follows: first the tuang-tuang was brought to the tongkonan in which the deceased puang lay in the death roll; there it was knotted to the door giving entrance to the Northeastern part of the house; next a number of bamboos were stuck in the ground in order to hold up the chain as it was strung out. One heard women wailing in the tongkonan while the tuang-tuang was being hung up. That morning, at about ten, the ma'kande had been enacted, the feeding of the dead.

After the tuang-tuang was in place, the to ma'randing entered the compound of tongkonan Buntu Kalando at about eleven to perform a war

Fig. 50. Alternate ways to cut bamboo.

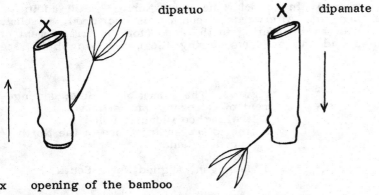

dipatuo   dipamate

x   opening of the bamboo

——→ direction in which the bamboo grows

With a bamboo which is cut dipamate, the direction of growth is
"wrong" or "opposite", i.e. towards the ground. This is perhaps an
allusion to the association which exists between death (mate) and death
rituals with "below", i.e. the underworld.

dance. Before they began, they uttered a war cry. The to ma'randing
who had ritually felled the bamboo for the tuang-tuang danced a war
dance, brandishing his sword while he sang of the heroic exploits of
the dead puang in poetic language.

Tuesday, December 5, 1972
This is the day designated for the ma'popengkalao alang, the lowering
of the corpse to the ricebarn, a custom that is part of all death rituals
of a high order in Tana Toraja. No one was in a hurry. After some
hours, during which those present dined on rice and morsels of pork
and a small group of men danced and sang badong under the overhang-
ing roof surrounding the tulak somba, a bonga ulu, a black buffalo
with a white head, was sacrificed. He was killed by a blow from a
sword. In the past the animal was speared to death; at present a spear
is merely laid across his back before he is slaughtered. The buffalo's
head went to (former) kaunan. Meanwhile a group of men had gathered
inside the tongkonan which was decorated out front with a red cloth
studded with coins; the men assembled in the room where until now the
dead had been on view. They lifted the bodily remains and started
jigging. Next, first of all a long red cloth to which old coins were fixed
was carried outside; a kain Rongkong was sewn to this cloth. The
fabric was attached to the death roll itself. Jigging and singing[22] the
men removed the corpse from the house. The dead puang was not
conveyed out the projecting part of the front facade, as Van der Veen
reports (Van der Veen 1965:19), but left the house through a door in
the East wall. This departure contrasts to what happens with dead com-
moners who leave the house from the West side. Already during his
lifetime a puang is associated with the deata, the gods situated in the
East of the cosmic order.

The bodily remains were then laid on the floor of the ricebarn opposite the tongkonan. At once female relatives of the deceased, and a grandson, began to wail beside the death roll, the women burying their faces in their arms which leaned on the death roll. Three kandaure and two gold krisses were placed on the shroud. One of the krisses had the customary handle in the shape of a doll; the handle was inlaid with diamonds. I was told that the krisses (at least the blade and handle) came from Balambangan in east Java. The names of the krisses were Gayang Tangmangka, The Unfinished Kris, and Gayang Tua, The Old Kris. According to tradition they had once belonged to the Torajas' seminal ancestor, Lakipadada. Before the krisses were put back in storage, muffled in a sack of grey cotton, they were held to the lips of certain women whose special task it was to "kiss" them. The krisses, indeed, do not lie on the death roll the whole day long. It was said that one of the krisses would be given to the deceased to take with him. It remained vague, however, whether the kris would be laid in the tomb temporarily, or permanently. I doubt it would be disposed of in this way for good.

The tau-tau which depicted Puang Lasok Rinding was set up in front of the ricebarn. Until now it stood before the tulak somba of tongkonan Buntu Kalando. The two craftsmen who were entrusted with carving motifs into the wooden sarigan had by this time completed their assignment. The master carver was the talented artist Pong Salapu who also made the tau-tau. The red cloth covering the death roll now had figures fashioned from goldleaf pasted to it. This work takes time. It doesn't have to be completed the same day, as long as everything is finished when the corpse is to be carried to the pantunuan. Nobele (1926:48) reports that for pasting a glue is used that comes from buffalo skin and the sap of the duayan-tree (a variety which I cannot further identify); the ingredients are boiled together. Among the goldleaf motifs is the barre allo (the sun burst) which is fastened to both extremities of the death roll. Application of the goldleaf is considered a separate rite, one for which a buffalo is sacrificed. In the evening, the ma'badong took place close to tongkonan Buntu Kalando (including the ma'badong to dolo[23] and the wilder dance described as ondo).

Wednesday, December 6, 1972
The next morning, the to ma'kayo brought food for the deceased (ma'-kande), his daily chore. The work done on the sarigan was finished. Today the unnolong was held, a ceremony which entails that a group of family members arrives with gifts, customarily rice. The close family members of the dead puang welcome them with pieces of pork after the arrivals have taken seats on the floor of one of the ricebarns. In addition to a pig, a buffalo is slaughtered. The Gayang Tua was strapped to the tau-tau during the morning as a special decoration.

Throughout the two days and nights that the bodily remains were displayed beneath the ricebarn, every morning some food was put down on a banana leaf in front of the wooden effigy. This was Pong Salapu's responsibility, the creator of the image. The effigy's clothing, moreover, became steadily fancier.

Also today, above and beyond the animals cited above, two black buffaloes (pudu') were killed. One served as an offering for the sambu' to balu ("the garment of the widow or widower"; the meaning of the expression is less than clear), the other for the simbuang batu, the monolith erected at great death rituals.

During the afternoon I seized my chance to take a walk to Suaya, the place where the puang and their family members are buried. The terrain consisted of a sheer cliff of rock in the face of which a number of burial chambers were situated. At various places mortuary effigies stood leaning against a balcony carved out of the rock. These portrayed dead puang. They were uncannily alive, with their outstretched hands and their staring eyes which were blind and yet all-seeing. The scene was an impressive burial site for a ruling class. Ordinary mortals were not consigned to these catacombs though, in the past, an exception was made for dead servants. They had, indeed, to serve their masters in the hereafter.

Thursday, December 7, 1972
The scene was full of bustle from early morning on, for today the ma'songlo' would take place, the carrying of the corpse in ceremonial procession from feast terrain I to II. Many guests had already assembled. The massailo' was danced, partly to entertain the crowd. Big bamboos (of the pattung-variety) had been collected to be used as supports for the bier and for the sedan chairs. Jigging and jogging, men placed the corpse in the sarigan.[24] The belo tedong had already been put together.

The final formation of the procession reflected the busy, festive ambiance intrinsic to great celebrations in Tana Toraja. The sequence of the escort follows below:
1. a file of buffaloes preceded the procession, with the tandi rapasan in front, a red maa'-cloth across its back;
2. the to ma'randing with the tuang-tuang;
3. the belo tedong;
4. a number of banners carried in the parade which had to be set up on feast terrain II (other flags had already been hung out there);
5. the tau-tau in its bedecked bullean (sedan chair);
6. the sarigan, in truth the largest object in the parade, carried on the shoulders of an estimated 40 men. Family members followed under a red cloth which was attached to the bier (see also the description of the ritual on December 30, 1972);
7. the sedan chair of the to balu, a sober black tent whose sole ornament consisted of a kandaure fixed to the top;
8. yet more sober, the tent-like sedan chair of the to ma'parandan;
9. the sedan chair of the next functionary, the to ma'peulli', was also without decoration.
(The sequence of the procession differs from that in Kesu', cf. Chapter XI.1-3.)

There were certain rules governing who should carry the various objects. The belo tedong was transported by people from the villages of Sarapung, Tongko, and Tu Manete. The tau-tau was conveyed by inhabitants of the settlements at Suaya, Katangka, Kaero and Raru. The sarigan was committed to men from Guali Bassi. The bearers of the to balu were from the same place, those of the to ma'parandan from the village of Turunan (for these areas, see Vol.I:84-9). The to ma'randing, the fine buffaloes, the impressive sarigan, the banners, the unfurled penants and the gold krisses fixed to the sarigan and the sedan chair of the tau-tau, bright metal glittering in the sun, made it a festal procession indeed. The dominance of red especially made the scene lively: the red of the parasols carried along and the long red cloth under which family members walked behind the deceased. The dense crowd that brought up the rear added to the vividness of the occasion.

The sarigan and the sedan chairs got jolted about continually. How this shaking of the sedan chairs differs from the smooth riding of the tumbang in their bullean; it must have been an ordeal for the to balu and the other ladies. At a jog trot the parade descended from Nuntu Kalando to the pantunuan at Lobe. The pace was brisk, the sight of gathering clouds perhaps lending added speed. First the procession passed along the sawahs to the North of Buntu Kalando and Lobe. One vast sawah was circled three times, clockwise. The answer to my enquiry whether this was a special rice field was negative. Next the parade struck out for feast terrain II where, upon arrival, three circuits were completed around the lakkean, once more in a clockwise direction. Originally the transit from feast terrain I to II was planned to last much longer, but the heavens had turned pitch black, a compelling reason to cut things short. The corpse had no sooner been placed in the lakkean then a cloudburst began. The to ma'randing found nonetheless just enough time to perform their war dance. And the to balu and the to ma'parandan, wrapped in black, were just in time to take up their positions in the lakkean (where they sat next to the death roll) while they were still dry.

This lakkean (tower for the corpse) missing during the first part at the ritual, was a recently completed structure shaped like a Toraja house. It had two floors and was decorated with red cloths which, together with kandaure and other ornaments, formed, as it were, the walls of the separate storeys. The tau-tau was stowed on the lower floor.

The arena for cock fights had already been built during the first part of the feast, in the middle of the terrain. Feast terrain II was hemmed in by the many guest accommodations (lantang) which, for the most part, had been put up in time for the first phase of the ritual. In part these had been restored and redecorated. Some new lodges had been added, including a vast hall for the reception of guests. Many of those who had been invited had already occupied their lantang.

Once the rain had blown over, the tuang-tuang was mounted. First it was attached to the Western side of the lakkean and stretched from there to the second simbuang batu in the first row of menhirs (why the choice devolved on the second stone could not be explained). Already very early in the morning the tombi had been hung out by female relatives of the dead puang. The tombi consisted of sarita and pio uki'. The Bate Manurun, so prominent during the first part of the death feast, failed to make an appearance during the second.

In the name of members of the family, four buffaloes were killed during the afternoon. In the course of this part of the feast, family members slaughtered a total of 22 buffaloes, including precious specimens. Seven were provided by Puang Sombolinggi' and his family. It should be observed that in puang-states there is no point in trying to outdo others by contributing more buffaloes in order to lay claim to a larger share of the inheritance. The sawahs of a puang who dies are not divided up in keeping with the number of buffaloes which various children slaughter at their father's death feast. In principle each child receives an equal share; the puang's successor inherits somewhat more, for many sawahs belong to tongkonan Kaero, the official residence of the puang. This at any rate was the rule in the past. Now that no new puang is appointed, I have no idea what happens with these sawahs. The rice fields which are not part and parcel of the tongkonan layuk, however, are shared evenly among the puang's children.

Once the buffaloes had been slaughtered, the to minaa divided their flesh on the bala'kaan.

During the afternoon of December 7, buffalo fights (silaga tedong) took place as well (Meyer 1972:801 (photo)). The animals didn't display much enthusiasm. Insiders attributed their lack of animo to the fact that they weren't pitted against each other on a sawah, but rather on dry land. In the evening, on feast terrain II, the ma'badong was celebrated.

The ma'parando deserves to be mentioned as a special rite which took place at night. Metuak is an alternate name. The deceased's grandchildren were carried around the lakkean, clockwise, seated on the shoulders of men. The small procession was torch-lit. Each grandchild held a torch in his or her hand. Should it burn long, then a long and prosperous life was in store. In addition each grandchild had a small basket (barasang) containing some food (a piong of pork, maize and millet) for the dead grandfather. Nobele (1926:51) explains the rite as a way of asking the dead puang's blessing. (One grandson did not participate, nor did he offer any explanation for his refusal.) The idea that a long-burning torch foretells a fortunate future is common to other Toraja rituals as well.

Friday, December 8, 1972
New groups of guests arrived. The formation of each party as it entered was the customary one: handsome buffaloes led the way onto the feast terrain; other gifts, including pigs and palm wine, followed. Each group also brought along the food which its members would eat, rice included. They brought firewood with them as well. Servants, family members, bearers ... all advanced in a line.[25] One after another the groups swarmed into Lobe. Each received a map. Gifts were duly entered in a record book. Then the guests were welcomed in the vast reception hall (see Fig. 48). Afterwards they were escorted to their own lantang.

In the afternoon the most important guests turned up, those from Ma'kale and Mengkendek, the other two puang-regions. The women from Mengkendek, in keeping with their local custom, wore a folded black cloth on their heads instead of a bamboo hat. Each cortege was preceded by fine buffaloes. The high point of the day was the arrival of a delegation from the Datu of Luwu' (Sangalla' and Luwu' have a special relation, see Vol.I:91).

The welcome of all groups featured the dances which have already been described. That morning, in vain, with the help of automative power, an attempt had been made to stand the menhir upright on the pantunuan. The many men who rushed to assist were unable to manoeuvre the vast stone onto its end.

A buffalo had already been slaughtered early in the day. Its carcass provided food for the guests.

Among the menhirs several buffaloes were tethered in the arrangement

customary to death rituals of a high order. Below I list first the buffaloes and then the trees which stood erected next to the monoliths:
- a bonga (dappled buffalo) stood bound to the simbuang kalosi, the
pinang-tree which was tied to a menhir with a strip of bark;
- a pudu' was tethered to a bamboo-betung;
- a sambao to a second bamboo-betung;
- a todi to an ampiri (pseudo sugar palm);
- a balian (an ox) to a bamboo-betung;
- a pudu' to seko (a special buffalo from Rongkong with short, broad
horns) to another bamboo-betung.[26]
All in all five buffaloes were slaughtered at first on the pantunuan,
followed later by four more. Many pigs were killed as well. These were
roasted late at night, giving off a tantalizing odour. After dark a con-
vivial, party-like feeling prevailed. High spirits continued the next day
as well, when cock fights took place.

Afterwards (upon completion of the massonglo') a rest period was observed which lasted some three weeks.

Thursday, December 28, 1972
About two in the afternoon the tau-tau were fetched from the family
grave of the puang at Suaya in order to be dressed in new clothes. All
in all there were six effigies portraying dead puang which were removed from the grave where only these princes may be buried. First of
all, the tau-tau of the father of Puang Lasok Rinding was brought down
from the cliff. He was carried on a man's back, just as subsequently
the other effigies would be. The rock grave towers some 30 to 40
metres above the ground, but this was no deterent to the agile Toraja
who scaled a colossal bamboo ladder to carry out their task - and
climbed back down again! On december 30 the same ladder would be
used to carry the dead puang aloft where, through a rectangular
opening gouged out of the cliff, he would be placed in the actual burial
chamber.

The mortuary effigies were carried to a place close by the grave
where their apparel was spruced up. Some tau-tau had old kain sarita
wound as turbans around their heads. A few effigies were carried
higher up the cliff and stood in a rectangular hollow hewn from the
face of the rock. There were other such niches, too, similarly fashioned
with a balustrade. A total of 20 tau-tau could thus be accommodated. A
wooden horse lay on the ground, the mount of one of the mortuary
effigies.[27] Close to this horse was a stone surrounded by a bamboo
fence. No one might touch this stone or try to sit on it; to do so was
to court certain death.

During my absence from Buntu Kalando and Lobe, the pantunuan had
hardly changed. Only the bala'kaan was gone. The tuang-tuang still
hung in the same place. The tau-tau still remained set up on the lower
floor of the lakkean, resting under a vast parasol with a fringe of
beads. The tandi rapasan stood tied under the lakkean throughout the
morning; later in the day he stood next to one of the simbuang.

Friday, December 29, 1972
The tau-tau at Suaya had acquired some new clothes. Preparations were
in full swing for carrying the deceased to the grave (meaa). Measures
were being taken to receive Sultan Hamengku Buwono, who would be
attending the rite, in style. Dancers were practising in earnest for the

ma'katia and ma'badong.

Saturday, December 30, 1972
The ma'badong had lasted until the early morning hours. Now a vast
triumphal arch had been constructed, decorated with a maa'-cloth and
swords. The horns of the tandi rapasan were draped with a red cloth
to which goldleaf figures were fastened. A saleko with enormous horns
was similarly decorated. From my vantage high in the guest house of
the family Sombolinggi' (Puang W.P. Sombolinggi' was one of the dead
puang's sons), I had a good view of the dressing of the buffaloes.
    The lakkean was also provided with a red cloth. Over this a
maa'-cloth was draped. A red carpet was unrolled leading to the main
guest house which was further decorated with strips of red and white
cloth.
    By ten, some twenty buffaloes stood on the pantunuan. Two groups
of badong-dancers and a group of female massailo'-dancers were ready
to perform. Their presence could be attributed to the anticipated visit
of Sultan Hamengku Buwono (who, unfortunately, because of illness,
was prevented from coming, to the deep disappointment of the organizers of the feast). The youths who waited to welcome eminent guests
were dressed with special distinction. Two men in black each held a
kandaure in one hand fastened to a staff. Four young girls in black
blouses wore kandaure over their backs. On their left hip, a gold kriss
was inserted in their waistband. Several wore a checkered Buginese
sarong. The young people who helped arrivals to refresh themselves
were just as graciously and fashionably dressed. The girls wore a red
headband with goldleaf figures, a belt which encircled a kris, and a
kandaure on the back. They carried red or blue braided baskets with a
cover. They were followed by a row of young men in black sarong and
white shirts. The girl who stood in front carried a sirih-set the most
important element of which was a nut from the Seychelles (an heirloom,
brought to Tana Toraja in the distant past by the famous ancestor
Lakipadada (see Vol.I:149 and 300, note 24).
    The tau-tau still stood displayed on the bottom floor of the lakkean
with its face to the North. On the level above lay the death roll. The
to balu and the to ma'parandan kept faithful watch over the dead, as
they already had for so long, accompanied by several other women.
They wore black and had knotted their sarongs under their arms. The
lakkean was decorated with yet more maa'-cloths. Under the pointed
roof of this lakkean, a maa'-cloth had been fixed to the façade, and
above it, a kandaure hung.
    The tandi rapasan was slaughtered after a spear was placed across its
hindquarters. A blow with a cleaver laid him low, after the performance
of the massailo'- and ma'badong-dancers.
    After several buffaloes had butted heads and one cock fight had
reached its climax, a to minaa recited a litany with the help of a loudspeaker (the text was not recorded). In this prayer he commemorated
the descent of the puang's ancestors from heaven. Now and then the
dancing of two to ma'randing, one to the North, one to the South of
the death roll, interrupted the recitation.
    Afterwards the death roll was lifted and with much singing and
jigging taken out of the lakkean, down the ladder to be laid in the
sarigan. The tau-tau, too, was by this time in its sedan chair. Family
members took their places under the long red cloth attached to the

sarigan. The procession advanced ahead of the sarigan so that the dead seemed, as it were, to be pulled forward.[28] The tau-tau led the way, surrounded, like the sarigan, by a mass of people. The to balu stayed behind and did not join the procession.

Upon arrival at the rock grave, the death roll was removed from the sarigan. Women, older family members, some five in all, with the to ma'parandan as one of their number, wept beside the dead for a final time. Granddaughters in black with a kandaure on their backs and red ribbons decorated with gold in their hair held handkerchiefs in front of their eyes. One was crying for real. A red and a white ribbon were wound around the roll. Two men lifted up the roll, assisted by four men from underneath. And thus they ascended the 40 m high ladder while the cry rang out: "Hoo jo milelle". Within a quarter of an hour, they had reached the rock chamber to which the dead would be consigned. Here Puang Lasok Rinding was carried inside. Some time later his tau-tau was placed lower down the face of the cliff together with other mortuary effigies portraying generations of dead puang.

Subsequently two more buffaloes were slaughtered on the rante. Burial in the grave was concluded with a number of ceremonies, including, for example, the ma'bolong that took place three days after the puang was installed in the funeral chamber.

Tandilangi' (1968-69) reports the ma'pakatua as a closing rite, a repetition of the preceding rite. He also mentions the ma'poli', previously described during the account of the first part of the puang's death ritual, and the parundun bombo, during which a pig is killed and food is offered to the soul of the deceased. The rites which Tandilangi' goes on to name, the malolo tangnga and the malolo tarru' are virtually identical to the kumande-rites in Kesu'. Those in mourning are gradually permitted to eat rice again. The ma'bai puyu' corresponds to the membase in Kesu'.

Salombe' (1972:37) mentions two rites: massapa'i, limiting closing the rites, and ma'pakande masero, a cleansing rite (cf. the untoe sero in Kesu', Chapter XI.1.3.). After harvest the ma'gandang (beating the drum) is celebrated. It is a joyful festival, because the puang's soul dwells in heaven (looking after the rice). Three pigs are sacrified. Ma'nene' follows after some time, but always after harvest (see Chapter X.5.).

2.3. Commentary

Celebrants, I pointed out, do not always abide by the sequence of events for a death ritual as prescribed by adat. The rites are, indeed, complicated and time consuming; when convenient, people may skip a rite or give more prominence to a ceremony which seems important. The cock fights are a case in point. The government may furthermore grant permission for cock fights at a time different from the proper ritual time.

Changing times have also affected other aspects of the death ritual. A limit is now set by the government to the number of buffaloes that may be killed (a limit which the organizers of a feast may do their utmost to subvert). A further complication is that not everyone who should attend the death ritual of a relative is free to take leave from his work to be there, especially not when the date set for the observance is frequently subject to postponement. If one is a Christian, moreover, appearing at the "heathen" death ritual of a friend or relative, what can you permit yourself, and what not? There are rules for such a situation but they do not cover everything, participation in the badong, for instance. A Christian may, for piety's sake, attend a burial enacted according to the aluk to dolo, but this will require a measure of personal initiative and soul-searching, perhaps even some compromising with his conscience.

Another factor related to new outside influences is the steadily rising expense of death feasts. Many older informants assured me that during the previous century funerals were comparatively inexpensive. Yet apparently the elaboration of these rituals began already during the last century, when, after 1870, the cultivation of coffee in Tana Toraja began to yield profits. The few things to be bought with money were either fancy goods (Indian textiles, batiks, kain sarita, Chinese pottery, gold and silver coins) or land. For the rest the rich could do little with their earnings except double their capital and spend extravangantly of feasts. By holding rituals they would exhaust their capital, investment was limited to the purchase of valuables or sawahs. Good coffee years used to be followed by good ritual years. The same still holds true. Moreover, nowadays, the expense of feasts is met in part by contributions which arrive from family members who work outside Tana Toraja.

Innovations shortly after World War II made traditional feasts more costly: facilities, for example, for electric lighting. Van Lijf estimates that the funeral of adat chief Rombelayuk in 1949 cost several hundred thousand guilders (Van Lijf 1951-52:372). Feasts after 1950 were hardly less splendid although an estimate of their cost is difficult because of the prevailing principle of reciprocity at work. That novelties from the outside world - glaring lights, amplifiers, loudspeakers - disturb the traditional sphere of the rituals is arguable. The Toraja themselves do not find the encroachment of technology disturbing. Even while they go to great lengths to dress themselves as authentically as possible in traditional style, they don't remove their wristwatches.

To what extent do the Toraja approve and support feasts that consume so many resources? In 1950 the younger generation and even several persons of eminence in the society did not hesitate to say that money could be better spent on other things. Yet by the 1970's the same people appeared more often than not to be wholly committed to death rituals on a grand scale. And as far as the deceased's inheritance is concerned: no one raised in such a society, with rare exceptions, enters the hereafter buried like a poor man. In addition we should realize that Toraja death rituals have become a vital tourist attraction. It is my impression that the government encourages them as such, securing in the process more of a voice in determining how rituals are to be carried out. A feast may be delayed, for example, if some high official or a foreign guest can not arrive on time - and all the to minaas' protests will be in vain. It is no longer conceivable that death rituals take place without tourists. They are often integrated into the proceedings. They walk in the procession of guests, in single file, leading a buffalo with them as their contribution (German tourist agency, late 1970s).

The danger is real that Toraja death rituals will increasingly turn into events for tourists, losing, as time passes, their own, intrinsic character.

View of death house from outside. On the scaffold set up in front of the tongkonan within which the dead puang lies in state, regalia are displayed, including the Bate Manurun. A portrait of the dead prince is fastened to an old maa'-cloth. Two kandaure hang from the scaffold as well. Behind the decorations can be glimpsed the drum and gong which are used during the ritual. To the right in the photo is a man with a loudspeaker who announces the rites as they are about to happen. See also pp. 283-285. (Photo: Hetty Nooy-Palm, 1970.)

Detail of a ricebarn. Above the buffalo-head motif, part of the tuang-tuang can be seen, small pieces of bamboo-bulo. See also p. 292.
(Photo: W.J.A. Willems, 1938; Oudheidkundige Dienst van Nederlandsch-Indië.)

Detail of a mounted tuang-tuang. A section of the giant bamboo chain strung up during the second part of the funeral of Puang Lasok Rinding of Sangalla'. See also p. 292. (Photo: Hetty Nooy-Palm, 1972.)

Tau-tau portraying Puang Lasok Rinding of Sangalla'. The tau-tau stands on the lowest floor of the ricebarn opposite tongkonan Buntu Kalando. The tau-tau is dressed in traditional Toraja clothing; a tali bate (batiked headcloth) and a gold kris which belongs to the regalia of the puang-dynasty, complete the effigy's costume. In its left hand the tau-tau holds a walking stick. Behind the tau-tau lies the death roll. To the effigy's left hangs the red cloth decorated with coins which is one of the pusaka (heirlooms) of the princely family. See also p. 297. (Photo: Hetty Nooy-Palm, 1972.)

Division of meat; first part of the death ritual for Puang Lasok Rinding
of Sangalla', 1970. The to minaa about to toss down the hindquarter of
a buffalo for the tananan basse. See also p. 286.
(Photo: Hetty Nooy-Palm, 1970.)

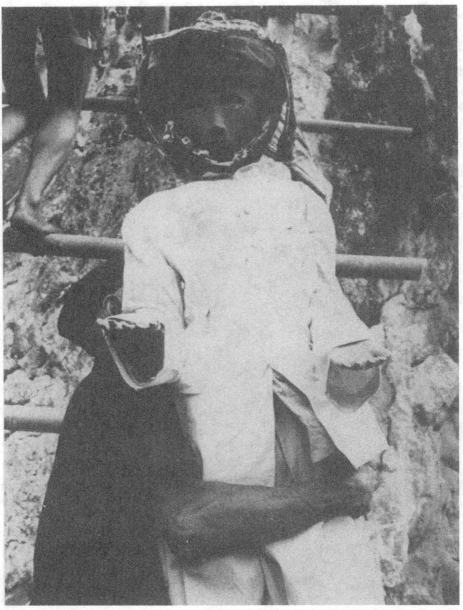

A tau-tau. This mortuary effigy, the image of one of the members of
the puang-lineage, is being carried back up to its cliff-side niche after
a change of clothing. A sacral sarita-cloth has been wound around the
tau-tau's head. See also p. 301.
(Photo: Hetty Nooy-Palm, 1972.)

Reinstallation of the tau-tau. The effigy is returned to the rock tomb after being reclothed. See also p. 301.
(Photo: Hetty Nooy-Palm, 1972.)

Chapter XIII

HEADHUNTING (MANGAUNG)

"In old times he a hero was,
In former times a fearless man.
A coconut took as he passed,
Bore cord-strung pangi on his way.
He cleft that was no coconut,
He split that was no pangi-fruit."

(The Chant:77)

1. Introduction

Once the Dutch actually established their authority in Tana Toraja early this century, headhunting was forbidden. Literature seldom mentions the practice. Our leading sources are A.C. Kruyt 1923-24:259-74, Kennedy 1953:173-4 and Wilcox 1949:326-31. Presumably headhunting never claimed many victims, in contrast, for example, to the scale of such killing known among the Iban on Borneo. This in no way diminishes the importance, however, which people attached to headhunting in certain areas of Tana Toraja. Headhunting, to be sure, was not universal throughout the region.

2. Areas where headhunting was customary

In the puang-territories, Sangalla', Ma'kale and Mengkendek, headhunting did not occur, with one exception. In Ma'kale - just as in Upper Binuang - headhunting would be undertaken to avenge the death of a fellow villager, friend or family member, fallen in battle. (Other information suggests headhunting was current at one time throughout the puang-states.) In Mamasa (an area inhabited by the Mamasa-Toraja, who are closely related to the Sa'dan), a headhunting expedition took place if many children were dying. Elsewhere, in the districts of Kesu', Balusu, Baruppu', Pangala' and in Tondok Litak (district Rantepao), headhunting typically was organized after the death of a prominent man. The deceased then had to belong to a certain tongkonan, e.g. tongkonan Banua Sura' in the village of Ba'tan, or tongkonan To Sullukan in Tonga or the tongkonan to which the great adat-chief Pong Maramba' belonged (about this latter tongkonan I have no information). When a leading figure died in Kesu', the deceased's family would purchase a slave in Lemo, a district of the former kingdom of Luwu', inhabited by Toraja. This slave was subsequently beheaded. Or perhaps a kaunan was ordered to cut off the head of someone in Pantilang, a region in Luwu' also populated by Toraja.

Sarungallo's interpretation of past practice disagrees with the above account. When in Kesu' somebody eminent died, a number of men from the same village went on a hunt; they searched for a victim who was out walking alone, or otherwise was by himself. One didn't take heads close to home, but in some distant place, preferably in Karunanga, for this region did not participate in the seventeenth century resistance against Bone. The headhunting expedition in Karunanga was thus also intended to be punitive.

3. Reasons why a headhunt would be undertaken

Preparations for a headhunt were called for whenever:
a. someone of high rank died;
b. someone had been killed in one's own territory;
c. certain epidemics raged.
As an example, let us consider the death of an adat chief as supplying the motivation for conducting a headhunt.

The intention behind the hunt was to provide the deceased, a man of importance during his life, with a servant to look after his buffaloes in the land of the souls. A man's own slave was never put to death for this purpose. A.C. Kruyt provides the following information (1923-24: 259-74): the hunters who go out to procure a victim after the death of a prominent person, do not belong to any specific family. In this regard, however, Kesu' was exceptional where headhunters had to be descendants of tongkonan To Kamiri in the village of Ba'tan. These men were called to ussobo'i pangala', "those who first enter the woods". If revenge was the purpose of the headhunt, the slain whose death required retalliation was first carried home. There friends and relatives danced about the house (menanna) dressed in old clothes. Women, too, took part in the ritual. Men wore their hair loose, like women, while women imitated the hairstyle of men. No explanation is offered for this

Fig. 51. Headhunter's jacket.
Simple version of a babu' executed in single pair twining technique; made presumably from rami-fibres (rami = Bochmeria nivea Gand). The "war shirt" consists of two layers; the inner layer has a natural colour; the outer layer is also largely natural, but is decorated with black and brown stripes. This jacket comes from the vicinity of Ma'kale, Tana Toraja. It is at present part of the collection of the Museum Pusat in Jakarta (Inventory no. 16730). (Drawing by Subokastowo.)

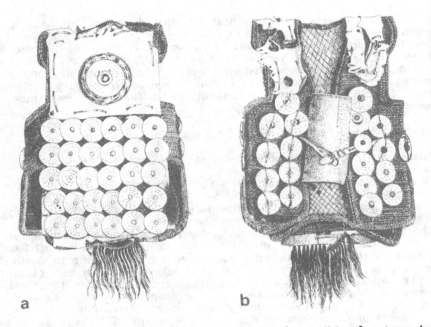

a   b

Fig. 52. Headhunter's jacket. Back (a) and front (b) of a to ma'randing's (war dancer's) "armour" (babu'). The jacket is made in the same way as the garment in Fig. 51. It is reinforced with pieces of leather and discs made out of shell; the placement of these materials produces a decorative effect. An ornament of human hair is attached to the lower edge of the jacket. The garment comes from Ma'kale and is at present part of the collection of the Museum Pusat in Jakarta (inventory no. 16709). (Drawing by Subokastowo.)

reversal (see Nooy-Palm 1980:172-3). Before the expedition departed, the men bound their hair up again. They sang a song which expressed the hope that the soul of the deceased might select a victim of higher rank than theirs (no text of the song is reproduced).

Kruyt's report indicates that it were the young men who went on headhunting expeditions. The to minaa and the to parengnge' spoke from the bala'kaan. The most important man was the last to address the group: this explains why he was known as to lolok kada, "he who has the last word". After his speech, a buffalo was killed. This was called the siilang bua (Kruyt 1923-24:264). (This title is the same as that of the buffalo slaughtered during the ma'batang rite of the death ritual.) Should the buffalo that was sacrificed fall with its feet in the air when the last blow was delivered, then it was believed that the fallen man would soon be avenged. Before the headhunting party left, a chicken was killed and its intestines studied (by the to minaa?) to see whether the moment was favourable for the undertaking. As in other places in old-time Indonesia (Kalimantan) attention was also paid to the cry, the flight and the behaviour of certain birds. Important was whether a bird came from right or left, regardless of the direction one was moving in

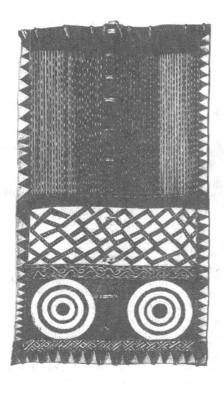

Fig. 53. Shield (balulang), part of the battle dress of a to ma'randing. These shields may only be made from the skin of buffaloes slaughtered during a death feast. The shield is decorated with concentric circles, zigzag-motifs, a series of triangles, a decoration consisting of stripes, a tendril motif and patterns deriving from plaitwork (such shields are also frequently decorated with a buffalo horn figure known as pa'tanduk rape). The decoration is produced by scraping off some of the surface of the hide. At times the motifs are coloured in with black and white paints.
The shield has more uses than warfare. It does not serve exclusively in rituals of the West (death rituals). It also provides the surface on which the to parengnge' brings an offering (a pig's head) before rice is sown (see Van der Veen 1924b:372).
This shield is part of the collection of the Museum Pusat in Jakarta (inventory no. 16739).
(Drawing by Subokastowo.)

oneself. Such augury was the task of the to minaa. The headhunters' wives were subject to all kinds of taboos (A.C. Kruyt 1923-24:269).
  Most men dressed themselves specially for headhunting expeditions. The typical outfit can be observed today in the costumes of the ma'-randing-dancers (see Figs. 51-55). It would seem this was ritual apparel only, however, for it strikes me as highly unlikely that the warriors would pass stealthily through the forest in such ornate finery. The ma'randing-dancers take part in the funeral rites at the burial of an important man. Their costume consists of a battle jacket or protective vest (babu') made of twined rope (karidi'). Usually there are kara (discs of shell, round, flat and white, with a hole in the middle) attached to the jacket for decoration. Similar kara are fastened, too, to the war cap of the to ma'randing; and a kara-motif is carved into the warriors' buffalo hide shields. The war cap is actually a hat made out of braided rattan (salulung), sometimes covered with the skin of a monkey, deer or couscous. Brass horns are affixed to the cap, imitation buffalo horns, known as tanduk gallang (brass horns). A headhunter's armament consisted of an ordinary cleaver (la'bo') and a lance (doke), possibly decorated with human or goat hair (doke pando). A shield of buffalo hide (balulang) was also part of his equipment. This shield may only be cut from the hide of a buffalo sacrificed during a death feast, not from one which has served as an offering to the deata of the East. (Similarly, from the skins of buffaloes sacrificed for the deata, only

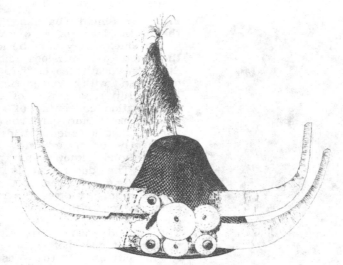

Fig. 54. Hat (salulung), woven from strips of rattan. It is decorated
with two sets of brass horns (tanduk gallang or tandu' allang). A
plume of human hair crowns the hat which is studded with discs of
shell. The hat is part of the collection of the Museum Pusat in Jakarta
(inventory no. 16720). (Drawing by Subokastowo.)

drumheads may be made for drums played during rituals of the East.)
The tora-tora, a necklace, is also part of the headhunter's complete
dress. For illustrations of the clothing and accessories the hunters wear
and carry, see Figs. 51-55.

    If the hunt was a success, one could hear that from the war cries
(sumapuko) of the returning warriors long before they came in sight.
Villagers would pour out to meet them, taking puffed rice (ra'tuk) and
dehusked, soaked rice with them. "The former were sprinkled over the
warriors, the latter was given them to eat. Until they had tasted these
raw grains, they might not eat cooked rice." (A.C. Kruyt 1923-24:270).
The corpse of the victim for whom revenge was required was then
brought to the rante. A coconut was hung from the bala'kaan. The
young might hack away at it. The nut represented the severed head of
the hunters' prey. Also in death chants and maro-songs the victim's
decapitated head is compared to a coconut or a pangi-fruit (Pangium
edule). The head is impaled on a stick that is implanted in the ground
in front of the bala'kaan. Men and women danced around the stick (the
dance was called sumengo). The dancing was accompanied by drums.
When in 1920, long after headhunting had been forbidden, the prominent adat chief Pong Maramba' died, the head of a deer was placed on
a stick when his death feast was celebrated. A number of men sung the
headhunting song that was customary for a human skull and danced
around the deer's head (information by Van der Veen).

    In precolonial days the return of a successful headhunting party led
to various celebrations. The tongkonan of the deceased would be decorated together with the entrances to the village. Young leaves from the
sugar palm were used. (Decoration with these pusuk falls within the

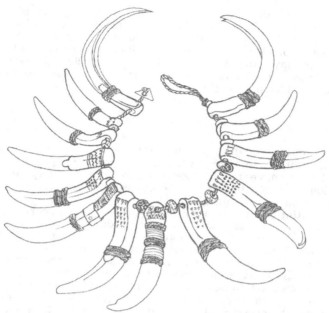

Fig. 55. Headhunter's neck ornament (tora-tora). This ornament consists of the teeth of a wild boar which have been threaded together.
Each tooth is set in a piece of wood that has been hollowed out to hold
it; each piece of wood is pierced by a hole through which the connecting thread can pass. On occasion the pieces of wood have been carved
to look like stylized human heads. At times the teeth of a crocodile are
used instead of those of a boar. The tora-tora shown comes from Kesu'.
(Drawing by Suzanne Taub.)

Eastern sphere.) Sham battles were then staged. Next the skull was
treated (A.C. Kruyt 1923-24:271). In Angin-angin, Kesu' district, a
kaunan prepared the skull, one whose family had traditionally performed
this task. Illustrations of captured heads are rare. Grubauer has
portrayed one; the eye sockets are plugged with roughly cut bits of
wood while a piece of woodcarving in the form of a fruit is inserted in
the nasal cavity. This large false nose makes the head look remarkable
(see Grubauer 1923:58). Elsewhere a severed head was decorated with
buffalo horns.

After a headhunting expedition ended, according to A.C. Kruyt, the
head taken as a prize would be mounted, once it had been prepared, on
the façade of the house. He does not report whether this was the house
where the deceased for whom the head was taken lay on view, or if it
was the dead man's leading tongkonan. Sometimes the skull was suspended from the ridge pole. Wilcox says that he saw a head trophy
hanging where otherwise the wooden bird's head (katik) is to be found
(Wilcox 1949:336). In 1925 Van der Veen saw skulls hanging on the
façade of several tongkonan. In the village of La'bo' (Kesu' District),
as late as 1966, I myself saw a severed head suspended from the front

of the eminent tongkonan Tanete. It hung high on the ridge and was
decorated with two buffalo horns like the head which Wilcox reported
seeing. This prize had been secured in connection with the death of a
respected member of this tongkonan. Allo Rante (Ne' Sangga) let me see
six heads which lay stored in his ricebarn (1969). He was going to
remove them from the ricebarn because as a Christian he found it no
longer fitting for him to preserve them.

4. The ritual implications of headhunting

Above I have outlined what people propose as the motivations which
underlay headhunting in Tana Toraja: the wish to provide a notable
dead man with a servent, to take revenge, or to allay an epidemic.
The motivation last mentioned was only reported of Mamasa; for the
connection between headhunting and illnesses, see Chapter VI.2.9., and
below. Headhunting had yet additional goals too. According to A.C.
Kruyt the scalp of a head that was taken would be placed in a durian
or coconut tree to cause it to produce a superabundance of fruit. Here
we appear to encounter the conviction that certain forces emanated from
the severed head. Possibly we also have to do with the notion, current
among other peoples as well, that life springs from death. Healing
properties were also attributed to the skulls; this emerges from the fact
that sick persons were made to drink from the cranium either of a defeated enemy or of someone who fell prey to headhunters (A.C. Kruyt
1923-24:272-3). Sometimes sick children were given to drink part of the
water in which the head was cooked to remove the soft parts during the
preparation proces. This explains the reference to headhunting and
skulls in the songs performed during the maro-ritual.
The hanging of a severed head on the North side of the house is
possibly connected to the fact that it is on this side of the tongkonan
that symbols appear which express power (cf. buffalo horns).
How should we classify headhunting with the sphere of the East or
West? The Toraja themselves couldn't say. Informants from Nonongan
said headhunting was an Eastern ritual, yet other adat experts clearly
had their doubts. In my opinion headhunting falls within the sphere of
the West. There are various indications that point in this direction: the
ritual is intimately associated with death; different rites take place on
the rante, the plain where death rituals are celebrated; the participants
in a headhunting party are forbidden for some time to eat rice; and the
to ma'randing-dancers who perform during important death rituals wear
the full dress of headhunters. There are, however, also associations
with the sphere of the East, with life. This would seem the conclusion
to be drawn form the appearance of pusuk as decoration, and the
placing of scalps in trees to promote fertility. References to headhunting occur in songs which belong both to the Western and the Eastern sphere (The Chant:39, 76-77; Van der Veen 1979:69, 71, 81, 133,
219).
The to barani who are praised during the great bua'-ritual, are not
only courageous in battle, but also headhunters. The verses which are
printed at the beginning of this chapter come from a satire (retteng)
sung during the death ritual celebrated for a person of note (The
Chant:16-7; 74-89).

Chapter XIV

CONCLUSIONS

1. Introduction

A variety of helpful sources have not yet been adequately exploited in attempts to reconstruct the origins and history of the Sa'dan-Toraja: prehistoric research, genealogies, myths and traditions, lontara of the Buginese and Macassarese, and European historical sources. Focussed prehistoric research has, unfortunately, hardly been attempted: we are merely able to point out the resemblance of the boat-shaped sarcophagus in the region of Duri, placed on rock ledges (see Vol.I, photo section), to coffins used by the Toraja.

As far as lontara are concerned: far from all have been examined. More intensive study might well yield new points of view.

European historical sources begin with Gervaise (Vol.I:9; Abidin 1982:64). They tell us very little about the past migrations of the Toraja. The first to pay some attention to this topic were the much later Memories van Overgave (cf. Nooy-Palm 1978:168-78; 187).

Attempts at reconstruction therefore have had to depend largely on myths, genealogies, and linguistic research. Let us begin with the last of these three. According to Mills, the various peoples of South Sulawesi (Macassarese, Buginese, the inhabitants of Luwu', the Duri, Sa'dan- and Mamasa-Toraja) originally belonged to a single language group: Proto South Sulawesi (Mills 1975:205ff.). The Buginese, Duri, Luwunese and the Toraja followed the course of the Sa'dan River when they settled on the peninsula. Apparently at first comprising a single subgroup, they later split apart: the Sa'dan-Toraja settled near the upper reaches of the river; the Mamasa-Toraja set out for Mamasa; the Luwunese built villages to the East of the Sa'dan-Toraja; and the Buginese migrated to Luwu' via the headwaters of the Sa'dan until they reached the coastal harbour of Palopo. From Palopo they sailed along the coast to the fertile plains which lay in the southern expanse of the peninsula, driving out, to some extent, the Macassarese who had formerly settled there. Like the Macassarese, the Buginese developed into merchants skilful at seafaring. Their gaze was consequently more fixed on the outside world than that of the isolated, "introverted" Toraja. The kingdom of Luwu' is still today considered the mythic fatherland of the Buginese dominions (Andi Zainal Abidin 1982:63; Mangemba et al. 1956:48f.). Yet the affinity of the Sa'dan-Toraja with Luwu' remained important, considering the form of homage which the puang of Sangalla' and dignitaries of other regions paid to the datu of Luwu' (melondong datu, see Chapter IV.4.). The Luwunese and Toraja moreover are not only related linguistically, but culturally as well: rice ceremonies among both peoples resemble each other, and the rice priest in Tana Toraja bears the same title as his colleague in Luwu': bunga' lalan. The Buginese and Toraja also demonstrate cultural similarities, yet as they drifted apart historically, their cultural and religious differences increased.

Turning back to the cradle of the Toraja and their related groups, let me cite Mills: "We can also tentatively posit a homeland area from which the dispersion of linguistic groups can be tied in with geographical factors: to wit, the lower course of the Sa'dan River" (Mills 1975:216). It was from here that the Sa'dan Toraja departed for the upper course of the river where they made their home and subsequently moved first East and then later West. This enables us to explain why social stratification is most marked in the valley of the upper reaches of the Sa'dan (roughly where Ma'kale is situated) and in the small states which lie to the East: the Tallulembangna. These regions were the most accessible and had the best soil and most favourable climate. Here the oldest tongkonan were established and genealogies stretch back farthest in time. This explains why in the Tallulembangna and in Kesu' family trees include some 34 generations, whereas dynasties in the Northwest of Tana Toraja (in Balla, Bittuang and Pali) can trace their ancestry back only some ten generations (Vol.I:67). The leading trade route to the South also followed the Sa'dan valley. It had a branch eastwards to the sea, the old route from Rantepao to Palopo which is still of significance today. Along this way Indian textiles and V.O.C. coins were imported into Tana Toraja. When, after 1870, cultivation of coffee began to flourish, this was the route along which coffee was exported to the South and East. The coffee crop brought new prosperity to Duri and Tana Toraja, not only in the river valley, but also, for example, in Pangala' and on the slopes of the Sesean, where the ground was particularly suited to growing coffee. We have already mentioned how proceeds from the sale of coffee contributed to the involution of Toraja feasts (see Chapter XII.2.3.).

Toraja myths and songs support Mills' theories. The trek he describes for the Toraja accords with place names that appear in the elegies: via Pongko' (= Lebukan, the mythic island which defies identification) they arrived at Karangan, the mountain Bamba Puang in Duri, Enrekang, Se'ke', Sinadi, Bangkudu, etc. - all readily identifiable locations (The Chant:25-7). Traditions and genealogies mention which tongkonan were the first to be founded and what fissions later took place. Such a break took place in an ambilineal group after about five generations (see Bigalke 1981:21 and Schmitz 1964:51). Taking as our point of departure a genealogical depth of some 34 generations, the conclusion seems justifiable that the first settlement in Tana Toraja took place between 700 and 900 years ago.

In districts where stratification is most pronounced, rituals are celebrated with great display. The splendor involved not only attracts tourists, it has meant that anthropologists have devoted themselves primarily to these regions as well.

2. *Myths and rituals*

At the core for a culture are its myths and rituals. Despite the fact that the rituals can be exceedingly spectacular, they do not include dramatization of myths: no masked play-acting takes place, no mummers portraying gods or spirits. Myth is recited during the ritual (bua', merok) and its recitation is the ritual act (cf. Van Baal 1981:162). For the Toraja the relation between myth and ritual is important; the recitation of the founding myth is the "pièce de résistance" of the merok, and - to somewhat of a lesser degree - of the bua'. "Most rituals are connected with such a founding myth, which can be looked upon as its charter" (Van Baal 1981:162).

Rituals and the social order are sanctioned by the founding myths; the Passomba Tedong from Kesu' (see Vol.I:134ff.), the Traditions concerning Heavenly Origins from Riu (see Vol.I:139ff.) and the History of Tamborolangi' in the puang-territories (see Vol.I:145ff.). The main theme of all three is the same descent to earth of divine ancestors from heaven who bring with them their possessions (including slaves), adat regulations, and rituals (with the exception of the death ritual, although, in veiled terms, it is referred to in the myths).

There is some variation: Tamborolangi's myth is more consonant with Buginese traditions, of which, indeed, it constitutes a part; Kesu' places less importance on the landing of the first inhabitant of earth on a terrestial hill, a moment which is more elaborated in Riu and Tikala; Riu particularly stresses the sin of incest. All the myths, however, emphasize that socio-religious structure is of celestial origin. The history of the tribe is commemorated during major rituals, the tale starting with the descent from the sky and the journey of important ancestors; they were gods and their descendants participate in this divinity; adat and aluk acquire their legitimacy.

Mankind, as inhabitant of the middleworld, should strive to maintain the balance between the upper- and underworld, East and West (North and South). In man's immediate vicinity there are spirits who can both aid and trouble him. Spirits of the underworld are also nearby, lurking in rivers, pools and wells, or directly beneath the surface of the earth. At more of a distance are the deata of the upperworld. Communication with all these gods and spirits takes place either directly, through a simple rite, or with the help of priests or shamans. If at the right time and in the right place the proper ritual is observed and the proper offerings are brought, evil will be kept at bay and the ancestors will extend their protective care over their descendants and see to it that they prosper. The relation of gods to men, ancestors to descendants, involves to a considerable extent the basic principle which plays such a fundamental role in mutual relations among the living.

Yet relations with upper- and underworld remain unstable; border zones are vulnerable, and security can disappear. An incestuous relation - behaviour considered to be one of the most culpable violations of adat - may be initiated, for example. Disease and epidemics can be the result. In the event of incest (with its mythical prototype in Rura), one makes an expiatory offering, mangrambu langi', "to cover the heavens with smoke", i.e. to darken, to obscure (cf. Merok:164-5).

The religious system seems to be logical, but it raises certain questions. It gives the impression of being well ordered, yet in fact there is little if any homology between gods in the upperworld and functionaries in the social-religious system in the world of men. The goddess of earthquakes has no equivalent figure who represents her in rituals. The Medicine Woman from the upperworld is perhaps better represented by the tumbang of the maro-ritual than by the to ma'dampi. The hermaphroditic priest who officiates in the great bua'-feast has no prototype in the upperworld, although mention is made of a first burake in

Table 4. Toraja rituals: artefacts.

Rituals of the East				Rituals of the West	
great bua'-feast	merok	maro	conversion rituals	headhunting	death rituals
anak dara	sendana	bate	palanduan	headhunter's tree	tau-tau
rice mortar	pair of drums		bate manurun		rapasan
gorang					bala'kaan
lumbaa langi'					lumbaa padang
					parangka (Ma'kale)
barana' sendana					simbuang kayu
parangka					simbuang batu
pair of drums					drum

The anak dara (tumba'), the fertility symbol in the bua'-feast, considered female, is guarded by the tumbang, its human – also female – counterpart. The "pendant" (sibali) of the tumba' is the tau-tau in Western (death) rituals. This effigy is placed in front of the rock-tomb, looking out over the ricefields. It represents the deceased, who in the meantime has reached heaven, becoming a guardian over the rice. The gorang in the Eastern sphere and its opposite, the bala'kaan in the death ritual, are cosmic symbols, used respectively for the laudation of the men in the bua'-territory and the distribution of meat according to rank at a death ritual. The squares, where these structures are erected (not mentioned in the table), are each other's opposites: the rante kala'paran (the plain for concluding rites of the bua'-feast) is the sibali of the rante or pantunuan, the plain for slaughtering the buffaloes for a deceased. A rice mortar, resting on the ground under the gorang is holding the lumbaa langi', the "pole of heaven". On top of this structure several bundles of paddy are suspended. The pole symbolizes the connection between heaven and earth; the rice is a food of heavenly origin. The sibali of the lumbaa langi' is the lumbaa padang in the death ritual, "the pole of earth", with a tombi on top. The bamboo is erected on the rante to honour a deceased of high rank. The rice mortar under the gorang may have its equivalent in the rapasan, used to contain the bodily remains of the deceased, the future guardian over the rice. The bate manurun has its counterpart in the parangka, a forked bamboo structure which has the same shape. The parangka is set up at death rituals in Ma'kale, to ward off evil. The parangka erected in the bua'-ritual is a different object: it is a stone, which is set (together with the sendana) in front of the house where the tumbang resides. Its ritual opposite is (probably) the simbuang batu in the death ritual. The simbuang kayu is the Western counterpart of the Eastern trees in the Eastern rituals (barana', sendana, etc.). The tongkonan, being the centre in nearly all rituals, is the link between East and West. The sequence observed in the table differs slightly from the one observed in the preceding chapters, for some Toraja do consider head-hunting an Eastern ritual. For the tongkonan as a link between rituals of East and West, see photo p.166.

heaven. The burake tattiku' and her helper, the to ma'gandang, may perhaps be considered as earthly counterparts of a divine couple.

From gold dust the divine smith created man, the sacrificial animals, rice, etc. Man, however, is in principle not a creator. He can merely do his best to maintain what the Creator has made. Only the smith can give anything its form; perhaps a potter can do the same, and Puang Matua is cited as a potter when he shaped the small clay doll that became the first female slave. Those who make pottery, however, are not particularly esteemed among the Toraja. Figures of authority, title-holders, however important their status, do not have creative functions; rather they are the preservers, or, like Toraja priests, the protectors of the community. Guardians of the order established in myth, the order which is time and again refreshed in memory through ritual recitation. Perhaps the burake tambolang by virtue of his ability to promote human fertility is closest to the gods.

3. Binary opposites and the tri-partite cosmos

When Toraja informants speak of their religion they call attention emphatically to binary opposites within rituals (of the East and West). Their presentation creates the impression that such polarity is of more significance than the tripartition of the cosmos. Dualism is something they grow up with and they point to the "pendant" (sibali) which every functionary and every artefact has in the ritual of "the other side" (for the artifacts, see Table 4).[1] Even myths have their counterpart; the theft in the upperworld is doubled by a theft in the underworld. The latter, however, proved less catastrophic: it did not lead to the severing of relations between the inhabitants of the earth and the gods or spirits of the other world (for these myths, see Vol.I:163ff.).

Oppositions to be sure find expression in the socio-religious sphere: one can pair off the highest in the land, as the heirs of the gods who descended to earth, against the lowest class, the descendants of those who because of their refusal to comply, because of their desire to be equal to their brothers, were reduced to slavery. "Those who strain like oxen under the yoke" are associated with mud; they wear an armband of clay, their buffalo is drab. Members of the upper class are linked with symbols of the upperworld: heavenly bodies, sun-screens, gold, the colour of yellow, precious buffaloes and valuable, even sacral possessions.

Priests, too, can be sorted into the categories of East and West: the death priest who in many regions is a member of the lowest class, can be seen as the pendant of the almost divine burake tambolang. One can also, however, see him in opposition to the rice priest:

West	East
to mebalun (wrapper of the dead)	to indo' (rice priest)
to burake matampu', the burake of the West[2]	to burake tattiku'
	to burake tambolang
	to burake matallo, the burake of the East

In the puang-states, the opposites are the following:

West	East
to ma'kayo (the name derives from the grey heron); he is identical to the to mebalun	to burake tambolang (the name derives from a black and white heron)

Opposites are not only characteristics of the religious sphere, however; they occur in the social sphere as well. As an example, let us take the settlement in Kesu':

"Upper"	"Lower"
sokkong bayu	
datu muane, "prince" (see Vol.I:97-100)	datu baine, "princess"

In the village structure "prince" and "princess" do not function as a couple that represents one pair or another of gods from the upperworld (or any cosmic pair at all). The pair probably represents the male and female principle within Toraja culture (cf. the to burake tattiku' and the to ma'gandang in the bua'-ritual, see Chapter II.2.). The recent construction of datu muane versus datu baine offers evidence that the creation of binary opposites here is still every bit as much alive as in many other Indonesian cultures. Although this duality is of recent origin according to Toraja informants, it is highly reminiscent of similar structures elsewhere in Indonesia and in Oceania.

House and compound belong together. During the merok and the mangrara banua, the prayer on the compound is delivered by the sokkong bayu (datu muane), inside the tongkonan the task falls to the datu baine.[3] Are we to deduce then that the "princess" should be more closely associated with the tongkonan, and the "prince" with the surrounding yard? The Toraja have nothing to say on the subject; nor did I pursue it. The conclusion, however, does seem probable. Ritually considered, the compound is more a man's place. Men are the ones who slaughter the sacrificial animals, divide the meat and cook it on the yard. "Daily" cooking is woman's work, in the kitchen inside the house. The house is the woman's domain, ritually seen as well. Here the anak dara is mounted[4], the symbol of woman (and of rice).

In Riu and Tikala we also come across a twofold division in the form of a "masculine" and a "feminine" chief. We might expand such oppositions still further: as a pendant to kaunan in the sense of slaves, one can identify the kaunan garonto', the predial slaves who belong to the tongkonan from generation to generation. In the puang-state Sangalla' this opposition could be extended still further, for certain kaunan, the "golden slaves", have been elevated there into a kind of court dignitaries. Such dependants can no longer automatically be categorized as belonging to the sphere of the West and of death. This obtains, for example, for those slaves who perform some task in the cultivation of rice on the royal sawahs. It is, to speak in the vein of Lévi-Strauss, very difficult to identify a dualistic structure, as each pair of opposites constantly conjures up a new opposition. A binary division is actually already threefold, which can be extended to a N-fold division. If, like the Toraja, we make a sharp distinction between East and West, then, in the religious sector, we can regard the to burake (the to burake tattiku' or the to burake tambolang) as in opposition to the death priest, and in secular affairs the puang or to parengnge' as in opposition to the kaunan. Yet parengnge' also take part in rituals, especially in those rites which are to sustain contact between the earth and the upperworld.

Up to this point I have confined myself to the dualism inherent in Toraja culture. How is the division of the world into three portrayed in incorporeal representations, in particular in myths? How is the tripartite nature of the cosmos embodied in rituals?

In founding myths recited during the great bua'-feast and the merok-feast three worlds are specified: the realm of Puang Matua, the world of man, and the kingdom of Pong Tulakpadang and the to kengkok, the folks with a tail. Yet in these rituals (aiming at prosperity, abundant offspring, much rice and many animals) the underworld remains in the background. It is in the maro-ritual, the most "marginal" ritual of the East which is the most closely associated with the sphere of headhunting, that the tripartite division of the cosmos receives its fullest expression. The tumbang, fallen in a trance, journeys through the skies, descends again to earth, and finally plunges into the pools of the underworld. Many binary and tertiary divisions in Toraja culture merit closer analysis, but in what follows we will confine ourselves to one single case, the opposition between rice (= life) and death. What emerges is that rice also plays a role in the death ritual, so that we can speak of a unity of opposites.

4. Food and rituals

Food for the Toraja is indeed important and is part of religious offerings. The colour, kind and number of sacrificial animals is specified in detail, as well as the kinds of crops which are to be used and the manner in which ritual meals or offerings must be prepared and served. Preparation of food during rituals is a task for both men and women, but as soon as meat is involved, men are entrusted with its distribution and cooking. Many rituals are characterized by a special sacrificial animal and special foods. Yams and maize, for example, are never part of any rite in the sphere of the East. In the closer analysis of food among the Toraja which follows, there will, however, be no distinction drawn along the lines Lévi-Strauss pursues in his dichotomy of the raw and the cooked, nature and culture (see De Ruijter 1977:203-7).

An attempt will be made to comment upon the diverse categories of food which figure in different rituals from the perspective of the Toraja's own religious system. The linked concepts of East-West, life-death, entail, on the one hand, opposition; on the other hand, they are complementary. A ritual of the West can, as it proceeds, reach a point where it embraces "Eastern" elements. Below I will try to illustrate this happening, using rice as my primary example.

In principle rice is kept far from the sphere of death: as long as rice still grows in the fields, no death feast may be celebrated. A rice priest should avoid death rites. Within the context of the annual cycle, we encounter the opposition rice and rice cult versus death and death feasts, an opposition which in part is based upon division of the year into wet and dry seasons, and which also has its practical aspects (see

Chapter I). The opposition rice-death also extends over a longer period: until all death feasts have been completed, no great bua'-feast may be held. In such a bua'-ritual rice plays a major role, given the symbolism of this crop in the feast: the rice vat in which the lumbaa langi' is placed; the sprigs of rice which hang about the neck of the wooden bird's head; the bird motif used to decorate the sedan chair of the tumbang. Rice is ritually winnowed, an act that is also part of the merok (cf. Merok:5). Last but not least is the anak dara, the female symbol in the bua'-ritual, the enormous "rice mother" which becomes pregnant, just like the rice itself (see Chapter II, note 28). In the bua'-ritual the important role of women in society is emphasized: they will bear the descendants of the future, and they have the harvested rice - the leading food crop - under their protection. Although the rice priests are men, they are designated by the name to indo' padang, "the mothers of the land". In the course of the bua'-feast there are also men who are praised, first and foremost men who - formerly - distinguished themselves as headhunters. By taking heads, these warriors made their contribution to promoting the growth of the crops, rice especially.

Rice figures not only in rituals of the East, but also in death rituals - a subject to which we turn below.

4.1. The death ritual and rice

Since funerals of a higher order are of special importance for the ancestor cult, I have chosen to limit discussion to such rituals. Not only must the deceased have been a person of considerable status and wealth, but his life, the length of time which he passed on earth before Pong Lalondong cut the thread of his days, must have been of more than brief duration. Whatever their class, dead babies and small children are buried with little ceremonial fuss.[5] Only a rich, adult Toraja who during his lifetime has thrown one or more feasts of merit can ascend to become a deata, a divinity who watches over the prospering of the rice and the well-being of his descendants.[6] The death feast, his final "rite de passage", reflects as it were - however paradoxical it may sound - the diverse stages of the human life cycle. We have observed how, in the first part of higher death rituals such as the dirapa'i, the deceased is portrayed as a child: he is taken in the arms (cf. the sword, symbol of the dead, in the silali'-ceremony, Chapter XI.1.2.). In Sangalla' and other puang-territories a dead prince (close to a god) is bound in the position of a foetus. In Kesu' and elsewhere, the ma'pasusu takes place in the first part of the death ritual (see Chapter XI.1.2.). The dead is as it were still in his childhood: at this stage he is not yet able to extend his protective care over the rice as a notable can for whom all the rites of his death feast have been completed. It is true that he can already exercise some power (he can cause rain), yet he is not yet "mature", he is not yet a deata who cares for the rice. This is reflected in the death ritual. This immature phase is stressed, as it were, by the significance of the food in the mourning ceremony, an important matter examined further below.

In the interval between the first and second part of a major death ritual the dead is laid to rest in a rice mortar (Kesu', Tikala). The parallel between the deceased and the rice is striking.

The first phase of the death ritual, its incompletion, finds its equivalent in the unripe food that mourning family members eat. Close relatives and those who tread on the sleeping mat of the deceased may only eat raw food. This consists principally of maize. This food - uncooked maize is in fact inedible - makes a stark contrast with cooked rice: the latter is the Torajas' preferred food, prepared from rice which the ancestors have stood guard over in the field. There is thus not only an opposition between maize and rice, but also between uncooked and cooked.

(Cooked) rice is considered so important that it has its own ancestor, Takkebuku, "He who has no kernel". A certain opposition is contained in this name: being without a pit or kernel is opposed to the skeleton (of the deceased). Takkebuku, like the first man, the buffalo, the chicken, the small rain and the poisonous ipo-tree, was created by Puang Matua from the gold that he placed in the divine bellows. It goes without saying that rice must be kept far from the sphere which surrounds the deceased who has not yet been laid in the rock grave; in this situation only raw maize may be consumed. This is especially true for a dead person for whom only the first part of the death ritual, the childhood phase, aluk pia, has been celebrated. Yet as the ritual advances the deceased is increasingly surrounded by symbols which have something to do with rice.

The deceased is placed in a rice mortar, his "golden vessel" as it is called in death chants. He travels to the land of the souls; he reclines in his death ship; yet from the fact that this "ship" has the shape of a rice mortar it appears that the dead is closely associated with the rice. This is manifest as well in the handling of the death roll and the tau-tau, the mortuary effigy which is an image of the deceased and in which the dead man's soul houses: during a certain rite of the feast the effigy is placed on the floor beneath the ricebarn (the alang of the deceased). The bodily remains themselves are also placed on the floor below the ricebarn (ma'popengkalao alang).

One of the last passages of the deceased is the circuit he makes around his sawahs. The concluding rite of the death ritual is the mangrara pare, "the sprinkling of the rice with blood", an important sacrifice that is made on one of the dead man's sawahs after the rice harvest.

4.2. Rice and headhunting

Headhunting is closely allied with death rituals. The search for a victim involves violent death, a dangerous sphere. To be sure whoever dies in battle and/or whose head is taken is numbered among the "dangerous dead".[7] For someone who is killed a buffalo (pundu paresa') is slaughtered on the rante beside a menhir; in addition a lansa' (Lansium domesticum) is planted. For a person who met a violent end no death feast could be celebrated until a head had been taken in revenge. The scalp of the trophy - portrayed in the ritual as a coconut, a fruit - was considered to have the power to increase the fertility of the fields (see Chapter XIII.4.). (Although this information pertains primarily to durian and coconut trees, the placing of severed heads in the ricebarn suggests that a similar line of thought obtained for rice.)

Headhunting also involved food taboos and restrictions with regard to rice. At a headhunting feast puffed rice and dehusked, soaked grains of rice were of prominence (see Chapter XIII.3.). This behaviour runs

parallel to the demands made of the to maro' - who may eat no (cooked)
rice - during a death ritual. Prohibitions are even more stringent,
however, for these ritual mourners; on the whole they may not eat any
rice, whatever state it happens to be in. Puffed or roasted rice is not
entirely uncooked; it is, at the same time, not cooked food. It has been
processed, true, but in a way that stops short of true cooking. Toraja
informants were unsure whether headhunting was a ritual of the East or
the West. In any event it is close to the death ritual that falls in the
sphere of the West, and yet is itself more Eastern than a death feast.
The party of headhunters found themselves in a taboo situation which
differed slightly from that of the close relatives of the deceased: the
warriors, too, were closely related to the deceased, yet the latter was
not yet "officially" dead since his mourning rites still remained to be
celebrated. In this phase he is no ordinary dead person.

4.3. Rice in the death ritual of the East

A deceased burake is also no ordinary dead person; his death ritual
falls beyond the rituals of the West. Yet not entirely: mourners may
also eat no rice. They eat yams during the mourning period. This is an
indication that the ritual is not considered altogether as a feast in the
Eastern sphere (see Chapter V.5.), for yams, a tuber, belong to the
West. This does not diminish the fact, however, that the burake
reaches heaven more quickly than other dead.

5. Rice and myths

The burake will occupy a place among the other ancestors who are part
of the constellation which is situated between the Seven Sisters
(Pleiades) and Ursa Major. These deata protect mankind, animal and
crops, rice in particular. These deified ancestors, to mebali puang,
"those who have become lords", the stars and the rice are, to the Torajas' way of thinking, closely related. The ancestor has become a star.
Stars are compared to grains of rice which have been roasted, as in the
following narrative: Kundailangi', the daughter of Tumba' Bena'
Kumpang and To Tanarangga, married Kambunolangi', the first to
minaa. She gave birth to Sambiralangi', a datu muane (god) who
entered into union with a yellow-shining star described as a grain of
rice burst open with roasting. From their marriage, the god Buralangi'
was born, "The Foam of Heaven, the Fruit of the Firmament"
(Merok:155). In Tikala Buralangi' is the forefather of Pong Mulatau, the
first man. In this instance the ancestor is the offspring of a star symbolizing rice (see Merok:155, verses 782-91).

The relation between mankind and rice is rendered most effectively,
however, in the myth of Tulangdidi' (Vol.I:166-8). She is alternatively
known under the name Indo' Samadenna, Mother Everything is in hand
(cf. Merok:71), or Mother Abundance (cf. Vol.I:141). The story is told
in Vol.I.166-8. The heroine, at first called Tulangdidi', "The Upright
Yellow One" (= the rice), is referred to at the end of the story as
"Mother all there is", Mother Abundance". Practically every ritual ends,
to be sure, with a prayer for many children, many buffaloes, many
precious possessions, abundant rice. In Tulangdidi's story it is a
mother figure who is looked upon as the agent who will confer bounty

even though the prayer asking for blessings is addressed to the gods in general. Indo' Samadenna is the Toraja version of the European figure Frau Holle (Mother Carey). it is above all a good rice harvest that will satisfy peoples' expectations. (Coffee has only played a role in the prosperity of the Toraja since 1870, relatively recently, and consequently this crop is not mentioned in the myths.) It is hardly coincidental then that the story of Tulangdidi' (and other tales of similar drift) are told at the time the rice begins to ripen (cf. Vol.I:162). The narrative begins with Tulangdidi' weaving; weaving, just as the phases of the moon, is compared symbolically with the rice cycle, or with the life cycle of man. Tulangdidi' interrupted her weaving because her father's dog made it dirty; this dog (a hunter, a chtonic beast) she struck dead with her "sword" (the weaver's beam) and buried under a mat (a truly rudimentary form of burial). A crow (certainly not the prototype of a celestial bird; an eater of waste and carrion) betrayed her to her father who thereupon killed Tulangdidi' by cutting her in two with his sword (a masculine weapon, the counterpart to Tulangdidi's weaving utensil (division in two suggests the dichotomy of life and death). The father buried his daughter upstream (cf. the irrigation water for sawahs which comes in Tana Toraja from the upper course of the Sa'dan). From the chicken's egg which Tulangdidi's mother had given to her daughter who was condemned to death, a cock emerged who picked the maggots out of Tulangdidi's corpse (cf. the to ma'peulli' who - symbolically? - removes the maggots during death rituals). The cock and the to ma'peulli' have the task of purifying the dead. Both are closely associated with rice. A notable who has died will watch over the rice once "the offering meal is converted". Tulangdidi' came to life again after her purification; an eminent deceased afterwards embarks on his journey to the hereafter.

Later in Tulangdidi's story the cock is struck down by men after pecking at the rice. Like mankind the cock, too, eats rice. Paralyzed in one wing, he is called the Flapper. Despite the attempt to prevent him from flying, he climbs to the firmament and becomes a constellation: The Cock of Tulangdidi', important for the cultivation of rice. The cock's ascent to the heavens is also a symbolic representation of the fact that although rice is grown on earth, it is inconceivable without the favour of the gods and spirits of the upperworld, the world where rice first originated.

The cock brings Tulangdidi' wealth; her father is punished in the fashion reserved for wrongdoers in Puya; her mother is buried with pomp. The cock bears Tulangdidi' straight to heaven as if she were a to burake who need not bother with the troublesome transit through Puya. She lands on the moon where she becomes the woman with a spinning wheel. The rotation of the wheel speaks of a cycle just as the changes of the moon itself. Like the rice, she grows constantly - and there is periodically once again an interruption. The moon goes dark, after the harvest for a time the fields lie fallow. In the myth there is also an interruption: Tulangdidi's death, followed by her being brought back to life. She is "awakened" just as the deceased is roused at the outset of the second part of a death ritual.

In the myth the opposition life-death is central. It is fused into a synthesis, a unity of opposites. The theme is expressed through the two protagonists: a human, a woman, who becomes a goddess in the upperworld and a cock that as a constellation, The Cock of Tulangdidi', is consulted during the cultivation of rice.

How long will people continue to obey the precepts of the deata of the
Northeast and the to matua of the Southwest? I dare venture no pre-
diction. There are indications, however, that the influence of what,
succinctly, may be called "modern times" has been eroding long-stand-
ing beliefs and practices (see Mattulada, Nooy-Palm et al. 1980). Sacral
goods said to come from heaven are already being sold to tourists and
art dealers. The parengnge' no longer eats from the hollow wooden
bowls which belong to his status. Considered old-fashioned for a long
time already, the bowls are objects coveted by outside collectors.
Indeed, the status of the parengnge' is not what it used to be. Here
and there he may still enjoy a certain spiritual authority, but he is no
longer the regent to whom his people look for guidance. Government
officials have supplanted him. His children no longer abide by the
precepts of adat law. They have new professions: doctor, lawyer, judge
or anthropologist. And representatives of the last of this new breed of
professionals are engaged in recording what still remains of autochthonic culture before it disappears.

Tulangdidi' portrayed on an old cloth. Tulangdidi' is shown at her
spinning wheel. The phases of the moon are also represented. Above
the moon, to the left, is the cock, the constellation The Cock of
Tulangdidi' containing a spinning wheel. This constellation is composed
of Orion, Sirius and the Pleiades; no attempt has been made to render
the exact number of stars.
(Photo: R. Kok, Amsterdam.)

NOTES

CHAPTER I

1   For examples of badong and retteng, see The Chant:19-20 and 74-84 respectively.
2   During the ma'pallin that is part of the merok-feast, a black hen is sacrificed to the West of the tongkonan (see Merok:3, 158; see also Vol.I:247).

CHAPTER II

1   Garatung, a clapper drum. See Vol.I:IX, notes 7, 8 and 13.
2   The notion of cleansing one sees unmistakably in the term la'pa' kasalle.
3   The pendant of the lumbaa langi' is presumably the lumbaa padang in the death ritual. Lumbaa padang means "pole of the earth". It is with this name that the tombi, the banners and textiles which are displayed in the house of the dead, are designated.
4   According to J. Kruyt 1921:48-71.
5   This might indicate that certain families in Pangala' come originally from Kesu' and Tikala.
6   V.O.C. = Verenigde Oostindische Compagnie (Dutch East Indies Company).
7   The contemporary name is Cordyline terminalis.
8   A tree which I am unable to identify.
9   True, too, in Riu; see section 4 below.
10   Young bamboo sprouts are an exception. In Riu the to tumbang eat bananas as well.
11   In the merok-feast, the sendana is the symbol of the ramage.
12   The gelong (sung during a trance) actually belongs to the maro-ritual. In the observance of Toraja rituals, however, elements from one are often taken over in others.
13   Apparently Kruyt means all the families in the bua'-community.
14   Aluk: rite or ritual; padang: land, soil. The meaning of the phrase is not clear.
15   It is not clear what a year encompasses according to Kruyt. A rice cycle? Two rice cycles? At least the rice must have been harvested. In Riu the big rites of the bua' are organized in September and October.
16   The yellow rice is piled into the cover of the rice basket (= tutu nase); such covers are rather often used to convey an offering.
17   The relation of the burake to each other is unclear.
18   Apparently Kruyt refers here to the to usso'boi bua', a member of another bua'-community. This functionary is the first to set foot on the feast terrain in order to cleanse it of evil influences (Woordenboek: v. so'bo).
19   For this rite, see also section 3 where another interpretation of the ma'parekke para is offered under 13.
20   No texts have been recorded for the mangkaro bubun and the succeeding rites, the massali alang and the membase kandean.
21   No mention is made about whether those unable in the past to have celebrated the manganta' also sacrifice pigs at this point, or whether all those guilty of the omission were indeed family members of the host.
22   These women are reminiscent of the to mangria barang; see sections 2 and 4.

23 A functionary from the village community; see Vol.I:72.
24 See Vol.I:VIII.1.5. During a later stage of this feast the ampang bilik, it was said, would be affixed to the tumbang's sedan chair (see below). It is also possible, however, that the ampang bilik is a part of the gorang, for it is another name for the object known as the ruma-ruma. For the ambiguity surrounding the ruma-ruma, see also J. Kruyt 1921:62. According to Van der Veen the object is called ruma-ruma before it is placed in the tongkonan as a sign that the bua'-feast has been celebrated. Afterwards it is called ampang bilik, "the treshold of the room". It separates the Southern room from the central and Northern ones, the rooms associated with Eastern rituals.
25 The informant had nothing to say about the manner in which the sacrifice is performed.
26 A sacrificial altar of four bamboo poles carved with figures (cf. Vol.I:119).
27 According to information from B. Sarungallo, these spirits include both the important gods and all deata, thus also all the dead for whom a conversion ritual has already been celebrated. He has never personally attended the ma'pangalukan but from what he has heard the to burake carries on as if she is "mad", i.e. possessed. It is not clear whether a real or pseudo-trance state is involved. In the feast presently discussed which took place in Riu, when the to burake invoked the gods, there was no trace of a trance.
28 The duration of this period of seclusion merits challenge. According to Zerner (1981:109), the anak dara (he does not use the phrase anak dara but speaks rather of a straw effigy; see his note 3b) becomes "pregnant" and is served food. If the anak dara is identified with rice (which might be one aspect of the bua'-ritual), then the time spent by the tumbang in isolation will last approximately as long as a single rice cycle. Another point to be questioned here concerns the age of the tumbang. It is my impression that in several areas (Kesu') younger women, and in others (Riu) older women who have passed child-bearing age are chosen as to tumbang.
29 Family members come from other villages to share in this feast.
30 In Riu several sedan chairs are made for the to tumbang and her companions; see section 4.
31 It seems more probable to me that the ampang bilik is attached to the sedan chairs in front (the way in Riu the carved plank is); see section 4.
32 This is not customary in Riu.
33 Instead of a bell, the dancers may also hold a la'pa-la'pa, a bamboo rattle, in one hand.
34 A similar rite occurs in the merok-feast (Merok:5) where it is known as ma'pasa', "going to the market". Food is only given out, however, to members of the ramage.
35 Unlike what J. Kruyt reports concerning Pangala' (1921:48), this is before the rice planting season.
36 This sequence for bua'-feasts differs from that provided for Nonongan.
37 The Mother of the Small Rice, a goddess from the upperworld; see Vol.I:120, 135ff.
38 Small pieces of the liver and other parts of these animals are removed as an offering for the gods and spirits (cf. Vol.I:206). The rest is consumed by the members of the host's family who are present.
39 J. Kruyt (1921:52-6) also describes the anak dara.
40 In 1970 approximately half a dollar.
41 Manglika' bua' might possibly signify the unification of the bua'-feast.
42 Literally: "Those who hold the winnowing fan on their laps".
43 In addition to the parts usually included in a pesung, on this occasion the offerer also selected a piece from the pig's front leg (tingkoran), its hind leg (lette undi) and a kollong.
44 Um (= unn); before a verb this prefix converts the verb into an active participle.

45   The text of this prayer was not recorded in writing. The banaa (see above) is once more filled and wrapped in a sacral maa'-cloth.

46   It is not certain whether a real market is meant or the feast plain. In the major rituals of the Toraja the word pasa' recurs regularly. At times it has a ritual significance (see Merok:5, and above), yet also at times an actual market is held on the feast terrain where a wide assortment of food is for sale. From this practice various permanent markets have developed in the course of time.

47   From J. Kruyt's account, one can conclude that the to mano'bo and the to ma'tanduk are two, distinct figures (see above). Which of the two is the to usso'boi rante?

48   Woordenboek: v. tampak pesung, "the remainder of the offering after the gods have claimed the essence for themselves; this sacrificial food is considered to have especially powerful magical properties; it is distributed among those who have participated in the sacrifice in tiny portions; they are forbidden not to taste of it."

49   Since there were several bua'-feasts under way at roughly the same time, this foursome, it should be understood, included ampu bua' from other bua'-feasts, who participated here as guests.

50   Division of the meat in Riu is the task of the saroan.

51   The to ma'gandang is usually the "brother" of the to burake. The family tree of the burake tattiku' in the region of Riu begins in heaven; a daughter always takes up the office of her mother. According to this family tree the to ma'gandang is her (classificatory?) brother.

52   Van der Veen maintains this mummery portrays the long "journey" which the bua'-feast itself has taken; in myth the feast changed location several times. See Chapter II.4.

53   For division of the meat, cf. rite 55 above. Batu Kamban had five saroan to divide the meat.

54   Beneath the gorang is a stone vessel used for pounding rice. In the empty mortar an egg is placed. Here at midnight assemble various and sundry spirits. Whoever, naked, dares to come and carry off this egg, will have all his wishes granted, but no one is brave enough to come without clothes and risk confrontation with the spirits. In the same vessel the lumbaa langi' is anchored. It rises through an opening in the laa(ng) (the platform on which the to minaa stands during the laudations) and sticks out far above the gorang.

55   According to some Christians who attended the feast, too, the devastation came because the "big day" of the feast was held on a Sunday.

CHAPTER III

1   A slave who has prospered can buy his own freedom (Vol.I:47). This is true, however, only for the unfree who became slaves because of a debt.

2   Literally: ma'rapu tallang, "a family group (rapu), numerous as bamboo tallang sprouting from one root". In some districts (Kesu') the term pa'rapuan denotes a ramage, rapu a subramage. In other districts the words pa'rapuan and rapu are used alternately, in the sense of a ramage.

3   Karaeng is an analogue of the noble title Datu in Macassarese.

4   The Chicken of Tulangdidi', also called: Londongna Tulangdidi', The Cock of Tulangdidi'; see Vol.I:166-8.

5   According to Van der Veen the sokkong bayu (or the to minaa) digs the hole; the implement used is a small spade, pesese.

6   The word is difficult to translate. Sipalakuan is the name of a rite in the merok-feast and the manganta' (a conversion ritual) during which the person enacting the sacrifice (the to sipalakuan) and one of those who help him hold tightly to the tail of a pig that is to be slaughtered and pray for a blessing for themselves. This takes place on the "big day" of the merok or the manganta' (information from H. van der Veen).

7   For the sarita, see Vol.I:257. The liana, rattan and cloth are plaited into

one (tallu basongna, "the three twisted ropes", see rite 13 below).

8   Van der Veen maintains the following actions precede the actual merok-
    feast:
    a. the maro, held as the final rite of the death ritual on the western slope
    of the mountain Sesean. During the maro sacrifices are made first to the to
    matua and later to the deata; the to minaa officiates.
    b. the manganta' (massura' tallang): sacrifices for the deata are offered to
    the Northeast of a small bamboo altar; cloths are hung out; here, too, the
    to minaa takes charge (see Merok:1-9).
    c. subsequently, the following rites of the feast are enacted: the ma'pallin,
    the likaran biang, the mangrambu langi', the mangrimpung.
    It is not so surprising that there is some difference between the sequence
    of rites as reported by Van der Veen and Sarungallo, for Van der Veen's
    informant came from Salu in the complex Nonongan. The more incidental sa-
    crificial rites can indeed vary from place to place. See also notes 9 and 10,
    and rite 6b, mangrara kombong.

9   For Van der Veen the mangrambu langi' is the third important rite; it
    serves to nullify the evil generated by a sin (see Merok:1-9). Afterwards
    the manglika' biang takes place.

10 The sequence of these rites differs from the order Van der Veen reports in
    his Merok Feast. His version: mangrimpung - membase kandian - ma'bubung
    - massali alang - mangkaro bubun. He places the mangrara kombong later.
    The membase kandian is equivalent to the ma'tadoran.

11 According to Van der Veen, "to introduce the drums into the ritual".

12 Van der Veen cites yet two more rites between the mangrara kombong and
    the ma'patama gandang: the langngan Kesu', which involves climbing up
    Kesu' Mountain where the important ancestor descended to earth; and the
    ma'pasa', "going to market", where women from the ramage offer rice and
    palm wine to members of the ramage whom they encounter at the market
    (Merok:5).

13 Van der Veen reports this as a separate rite, tallu basongna (Merok:6). He
    contends a rattan is part of this tallu basongna; in Buntao', I saw that to
    bind the buffalo a combination was used of a liana, a rattan and a sarita
    twisted into one. Leaves from the sugar palm were not used.

14 Suru': an expiatory offering to atone for sins; rassa papa, a compact roof
    covering of bamboo shingles.

15 Presumably the pesung are placed at a crossroads.

16 In Kesu' the sacrifice during the ma'pallin consists of a black chicken. In
    Kesu' the rite is to drive out evil. For the significance of the colours of
    chickens, see Vol.I:290ff.

17 Presumably this rite is identical to the manglika' biang in Kesu'; see Merok:
    158-64.

18 A black chicken. It is not clear why the chicken must be black, for the
    merok is a ritual of the East. This colour possible is chosen as appropriate
    to an expiatory rite.

19 It is Van der Veen's opinion that such an array of sacrificial foods and
    colours only occurs in the course of the bua' kasalle-feast (Woordenboek:
    v. rangga). In Buntao' this usage also is part of the merok-feast; it
    deserves mention, however, that the great bua'-feast is less frequently
    celebrated here than, for example, in Riu.

20 Pata': the beam that runs lengthwise under the house and supports the
    floor. The front end juts out from the facade.

21 This is a sign that guests are expected for the "big day" of an important
    ritual. The pounding of rice is also a feature of the "big day" of a death
    ritual, but the rhythm is then different.

22 To mangimbo: he who speaks the prayer (at this rite, however, I have
    never noticed recitation of a prayer).

23 In point of fact the to minaa, as the Issong Kalua's replacement, wore the
    ritual clothing that was appropriate; the Issong Kalua also, however, was in

festal apparel.

24   The buffalo's jaw was not clamped shut during the invocation the way it is
      in Kesu' (Merok:7).

25   The head of the lembang, here a synonym for kecamatan, a modern adminis-
      trative unit (sub-district).

26   A sirih-pouch was also among the hanging cloths. The arrangement was
      strongly reminiscent of cloths displayed during the manganta' (as conver-
      sion ritual). It made me wonder whether this merok-feast was not really a
      conversion ritual as observed at the end of a death feast.

27   The to ma'sanduk who portioned out the meat of the sacrificed buffalo, the
      pig and the chicken, was a descendant of the female ancestor who (together
      with her husband) had founded the tongkonan.

28   It is conceivable that the areca-nut is a symbol of the prohibition against
      incest; see Vol.I:160.

CHAPTER IV

1   Mengkamma' and Ma'loko-loko both have the meaning of "to keep silent". For
      the meaning of keeping silent in the ritual context see rite 8 below.

2   This title also is in general use in Luwu' for the leading rice priest or
      guardian of the land, even beyond the territory which the Toraja who live
      there occupy.

3   For the tongkonan to which functionaries 2 through 5 belong, see Vol.I:
      102.

4   Until the arrival of the Dutch and for a short while thereafter, it was con-
      sidered taboo to grow rice on dry ground. Plagues and diseases would
      ravage the crop. This prohibition is no longer in effect. It should be stated
      that to a high degree the sawahs depend on rainfall; this is true of 13,076
      ha of the total surface area of 17,686 ha sawah-land (Yacobs 1971:10).

5   The tools described here, the hoe, peleko' and iron staves are also used at
      present for roadwork. Another implement used to cut grass is the kabom-
      bongan, a spade with a short handle.

6   Elsewhere rice is sometimes planted according to a different scheme; see
      Woordenboek: v. pare kasalle and pare dolo.

7   La'bo' is the name of a complex of villages in the territory of Kesu'.

8   In the territory of Tikala, Pong Maramba' tried to organize an irrigation
      system.

9   The publication of the first author, in Indonesian, provides a complete ac-
      count of rules and procedures.

10   Also in other territories when blast affects the rice, or if there is a plague
      of mice, an attempt is made to find out who is guilty of a sexual trans-
      gression (especially intercourse between close relatives, sampu pissan,
      sampu penduan, see Vol.I:28, 31ff.).

11   Marra': to tie as tightly as possible (Woordenboek: v. marra'). Probably the
      ma'kambuno'i, another rite, precedes the mantanan pemali. This is an offer-
      ing performed on the sawah dike on the Northeastern side of the rice field.
      See rite 1 of the mangrara pare, Chapter VII.2.8.

12   This melondong datu is different from the ritual described in section 4
      below.

13   According to information from 1969: these leaves and packets are hung on
      both the front and back of the tongkonan. Someone showed me one sus-
      pended from the neck of the katik (a wood-carving representing a bird).

14   The name pare deata, gods' rice, is also in use. The celestial pendant of
      these three rice plants is the pare tallu bullina, the mythical "three-eared
      rice" (see above).

15   According to tradition, after the murder of Palonga', the puang areas broke
      off relations with Luwu'; see Vol.I:153. In Kesu' and other territories the
      melondong datu is a rite which involves sacrifice of a rooster when the rice
      seedlings take root in order to promote their growth; see rite 11 above.

16   A term which causes confusion because the celebration of the great bua'-

feast in Riu is designated in the same way.

17 The to menani wears buffalo horns on his head, but these do not branch out to either side like the copper horns of the ma'randing dancers; instead they stick straight up and are decorated.

CHAPTER V

1 Rituals examined in this chapter are concerned exclusively with mankind. Ceremonies related to animals, those rites, for example, which have as their goal the prosperity of livestock or the healing of sick cattle, will not be discussed here.

2 A.C. Kruyt maintains that the navel wound is covered with chewed tumeric on top of which a sirih leaf is laid (1923/24:133).

3 Nobele (1926:37) reports that this period of rest lasts for three days; his information concerns childbirth in Ma'kale.

4 This is where Arrang diBatu, the god's wife, lived; see Vol.I:118.

5 A basket or plate of woven bamboo covered with leaves on top of which rice and chicken are served.

6 The to minaa sando is the highest order of to minaa.

7 In Tikala, the passurak tedong is not differentiated from the Passomba Tedong.

8 Such trances, a standard feature of the maro- and bugi'-feasts, are difficult to explain here. Perhaps the performance has to do with the fact that before he or she became a priest, the to burake will have lived for some time in seclusion, a period during which he or she will have gone into a trance or dreamed a great deal (personal interpretation).

9 = rante to tumbang. The to burake, to minaa sando and the to menani have a feast plain (rante) of their own where some of the funeral rites are observed.

10 = the to menani (see Vol.I:279).

11 Through verse 21, Tumba' Sanda landi Patong, the names recited are presumably those of all the burake who lived in certain places and enjoyed some renown. The prefix Tumba' indicates that the person mentioned was a to burake. The next verses have not been repeated in the translation.

12 In Mendetek there is a priest entitled sando; see Vol.I:275.

CHAPTER VI

1 In the Toraja language to double a word often weakens it or changes the original meaning.

2 The to parengnge' are also able to pinpoint a transgression.

3 Conversely, a slave may not use the eating or drinking vessels of his master.

4 Someone other than the medicine-man may also let a woman rotate on the sword.

5 The final rite has given its name to the feast as a whole.

6 The significance of the name Benevolent Mother Blossom is not altogether clear.

7 With the assistance of J. Tammu, Van der Veen has translated two maro-songs into Dutch, both with an introduction from his hand: "De Maro-zang van Ne' Nora'" and "De Maro-zang van Sangayu'" (Van der Veen 1979: 38-109 and 109-29).

8 This happens also to the burake tambolang at the time that he prepares for priesthood; he is then created anew by the gods.

9 The sequence of verses reproduced here in the text has been chosen for the sake of rendering the narrative in as clear and continuous fashion as possible; citations from the Toraja source should make it clear, however, a different sequence occurs in the original.

10 According to information from Van der Veen, at maro- and bua'-feasts men who have distinguished themselves in battle may wear a wreath made of padang-padang, a variety of grass with blades so sharp they are like

needles, and with small fruits which stick to the clothing like burs.

11   Since 1972 Christian Toraja have been forbidden by the church to attend
      maro- or bugi'-rituals.

12   The blood-wort leaves often serve as a "path"; see J. Kruyt's report of the
      maro-ritual to heal the sick (J. Kruyt 1921:177) during which the patient
      follows the "path" of blood-wort leaves. During the great bua'-ritual the
      tumbang on her way to the feast square walks on the leaves of these
      tabang thrown down before her. Tabang-leaves used for a pesung should
      perhaps be regarded as more than merely a receptacle for an offering, but
      as a kind of place marker for the gods or spirits as well.

13   Kebali'bi derives from bali'bi, to have a fin or fins. Eels and underworld
      monsters have these fins. This indicates that pools and rivers with their
      finny denizens belong to the underworld. The to kebali'bi, "creatures with
      a fin or fins", equivalent of the to kengkok, "creatures with a tail", are
      residents of the underworld (Vol.I:107).

14   Or: "to free oneself from the paddy bird"? in the sense of: "from a plague
      of paddy birds"?

15   Bakku' are often made from bamboo-strips interwoven with tarra'-leaves
      (tarra': Artocarpus Blumei).

CHAPTER VII

1   Bua' Sarungallo maintains that the offering meal on the lower level is placed
      there for the three gods Pong Tulakpadang, Pong Banggairante and Gaunti-
      kembong; the food on the upper floor of the pentingaran was meant for
      Puang Matua. See, too, Vol.I:272.

2   The manganta' can also be held some time after a transgression has been
      committed. It is then not a conversion ritual, but more of a thanksgiving.
      One gives thanks for prosperity enjoyed after paying for one's sins (by
      holding a previous ceremony). In its diversity of functions manganta' is
      comparable to merok.

3   In the merok-ritual, but not in this feast, these have the function of the
      mangrande londong. For the function of matua ulu, sipalakuan and mang-
      rande londong, see Vol.I:99-105.

4   As used here the title parengnge' can be differentiated from the traditional
      to parengnge'. The former was conferred on a district head by the Dutch
      colonial administrators. Colloquially such a district head was called kepala
      lompo, the big head, as distinct from kepala, village head (information from
      Van der Veen).

5   Poya-poya literally means that which looks like a noose. The sense of this
      usage here could be that the poya-poya ensnare the spirit (soul) of the
      former owner of the sawah and keep it at the rice field (a reference to the
      significance of the ancestors of the rice cult?).

6   The place of ancient blood-wort is where the parangka is situated; this
      is the stone set up in front of the house where a great bua'-feast is cel-
      ebrated. Here a sandal tree is planted, a blood-wort and a Cordyline (see
      Merok:102 and 149, the notes to verses B510 and B764 respectively).
      Tabang tua is used at times as an equivalent for parangka.

7   Ma'papa' merangna dao: the literal translation is "in the layer like honey on
      high". The phrase may also be translated: "in the layer on high like a
      yellow-gold bee". The verse is a description of Puang Matua enthroned in
      heaven.

8   Cf. Merok:36 verse B103 and the note which belongs to it.

9   The image entails a container brimful with palm wine in which bits of white
      sediment rise to the surface.

10   Dewata (deata) here means the sky that has been made divine.

11   The "scale with the favourable portent" refers to the scales on the feet of a
      fighting rooster, a portent which has to be observed.

CHAPTER VIII

1 An account of several funeral rites for Christians carried out in traditional style can be consulted in Nooy-Palm 1966-1972.

2 It would seem that when speaking of this (second) great death feast Van Wouden refers to the feasts connected with the second burial of the corpse.

3 In this context we should call attention to the special position of these people from Baruppu' who refer to themselves neither as Sa'dan nor as Toraja, but rather as To Baruppu'. The inhabitants of other districts in Tana Toraja, they designate as Toraa.

4 The burial prescribed for the burake tambolang and the to minaa sando, as explained in Chapter V, is not a ritual of the West.

5 A.C. Kruyt reports that for a dead person of note in addition to a chicken a pig was also slaughtered and hung up on the West side of the house until it decayed. It is unclear whether this pig is the same as Van der Veen's ma'karu'dusan or ma'puli. None of my Toraja informants mentioned the practice. It is possible that the practice has been discontinued because of the revolting stench the pig will have generated.

6 At times the "coffin" with the corpse is set on scaffolding erected to the South of the house. The moisture drained from the body accumulates in a bamboo (ma'borro') which is placed far from the house. With its contents the bamboo is later set down in the death chamber. The coffin here is not the same as the rapasan (see also Chapter X.1.2.).

7 When a puang dies, the fluid from his corpse is collected in the leafy sheath of a pinang tree.

8 Perhaps this explains the origin of the term ma'batang, "to make into a tree trunk", the name of one of the most significant rites observed during the death ritual; cf. Chapters IX.2.2. and X.7.

9 Nobele (1926:40) does not mention the "sitting" in fine raiments of deceased puang. In other respects he is rather exhaustive in his treatment of how the dead are cared for, reporting, for instance, how the faeces of a dead puang are cleared from the corpse through massage.

10 In Kesu' the to balu may eat the flesh of a coconut, bananas (which may not be boiled or fried), the raw kernels of young maize, sugar cane and fruits.

11 This should signify that the widow is considered to be guilty. Apparently among the Toraja, too, widows are seen as more culpable than widowers.

CHAPTER IX

1 One would expect this to take place to the West of the house.

2 According to Van der Veen, disilli' is the term for a death ritual observed for poor people (Woordenboek: v. silli').

3 The to balu also sleeps to the West of the deceased. Should the death ritual be of long duration, then the rules of "keeping watch by the dead" are not so strictly obeyed; the to balu then enjoys somewhat more freedom of action. He or she will seldom leave the house, however.

4 Van der Veen's information about this practice differs. He asserts this rite only occurs during the tallung bongi or even more elevated rituals and that people continue to eat no rice until on the third day of the ritual a pig is killed. Until then no rice may be kept inside or even near the house of mourning.

5 The rite is known as ma'karu'dusan. Prior to 1920 the pa'karu'dusan was not part of the three nights death ritual; in later years people had more buffaloes at their disposal.

6 The crowd consists for the most part of residents of the village where the death feast is being held. They are usually ex-slaves or belong to the group of the relatively needy. In the past the buffalo was hacked to pieces while still alive, but once Dutch Administration had been established this practice was forbidden. There are regions, however (Sangalla'), where the former practice is still observed during great death rituals.

7   He is the counterpart of the to ma'pemali but in contrast to this woman he
        is not obliged to stay in the immediate vicinity of the corpse.
8   This buffalo's head must be sent to the tongkonan of the sokkong bayu.
        The meat which remains after the death priest and his helper have received
        their share and the dead himself has been provided for, is divided among
        the other tongkonan in the village. The buffalo head "supports" the
        tallang, i.e. the tongkonan of the sokkong bayu; the adat-house is thus
        compared here to this variety of bamboo.

CHAPTER X
1   See Geertz 1970:81. Geertz borrows the core of his argument from Golden-
        weiser 1936.
2   Erecting the monolith on the rante was not reported as a separate rite in
        this ritual. My informant apparently forgot it. The huge stone is set on end
        shortly before the buffaloes are led to the rante to be slaughtered, pre-
        sumably one or two days.
3   The slaughtering of a dog was also reported as part of the preceding
        rituals. Van der Veen maintains that this dog accompanies the deceased to
        Puya and there chases off the cat who checks the dead person's possessions
        to see if anything has perhaps been pilfered (see Vol.I:218).
4   Mantunu (Kesu' and other districts) or pantunuan as people say in the
        puang-areas, derives from tunu or mantunu, the slaughter of animals on
        behalf of the dead. Some of the buffaloes slaughtered will have been the
        possessions of the deceased; family members and friends present the re-
        maining ones.
5   Sapu randanan: the highest of all, reaching up to the rim, unsurpassed.
6   Also called erong. In Sangalla', Mengkendek (Silanan), Taleon, Malimbong,
        Palesan, Rano and Buakayu a coffin is known as duni. The term issong is
        used in Tikala for the (temporary) coffin.
7   During the first phase of the death ritual which I attended in Tandung, the
        dirapa'i sapu randanan-ritual, the ma'bolong was the final rite of the first
        phase.
8   Ma'palangngan ba', to fasten the bodily remains to the ba'; ma'popengkalao
        do mai ba' = to let the bodily remains come down from the ba'. The names
        of these rites indicate that also during the second phase of the death ritual
        the corpse in its wrappings is fastened to the roof for a short period.
9   In the death chants (badong) which begin already before the deceased's
        soul is led out, the departure of the dead man's soul from his relatives is
        described, as well as the start of the soul's journey to the hereafter. These
        badong commence in the night following the ma'karudu'san, the "death" of
        the buffalo and of the deceased. This passage to Puya should therefore
        begin earlier than that which occurs after the dead man's soul has been led
        out of the village. Yet people do not appear to be so literal-minded.
10   Nanai = the place where; umpopengkalao = to let descend; pangngan = the
        offering of betel and pinang.
11   Sometimes a buffalo is killed. In that case a sandal-tree is also planted.
        Whether this tree comes to stand beside the tongkonan or the grave is
        unclear to me.
12   The origins of this meat are not clear: from the pemanala, or from the flesh
        that is left over?

[Notes 13-39 are by Van der Veen.]

13   Nanai umpopengkalao pangngan: "the place where one puts down the sirih-
        pinang" (literally: let descend). Nanai: place where, not a special gathering
        place; it is a relative locative. The barana' is the banian tree, Ficus
        benjamina.
14   Dipatayang lamba', literally: "will be elevated like a fig tree which sticks
        out above the other trees".
15   Lan kapuran pangngan, "at the sprinkling of the lime on the sirih-pinang"

has the meaning of "at the presentation of the sirih-pinang".

16 Pelambaran dibaolu, literally, "the taking up leaf by leaf of the sirih-leaves", i.e. at the presentation of the sirih-pinang.

17 To ma'rara tiku, literally, "folk who have blood from all around".

18 Lolosu kandaure, literally, "progeny, noble as the kandaure".

19 Bolu tang silenda ura'na, literally, "betel leaves whose veins do not miss each other", a special sort of betel leaf, for, as a rule, the veins do not touch.

20 The meaning of this strophe is that forefathers from all around are invited to enjoy the betel quid. "His enclosure", i.e. the enclosure of the buffalo stable. "Plucking the stringed instruments", i.e. making the invitation audible.

21 Ma'pakatua: to ensure firmly, to make a fixed, immutable promise, to make an assignment which is absolutely binding, which may neither be disregarded or forgotten.

22 Ma'pabanu' karurungan, literally, "to ensure in a powerful way, hard as the hard pith of the old trunk of a sugar palm".

23 Tetean tampo: "the walking on the sawah dikes", i.e. work in the sawah.

24 Pananda uai: dam in the irrigation drain.

25 The meaning of this strophe is that a tasty meal suits the delicious pork. Bonde' is the herbaceous cotton plant, Gossypium obtusifolium.

26 Lolosu: "small tip, shoot of beginning new leaves".

27 Batang kale, literally, "the bulk torso, the body in contrast to the soul", batang dikalemi, literally: "the bulk of your body", i.e. "yours", "on you".

28 Dete', literally, "climb" (e.g. a tree).

29 Tondon, literally, "edge, up to, close by". Lako tondon to batangmi, "up to the edge of your body", i.e. "as far as you".

30 Sulu': bolt. Sisulu' basse: "seal off mutually with a promise pledged under oath".

31 Pindan: porcelain dish or tray, metaphorically: "upright promise, sacral promise".

32 Lumokkon lalanna, literally: "they folded their path".

33 Urria, literally, "hold on the lap".

34 Tangke: branch, limbs, hand, foot.

35 Tikkondo': relax, become loose.

36 Matombe': to sink down because of weight, the lax drooping of a rope that is not taut. La'pa-la'pa: split bamboo rod which when shaken sounds like a rattle; it is set up on the sawah to chase away "rice thieves" (small birds); the rattle is put in motion by pulling on a long rope tied to the bamboo. The la'pa-la'pa is also used as a musical instrument during the manganda'-dance at the la'pa kasalle-celebration. In this context the la'pa-la'pa has undergone a transformation of meaning into "long rope".

37 Buntu rengnge': "heavy responsibility, high as a mountain". Rengnge': "to carry a load with a band worn around the forehead".

38 Patondon: "that which is as an abyss, abyssmal, that which is an extreme burden (sickness, cares)".

39 Sariri: "load which is carried with a band slung over one shoulder".

40 Van der Veen's Woordenboek: v. lao states that the belo tedong is worn during the ma'palao. None of my informants, however, listed this as a rite belonging to the dipalimang bongi. The ma'palao indisputably is part of the dipapitung bongi and of the dirapa'i, however. One gets the impression that in Sangalla' elements from a death feast of higher order have been introduced into this dipalimang bongi because the deceased belonged to the puang lineage. The ritual enacted was extremely reminiscent of the dipalimang lompo (ditombi padang) as described by Tandilangi' (1967:22-3).

41 Sailo' is the name of a song form consisting of two lines; the first line ends with the words le' sailo' le, the second begins with the word ole. Such a song form is employed at rituals for the dead as commemoration for the deceased (Woordenboek: v. sailo').

42   For this ma'badong, cf. Holt 1939:115 and The Chant:1-17 and 19-73.
43   For these relatives, see Vol.I:27.
44   For the simbuang kayu, see Vol.I:266.
45   As a rule the bala'kaan does not rest on sandal-trees.
46   Bulls and oxen are usually slaughtered during funeral rites; cows are
      rather exceptional.
47   Also spelled ma'aparando (see Wilcox 1949:87).
48   My Toraja informants said that it was prerequisite that the dead person
      have cucu tiga lapis (Indonesian, literally: "three layers of grand-
      children"). Wilcox asserts great grandchildren are sufficient.

CHAPTER XI

1   One informant told me Sa'pang died in tongkonan Langsa'; another well-in-
      formed source claims death occurred in tongkonan (Bangko) Tandung. My
      choice here has been to side with the second report.
2   Sa'pang's mother belonged to tongkonan To' Sendana (The Sandal-Tree), an
      important house, originally situated in the village of Tonga in the Tikunna
      Malenong, Kesu'. This tongkonan, however, together with tongkonan Salle-
      bayu, was moved later to the village of Ke'te' in Bonoran (see Vol.I:74ff.).
      The eminent status of To' Sendana can be deduced from the presence of
      both an a'riri posi' and an ampang bilik (Vol.I:240f.).
3   Informants from Nonongan told me the death priest beat a drum, keeping to
      the rhythm usual for rituals of the West (ma'tenten pungpung).
4   The Christian Party of Indonesia, one of the country's major parties.
5   The ma'katia had to be performed here because the organizers of Sa'pang's
      funeral had rejected the possibility of staging the ma'gellu', another dance
      often executed nowadays during death feasts. Their rejection of the ma'-
      gellu' was based on the grounds that, originally, the gellu' was exclusive to
      the maro, a ritual of the East.
6   Called to mariu in Bittuang, Balla and Pali.
7   No examples of these lamentations were recorded.
8   This textile originates from the region of the To Mangki; it is purely
      decorative, according to my information, with none of the sacral importance
      of maa'-cloths.
9   Money is never given in payment at a death ritual. Even those who helped
      to build guest accommodations for the feast, received simply rice, cigaret-
      tes, tobacco, betel and tuak in return. Work in connection with rice culti-
      vation is today usually paid for with cash so that the old system of an
      exchange of services remains intact solely in relation to funeral celebrations
      (cf. note 17). Even prior to World War II, however, female dancers re-
      ceived a sum of money for their performances - from guests! The amounts
      involved can be considerable.
10   Three of this total were not slaughtered: two were delivered alive as a form
      of taxation to the government; one was handed over to the group of badong
      performers.
11   Cloths are similarly displayed during the "conversion" ritual for a dead
      person (see Chapter VII.2.7.).
12   For the most important family members and guests, see section 1.4. below.
13   These family members were part of the "cognatic descent group" to which
      the deceased belonged. Members of the deceased's spouses' families also
      bring gifts with them to the funeral (see Vol.I:27-8).
14   The young people serving refreshments were relatives of the deceased for
      the most part, some more closely related than others. They belonged to the
      anak pare-pare nangka'-group.
15   This is a special name for this buffalo. Silang bua or siilang bua means "to
      rub against each other"; the name presumably alludes to buffalo and sugar-
      palm trunk, but the total significance remains not altogether clear. See
      further Woordenboek: v. ilang.
16   Instead of a sugar palm, the Arenga saccharifera may be used. In response

to my question why these palms were specified, I received the answer that they were a sign that the deceased came from a noble family. The same trees are used in the dipapitung bongi- and the dipalimang bongi-rituals, but not in death feasts of a lower order.

17 Thus they receive payment in cash!

18 These titles, however, are confusing. To silali' derives from lali', fly, and can be translated as "those who shoo away the flies" (symbolic, for at this point the corpse in its bale of cloth attracts few flies). Removal of maggots (to ma'peulli') and chasing away of flies are activities which take place in the sphere of the care for the (still impure) dead. This would confirm that the to ma'peulli' plays a role in the ritual. She then possibly is called to dilali', "she who shoos away the flies" in the metaphoric sense of "she whose shoulders are weighted down with care". Yet, who is she? The to dibulle tangnga? Then who is the to dipandanni bassi in the ritual, "she who is laid down like iron"? The to ma'pemali?

19 The cutting with one blow of the suke, small bamboo cylinders, used for offerings and in this case also for the baratu, the tax of 10 % imposed on the cock fights from which the deceased family meets part of the costs of the death ritual.

20 The name of the rite is somewhat confusing, for in Chapter X.4. ma'kayu is mentioned as one of the first rites. Ma'kayu and mekayu differ in significance as well.

21 Derived from mengkalao, "to go down".

22 They are inserted into the cylinders.

23 The arrangement varies in different districts.

24 The effigy is indeed the bombo dikita, the "visible soul of the dead". It is possible that the naturalism of this image among the Buginese has instilled in them the ineradicable belief that a dead Toraja "wanders" to his grave.

25 After slaughter during the mantunu, the heads of the other buffaloes tethered to various simbuang are distributed among the important tongkonan in the village; the following order of precedence is strictly observed: tongkonan of the sokkong bayu, tongkonan of the datu baine, etc. (information form Nonongan).

26 In point of fact the demand applies solely to Ne' Marini; the expression "group" relates to the expectation that children, if they are able, support their parents in delivery of requisitioned buffaloes.

27 This pertains to Lai' Koko and her children.

28 Elegies are also sung at Christian funerals but then, to be sure, their content is different.

29 This title originates from Nonongan. Like the to parengnge' in Kesu', these to bara' may bring a sacrifice.

30 Illness is always considered the consequence of the violation of a taboo.

31 Ne' Sara is the name of a well-known death priest from Nonongan, the place from which this badong comes. The "dried areca leaf" refers to the headdress of the death priest.

32 The rapasan.

33 The rains which fall during and shortly after the period usually reserved for death feasts are important for rice cultivation. According to Toraja belief, a notable who has died already has the power to let these rains fall, rains so important for the rice, shortly after his death. People wait to begin sowing rice and performing rice rituals until the deceased has been buried in the rock grave (or the ritual is interrupted by a pause). In a nearby village which, however, falls outside the bua'-circle to which the deceased belonged, cultivation of rice can begin prior to his burial.

[Notes 34-48 are by Van der Veen.]

34 Sitangnga silolok, literally "one by one, each who finds himself in the middle, each who finds himself on the top".

35 Malaa': long-jointed (of a bamboo). Pa'palumpun: that which is stowed away, preserved. Sangka': example, model, antecedent. Dipamangka salaga:

finished for all time, like a rake which is not used merely once but constantly serves again. A parallel expression is dipondok tengko: "which is
determined or fixed as a plough, which also is constantly put back into
use".

36   The parts of the slaughtered buffalo, nourishment for the deceased on his
      way South to the realm of the souls, are offered to the forefathers and set
      before them as a sacrifice to acquire a blessing from them.

37   Lambanan: place where one makes a crossing. Mendalelona: sway constantly,
      flutter without end; mendalelo, with the infix al, derives from mendelo;
      mendalelona-mendalelona: "that which sways constantly" is a parallel to
      engkokna, "tail" with the meaning of "the hindmost part", "the extremity
      of".

38   Lalanna sukaran aluk: "the way of the sacrificial ritual", i.e. the way along
      which the sacrificial ritual is passed down to us. Pantiran is a variant of
      patiran.

39   Anak nakombong diong lisunna pala', literally: "children whom he gave
      shape to in the centre of the palms of his hands by smelting"; the meaning
      is that the dead will hand down the sacrificial ritual to the children whom
      he procreated and that they will abide strictly by the ritual. Lisu: centre
      of anything which turns. Ma'tengko tiranduk, literally: to plough so that
      the plough is driven in. This expression signifies: "to try to earn his
      living". Bongsu: youngest child; poetic equivalent for anak, child. Natakko
      bumbungan: "he who let take shape", literally: whom he like milk let
      curdle. The significance is: whom he procreated. Diong se'ponna kanuku
      malotong is an equivalent of diong lisunna pala': "in the middle of the palms
      of his hands". "Straining with a yoke which pulls true" has the significance
      of "working with a team of buffaloes which pulls straight ahead so that the
      field produces a good harvest". Ma'ayoka: "ploughing with a yoke of buf-
      faloes".

40   Passangayokan: "as many times as a yoke", i.e. twice.

41   The triple sacrificial ritual was accorded by Tangdilino' in Morinding to
      each of his three descendants who established the adat regulations in the
      regions where they journeyed. These three were: Pasontik, who went to the
      East to the area stretching from the adat-community Pantilang (in Luwu') to
      the Sa'dan river; Tandililing who travelled West to the area extending from
      the territory of Banga to the territory of Baruppu'; and Pabane', who
      struck out North for the area that was "in between", Tangnga padang,
      "intermediate region", or Pata'na padang (literally: "The longitudinal beam
      of the land", "The longitudinal (section of) land"), skirting the rock
      complex Sarira (i.e. the area surrounding Mt. Sarira in Kesu' territory as
      far as Tikala). Tallulembangna, the territories under the administration of a
      puang, are omitted from mention. These had their own adat provisions, aluk
      Puang: adat regulations which are valid for the puang. Another explanation
      for the term triple ritual is possible: aluk to mate: ritual for the dead, aluk
      tau: sacrifice for the well-being of man, and aluk padang: agricultural
      ritual. Samma', an alternate form of samba': stake, boundary marker,
      boundary. Kadaang: strip, e.g. a long strip of cultivated land situated like
      a dike between two trenches; furrows from ploughing.

42   Nasakendek-kendekna and nasalangngan-langnganna, forms with repetition
      of words; the prefix sa and the suffix na are excessive forms with the
      meaning "ever more".

43   The sacrificial ritual of the West is the ritual for the dead and the ritual of
      offerings to the ancestors during which celebrants face the Southwest. The
      sacrificial ritual of the East is that of offerings to the gods; then cel-
      ebrants turn to the Northeast. Pollo'na, literally: the hindmost, viz. the
      lower reaches of a river, here the Sa'dan River, which flows South.
      Pollo'na and ulunna are elliptical expressions. The complete phrases are
      pollo'na uai, "the lower reaches of the water, the South" and ulunna uai,
      "the upper reaches of the water, the North". Comparable to pollo'na is the

expression engkokna padang, "the ends of the earth", literally: "the earth's tail", another way of indicating the South.

44 Paria, literally: "who holds on her lap", "who cuddles".

45 Ma'ti ditari', literally: the dry land, that is trimmed in order to give it a certain form. Pataranak, just as paria in verse 23, has the meaning of "who cuddles, who looks after".

46 The deceased is "He" in this verse; the grandchildren are his.

47 The phrase ma'kambuno lumu', "which has a sunshade of duck-weed" indicates a sawah with much water which produces a good yield.

48 Tutungan bia': "the kindling of the torch"; this expression has the metaphorical significance of bringing an expiatory offering to discharge whatever guilt may still remain from the act of incest committed in Rura; dispelling the cloud of this guilt hanging over Torajaland, the offering seeks health and benediction. Tutungan bia' can also have the general meaning: happiness and prosperity.

CHAPTER XII

1 This introductory text is based on a stencilled biography in English which was distributed to foreigners during the puang's funeral.

2 For Tamborolangi', see Vol.I:145-53.

3 The state, founded during the Den Pasar Conference (December 1946), dissolved by the Republic of Indonesia in 1950.

4 The text concerning this rite derives from the article written by Puang Paliwan Tandilangi', son of the late Puang Lasok Rinding, who appears to have inherited his father's special interest in adat-ceremonies (see Bingkisan 1968-69, nos. 2, 6, 7, 8, 9).

5 The picture presented is thus contradictory. Crystal's statement would seem to make better sense: the dying Puang Lasok Rinding from Sangalla' was taken by his family members on their knees to prevent his touching the ground (Crystal 1972:28-32).

6 The word sampung was unknown to Van der Veen, who translated the Toraja text.

7 No mention was made when or if a ceremony was held to consecrate the new house. These rites, to be sure, are rites of the East which must be held far from the scene of any death ritual.

8 In contrast to usual procedures at funerals in Kesu', during a death feast in Sangalla' no clothing is worn which is made from pineapple fibres.

9 Her position thus differs from that of a widow in Kesu' who sits facing the deceased; see Chapter XI.1.2.

10 Rimpisan: a device for clamping something tight; bia': torch. The relevance of these words to the rite itself is unclear to me. Nobele reports that the pig which is offered is killed by a kaunan (1926:44).

11 The part of the cloth that hung outside was decorated with coins, with old V.O.C.'s as well as gold pieces of recent mintage. Where the red cloth lay over the corpse, it had been covered by old, sacral fabrics, which had been stitched together.

12 The buffaloes differ in colour and markings. The one tied to the simbuang kalosi was a bonga.

13 Tananan basse: a group of people, usually from a single lineage, who are related to the puang in a way fixed by tradition. In the past a sacred oath (basse) was concluded between the puang and the tananan basse which has remained in effect until today. One such group, for example, is the Basse Maruang, a class of kaunan (see Vol.I:86).

14 From Tandilangi' 1968-69. Ma'pakatua, to use the pakatua, derives from the name of a plant, pakatua, which is used in the rite (Homalanthus populnea).

15 Poli': to sweep aside.

16 For the tandi rapasan, see also Vol.I:197.

17 This verse is difficult to translate.

18   See previous note.
19   The reference here is apparently to the establishment of adat-decrees
      governing the rituals of the living and the death ritual (Van der Veen).
20   Tandilangi' (1968-69) writes that these to ma'randing always come from the
      same area, from the region of Salu Tadongkon in Nonongan, thus outside
      Sangalla'. They belong to the class of ordinary people. This designation
      does not indicate whether the war dancers are kaunan or free farmers.
      Tandilangi' reports that the function passes from generation to generation,
      but omits mentioning whether leadership of the group is inherited as well.
21   A pig was slaughtered early in the morning before the tuang-tuang was
      mounted. This sacrifice should have taken place the preceding evening but
      it was then raining too hard. Meat from this pig was offered to the deata
      (not to the to matua); it was placed to the Southeast of the easternmost
      shed belonging to the tongkonan. The offering lay on two banana leaves in
      the middle of four stalks of a certain variety of reed that were knotted
      together (biang).
22   Nondo was the name given for their song and dance. In fact the ondo- or
      nondo-dance is performed at maro- and bugi'-feasts.
23   A badong chanted in traditional style.
24   Also called paladura or paradura in Sangalla'.
25   For slight variations in the sequence of different processions, see Tandi-
      langi' 1968-69.
26   Tandilangi' reports the following additional trees: simbuang Buangin,
      simbuang Induk, simbuang Kandinge'. The head of the buffalo tied to the
      simbuang kalosi goes to the leading tongkonan in Sangalla'.
27   Although the soul of the dead rides to Puya on a buffalo, some mortuary
      effigies are provided with a wooden horse. The tau-tau, moreover, reflect
      modernification. Even prior to World War II, the effigy of someone fond of
      automobiles was installed in a wooden car; the effigy of a dead teacher was
      placed on a school bench.
28   This contrasts with procedures reported in Nonongan: should the deceased
      be a man then the bier is followed by relatives who walk under a long,
      narrow cloth. The dead thus has them in tow.

CHAPTER XIV
1   Among the Sa'dan Toraja the word bali may have a number of meanings; see
      Blust 1980:222: a. companion, mate; b. partner, whenever two parties
      oppose each other, as in a cock fight; c. opponent; d. answer, oppose,
      resist; e. in to pabalian, assistant, helper; f. the slave who stands at the
      side of the to mebalun, the slave who stands at the side of the to minaa;
      g. sibali, become a pair, marry. The meaning varies from friend, helper, to
      opponent and adversary. At first this may seem to be self-contradictory.
      We should remember, however, that bali in the sense of foil, opponent,
      functions within the context of two rituals, East-West, in which a unity of
      opposites is inherent.
2   The death priest bears this title only during the time that he officiates
      during the death ritual.
3   Here we can notice a controversion: the datu baine who lives in the "lower"
      part of the village functions in something which is higher than the ground,
      i.e. in the house. The sokkong bayu leads prayers on the compound (a
      place lower than the house).
4   The anak dara and tumbang can be placed in opposition to the deceased and
      the to ma'pemali. The deceased, like the anak dara, is associated with the
      rice. The function of the to ma'pemali and of the other women in the death
      ritual who enfold the deceased with care is comparable to the function of
      the tumbang and her escorts who look after the anak dara and provide it
      with food. During a late stage of the bua'-ritual, the tumbang is carried
      out of the Eastern door of the tongkonan in an erect position, wrapped in
      sacral maa'-cloths. A deceased of eminence, covered with a sacral cloth, is

carried out of the Western side door of the death house.

5   The symbol of the buried chicken's egg gives pause for thought; see Chapter IX.1.1. No chick comes from the egg.

6   Nevertheless: conversion rituals also take place for "lower" dead, a fact which does not fit into the line of thought pursued in my comment. Perhaps the explanation for such observances is that these "conversions" are for safety's sake; people remain afraid of the souls of all dead which remain flitting about the compound until they have been "converted". Another possibility is that in the past the status of deata was accessible to all souls and only later as stratification became more elaborate and more rigid, developed into the special prerogative of the more eminent (cf. Vol.I: 123-4).

7   In a certain sense every dead person is dangerous until he has been ritually buried. This is true to a far greater degree, however, for someone who has fallen in battle or had his head cut off, as well as for a few other categories of dead. For the ritual for a dead man who has been killed in battle, see Merok 130-131.

BIBLIOGRAPHY

Abbreviations:
AdV   Alle den Volcke, Maandblad van de Gereformeerde Zendingsbond.
BKI   Bijdragen tot de Taal-, Land- en Volkenkunde van het Koninklijk
         Instituut voor Taal-, Land- en Volkenkunde
TBG   Tijdschrift voor Indische Taal-, Land- en Volkenkunde van het Bata-
         viaasch Genootschap van Kunsten en Wetenschappen. [Continued as
         Madjalah untuk Ilmu Bahasa, Ilmu Bumi dan Kebudajaan.]
TNAG   Tijdschrift van het Koninklijk Nederlandsch Aardrijkskundig Genoot-
         schap.

Abidin, Andi Zainal
1982   "The migration of the people of South Sulawesi in the Pacific region",
          The Indonesian Quarterly 10-2:63-94.
Andi Lolo, G.K.
1969   "Semba', olah raga adu kaki specifik Toraja", Bingkisan 3:76-101.
Baal, J. van
1981   Man's quest for partnership; The anthropological foundations of ethics
          and religion. Assen: Van Gorcum.
Belksma, J.
1922   "Lijkbezorging bij de Sa'dan-Toradja en Rante Pao, inzonderheid in het
          district Pangala'", AdV 16:42ff., 53ff., 64ff.
1923   "Een Zondagmorgen (een doodenfeest te Kande Api)", AdV 17:29ff.
1923-24   "Verbodsbepalingen bij de Toradja's", AdV 17:111ff., 125ff.; 1924:
          5ff., 15ff.
Belo, Jane
1960   Trance in Bali [with a preface by Margaret Mead]. New York.
Bigalke, Terence William
1981   A social history of "Tana Toraja", 1870-1965. Ann Arbor: University
          Microfilms International.
Blust, Robert
1980   "Notes on Proto-Malayo-Polynesian phratry dualism", BKI 136:215-48.
Bodrogi, Tibor
1970   "Beiträge zu den Bestattungsbräuchen der Sa'dang-Toradja (Zentral-
          Celebes)", Scientiarum Hungaricae 19:21-38.
Chabot, H.Th.
1950   Verwantschap, stand en sexe in Zuid-Celebes. Jakarta.
Crystal, Eric
1970   Toraja town. Berkeley: University of California, Department of Anthro-
          pology. [Dissertation.]
1972   "A death in the tribe", Orientations 7:28-32.
1974   "Cooking pot politics: a Toraja village study", Indonesia 18:118-52.
Crystal, Eric and Shinji Yamashita
1982   Power of the gods: ma'bugi' ritual in the Sa'dan Toraja. [Draft; paper
          presented as a contribution to the Conference on religions of
          Indonesia; Ohio University; unpublished.]

Geertz, Clifford
1970   Agricultural involution; The process of ecological change in Indonesia.
          Berkeley and Los Angelos. [1st ed. 1963.]
Gervaise, Nicolas
1688   Description historique du royaume de Macaçar. Paris/Regensburg/
          London.
Goldenweiser, A.
1936   "Loose ends of a theory in the individual pattern and involution in
          primitive society", in: R. Lowie (ed.), Essays in anthropology pre-
          sented to A.L. Kroeber, pp. 99-104. Berkeley: University of California
          Press.
Grubauer, A.
1923   Celebes; Ethnologische Streifzüge in Südost- und Zentral-Celebes.
          Hagen/Darmstadt.
Hekstra, G.
1970   Sociaal-ekonomische survey van West-Toradja; het gebied van de
          Geredja Toradja. Salatiga. [Stencilled report.]
Holt, Claire
1939   Dance quest in Celebes. Paris: Les Archives Internationales de la
          Danse.
Jannel, Claude and Frédéric Lontcho
[n.d.]   Laissez venir ceux qui pleurent; Fête pour un mort Toradja (Indo-
          nésie). Aix-en-Provence.
Kadang, K.
1960   Ukiran rumah Toradja. Jakarta.
Keers, W.
1939   "Over de verschillende vormen van het bijzetten der doden bij de
          Sa'dan-Toradjas", TNAG:207-13.
Kennedy, Raymond
1953   Field notes on Indonesia; South Celebes 1949-1950. New Haven: Human
          Relation Area Files.
Koubi, Jeannine
1975   "La première fête funeraire chez les Toradja Sa'dan", Archipel 10:
          105-21.
1979   "Le maladie, le mort et son 'double' visible en pays Toradja", in: Les
          hommes et la mort; Textes ressemblés et presentés par Jean Guiart le
          Sycamore, pp. 160-70. Museum National d'Histoire Naturelle. Objects et
          mondes.
1982   Rambu Solo', "La fumée descend"; La culte des morts chez les Toradja
          du Sud. Paris: Centre de Documentation et de Recherches sur l'Asie
          du Sud-est et le Monde Insulindien.
Kruyt, A.C.
1923-24   "De Toradja's van de Sa'dan, Masoepoe- en Mamasa-rivieren", TBG 63:
          81-175.
1935   "Het stamfeest op Midden-Celebes", TBG 75:550-604.
Kruyt, J.
1921   "De Boea' en eenige andere feesten der Toradja's van Rantepao en
          Makale", TBG 60:45-77; 161-87.
Lijf, J.M. van
1951-52   "Tana Toradja 1905-1950", Indonesië 5:352-75.
1952-53   "Tana Toradja 1905-1950: Technische voorzieningen en hun gevolgen",
          Indonesië 6:352-75.
Mangemba, H.D.
1956   Kenallah Sulawesi Selatan. Jakarta.
Matthes, B.F.
[n.d.]   Ethnographische atlas, bevattende afbeeldingen en voorwerpen uit het
          leven en de huishouding der Boeginezen.

Mattulada, C.H.M. Nooy-Palm et al.
1980   Torajan migrants in Ujung Pandang. Occasional Paper of the Tropen-
            instituut Amsterdam.
Meyer, Pamela and Alfred
1972   "Life and death in Toradja", National Geographic 141-6:703-815.
Mills, R.F.
1075   "The reconstruction of Proto-South-Sulawesi", Archipel 10:205-25.
Nobele, E.A.J.
1926   "Memorie van Overgave betreffende de Onderafdeeling Makale", TBG
            60:1-144.
Nooy-Palm, C.H.M.
1966-72   Enige Christelijke dodenrituelen. [Unpublished.]
1969   "Dress and adornment of the Sa'dan-Toradja", in: Tropical man [Year-
            book of the Anthropological Department of the Royal Tropical
            Institute], pp. 162-94. Leiden: Brill.
1975a   "Introduction to the Sa'dan Toraja people and their country", Archipel
            10:53-92.
1975b   De karbouw en de kandaure. Delft: Ethnografisch Museum Nusantara.
1978   "Bibliography; survey of studies on the anthropology of Tana Toraja,
            Sulawesi", Archipel 15:163-92.
1979   "The role of sacred cloths in the mythology and ritual of the Sa'dan-
            Toraja of Sulawesi, Indonesia", in: Indonesian Textiles, pp. 81-96.
            Washington: The Textile Museum.
1980   "Man en vrouw in de rituelen van de Sa'dan-Toraja", in: R. Schefold
            a.o. (eds.), Man, meaning and history; Essays in the honour of H.G.
            Schulte Nordholt, pp. 140-78. The Hague: Nijhoff, VKI 89.
Nooy-Palm, C.H.M. and R. Schefold
[forthcoming]   Colour and anti-colour in the death ritual of the Toraja.
Pakan, L.
1973   Rahasia Ukiran Toradja; The secret of typical Toraja's patterns.
Pronk, L.
1935   Memorie van Overgave van de onderafdeling Palopo. [Stencilled
            report.]
Ruijter, A. de
1977   Claude Lévi-Strauss: een systeemanalyse van zijn antroplogische werk.
            Utrecht, ICAU Mededelingen 11.
Salombe', C.
1972   Orang Toraja dengan Ritusnya: in memoriam So' Rinding Puang Sangal-
            la'. Ujung Pandang.
1977   "Pengertian dan perkembangan siriq dalam seminar tentang masalah siri
            di Sulawesi Selatan", Bingkisan I-2:75-100.
Schmitz, Carl
1964   "Grundformen der Verwandschaft", Basler Beiträge zur Geographie und
            Ethnologie, Ethnologische Reihe 1:39-56.
Stöhr, W.   ·
1965   "Die Religionen der Altvölker Indonesiens und der Philippinen", in:
            Die Religionen Indonesiens, pp. 1-208. Stuttgart, Berlin, Köln, Mainz:
            Kohlhammer.
Tandilangi', Puang Paliwan
1967   "Datu Laukku' dan Pong Mula Tau", Bingkisan I-21:21-37.
1968   "Tananan basse", Bingkisan I-6:33-5.
1969   "Rapasan doan", Bingkisan II-6:2-16.
Tangdilintin, Paulus
1981   "Padang bombo', the heaven of the Torajanese", Indonesia Magazine
            Nov.-Dec.:43-49.
Veen, H. van der
1924   "Aanteekeningen van Dr. H. van der Veen over blaasroer, schild en
            pijl en boog bij de Sa'dan- en Binoeang-Toradja's", TBG 63:368-73.

1929a   "Een wichel-litanie der Sa'dan-Toradja's", in: Feestbundel Koninklijk
           Bataviaasch Genootschap van Kunsten en Wetenschappen II. Batavia.
1929b   "Nota betreffende de grenzen van de Sa'danse taalgroep en het haar
           aanverwante taalgebied", TBG 69:50-97.
1940   Tae' (Zuid-Toradjasch) - Nederlandsch woordenboek. Den Haag:
           Nijhoff.
1950   "De samenspraak der beide priesters, de woordvoerders van bruid en
           bruidegom bij de huwelijksplechtigheid der Sa'dan-Toradja's", Bing-
           kisan Budi: 291-306.
1965   The Merok feast of the Sa'dan-Toradja. The Hague: Nijhoff, VKI 45.
1966   The Sa'dan-Toradja chant for the deceased. The Hague: Nijhoff, VKI
           49.
1976   "Ossoran Tempon Daomai Rangi' (naosso' Ne' Mani', to minaa daomai
           Sereale); (Overleveringen van den beginne vanuit de Hemel, in gere-
           gelde volgorde meegedeeld door Ne' Mani', priester uit Sereale)", BKI
           132:418-39.
1979   Overleveringen en zangen der Zuid-Toradja's. The Hague: Nijhoff, VKI
           85.
[Unpublished a]   Ma'biangi, part of which is the Pangimbo likaran biang.
[Unpublished b]   Pangimbo Manuk, The Prayer over the Hen Sacrifice (KITLV
           Or.515 no.83).
[Unpublished c]   Ethnografie Sa'dan-Toradjas. 354 blz. (KITLV Or.515 no.17a).
[Unpublished d]   Ossoran nene' lan lino (KITLV Or.515 no.84).
Volkman, Toby
1979a   "The riches of the undertaker", Indonesia 28:1-28.
1979b   "The arts of dying in Sulawesi", Asia July-August:24-30.
Wilcox, Harry
1949   White stranger. London.
Wulfften Palthe, P.M. van
1940   "Over trance", Geneeskundig Tijdschrift voor Ned.-Indië 36-80:
           2123-53.
Yacobs, Yan
1971   Data-data perekonomian sosial, wilayah BRI, Tjabang Makale. Makale:
           Bank Rakyat Indonesia. [Stencilled report.]
Zerner, Charles
1981   "Signs of the spirits, signature of the smith: iron forging in Tana
           Toraja", Indonesia 31:89-112.

GLOSSARY AND INDEX

aa'	slope 87
aa' uma	a small sawah nestling against the mountain side 87
aak	a slab of meat which clings to the spine joint above the hip joints, midrif 45
ada'	the complex of habits and customs, customary law see adat
a'da'	a kind of grass 100
adat	customary law (Indonesian) 164, 216, 275, 283, 288, 302, 321
adat-chief	the head of an adat-community 27, 63, 71, 154, 171, 236, 276, 287, 313, 314, 316
adat-community	139, 140, 142
adat-decrees, adat-usage, adat-performances 10, 174, 276-7, 280, Ch.XII note 19
adat-functionary	27
adat-head	see adat-chief
adat-house	Ch.IX note 8
ala-ala	cockpit 241
alang	ricebarn 100, 217, 251-3, 279, 327
allo datuna	"the day of the lord", a rite in death ritual 212
allona	the high-day of a ritual 64, 159-60
allona kaperaukan	a high-day of merok 64, 68, 71-6
aluk	ritual, sometimes used in the sense of adat-precepts or adat-regulations 34, 173, 179, 224, 321, Ch.II note 14; see also sukaran aluk
aluk matampu'	see aluk rampe matampu'
aluk padang	the ritual (or the adat and ceremonies) connected with arable land (ricefields)
aluk pembalikan	see pembalikan
aluk pia	"the child ritual", the first part of an important death ritual 225-43, 250, 280, 290, 327
aluk rampe matallo	"the Ritual(s) of the East", the rituals for the living 3
aluk rampe matampu'	"the Ritual(s) of the West, comprising rituals connected with death 3, 124
aluk susu	death ritual observed by the mother's side of the deceased's family 224, 238
Aluk to Dolo	"The Belief of the Forefathers", "The Faith of the Old", the autochthonous religion of the Toraja 304
ambe' bugi'	"the father of the bugi'"-ritual, an important function-ary in the bugi'-ritual 142
ambe' tondok	members of the village 257
ampang bilik	"the threshold of the house (or of the room)", a decor-ated plank functioning in the bua'-ritual, which is placed in a tongkonan of status after the ritual is finished 27-9, 31, 42, Ch.II note 24, Ch.XI note 2
ampiri	the pseudo-sugar palm 16, 36, 284, 286; see also lambiri

ampu bua'	"the Host of the bua'-feast" 11, 13, 16-9, 21-2, 42, 45, 47
ampu padang	"the Lords of the Earth", earth spirits 15, 19, 22, 92, 244-5
anak	child Ch.XI note 39
anak dara	1. virgin, sister, a name used for the principal functionary in the bua'-ritual 12, 16, 22, 24-5, 28, 32, 35-6, 47
	2. a fetish in the bua'-ritual 12, 24, 33, 37-8, 40, 46-7, 129, 322, 326, Ch.II notes 28 and 39, Ch. XIV note 4
anak disarak	foster child 225, 259
anak pare-pare nangka'	a category of nobility, people of rank 85, 95, 126, 134, 142, 224
anak passarak	see anak disarak
anak patalo	a category of nobility, people of rank (Kesu') 6, 30, 85
anak sangtepo	a child who inherits one fourth of the inheritance 259
andoa'	yam, Dioscorea alata L. 86, 238
angat	hot (Indonesian) 129
anta'	to accompany 187
antolong	a tree used for the burial of a baby 183, photo p.192
ao'	bamboo-ao' or bamboo-aur (Indonesian), a bamboo variety, Dendrocalamus strictus 18, 22, 29, 31, photo p.51, 104-5
a'riri posi'	the central pillar under the house of a tongkonan of importance 25, 26 (Fig.1), 71, Ch.XI note 2
Arrang diBatu	"The Radiance in the Stone", the spouse of Puang Matua 114, Ch.V note 4
ayoka	the yoke of a plough 87 (Fig.6), 88
ba'(teng)	a beam running parallel to the ridge beam about halfway between the floor and the roof 199, 243, Ch.X note 8
ba'ba	door 199
ba'ba sade	a door in the Western wall of a house used in mortuary rites 246
babo bo'bo'	the conversion ritual for dikaletekan tallu manuk-ritual 153
babu'	a headhunter's jacket 313 (Fig.51), 314 (Fig.52), 315
badong	death song(s) 7, 178, 196, 210, 212, 217, 230, 231 (Fig.35), 243, 248, 262-5, 281-2, 286, Ch.I note 1, Ch.X note 9, Ch.XII note 23
badong-dancers	230 (Fig.34), 231 (Fig.35), photo p.271, 302
badong diossomo	a special kind of badong 262
badong to dolo	"the badong of the old", a special type of death song 231, 282, 297
badong to songlo'	the badong sung when the deceased is carried to the rante 262
bai a'pa'	"four pigs", a low order of death ritual 5, 7, 153, 184, 186
bai to balu	the pig of the widow (widower) 286
bai tungga'	see dibai tungga
baine	woman 36
baisen	mutual parents-in-law 113
baka bua	large baskets woven out of rattan 117
bakku'	a basket 36, 142, Ch.VI note 15
bala'kaan	the scaffolding which serves for the distribution of meat by the to minaa during a ritual for the dead 103, 116,

Buntao'	a region, a patang penanian (= four bua'-circles) 40, 64, 68, 72-3, 74 (Fig.5), 75, photos pp.77-82, 99, 171, 175, 257, Ch.III note 13
buntu	hill 125
bunu'	strips of bamboo 85
bupati	(Indonesian) regent 173
burake	see to burake
camat	district head 158, 226, 257
cendana	(Indonesian; Toraja: sendana) a sandalwood tree (Santana album) 8, 17-8, 26, 39, 48, 65, 67, 69, 72-3, 74 (Fig.5), 76, 322
Cordyline terminalis	see tabang
cucu tiga lapis	(Indonesian) "three layers of grandchildren", great grandchildren Ch.X note 48
daha	(Balinese) virgins in a Bali aga community 28
dalle	maize 212
danga-danga	a kind of gladiolus 159
dapo	kitchen 288
darinding	a plant used in religious ceremonies 100, 156
datu	lord, prince 25, 85
datu baine	"the female lord", a functionary in Kesu' and elsewhere 27, 97, 157, 324, Ch.XIV note 3
datu bua'	a functionary in the bua'-ritual 38
Datu Maruru'	"The Righteous Lord", a spirit 139-41
Datu Matallo	"The Prince of the East", the Datu of Luwu' 101
Datu Mengkamma	the first rice priest in heaven 63, 84, Ch.IV note 1
datu muane	1. deity 328
	2. "the male lord" see sokkong bayu
Datu of Luwu'	300
daun bolu	sirih-leaves 73
daun pusuk	see pusuk
daun tabang	see tabang
deata	god(s), goddess(es), spirit(s), ancestors of the East 3, 18-20, 22, 25, 33, 38, 40, 50, 65, 75, 95, 100, 122, 124, 126, 128, 131, 134, 136-7, 141-3, 152-3, 156, 178, 243-6, 295-6, 315, 326, 328, Ch.VII note 10, Ch.XII note 21, Ch.XIV note 6
deata-feast	feast in honour of the deata, deata ritual 17, 49, 69, photo p.55, 126, 138, 142-4
dibai a'pa'	see bai a'pa'
dibai tungga'	"he - or she - is treated in keeping with the ritual of a solitary pig", a simple death ritual 5, 153, 184
diba'gi	to consign 261
dibarira	see diremba'i
diba'rui bua'	the renewal of the bua'-ritual 42
didedekan pangkung bai	a low death ritual 153, 183-4
didodoi pusuk	to decorate with the young leaves of the sugar palm 25
dikaletekan tallu manuk	the death ritual for still-born infants 153, 183
dikaroan dapo	name of the pig sacrified at ma'bolong 288
dikiki'	small pieces of meat offered to the ancestors 25, 215
diongan (diongna)	low 85
dipalimang bongi	"that what happens during five nights", a death ritual of a higher order 5, 62, 117, 154, 194, 216, Ch.X note 40, Ch.XI note 16
dipalundan	to lay out 17
dipalundan sendana	"to lay out the sandalwood tree", a rite in the bua'-ritual 17

dipalundan to tumbang	"to lay out the tumbang", a rite in the bua'-ritual 17
dipamate	a special way of cutting a bamboo joint 296 (Fig.50)
dipantunuan pia	see ma'batang
dipa'pea	to send, to dispatch 202
dipapitung bongi	"that what happens during seven nights", a death ritual of high order 5-6, 117, 154, 172, 196, 289, Ch.XI note 16
dipasang bongi	"that what happens in one night", a death ritual of low order 5, 7, 153, 172, 186
dipatallung bongi	"that what happens during three nights", a simple death ritual 5-6, 62, 117, 172, 186, 195, Ch.IX note 4
dipatuo	a special way of cutting a bamboo-joint 296 (Fig.50)
dipeantolong	to deposite the dead body of a baby in a tree 183
dipiong	food cooked in a bamboo-joint, used as an offering 15
dipodoi to' laang	an offering for the laang-laang, a rite in the bua'-ritual 40
dirapa'i	a death ritual of the highest order 5-7, 35, 62, 101, 103, 134, 158, 171-2, 196, 198, 203, 224-5, 231, 233, 237-8, 242, 246, 255, photo p.272, 292, 326
dirapa'i dilayu-layu	"the dirapa'i that brings out wilting or fading", the lowest order of dirapa'i 5-6, 154, 198, 231
diremba'i	a rite in death ritual 175, 184
disanga anak	adopted child 258
disilli'	a low death ritual 153, 183-4, Ch.IX note 2
disilli' bai	see dipeantolong
disissik	a special way of folding a head cloth 103, 225
disuru'	see ma'suru'
doan	high 84
dodo	sarong 214 (Fig.30)
doke	spear 73, 235, 236 (Fig.38)
dolong-dolong	a wooden vessel 36
dongka	a Colocasia species 98
doti	a cross 245
doti langi'	"spots of heaven", a motif 235, 249 (Fig.42), photo p.273
dua'	see andoa'
duba-duba	a shelter covered by sacral cloths 235, 236 (Fig.38)
dulang	a dish or plate on a (high) pedestal 50, 97-8, 157 (Fig.20), 158, 188, 98
duni	the name of an old coffin in Sangalla'; see erong, issong and rapasan
Duri	a district 319-20
engkok(na)	tail Ch.XI note 37
engkok(na) padang	"tail (end) of the land" Ch.XI note 41
eran to tumbang	the staircase of the tumbang 118
erong	see issong
Flores	93
galla'	a small platform of woven bamboo 29, 104
galung	a wet ricefield 86
gandang	drum 67, 75, 186
garatung	clapper drum photo p.54, Ch.II note 1
garentong	pieces of bamboo and scraps of tin, joined to a rope, to scare away birds 90
Garuda	a mythical bird 287
Gauntikembong	"Self-expanding Cloud", a god of the upperworld 143
gayang	kris 31, 210, 217

gelong   a song sung at the maro-ritual, invoking trance   36,
                              Ch.II note 12
gelong bate   a maro-song   134
gellu'(-dancers)   a dance, performed at the maro-ritual   126, 128, 136,
                              140, photo p.149, 282, Ch.XI note 5
gorang   an elevated platform used in the bua'-feast   12-3,
                              19-20, 22, 28-9, 42, 44, 47-9, 48 (Fig.4), photos
                              pp.51-2, photo p.54, photos pp.58-61, 140, 322
gorang bulaan   "the golden gorang", the platform used for the division
                              of meat and other ceremonies in the burials of the
                              Eastern sphere   116, 118, Ch.II note 24
gusian   a fishpond in the ricefields   91

ijambe   a death ritual of the Maanyan-Siung   171
ikko'na   the part of the pig which after slaughter is returned to
                              the owner   158
inan rari'   "the place (holder) of the rope"   88 (Fig.7)
indo' bugi'   "the mother of the bugi'", a functionary in bugi'-ritual
                              142
indo' mangrakan   "the rice mother"   85, 98-9
Indo' Belo Tumbang   "Mother who dances (hops) beautiful", the patroness of
                              the medicine used in maro-ritual   122, 127
Indo' Pare-pare   "Mother of the Small Rice", a deity   34, Ch.II note 37
Indo' Samadenna   "Mother of Everything in Hand", a deity   329
induk   sugar palm (Arenga saccharifera)   36, 250
ipo-tree   Antiaris toxicaria Lesch., a tree used for making poison
                              327
isi salaga   "the teeth of the harrow"   88 (Fig.7)
issong   coffin in the shape of a rice mortar   215, 215 (Fig.31),
                              231, photo p.273, 289, Ch.X note 6; see also duni and
                              rapasan

jambu   (Indonesian) Eugenia malaccensis   113
juru tulis   (Indonesian) a clerk in the village head's office   158

kain Sekomandi   an ikat-cloth woven by the northern Toraja   230, Ch.XI
                              note 8
kala'paran   see rante kala'paran
kaledo   packet of folded banana leaf containing sticky rice   20,
                              22, 76, 93, 94 (Fig.11), 95, 105
Kalimantan   314
kaloko'   a kind of cuckoo   84
kalosi   an areca-tree or areca-nut   40, 236, 250, 284, 286
kamban-kamban   a creeper   24, 36
kamboti   a plaited bag   104
kambuno   Livistona rotundifolia   159
Kambuno Langi'   "The Sunshade of Heaven", the first to minaa in myth
                              127, 328
kamiri'   candle-nut tree, Aleurites moluccana   195
kampa banaa   the guardian of the banaa, a functionary in the bua'-
                              ritual   17, 38, 42
kampung   (Indonesian) village   158
kandaure   an ornament fashioned from beads   75, photo p.85, 188
                              (Fig.21), 210-1, 214, 217, photo p.219, 234, 235
                              (Fig.37), 247, 285, 298-9, 302, photo p.305, Ch.X note
                              18
kandean   plate   212
kandean lau   a dish from half a gourd   85, 141, 144
kandeatan   possessed ("eaten") by spirits   132-3

kaniala'	a kapok tree 195, 244
kapa'	the penalty or fine which has to be paid when one of the marriage partners commits adultery 116
ka'panan balang	see mantaa' bati'
kapipe	a plaited bag 111, 183
kapuangan	puang-ship 275
kara-motif	a motif representing discs cut out from shell 315
karerang	basket 295 (Fig.49)
karidi'	twined rope 315
karu'dusan	see pa'karu'dusan
karurung	a chicken whose light brown feathers, which has black speckles 69
kasalle	great 10
kaseda	a very long cloth, red or white, used in rituals 103
kasongloran ma'mulle	the descent to the feast terrain in sedan chairs in the bua'-ritual 44
kasongloran tama kala'paran	the descent in procession to the place of the feast 45
kassok	cylinders 246
katik	a woodcarving representing a bird with a long neck 43, photo p.56, photo p.58, 317, Ch.IV note 13
katupa'	steamed rice wrapped in a packet of the braided strips of young sugar palm leaves 94 (Fig.11)
kaunan	the unfree, the slaves 6, 113, 141, 158, 240, 278-9, 296, 317, 325, Ch.XII notes 10 and 20
kaunan garonto'	hereditary slaves 240, 324
kaunan tai manuk	"chicken shit slaves", a low order of unfree 279
kayu ampiri	see ampiri
kayu buangin	see buangin
kayu kamban	see kamban
kayu kole	see kole
kayu mate	see antolong
kayu nanna-nanna	see nanna-nanna
kebali'bi	ghosts of the underworld Ch.VI note 13
kecamatan	a modern administrative unit Ch.III note 25
kepala desa	(Indonesian) village head 158, 225, Ch.VII note 4
kepala lembang	(Indonesian) head of a district 48, 75
kepala lompo	"big head", the district's head Ch.VII note 48
Kesu'	a territory, a federation 5-7, 11-2, 14, 16, 20, 23-4, 26-8, 32-3, 35, 40, 42, 47, 62-4, 66, 69, 71-3, 89-90, 92-5, 98, 100, 102-3, photos pp.106-8, 115, 126, 133, 137, 140, 157-8, 171-3, 175, 177-8, 183, 187, photo p.192, 198, 201, 212, 216, 218, 224, 232, 236 (Fig.38), 249 (Fig.42), 252 (Fig.44), 255, 257, 262, 278, 281, 287, 289-90, 298, 312-3, 317, 326, Ch.II notes 5 and 28, Ch.III notes 12, 16 and 24, Ch.IV notes 7 and 15, Ch.VIII note 10, Ch.X note 4, Ch. XI notes 2, 29 and 41, Ch.XII notes 8 and 9
kinallona pesungan banne	three heads of rice, standing at the pesungan banne 86, 100
kole	a tree which yields excellent timber, used for the anak-dara fetish 36
kollong	the ring of flesh around the neck 18, 25, 45, 48
kollong arae	a chicken with a prominent comb 69
komba	a gold bracelet 176, 208-9
kris	a weapon 28-9, 31, 50, 123, 126, 176, photo p.181, 210, 217, 227, 234, 247-8, 269, 283, 297-8, 302, photo p.308
kuda kepang	(Indonesian) hobby horses 233

kumande	repeal of the prohibition against eating rice for those observing strict mourning rites 185, 195, 212
kumande bunga'	the first of the kumande-rites 190, 201-2, 250-1
kumande tampak	the last of the kumande-rites 190, 201-2, 251
kumande tangnga'	the middle of the kumande-rites 109, 201, 251
kurin	an earthenware crock 36, 241
kurrik	1. scratching or scraping 88
	2. a small harrow 88
laa	a platform on the gorang 44
laang-laang	a bench used in the bua'-ceremony 18, 20, 39 (Fig.3), 39-40
la'bo'	a machete, a cleaver 36, 62, 88, 229, 238, 315
la'bo' penai (la'bo' to dolo) an old, sacral sword photo p.56, 128, 238	
lakkean (lakke-lakkean, lakkian) a tower on the rante containing the remains of the deceased 174, 200-1, photo p.222, 247-8, 250-1, 291 (Fig.48), 299-302	
lali'	fly Ch.XI note 18
lambiri	see ampiri
lampa	a large bamboo joint, a bamboo used for carrying water 36
langi'	heaven 131
langko'	a basket of woven bamboo 116
langngan	a "spit", a construction of wood or bamboo used for roasting meat and cooking food, an object used both in rituals of the East and West photo p.32, 40-1, 45, photo p.53, 72, 75 (Fig.5), photo p.80, 104, photo p.182, 239, 281, 295 (Fig.49)
langngan buntu	"the climbing of a hill" in order to make a sacrifice on top 25; see also melondong datu
lansa'	Lansium domesticum 327
lantang	a shed, an accommodation for guests 226, 244, 252-3, 252 (Fig.44), 257-8
lantang bunu'	a shed in the rice ritual 85, 98-9, 158, 160
lantang pangngan	"guest house for sirih-pinang", a construction functioning in death ritual photo p.193
lantang pare	a shed for the ripe rice 100
lao'	see ma'palao
la'pa'	to loosen 10
la'pa' banua, la'pa' kasalle see bua' kasalle	
la'pa' bugi'	the final rites of the bugi'-ritual 142
la'pa' gandang	"letting go of the drum", a concluding rite of the death ritual 213
la'pa' dena	"the freeing of the paddy bird", the final rite of the bugi'-ritual 141
la'pa-la'pa	rattles of bamboo 90, Ch.II note 33, Ch.X note 36
Laso' (Lasok)	prefix of a boy's name 112
lau	a dish from a calabash 73
lau'	see lao'
layu	wilting 198
layuk	principal, see tongkonan layuk
lembang	1. a wooden sled 89
	2. a proa 89
	3. a district 32, photo pp.51-7, Ch.III note 25
lemun padang	a rite 102
lette undi	hind leg Ch.II note 43
lettoan	a litter for pigs 284
liang pia	a rock grave for a child photo p.192
likaran biang	see manglika biang

mangaluk — invocation of the deata by the to burake 18, 20

manganda' — a dance; the dancers wear the heavy headgear of real buffalo horns, sacral cloths and coins 31, 43, 118, 120

manganta' — "to accompany", the name of a conversion ritual 6, 24-5, photo p.83, 102, 133, 153-8, 187, 198, 213, Ch.II note 21, Ch.III notes 6, 8 and 26, Ch.VIII note 2

mangaro — to lift the corpse out of the rapasan 200, 245

mangarra'i pemali — see mantanan pemali

mangaru — a war cry 31, 103

mangaung — headhunting 312-8

mangeka — see ma'nene'

mangimbo — to say a prayer 8, 43, 102-3, 143, 160

mangimbo sisarak — a prayer in the ma'nene' 204

mangkaro bubun — "the cleansing of the well", a rite Ch.II note 20, Ch.III note 10

mangkaro kalo' — "the cleansing of the ditch", a rite 93

mangke'te bambalu — "cutting off the bambalu-liana", a rite 25

manglassak tau-tau — the mortuary effigy is given sexual parts 200, 246

manglelleng anak dara — the cutting down of the banana tree and the bamboo necessary to make the anak dara, a rite 24

manglelleng bunu — to cut down the bunu 97

manglelleng sarigan — the hewing of the wood for the bier, a rite in death ritual 196, 200

manglelleng sendana — cutting down the sandalwood tree, a rite in bua'-ritual 25

manglelleng sendana pa'tangdo' a rite in bua'-ritual 39

manglelleng tallang — the hewing of the bamboo tallang for the bate, a rite in maro-ritual 35

manglelleng tau-tau — the hewing of the wood for the tau-tau, a rite in death ritual 200, 244

manglese roa (manglese roaya) treading on glowing coals, a rite in the bua'-ritual 39

manglika' biang (likaran biang) an offering of intertwined biang-reeds, a rite in several Eastern rituals 7, 24, 26, 66, 74 (Fig.5), 112, 153, 155 (Fig.18), Ch.III notes 8 and 17

manglika' bua' — a rite of the bua'-ritual 38, 45, Ch.II note 41

manglossokan — "freeing oneself of the death ritual", a rite 200

manglullu' — the treading process of releasing grains for sowing the rice 91, 94, photo p.106

mangnganan barodo — a rite in rice ritual 85

mangrakan — to harvest the first bunches of rice 98, 158

mangrambu bulisak — to blacken the wood chips with smoke 200, 246

mangrambu langi' — "covering the heavens with smoke", an expiatory offering 16, 24, 33, 70, 321, Ch.III notes 8 and 9

mangrapu — see mangrimpung

mangrara banua — "to cover the house with blood", a ritual organized by the members of the ramage when the tongkonan has been renewed 24

mangrara kombong — "the covering of the sugar palms of the tongkonan with blood", a rite 6, Ch.III note 10

mangrara pare — "to cover the ripe rice with blood", a conversion ritual 5, 66, 98, 158-9, 161, 204, 327, Ch.III note 11

mangremba' — "to chase away", a rite in death ritual 175

mangrenden bua' — "the pulling (or the pulling onwards) of the bua'-feast", a rite 38

mangrera — feeding the dead 200, 246

mangria barang — see to mangria barang

mangrimpung (mangrapu) assembly of the ramage 23, 66, 123, Ch.III notes 8 and 10

mangrinding   "the erection of a wall", a custom in death ritual 262
mangriu batu   hauling the monolith 244
mangrompo tondok   "to enclose the village", a rite in rice ritual 100
mangrondon   to unwrap the corpse and wrap it again 282, 292
mangrondon bota   letting grains of rice fall down, a funeral rite 185,
                           190, 195, 197, 202
manik ata   a necklace of golden or gilded beads, alternating with
                           beads of red coral 26, 38, photo p.58, 91, 136, photo
                           p.181
manik riri   a yellow bead 19
manik tedong   "the beads of the buffalo", a neck ornament of a bull
                           which will be slaughtered in a death ritual 209-10, 209
                           (Fig.25)
manimbong   a song in Eastern rituals 20-1, 39, 116, 118, 120
mantaa' bati   the division of the sacrificial meat among the descend-
                           ants, a litany 101, 265-70
mantaa' tuo   the division of meat among the living 250
mantanan lolo   the burying of the umbilical cord 42
mantanan pemali   the taboo in the plants, a rite in rice ritual 95, Ch.IV
                           note 11
mantunu   the killing of the buffaloes on the rante for the de-
                           ceased 185-6, 195-6, 201, 212, 216, 250, Ch.X note 4,
                           Ch.XI note 25
mantunu parepe'   the slaughter of the parepe'-buffalo 251
manuk   chicken 70, 153
Manuk na Tulangdidi'   the Rooster of Tulangdidi', a constellation 63, 329-31
manuk rame   see rame
ma'nunu   a rite of the mangrara pare-ritual 159, 166
Manurun diLangi'   an ancestor descending from heaven 15, 19, 22
ma'ondo   a dance in maro-ritual 123, 126, 138, 144, 297
ma'padoloi   "transplanting (some rice plants) before proceeding to
                           plant the entire sawah" 95
ma'pakalapu   a rite in rice ritual 99
ma'pakande   to give food (in the sense of feeding an effigy) 69,
                           199, 242, 287, 295, 297
ma'pakande nene' (ma'pakande to matua) "giving food to the ancestors of the
                           (South) west", an offering 20, 22, 24-5, 43-5, 67, 71,
                           95, 97, 142, 154-5, 157, 159-60, 199
ma'pakande padang   "giving food to the earth", a funeral rite 189, 190
                           (Fig.22)
ma'pakande Puang   an offering dedicated to Puang Matua 127
ma'pakande to matua (umpa'kande to matua) see ma'pakande nene'
ma'pakatua   see ma'bolong
ma'pakise   a rite in rice ritual 99
ma'palangngan ba'   to suspend the body from the ba' 200, 245, Ch.X note
                           8
ma'palangngan panganta'   the suspending of textiles from a bamboo in death ritual
                           187, 188 (Fig.21), 196, 232
ma'palangngan para   a conversion ritual 7, 112, 133, 153, 191
ma'palangngan sarigan   "to lift the dead onto the bier" 200, 246
ma'palao (massonglo')   the buffaloes and the deceased are led to the rante
                           189, 196, 201, 247
ma'palimbong   a rite at the end of the maro-feast 127
ma'pallin   an expiatory offering performed in many rituals,
                           whether East or West, as an initial rite 8, 23, 66, 69,
                           93, 121, 134, 184-5, 189, 195, 197, 212, Ch.I note 2,
                           Ch.III notes 8 and 16
ma'palumbung   "the piling of bunches of rice", a rite in death ritual
                           250

ma'tenten pungpung | beating the drum, keeping a special rhythm Ch.XI note 3
ma'tete' (ma'tete' uo') | "to make a bridge" (of the bamboo aur), a sacrifice to the gods 19, 24, 133
ma'tomatua | see ma'nene'
ma'tombi | carrying the sacral cloths to the rante, a rite in a death ritual of high rank 194-5, 207-13, 282
ma'tombi banua | display of holy fabrics in and around the house 280, 283-4
ma'tongkonan | 1. a meeting 95
| 2. a female relative of the deceased who has to observe taboos 178; see also to ma'pemali
ma'torroi | "to stop with something" (with the bua'-ritual) 42
matua ulu | "the old heads", the village elders 26, 104, 158, Ch.VII note 3
ma'tundan | "to wake" (the deceased) 200, 243, 292
ma'tundan gandang | "to wake the drums" 102
ma'tutu ba'bai | "to close the door" (= closing the rapasan) 199, 242
meaa | to carry the corpse (or the remains of the deceased) to the rock tomb 189, 195, 197, 201, 212, 251
mebala'kaan | constructing a bala'kaan 195-6, 200, 244
mebala kollong | "embracing the neck", a prayer to protect the community 27
mebalun | to wrap (the corpse) 183, 212, 282-3
megorang | to construct a gorang 29
mekayu | "the gathering of the wood" (= the firewood for the second part of a high-ranking death ritual) 243
mekayu busa | a rite in the bua'-ritual 39
melakkean (melakkian) | preparing the lakkean on the rante 200
melantang | the building of the guest houses 102, 196, 200, 244
melondong datu | "to offer a rooster to the gods" 25, 96, Ch.IV note 12
memala | a sacrifice 33
membali puang | "to return to the lords (gods)", to become a deity 262
membase | "to wash", a cleansing or purificatory rite 123, 185, 191
membase kandian | "the cleansing of the eating bowls", a rite in bua'-ritual 24, Ch.II note 20, Ch.III note 10
membase mairi' | "the cleansing of everything", a rite in the rice ritual 95
membase sali | the purification of the central room of a house, a rite in death ritual 197, 251
menammu pare | "to meet (= to receive) the ripening rice", a rite 97
menani pare | to celebrate the rice in song 101
mendio' | ritual bathing 127; see also ma'dio'
Mengkendek | a puang-state 142, 173, 278, 300, 312, Ch.X note 6
merok (merok-feast) | a ritual organized by the ramage, or by a person of status who for a long time has been prosperous and who wants to express his gratitude; or by an unfree who bought himself out of slavery 3-4, 6-8, 24, 26-7, 30, 30 (Fig.5), 32, 40, 45, 62-84, 103, 117, 133, 137, 140, 159-60, 202, 204, 321-2, 325, Ch.II notes 11 and 34, Ch.III notes 6, 18 and 26, Ch.VII notes 2 and 3
mesarigan | to prepare a bier, which is accompanied by a rite 187, 195, 243-4
mesimbuang | to erect a menhir 201
metangdo'-tangdo' | the construction of a small gallery in front of the house during the bua'-ritual 28
metena | a rite of the bua'-ritual 47
mewaka' pare | a rite in the rice ritual 95

parangka	1. artefact in bua'-ritual 322, Ch.VII note 6 2. artefact in death ritual 322
pa'rapuan	a family group; the belongings of a family group 12
pare	rice (nearly ripe or ripe) on the fields, the first cut 86
pare dolo, pare kasalle	different varieties of rice Ch.III note 6
pare pangrakan	bunches of rice 85
pare papanuku	bunches of rice, used in ritual 85
parepe'	1. a pig, a sacrificial animal in death ritual 103, 244, 246 2. a buffalo playing a role in death ritual 195, 210-1, 216, 244-5, 248, 250, 284-7, 289, Ch.XII note 16
pare tallu bullina	the three-eared rice (in myth) 86, Ch.III note 14
Parkindo, Partai Keristen Indonesia	the Christian Political Party of Indonesia 226
pasa'	a (ritual) market 56, 241, Ch.II note 46; see also ma'pasa'
pasa' rambu tuka'	"the market of the ascending smoke", the plain where the rituals of the East are held 126, 142
passakke	a plant with cooling (healing) capacities 68, 100, 144, 156, 160
passaseran	a trough with a handle 71
Passomba Tedong	the laudation (consecration) of the buffalo in Eastern rituals, a litany 8, 11, 13, 26-7, 63-5, 67, 73, 84, 86-7, 103, 117, 321, Ch.V note 7
passurak tedong	the litany for the buffalo to be killed at a death ritual 117, Ch.V note 7
pata'	the horizontal floor beam which runs parallel to the ridge of a tongkonan 71, Ch.III note 20
patane	a boulder in which a grave is hewn 251
patik	a daubing with pig's blood 68
pa'tinggoro	a functionary who kills buffaloes at a death ritual 231-2
pa'todiran	a small stick used to apply pig's blood on the forehead of ramage members 40
pa'tondokan	those who belong to the village 212
patotti	an ornament of human hair 30 (Fig.2a,b), 246
pattung	(Indonesian betung) Dendrocalamus flagellifer, a bamboo 64, 286, 298
payo-payo	a scarecrow 90
payung	umbrella 213
pekali	to dig 89
pekali bassi	a crowbar or iron digging "stick" 89
peleko	a shovel 89, Ch.III note 5
pemanala	pieces of meat from internal organs of the sacrificial animal used for offerings 105, 118, 203, 250
pembalikan	a conversion ritual 152
pembalikan bua', pembalikan la'pa'	to reverse the bua', a ritual 103
pembalikan pesungna	"the offering meal is turned around", the deceased is conveyed from the sphere of the West to the sphere of the East 152
penjaga mayat	(Indonesian) guardian of the corpse 176
pentingoran	see massura' tallang
permissi	(Indonesian) permission (for organizing a cock fight) 240
peruru	a ribbon to bind a woman's hairknot 36
pesangle	a serving spoon for rice 36
pesung	an offering on torn pieces of banana leaf, which are laid upon each other; in bua'- and maro-rituals a blood-

Puang Matua   "The Old Lord", the high-god of the Toraja 8, 15-6,
                               20, 22, 42, 47, 63, 66-7, 76, 100, 114-5, 118, 122, 127,
                               160, 276, 325, 327
puang-regions, puang-state, puang-territories the three statelets in the South
                               of Tana Toraja, the Tallulembangna 5, 88, 98, 100,
                               140, 173, 186, 216, 275, 278, 283, 289, 299-300, 321,
                               325-6, Ch.IV note 15
puaro   a brazier made from a cooking pot from which the top
                               has been hacked off 160
pudu'   a black buffalo 195, 212, 231, 281, 284, 289, 301
pulu   glutinous rice 143
punti   banana 40
pusaka   (Indonesian) heirloom 259
pusuk (daun pusuk)   young leaves of the Arenga saccharifera 16, 36-7, 43,
                               48, 104, 208, 318
Puya   the Realm of the Dead 113, 178, 187, 202, 238, 248,
                               259, 277, 287, 329, Ch.X note 3, Ch.XII note 27

raki'   raft 89
rambu solo'   "smoke that descends", the Eastern rites or ritual 4,
                               116
rame   a yellow chicken with brown spots 24-5, 66, 69, 94
rami   a fibre from Bochmeria nivea Gand. 313 (Fig.51)
rampean   in-laws 212
Rangga Ulu   "Having Branches", name of a sacral (maa'-)cloth in
                               Sangalla' 290
rangkapan   a rice knife 90, 90 (Fig.9)
rangking   a loosely plaited offering holder 142
rante (pantunuan)   the plain where the rites for the deceased are carried
                               on 187-9, 195, 200-1, 210-1, 215-7, photos pp.222-3,
                               236, 246-8, 251, 275, 283, 285, 287, 290, 297, 299, 327,
                               Ch.V note 9, Ch.X notes 2 and 4
rante bua'   a functionary in the bua'-ritual 38
rante bulaan   a region in myth 32
rante kala'paran   the great plain for feasts (rituals) of the East 11-3,
                               19-22, 29, 31, 42-6, 102, 118
rapa'   to be still, to stop speaking or to cease doing
                               something 198
rapasan   temporary coffin in which the dead person's earthly
                               remains lay for some time 5, 199-200, 214-5, 234, 239
                               (Fig.40), 240, 243, 289, Ch.VII note 6, Ch.XI note 32;
                               see also duni, erong, issong
rapasan sundun   the highest order of death rituals 5, 172, 198, 245,
                               photo p.273, 287
rapu   a family group, tracing its origin to the founder of a
                               tongkonan, a (sub)ramage 6; see also marapuan
rara'   a necklace, a neck ornament 31, 38, 48, 126, photo
                               p.181, 282
rari   rope or string 88
rassa papa   see pesuru
ra'tuk   popped rice 129, 316
rauk   see rok
rekke   northern 153
retteng   recitation of topical or satirical poetry at death feasts
                               7, 229, 234, 318
rimpisan bia'   a rite in the funeral ritual of Sangalla' 281, Ch.XII
                               note 10
Riu   a region, a district 14, 23, 30, 32, 34-5, 37, 39, 47,
                               48 (Fig.5), 133, Ch.II note 9, Ch.IV note 16

setan	(Indonesian) devil 137
sibali	partner, companion, male opponent 322, Ch.XIII note 1
sibali banua	a tongkonan which has a special relationship with another tongkonan 236, 251
siilang bua	a special buffalo in death ritual 236, 314, Ch.XI note 15
sikambi lindo banua	the guardians of the face (front) of the house 69
silali'-ceremony	a rite in death ritual 238, 325-6
Simbuang	a region, a district 288
simbuang batu	a menhir photo p.181, 188, 214-5, photo p.220, 237, 245, 248, 250, 279 (Fig.46), 291 (Fig.48), 298-9, 322, Ch.XI note 25
simbuang kayu	a tree trunk (buangin, kalosi) functioning in death ritual of high order 236, 250, 286, 291 (Fig.48), 301, 322, Ch.XII notes 12 and 26
singgi'	eulogizing the brave, the important men, the children or the slaves at Eastern rituals 7, 29, 31, 44, 46, 49-50, photo p.59, photo p.61, 103, 171
sipalakuan	a rite of the merok-ritual 75, photo p.83, Ch.III note 6
sipalakuan	"the helper", an assistant to a functionary in rituals 27, 112, 198, Ch.VII note 3
sirih	(Indonesian) Piper betle 76
sirih-pinang	(Indonesian) betel and areca, an offering 68, 76, 105, 188 (Fig.21), 202-3
sirih-pouch	189, 259, Ch.III note 26
sirri bua'	a functionary in the bua'-ritual 38
sirri-sirri	a plant, functioning in ritual 40
sisaong	cock fighting 240
sisemba'	calf-kicking 46, 49, 93, 100
sissarean	the backrest for the deceased, used in the first part of a dirapa'i-death ritual 232, 232 (Fig.32)
sitami patilli'	"to keep silence" (peace) 44
So'	see Laso'
sokko kalele'	a buffalo in myth 34
sokkong bayu (datu muane)	"the collar of the jacket", a title in Kesu' and elsewhere 26-7, 45, 62, 64, 67, 95, 97, 99, 102-5, 127, 154, 157, 226, 236-7, 324, Ch.IX note 8, Ch.XI note 25, Ch.XIV note 3
sondong para	a triangular ornament which resembles the para of a house 20 (Fig.2a)
songlo'	see massonglo'
sporran	(Scotch) a pouch for men 233
Suaya	the cliff with rock graves of the puang-family 291, 301
subak	an agricultural and irrigation society on Bali 92
suke	a bamboo joint 36, 40, 156, Ch.XI note 19
suke dibonga	a spotted suke 36
Suloara'	an ancestor from Tikala and Riu 34
Suboara'	a lembang (district) photos pp.52-5
sumapuko	war chants or cries, headhunter's cry 17, 247-8, 316
sumbung	the room at the rear of the tongkonan 37, 115, 225, 227-8, 228 (Fig.33), 239 (Fig.40)
sumbung penaa	"the appendage of the soul", a buffalo in death ritual 195, 198, 229, 281
sumengo	headhunter's dance 316
suru'	see massuru'
suru'na mellolo tau	"the cleansing of the umbilical cord", rites concerning mankind 109
suru'na rampanan kapa'	the marriage ritual 114-6

suru' padang	"the combing (cleansing) of the land" 102
suso	a snail 100
susu	woman's breasts 240
taa baine	the share of meat of important women in death ritual 189, 198, 235
tabang	bloodwort (Cordyline terminalis, Draecana terminalis) 16, 21, 24, 36, 39, photo p.56, 113, 118, 122-3, 126-8, 134-6, 141, 144, 155, 216, 284, Ch.VI note 12
tabuan	a wasp 50
tadoran	a bamboo with an offering in top 97, 155
tagari	a fragrant grass (Dianella ensifolia) 85, 98, 160
Tallebuku	the ancestor of the (cooked) rice 86, 327
tali bate'	a batik cloth used as a headdress 136, 227, 233, 236 (Fig.38), 236, photo p.308
talimbung	an object used in the bua'-ritual 37
tali padang-padang	a kind of laurel-wreath 46
tali sissik	headdress folded like the scales of a fish photo p.180
tallang (bamboo tallang)	36, 68, 75, 125, 156, photo p.182, 189
tallu basongna	"the three twisted ropes", a sarita and two liana used in merok 67, Ch.III note 13
Tallulembangna	"The Three Proas", the three states governed by a puang 6, 111, 177, 275, 288-9, 320, Ch.XI note 41
tallu manuk	chicken's egg(s) 50, 183
tallung bongi	see dipatallung bongi
tambolang	a stork 14
Tamborolangi'	the important ancestor of the puang-regions 276, 321, Ch.XII note 2
tambuk	the stomach 45
tampak pesung	sacrificial food Ch.II note 48
tananan basse	a class of people in Sangalla' 286, photo p.309, Ch.XII note 13
tanan laa kala'paran	"the bringing of the laa to the (rante) kala'paran", a rite in the bua'-ritual 44
tandi rapasan	see parepe'
tanduk gallang	copper horns 315, 316 (Fig.54)
tanduk tabang	horns from tabang-leaves 292
tangdo'	the room in the North part of a tongkonan 228 (Fig. 33), 239
tangdo'	a small house constructed for the tumbang in the bua'-ritual 25, 28, 43, 45
tangdo'-tangdo'	a small, square platform, a construction in bua'-ritual 19-22
tangdo' kalua'	"the great tangdo'", a construction in the shape of a front gallery added to the Northern part of a tong-konan, used in bua'-ritual 18-22, 27-9, 40
Tangdona Sulle Gayangna Bullu Matua	the swearing of the oath by the majestic successor to Bullu Matua 276
tarrung	Solanum melongena 48, photo p.56, 126, 128, 209
tasik	sea 31
tattiku'	a small bird 84
tau-tau	mortuary effigy photo p.168, 170, 174, photo p.181, 188-9, 204, 242, 248, 250, 297-9, 301-3, photo p.308, photos pp.310-1, 322, 327, Ch.XIII note 27
tau-tau lampa	a tau-tau made from a bamboo frame photo p.181, 188-9, 282-3, 290
teba	a portion of meat 97, 98 (Fig.14)
tekkenan doke	"the holding of the lance", a rite in death ritual 236
teng	see ba'

Printed in the United States
By Bookmasters